MELVILLE'S QUARREL WITH GOD

. . . that speech of Adam unto God . . .
as implying God the author of sin, and
accusing his maker of his transgression.
. . . This was a bold and open accusation
of God, making the fountain of good the
contriver of evil; and the forbidder of the
crime, an abettor of the fact prohibited.

BROWNE, *Vulgar Errors*

MELVILLE'S

QUARREL WITH GOD.

BY LAWRANCE THOMPSON

PRINCETON UNIVERSITY PRESS · 1952

PRINCETON, NEW JERSEY

To J. A. T.

CONTENTS

TO THE READER

The reason the mass of men fear God, and at bottom dislike *Him, is because they rather distrust His heart, and fancy Him all brain like a watch. (You perceive I employ a capital initial in the pronoun referring to the Deity; don't you think there is a slight dash of flunkeyism in the usage?)*

MELVILLE TO HAWTHORNE

Nay, it is more strange that Heathen Idolaters should do good Actions, than that Atheistical Philosophers should live like Virtuous Men: For the former must have been led to Crimes by their very Religion; it must have been a Point of Faith with them, That to make themselves Imitators of God, which is the End and Substance of Religion, they ought to be Cheats, Envious, Fornicators, Adulterers, Pederasts.

BAYLE, *Dictionary*

But it is this Being *of the matter; there lies the knot with which we choke ourselves. As soon as you say* Me, *a* God, *a* Nature, *so soon you jump off from your stool and hang from the beam. Yes, that word [God] is the hangman. Take God out of the dictionary, and you would have Him in the street.*

MELVILLE TO HAWTHORNE

TO THE READER

THE RIDDLE of man's relation to God has evoked many brilliant answers which are engrossing in whatever forms they find expression; but some of the most vivid answers are dramatically represented in the total actions of literary narrative. Of course, our enjoyment of such answers is largely dependent on our ability to read with detachment and to set aside, temporarily, our own private belief as to just which answer happens to satisfy our own peculiar spiritual needs. We naturally try to avoid the danger of letting our personal bias get in our own way, lest such interference should block off our vision and perception of that approach or viewpoint dramatized by the action. Unfortunately, however, most of us have fallen prey to that particular danger when we have tried to contemplate that engrossing progression of answers which Herman Melville has represented in the vivid actions of his novels.

We have fallen prey, partly because Melville deliberately arranged to help us do so. He took wry and sly pleasure in the irony of disguising his riddle-answers behind the self-protective riddle-masks of his ingenious art; behind various subterfuges of rhetoric and symbol; behind naughty uses of Bible quotation or allusion which may have one meaning in a Christian context and quite a different meaning as controlled by Melville's anti-Christian context.

To correct our misunderstandings, here, it should be helpful to remember that other authors have taken advantage of literary artifice for purposes of self-protection. It should also be helpful to place Melville's answers within a pertinent framework of con-

3

flicting concepts as to man's relation to God. Thus we may recognize the close kinship between his heretical views (as all who disagree with him may call them) and those views of earlier heresiarchs. For such purposes of orientation, we need to go back at least to the sixteenth century, when two opposed concepts clashed violently: the Reformation answer and that anti-Reformation assumption which I choose (quite arbitrarily) to designate as the Renaissance answer.

The typical Reformation riddle-answer was that man could achieve his ultimate salvation and atonement only through abject and self-effacing bondage to God; through strait obedience to the laws of God, as revealed in the Bible. By contrast, the ancient pagan contention which returned to popularity during the Renaissance was that man could achieve his ultimate self-realization and fulfillment as a "natural man," through the liberating assertion of his own natural powers of body and mind and spirit, without any necessary reference to supernatural powers. Although these opposed views were subjected to endless permutations, and were sometimes formulated in combination with each other, before and during and after the sixteenth century, these answers (in their pure forms) were poles apart because one emphasized the supreme sovereignty of God, while the other emphasized the supreme sovereignty of natural man.

In his youth, Melville inherited the Reformation dogma of John Calvin, in a quite undiluted form. His devout and pious parents were members of the Dutch Reformed Church in America, and they taught their son to believe that God had created him innately depraved and predestinately damned to eternal Hell; but that he might possibly be saved from such damnation, through divine grace, if he threw himself submissively and abjectly on the mercy of God, as revealed through Jesus Christ.

Until he left home, at the age of eighteen, Melville seems to have developed a deeply-rooted belief in the essential truth of his religious heritage. Although disappointments and disillusionments began to accumulate, during his first sea voyage, and although these disillusionments increased ominously during his later voyages, Melville did not completely rebel against his Calvinistic heritage until after he had written and published his first two travel-narratives, *Typee* and *Omoo*. Even during his writing of

Mardi, when the struggle between his beliefs and his doubts reached a crisis, he still managed to salvage a modified assertion of mystical religious affirmation, short-lived, because it did not satisfy and sustain him.

Disillusionment with one's inherited (and therefore second-hand) religious beliefs is such a familiar phase of human growth that one might suppose Melville could have worked out his own religious readjustments without carrying into later life any ineffaceable scars; that his own personal and firsthand religious experience might have modified his inherited beliefs until he could have arrived at some concept of God more acceptable and congenial to his temperament. By contrast, one might fear that Melville's concept of the Calvinistic God might gradually have become so repulsive that he might have moved through doubt and skepticism to a denial of the existence of God. This final step he never took. As it happened, however, Melville actually experimented with several different kinds of resolution, without achieving any lasting comfort or consolation. Mystically inclined, he preferred or wanted to think of God as that benevolent and personal source of Truth, to whom each individual could talk directly; and this attitude was an important part of his Protestant heritage. Nevertheless, while writing *Mardi*, he seemed to toy with the wavering and unpleasant suspicion that God could not possibly be what Melville wanted him to be. As a result, the asserted affirmation in the tableau-conclusion of *Mardi* was merely an assertion: it lacked conviction.

Increasingly embittered by a conjunction of unfortunate experiences, immediately during and after the writing of *Mardi*, Melville arrived at a highly ironic conclusion: believing more firmly than ever in the God of John Calvin, he began to resent and hate the attributes of God, particularly the seemingly tyrannous harshness and cruelty and malice of God. Thus, instead of losing faith in his Calvinistic God, Melville made a scapegoat of him, and blamed God for having caused so many human beings to rebel. In this sense, then, we might say that Melville became an inverted mystic as soon as he began to be angry with God for being the harsh and logical punisher that the Calvinists said he was. Still influenced by the Calvinistic dogma that God did indeed try to exact from mankind a rigid letter-of-the-law obedience, and

5

that Adam's fall was indeed the first indication of the unjust ruth-
lessness of God's punishment, Melville came to view God as the
source from whom all evils flow, in short, the "Original Sinner,"
divinely depraved. But this riddle-answer was no more consoling
to Melville than any of the others which he had explored, and
at times during his life he continued to investigate the validity of
other possible answers. Nevertheless, his inverted mysticism became a fixed idea, an obsession, which persisted during most of
his life.

As I shall demonstrate in the following chapters, I am interested
in Melville's spiritual idiom primarily because it controlled and
determined his artistic idiom. The tensions of Melville's peculiar
and inverted religious beliefs prompted him to give them outlet
in some kind of literary expression, and yet he hesitated to express
himself frankly. He knew very well that his contemporary reading
public was too deeply committed to Christian beliefs in the goodness of God to tolerate any open assertions as to the malice
and evil of God. He also knew that if he should announce that
he had declared his independence from the sovereignty of God,
and that he had declared war against God in order to fight for his
own freedom as a natural man, his Christian readers would tell
him that he was being ridiculous; that it takes two to make a
quarrel, and that God is above quarreling with a human being.

Still craving the satisfaction of giving literary vent to his secret
and heretical beliefs, Melville gradually formulated a complex
variety of stylistic and structural methods for expressing himself in
such a way as to protect himself from heresy hunters. The two
distinct elements with which he could experiment, in his narratives, were the stories he chose to tell, and the way in which he
chose to tell them. The plots of his novels were frequently selected
to represent, in vivid and dramatic pictures, his so-called heretical
and blasphemous views. The way in which he chose to present
these plots was not uniform; but he ingeniously arranged to pretend, in the telling, that no matter how much he indulged in
occasional religious doubts and questionings, his ultimate goal was
to praise and honor the orthodox Christian viewpoint. This pretense was very convenient for purposes of sarcasm and satire and
irony, because the pretense gave the illusion of proceeding in a

direction exactly opposite from the anti-Christian direction of the story itself, the plot itself. Within this flexible formula of sustained irony, Melville achieved ample elbowroom for playing with innumerable artistic devices for defensive concealment, subterfuge, deception, hoodwinking, ridicule.

To the best of my knowledge, this fundamental aspect of Melville's artistic method has never been fully explored by any of Melville's reviewers, critics, interpreters, biographers. Those who do not like my presentation of his method will of course be inclined to dismiss it as merely another fly-by-night theory, which cannot be substantiated by scholarly and documentary evidence. But I am willing to risk being attacked, because I think the evidence is pretty strong, even when it is only circumstantial. Although I must have made some mistakes in my interpretations of the evidence, I feel quite confident that the validity of my general thesis will not be injured seriously by my specific mistakes.

I am also aware that some critics may choose to attack me for indulging in what they like to describe as the "intentional fallacy." I am also willing to take that risk. I have tried to demonstrate, in the following chapters, that no completely valid interpretation of Melville's novels can be made by any reader until that reader recognizes, and learns to cope with, Melville's intention and method of employing artistic devices to deceive certain categories of readers, even including those who like to talk, in any age, about the "intentional fallacy."

Because my ultimate concern is with Melville's artistic effects, rather than with the causes of those effects, I here propose to describe the accidental way in which I happened to become interested in the close relationship between Melville's artistic idiom and his spiritual idiom.

Some years ago, while reading *Moby-Dick* with more care than I had previously given it, I had finished only a few pages of the first chapter when I thought I noticed that Ishmael was particularly fond of sarcastically saying two things at once: of insinuating a meaning which was quite contrary to the superficial sense of the overt statement. As I watched the growing effect of this device, I also noticed that Ishmael's overt meanings reflected a sympathy with the Christian doctrine of obedience and acceptance; but that the underlying and insinuated meaning hinted at a deliberate

7

and slv ridicule of concepts sacred to Christian doctrine. Here is a subtle example, from Chapter One of *Moby-Dick*:

"No, when I go to sea, I go as a simple sailor, right before the mast, plumb down into the fore-castle, aloft there to the royal mast-head. True, they rather order me about some, and make me jump from spar to spar, like a grasshopper in a May meadow. And at first, this sort of thing is unpleasant enough. It touches one's sense of honor, particularly if you come of an old established family in the land, the Van Rensselaers, or Randolphs, or Hardicanutes. . . . But even this wears off in time.

"What of it, if some old hunks of a sea-captain orders me to get a broom and sweep down the decks? What does that indignity amount to, weighed, I mean, in the scales of the New Testament? Do you think the archangel Gabriel thinks anything the less of me, because I promptly and respectfully obey that old hunks in that particular instance? Who ain't a slave? Tell me that. Well, then, however the old sea-captains may order me about—however they may thump and punch me about, I have the satisfaction of knowing that it is all right; that everybody else is one way or other served in much the same way—either in a physical or metaphysical point of view, that is; and so the universal thump is passed round, and all hands should rub each other's shoulder-blades, and be content."[1]

That cheerful and garrulous passage, pivoting on the word "indignity," might make a distinctly different appeal to at least three categories of readers. He whom Melville called the "superficial skimmer of pages" might hurry impatiently through this interruption of the story itself. A second category of reader, represented by a mature and devout Christian, might respond pleasurably to the Biblical references and (unconsciously guided by personal beliefs and prejudices) might be inclined to like Ishmael because he seems to reflect at least a vague Christian belief in submission, obedience, acceptance, and a seemingly positive Christian hope that everything is going to be "all right" in the end. A third category of reader, represented by anyone who maintains even a mild personal bias of skepticism, might be prompted to proceed more cautiously by remembering that Christian literature delights in representing life as a voyage and the world as a ship and God as the captain—tropes which Melville had played with, mischievously, in *White-Jacket* (written just before *Moby-Dick*). Thus placed on guard by remembering, such a reader might suspect that Ishmael *could* be speaking with tongue in cheek; that Ishmael *could* be merely *pretending* to honor and praise an attitude closely allied to the Christian concept of submission and obedience and faith in the fitness of things. Such a reader, lingering over his memory of the conventional Christian trope, might be forgiven for wondering just how reverent Ishmael was when he referred to the captain, in this context, as an "old hunks."

Although these thoughts occurred to me in random form as I was rereading the first chapter of *Moby-Dick*, I had previously acquired only a superficial acquaintance with the life and writings of Melville. Consequently, as soon as I began to suspect that Ishmael was a little naughty in his insinuations, I also began to suspect myself of reading into that passage, and into all of that first chapter, certain insinuations which might have been entirely foreign to Melville's purpose and method. Nevertheless, as I continued to read, I found many passages which were far less subtle in their suggestive naughtiness, and such passages accumulated until they encouraged me to stop suspecting myself.

Still wondering whether Melville intentionally made an appeal to three categories of readers, I realized that Melville's (or Ishmael's) rhetorical seas could easily be skimmed over, sailed over, by the fast-cruising reader, without any concern for any currents of meaning, either above or below the surface. For such a novice, the mere story might be interesting enough, and certainly there is no harm or wrong in reading *Moby-Dick* superficially. For the second category of reader, however, there might be a hypnotic delight in watching Ishmael pick up, toy with, toss off, one Biblical chip after another until such chips formed quite a long line, floating astern. Thus hypnotized, the devout reader could easily indulge the illusion that this backward-moving line of chips established a permanent and meaningful association with the shore of orthodoxy, God. By contrast, the more skeptical reader would be inclined to pay less attention to the illusory drift of the chips than to the less easily determined direction and motion of the craft itself, the piquant direction and motion of the *Pequod's* bow.

Still cautiously evaluating my own response to Melville's stylistic effects, as I continued to read, I became more and more convinced that the forming or informing principle of Melville's many stylistic devices was closely related to the forming or informing principle of his many structural devices. It occurred to me, gradually, that Melville was developing a subtle triangulation among three distinct whale stories: Ahab's adventures with a whale, Jonah's adventures with a whale, Job's adventures with Leviathan. Again I realized that the "superficial skimmer of pages" would become so absorbed in Ahab's vengeful quest that he might not notice any suggested analogies between the adventures of Ahab and those of Jonah or Job. By contrast, the mature Christian reader could not help but admire, and take delight in, the splendid rhetoric of Father Mapple's sermon on what happened to Jonah when "God came upon him in a whale." It also occurred to me that such a reader would be shocked and horrified if I or anyone else should even so much as suggest that perhaps Melville had written that entire sermon with tongue in cheek, for ultimately ironic and sarcastic and satirical purposes; that perhaps the devout and sincere Father Mapple had been permitted to preach that sermon, in a novel, so that the sermon itself could serve Melville as a way of testing the discrimination of his readers; as a further way of separating the sheep from the goats; even as a stylistically contrived sheeptrap or mousetrap.

Trap? In what sense? It was just possible, I thought, that a reader who was consciously or unconsciously bias-bound by his Christian heritage might conclude that Melville had deliberately arranged to establish a contrast between Jonah's ultimate obedience to God and Captain Ahab's ultimate defiance; that such a reader might finish *Moby-Dick* with the feeling that, in some sense or other, Melville had created of his materials an elaborate Christian parable, an *exemplum*; an object lesson, to illuminate the validity of Christian teachings on the rewards for "right reason" or obedience and the punishments for wrong reason, stubbornness, defiance.

As it happens, this Christian-parable interpretation is actually the interpretation generally agreed on, and fostered, by our most distinguished Melville scholars;[2] the interpretation generally accepted at home and abroad, just when we have finished celebrating the one hundredth anniversary of the publication of *Moby-Dick*. Could it be possible, I wondered, that Melville's stylistic "wile and guile" had been even more successful than he had intended them to be? If so, *Moby-Dick* might eventually be acclaimed not only as the American classic of the century but also as the most elaborate and Barnum-eclipsing, play-on-words joke of the century. Each of these jokers may have found his own contrasting devices for saying, "This way to the Egress."

Ahab, Jonah, Job. Again I paused, as I was reading, to notice another kind of effect which Melville achieved by piling up various references to Job; particularly by letting Ishmael quote tauntingly, and more than once, from God's own words to Job, uttered when God had established that celebrated analogy between his own incomprehensible power and the obviously, visibly incomprehensible power of God-created Leviathan, or the whale, as the word "Leviathan" was interpreted in Melville's day. Furthermore, Melville himself forced me to notice that there were some striking analogies between the religious disillusionment of Job and the religious disillusionment of Captain Ahab; that each had puzzled over the mystery of death; that each upbraided God for permitting innocent believers to suffer; that Captain Ahab even carried out, symbolically, the blasphemous suggestion made by Job's wife: "Curse God and die."

After I had finished this reading of *Moby-Dick*, and after I had become more interested in the possibility that Melville had consciously worked out stylistic and structural devices which might serve as deceptive sheeptraps and mousetraps, particularly for readers who might otherwise become vituperative heresy hunters, I wondered whether Melville had said anything in his other writings to corroborate my suspicion that he was obsessed with the subject of stylistic and structural deception. I also wondered how familiar Melville might have been with the writings of other authors who had protected themselves from heresy hunters; the writings, for example, of Rabelais, Montaigne, Voltaire, Pierre Bayle—the French being past masters at this game.

Although I turned to the best scholarly treatises on Melville, confident that they must have much to say about Melville's preoccupation with stylistic deceptions and hoodwinkings, I was surprised to find that no Melville scholar had bothered to mention this problem, which seemed to me so important and fundamental. But as soon as I began to read Melville's own writings, particularly his letters and book reviews and journals, I found considerable circumstantial evidence. For example, it seemed to me that Melville had unintentionally told his readers more about himself than about Hawthorne when he asserted, in a well-known review of *Mosses from an Old Manse*, that Hawthorne employed literary devices "directly calculated to deceive—egregiously deceive—the superficial skimmer of pages." I also suspected that Melville was consciously including himself when he insisted, in that same review, "The truth seems to be, that *like many other geniuses* [italics added], this Man of Mosses takes great delight in hoodwinking the world—at least, with respect to himself."

I was also pleased to find that while Melville was writing *Moby-Dick* he had summarized for Hawthorne, obliquely but concisely, his own private belief that natural man should declare his independence from God, and then should fight for that independence. I was also interested (to put it mildly) when I found that in yet another letter Melville had confided to Hawthorne that the "secret" motto for *Moby-Dick* began, "*Ego non baptizo te in nomine . . .*" Secret motto? In what sense secret, I wondered, unless Melville should have preferred (and should have arranged) to deceive some readers mistakenly into assuming that he himself was not at all in sympathy with the so-called "mad" old Captain Ahab's declaration of independence from God, particularly when that so-called blasphemer had made highly appropriate and symbolic use of the same Latin quotation, unexpurgated?

I have told this story of my own accidental stumbling into an awareness of Melville's conscious employment of artistic deceptions, because I want this story to provide the reader with a brief orientation. After my curiosity on this subject had become fully aroused, I went on to make an extended study of Melville's writings. The more I read, the more evidence I found to support and justify my initial hunch; even to justify the presentation of my findings, in the following chapters.

I must add one warning as to my method of approach in the following chapters. Although I have tried to abide by my own suggestion that the detached reader always endeavors to set aside his personal bias and prejudice as he contemplates or discusses the artistically represented viewpoint of an author like Melville, I have not been consistent in this regard. At times I have been able to indulge an illusion of sympathy for his viewpoint, to such an extent as to give the additional illusion that I am not only representing but also defending his viewpoint. At other times I have been guilty of losing my detachment so completely as to evaluate Melville's viewpoint in terms of my own prejudices. One such example may be found at the end of Chapter Two, another at the end of Chapter Four, and at last, deliberately, in the Conclusion and throughout the Notes. Obviously, my own bias is decidedly different from the bias of Herman Melville.

FRUIT OF THAT FORBIDDEN TREE

CHAPTER I

*Of Man's First Disobedience, and the Fruit
Of that Forbidden Tree, whose mortal taste
Brought Death into the World, and all our woe,
With loss of EDEN, till one greater Man
Restore us, and regain the blissful Seat,
Sing Heav'nly Muse . . .*

MILTON, *Paradise Lost*

*Foolish mortals enter into many contentions
with God, as though they could arraign him to
plead to their accusations. In the first place they
inquire, by what right the Lord is angry with his
creatures who had not provoked him by any
previous offense; for that to devote to destruction whom he pleases, is more like the caprice
of a tyrant than the lawful sentence of a judge;
that men have reason, therefore, to expostulate
with God, if they are predestinated to eternal
death without any demerit of their own, merely
by his sovereign will. . . . The will of God is the
highest rule of justice; so that what he wills must
be considered just, for this very reason, because
he wills it. When it is inquired, therefore, why
the Lord did so, the answer must be, Because he
would.*

JOHN CALVIN, *Institutes of the Christian Religion*

FRUIT OF THAT FORBIDDEN TREE

IF HERMAN MELVILLE had become a painter instead of a man of letters, he would probably have made at least one study of Adam and Eve in the act of sharing bites while the Serpent lingered in the lower left foreground and God watched permissively from behind the Tree of Life in the upper right background. Perhaps, in a later study, he might have arranged another grouping of this complex image, to represent a more pronounced sense of defiance, on the parts of the orchard thieves.

As it turned out, Melville did make elaborate literary uses of the Genesis story, and any reader who wishes to appreciate those uses should have in mind at least a few other extensions—historical, theological, dramatic, poetic—made of that same story by other authors, starting at least with Martin Luther and John Calvin. To direct our interest, here, we may begin with one of Melville's own covert allusions, in *Moby-Dick*. When Ishmael decided that not all of Queequeg's religious rituals were charming, he gave Quee-queg a brief course in comparative religions:

"Now, as I before hinted, I have no objection to any person's religion, be it what it may, so long as that person does not kill or insult any other person, because that other person don't believe it also. But when a man's religion becomes really frantic; when it is a positive torment to him; and in fine, makes this earth of ours an uncomfortable inn to lodge in; then I think it high time to take that individual aside and argue the point with him.

"And just so I now did with Queequeg. . . . I then went on, beginning with the rise and progress of the primitive religions, and coming down to the various religions of the present time,

17

during which time I labored to show Queequeg that all these Lents, Ramadans, and prolonged ham-squattings in cold, cheerless rooms were stark nonsense; bad for the health; useless for the soul; opposed, in short, to the obvious laws of Hygiene and common sense. . . . In one word, Queequeg, said I, rather digressively; hell is an idea first born on an undigested apple-dumpling; and since then perpetuated through the hereditary dyspepsias nurtured by Ramadans."[1]

For the moment, never mind that Melville had previously and privately been saying much the same thing to his Calvinistic self. Part of Melville's immediate jesting, there, probably lay in the use of the words, "rather digressively," because the ancient mysteries explored in the Genesis version of the apple-dumpling story are the identical mysteries explored in terms of whaling symbols throughout *Moby-Dick*. Furthermore, Melville can only pretend to be superior to those who have suffered from this hereditary form of bellyache. The truth of the matter is that his own apple-dumpling indigestion lasted all his life. Fortunately, his excellent sense of humor provided him with a reliable cushion to recline on, and to help him absorb the painful shock of his Calvinistic ailments. But it would be a mistake to conclude that, merely because his sense of humor frequently permitted him to take pride in his lofty sense of detachment concerning man's various quests for God, he was ever completely free from spiritual gastritis. In his humorously buoyant moods, of course, he could actually view the entire Genesis story as a myth not unrelated to the myths of Babylonia, Persia, India, and Greece; but such a historical perspective was never so absorbing to him as that Calvinistic interpretation which he had acquired not only from his parents but also from that Dutch Reformed Church which clung to "the old-fashioned orthodoxy as well as, if not better than, any other denomination."[2] In that church, during Melville's youth, all American ministers were literally required to preach frequent exegetical sermons on the Genesis story, starting always with man's first disobedience. And the American branch of the Dutch Reformed Church prided itself on having permitted no changes in its standards of Calvinistic doctrine since the formulation of that doctrine in the Synod of Dort in 1619—exactly two hundred years before Melville was born. We are told that the doctrine, as preached in American churches, placed particular emphasis on "the fact and the cause of man's misery, the method of redemption, and the gratitude which is due to God therefor."[3] Many of Melville's paternal ancestors in New England cut their educational eyeteeth on the *New England Primer* or its equivalent, and of course "A" stood for "Adam" as a fit beginning, and "In Adam's fall we sinnéd all." Just how lustily Melville's father had imbibed Calvinistic dogma, we may gather from this passing justification of the inscrutable ways of God to men, in one of Allan Melville's letters: ". . . that divine first cause, who always moulds events to subserve the purposes of mercy & wisdom, often subjects poor human nature to the severest trials, that he may better display his sovereign power. . . ."[4]

There, in brief, Melville's father showed his deeply-rooted belief in John Calvin's dogma that no man can trust in his own power to achieve the good; that man must rather rid himself of any sense of self-importance as a "natural man." Martin Luther had set the pace for Calvin, and Luther's own words on "natural man" are worth remembering: "Man by nature does not want God to be God; he would much rather that he himself were God and that God were not God."[5] Luther added that natural man, because of his sense of self-sufficiency, is actually God's enemy; that because natural man prefers not to acknowledge himself to be a created being, responsible to his creator, this refusal is sin.

Both Luther and Calvin were well aware that the Renaissance humanists were as much their enemies as were the theologians of the Catholic Church. In order to understand the direction of the attacks against the natural man, made by Luther and Calvin, it is also worth remembering that Catholics and Protestants alike waged war against the Renaissance humanists; that many years after the Spanish physician Michael Servetus published his attack on the doctrine of the Trinity in 1531, he was arrested by the Inquisition, in Lyons, and escaped from the Catholics, only to be burned at the stake by Calvin, in Protestant Geneva. It is also worth remembering that the French physician François Rabelais was bitterly attacked by both Catholics and Protestants for his humanism and for his satirical *Gargantua and Pantagruel*, which Melville greatly admired, and of which Calvin seemed to be thinking particularly when he included Rabelais by name among the "curs who assume the attitudes of comedy in order to enjoy greater freedom to vomit their blasphemies."[6] It is also worth re-membering that the prominent humanist Eugene Dolet, intimate friend of Rabelais, was hanged and burned because he published a dialogue, attributed to Plato, which denied the immortality of the human soul. If we keep only a few of these sixteenth-century humanists in mind, we are better able to understand the reitera-tive insistence of the following passage from John Calvin's *Insti-tutes of the Christian Religion* (1535):

". . . be not conformed to this world; but be ye transformed by the renewing of your mind, that ye may prove what is that will of God.

"This is a very important consideration that we are consecrated and dedicated to God that we may not hereafter think, speak, meditate, or do anything but with a view to his glory, for that which is sacred cannot without great injustice toward Him be applied to unholy uses. If we are not our own but the Lord's, it is manifest both what error we must avoid and to what end all the actions of our lives are to be dedicated. We are not our own. Therefore, neither our reason nor our will should predominate in our deliberations and actions. We are not our own. Therefore, let us not propose it as our end to seek what may be expedient for us according to the flesh. We are not our own. Therefore, let us as far as possible forget ourselves and all things that are ours.

"On the contrary, we are God's. To Him, therefore, let us live and die. . . ."[7]

Although the skeptical humanists in the sixteenth century took great delight in challenging either Calvinism or Catholicism (or both) for assuming to have full knowledge as to "the will of God," and as to the proper relation of mankind to that will, they were always aware that death might be their immediate punishment, not from the hands of God but from the hands of either Calvinists or Catholics. As a result, the skeptical humanists took pleasure and comfort in being able to make use of various rhetorical and stylistic devices which would protect them from their enemies. Perhaps their greatest inspiration, in this regard, may be traced to the writings of one of Melville's favorite authors, Lucian, the sec-ond-century Greek satirist who ran the gamut of appropriate rhetorical devices (scurrility, irony, burlesque, parody, satire, mock-heroic, fantasy) while poking fun at the religious, philo-

sophical, and social vanities of his time. The Renaissance humanists must have been largely responsible for the demand which
produced thirty-five publications of parts of Lucian's works, either
in the original Greek or Latin, before 1500. The tone and temperament of Lucian may be gathered from one title page: "These are
the works of Lucian, who knew that folly is of ancient birth, and
that what seems wise to some men appears ridiculous to others;
there is no common judgment in men, but what you admire others
will laugh at."[8]

Sebastian Brandt's *Ship of Fools* (1494) owed something to
Lucian; Erasmus' *Praise of Folly* (1512), aimed largely at theologians, was perhaps chiefly inspired by Lucian, partly by Brandt;
Montaigne's *Essays* (1580) rest on the assumption that "there is
no common judgment in men."

Because Melville showed especial interest in both the style and
the subject matter of Montaigne's most celebrated essay, the
"Apology for Raimond Sebond," it is further worth remembering,
in this context, that Montaigne's reiterated question, "Que sais-je?"
suggests his deeply skeptical attitude as to the advisability of
pretending to know what goes on in the mind of God, and just
what the proper relationship is between man and God. Sebond's
orthodox thesis (that Christian faith could be established on a
solid foundation of rationalism) appeared ridiculous to Montaigne; but for self-protective reasons Montaigne employed sustained irony in his "Apology" by pretending to praise Sebond's
thesis. A modern authority on Montaigne says in effect that many
careless or bias-bound readers of the "Apology" have failed to
pierce the subterfuge and thus have misunderstood it: "A careful
reading of this, the most important and most interesting of the
essays, seems to make it pretty clear (if we keep in mind Montaigne's hints to the wise to 'catch his meaning' and read between
the lines) that the title was intentionally misleading, and that the
whole essay is an attack on Christian belief in general."[9]

While the Calvinists were being assailed from outside sources as
different as the orthodox Catholics and those unorthodox Renaissance humanists who yet paid lip-service to Catholicism (even as
Montaigne and Rabelais did), they were also assailed from within,
by individuals whose differences were formulated into dogmas,
sects, schisms. Many of these sects or schisms, in turn, established

their differences from Calvin by appealing to doctrines first formulated by Christian theologians in the second, third, and fourth centuries. For example, the theologian Arius, who died in 336, had been excommunicated for heresy because he taught that the orthodox doctrine of the Trinity was not valid; modifying his teachings, the so-called Arians of the sixteenth century arose to dispute Calvin. For another example, the Dutch theologian Jacobus Arminius (1560-1609) founded an anti-Calvinistic schism of the Reformed religion and called it the Remonstrant Church, accusing Calvin of developing the doctrine of predestination in such a way as to make God the Author of Sin. Arminius answered Calvin by insisting that man's freedom of will was a self-determining power which gave the individual sovereignty over one's own self, one's own actions, one's own volitions, and that this will was not predetermined by anything prior to this will. Back of Arminius' teachings may be found the related concepts of Pelagius, the fourth-fifth-century English monk who denied the validity of the doctrine of inherited original sin and insisted on the freedom of the will; back of Pelagius' teachings lie those of the second-century theologians of the Alexandrian School, Clement and Origen, who had taught that moral evil was the necessary result of that freedom of agency in created beings, without which those beings could not be subjects of praise or blame. Clement and Origen had also taught that God might mistakenly be considered the Author of Sin, but that the so-called evils proceeding from God were actually disciplinary and corrective admonitions and chastisements such as a father might administer to a child. The endless permutations and combinations of these theological and humanistic concepts are of interest to us, here, only because they were familiar to Melville and because he subserved and adapted them to his own spiritual and artistic needs.

While the anti-theologian writers of the sixteenth and seventeenth centuries were employing self-protective forms of rhetorical and stylistic indirections, the Calvinists themselves employed related forms of indirection to defend and illuminate their own beliefs. Placing so much stress on the fundamental importance of the Word of God, as "revealed" in the Bible, and insisting on a literal reading of the Bible, Calvinistic writers might have displayed no interest in the ancient and medieval Christian preoccupation with allegorical interpretations of Bible stories. But, among the many unintentional contradictions and paradoxes in Calvinism, one of the most obvious was that Calvin, while urging a literal reading of the Scriptures, had actually borrowed from Catholicism an allegorical cosmology, based on the Scriptures. And in England this essential contradiction helped pave the way for the allegorical qualities of Bunyan's *Pilgrim's Progress* and Milton's *Paradise Lost*.

Because Melville became fascinated by the possibilities of self-protective indirection inherent not only in the writings of the Renaissance humanists but also in the writings of the essentially Calvinistic Milton and Bunyan, it may be well to keep in mind Bunyan's own words as to the effect which his literary form and method might have on his readers. In his "Author's Apology" for *Pilgrim's Progress*, he justified his method in terms of the Bible:

> I find that Holy Writ in many places
> Hath semblance with this method, where the cases
> Do call for one thing, to set forth another:
> Use it I may, then, and yet nothing smother
> Truth's golden beams: nay, by this method may
> Make it cast forth its rays as light as day.

In his conclusion to the first part of *Pilgrim's Progress* he added this:

> Now, Reader, I have told my Dream to thee;
> See if thou canst interpret it to me,
> Or to thyself, or neighbor; but take heed
> Of misinterpreting, for that, instead
> Of doing good, will but thyself abuse:
> By misinterpreting, evil ensues. . . .
> Put by the curtains, look within my veil;
> Turn up my metaphor, and do not fail.
> There, if thou seekest them, such things to find
> As will be helpful to an honest mind.

Milton's indirections, on the other hand, are far more complex and elaborate than Bunyan's. As a scholar, he was much better aware than the humble Bunyan could have been that the "great argument" which he undertook in *Paradise Lost* was closely re-

lated to the entire controversy waged between the Reformation
Calvinists and the Renaissance humanists. One major aspect of
the controversy centered on the word "freedom," and on the ancient question as to how it was possible for a human being to assert
any free will if all was predestined; on the equally ancient question as to the source of evil, if the universe were created by an
all-good God.

Before writing *Paradise Lost*, Milton put his own theological
house in order by elaborating his personal views in his essay on
The Christian Doctrine, which might be viewed as Milton's attempt to reconcile and correlate and harmonize the conflicting
views of Reformation Calvinism and Renaissance humanism, by
elaborating the Pauline doctrine of freedom within the law: freedom of will within the law of divine predestination. *Paradise Lost*
represents an artistic projection, in epic form, of those same personal convictions which Milton had previously elaborated in *The
Christian Doctrine*. Adapting to his own prejudices the conflicting
arguments previously advanced by Calvinists, Arminians, Clement, Origen, Milton made his precarious scales balance by placing
his own hand somewhat heavily on the Calvinistic side. Those who
have tried to claim for Milton a right to be viewed as a Renaissance humanist are fighting a hopeless battle. Although he permitted his "great argument" to include opposing views, such a
device was purely rhetorical, in order to squelch the so-called
Pelagian views of the Renaissance humanists. As though to put
those humanists in their place, Milton arranged to let Satan act
out the part of the Renaissance humanist, in one sense, and consequently get damned to Hell for holding such preposterous notions; to let Adam and Eve assert their own humanism, briefly,
and consequently bring on themselves the wages of their so-called
sin. In these closely parallel symbolic actions, as represented in
Paradise Lost, Milton revealed that his indignation against the
humanists was similar to that which Luther had in mind when he
wrote, "Man by nature does not want God to be God; he would
much rather that he himself were God and that God were not
God." In other words, while the positive side of Milton's thematic
coin was designed to justify the ways of God to men, the negative
side of that coin was designed to illustrate the folly, as Milton

24

saw it, of natural man's attempt to turn his back on Milton's concept of God. To Milton, any such sinful back-turning brought its own retribution: the fault could not be imputed to God. How ironic, Milton implied, for man or Satan to blame God, or to quarrel with God; how ironic for Satan to hurl defiances at God in the following Promethean terms:

> . . . yet not for those
> Nor what the Potent Victor in his rage
> Can else inflict do I repent or change,
> Though chang'd in outward lustre; that fixt mind
> And high disdain, from sense of injur'd merit,
> That with the mightiest rais'd me to contend,
> And to the fierce contention brought along
> Innumerable force of Spirits arm'd
> That durst dislike his reign, and me preferring,
> His utmost power with adverse power oppos'd
> In dubious Battle on the Plains of Heav'n,
> And shook his throne. What though the field be lost?
> All is not lost; the unconquerable Will,
> And study of revenge, immortal hate,
> And courage never to submit or yield:
> And what is else not to be overcome?[10]

From Milton's viewpoint, the ironically heroic and defiant attitude of Satan was closely related to the ironic pretentiousness of any humanistic attempt to deny the validity of God's law, as the Calvinists said that law had been "revealed" in the Holy Scripture. To the humanist, on the other hand, there was something far more ironic and pretentious in Milton's Calvinistic notion that God had actually "revealed" the letter of the law, in any sense; something additionally ironic in Milton's notion that he had succeeded in justifying the ways of God to men. In fact, the basic problems in the "great argument" had only been complicated by Milton's attempt to resolve those problems. For example, when Milton arranged his myth in such a way as to let Christ ask God some rhetorical questions, merely for the purpose of letting God give the right answers (after the manner of the catechism), some of Milton's unsympathetic readers could not help but believe that the questions came nearer the truth. These are some of the ques-

tions which Christ is permitted to ask God in Book Three of
Paradise Lost:

> For should Man finally be lost, should Man
> Thy creature late so lov'd, thy youngest Son
> Fall circumvented thus by fraud, though join'd
> With his own folly? . . .
> Or shall the Adversary thus obtain
> His end, and frustrate thine, shall he fulfil
> His malice, and thy goodness bring to naught,
> Or proud return though to his heavier doom,
> Yet with revenge accomplish't and to Hell
> Draw from him the whole Race of mankind,
> By him corrupted? . . .
> So should thy goodness and thy greatness both
> Be questioned and blasphem'd without defense.

One of Milton's most brilliant opponents, in spirit if not in letter,
was one of Melville's favorite authors: a seventeenth-century
Frenchman, back-slidden from Calvinism, named Pierre Bayle.
After having sought refuge in Rotterdam from Catholic persecu-
tion Bayle soon discovered that his fondness for ridiculing all
theological pretentiousness was likely to get him into equally
serious trouble with the Dutch Calvinists. A great admirer of Montaigne, Bayle developed his own varieties of self-protective stylistic equivocations and employed them with devastating effective-
ness in his anti-theological *Dictionnaire historique et critique*,
published at Rotterdam in French in 1697, and issued in English
translation at London in 1710.

Because Melville owned a set of Bayle's folio volumes and made
extensive use of Bayle's matter and manner, there is justification
for lingering a while here. Anticipating the Encyclopaedists, Bayle
set out to summarize such historical knowledge as enabled him to
display his own amused contempt for superstitions of all kinds,
and to display his witty awareness of the human tendency to let
all evaluations be controlled by personal prejudices and bias. Like
Lucian and Montaigne (to name but two), Bayle took skeptical
delight in showing that "what seems wise to some men appears
ridiculous to others." But the apparent diffuseness of his satirical
method was actually a self-protective way of going around Robin

26

Hood's barn to pounce on his *bête noire*: Calvinistic dogma. Because the Calvinists made so much of their understanding exactly how to interpret "the word of God" as revealed in the Bible, Bayle borrowed from Montaigne the dead-pan trick of quoting or paraphrasing a familiar scriptural passage in a context which made the orthodox interpretation of that passage appear ridiculous. Again, he would summarize an entire Bible story (such as the life story of David or of Abraham) in order to hint that the facts concerning these sacred figures raised some question as to whether these figures should be held up as models of human conduct, or whether their God deserved to be worshiped.

A more elaborate example of Bayle's matter and manner may be illustrated by recalling an incident which occurred soon after the *Dictionary* was published. At the instigation of certain rabid Calvinistic theologians in the Dutch Reformed Church, Bayle was arraigned in court and accused (among many things) of having presented the views of ancient heresiarchs in such a way as to reveal his heretical sympathies. Particularly, his accusers said, Bayle seemed to believe the heretical notion of the Manicheans and Paulicians and Zoroastrians that the problem of evil could best be explained by means of the hypothesis that there were two coeternal Principles in the Universe: a Good Principle and an Evil Principle. In his own mock-serious defense, Bayle protested that his beliefs were "orthodox," and that his detached concern for historical truth had been misunderstood. If Bayle had dared tell the truth, in that bigoted court, he might have explained that the major error on the part of his accusers had been their failure to pierce the ironic and self-protective subtlety of his rhetorical and stylistic methods. He had indeed devoted a great deal of space to ancient heresies, not because they interested him, as such, but because they enabled him to contrast the pretentiousness of those heresies with the even greater pretentiousness of Calvinistic dogma. An excellent example of Bayle's rascality, in this regard, may be found in the first part of his article on the heretical sect known as the Paulicians:

"PAULICIANS. Thus were the *Manichees* in *Armenia* call'd, when one *Paul* became their Head in the VII. Century. . . . Their fundamental Doctrine was that of Two Co-eternal Principles, and independent one upon another. This Doctrine at first hearing creates Horror, and consequently 'tis strange, that the *Manichean* Sect could seduce so great a Part of the World. But on the other Side, 'tis so difficult to Answer their Objections, about the Origin of Evil, that we must not wonder that the Hypothesis of the two Principles, the one Good and the other Bad, should have dazzled the Eyes of many Ancient Philosophers, and then found so many Followers in Christendom, where the Doctrine which teaches the Capital Enmity of the Devils to the true God, is always accompanied with the Doctrine, which teaches the Rebellion and Fall of one Part of the good Angels. [Note well!]

"This Hypothesis of the Two Principles would probably have made a greater Progress, if the particulars of it had been given less grossly, and if it had not been attended with many odious Practices, or if there had been then as many Disputes about Predestination, as there are at this Day, in which the Christians accuse one another, either of making God the Author of Sin, or of depriving him of the Government of the World.

"The Pagans could better answer than the Christians to the Objections of the *Manichees*; but some of their Philosophers found it a difficult thing. I shall observe in what Sense the Orthodox seem to admit of the Two First Principles, and in what Sense it cannot be said that according to the *Manichees*, God is the Author of Sin. I shall also criticize a Modern Author, who says that the Doctrine, which makes God the Author of Sin, does not lead a man to Irreligion. Nay, he says, that Doctrine raises God to the highest Degree of Glory that can be conceived.

"The Ancient Fathers were not ignorant that the Question concerning the Origin of Evil, is a most perplexing one. They could not resolve it by the *Platonick* Hypothesis, which was at the Bottom a Branch of *Manicheism*, seeing it admitted of two Principles: they found themselves obliged to have recourse to the Privilege of the Free-Will of Men; but the more we reflect on that manner of resolving the Difficulty, the more we find that the natural light of Philosophy ties and intangles that Gordian Knot. . . ."[11]

Considering the time and the place, Bayle's article on the Paulicians should be recognized as a very clever and saucy piece of writing, packed with insinuations highly uncomplimentary to Calvinistic dogma. Bayle's footnotes to his articles are usually the frosting on the cake, and one footnote to the "Paulicians" article may serve as a pertinent example. In reference to the statement, "I shall observe in what Sense the Orthodox seem to admit of Two First Principles," Bayle subtends:

"It has been a constant Opinion amongst Christians from the Beginning, that the *Devil* is the Author of all false Religions; that he moves the Hereticks to dogmatize, and inspires Men with Errors, Superstitions, Schisms, Lewdness, Avarice, Intemperance; in a Word, with all the Crimes that are committed amongst Men: That he deprived *Adam* and *Eve* of their Innocency; from whence it follows that he is the Cause of Moral Evil, and of all the Miseries of Man. He is therefore the first Principle of Evil; but because he is not Eternal nor uncreated, he is not the first Ill Principle, in the Sense of the *Manichees*: which afforded those Hereticks I know not what manner of boasting and Insulting over the Orthodox. They might have told them,

" 'Your Doctrine is much more prejudicial to the Good God than ours; for you make him the Cause of the Ill Principle; you assert that he produced him and that tho' he could stop him at the first Step he made, yet he permitted him to usurp so great a Power in this World, that Mankind having been divided into two Cities, that of God and that of the Devil, the first was always very small, and even so small for many Ages, that it had not two Inhabitants, when the other had two Millions. We are not obliged to enquire into the Cause of the Wickedness of our Ill Principle; for when an uncreated Being is so or so, one cannot say why it is so; it is its Nature, one must necessarily stop there; but as for the Qualities of a Creature, one ought to inquire into the Reason of them, and it cannot be found but in its Cause. You must therefore say that God is the Author of the Devil's Malice, that he himself produced it such as it is, or sowed the Seeds of it in the Soul that he created; which is a thousand times more dishonourable to God, than to say that he is not the only necessary and independent Being.'

"This brings in again the above mention'd Objections concerning the Fall of the first Man; it is not therefore necessary to insist any longer upon it. We must humbly acknowledge that Philosophy is here at a stand, and that its Weakness ought to lead us to the Light of Revelation, where we shall find a sure and stedfast Anchor."[12]

Part of Bayle's slyness, there, is his deliberate avoidance of quotation marks (which I have added) when he begins to tell what arguments the Manichees *might* have used, and which Bayle therefore feels called on, in all historical accuracy, to state! The possible confusion, near the end, is not entirely accidental, and the appeal to the "Light of Revelation" as a "sure and stedfast Anchor" is ironic, sarcastic. Yet whenever irony is thus used, some readers are bound to miss it. A modern scholar, who agrees, cites Bayle's almost too great success in this regard:

"Bayle was also faced with the criticisms of men who were ordinarily on his side. Leibnitz, the German philosopher, LeClerc, the journalist, Jaquelot, the liberal theologician, called in question Bayle's assumption that reason was a useless defense of Christianity, that the only recourse was to retire behind the defensive walls of Holy Scripture, where divine inspiration was an impregnable fortification."[13]

What factors contribute to the possibility that we may make the mistake of reading literally a statement made ironically, or sarcastically? The major factor is usually our tendency to read into a statement exactly the value or meaning we prefer to find. Another factor may be our limited sense of the humorous, the comic, so that slyness passes unnoticed. Melville prided himself on being a "lynx-eyed" reader, and yet there is the strong possibility that he himself sometimes misinterpreted Bayle's ironic and sarcastic references to God as the Author of Evil; that Melville's disillusionment made him prefer to think that he and Bayle (and Hawthorne) actually and seriously shared that somber view. Although Melville was of course wrong about both Bayle and Hawthorne, he found in Bayle and in other writers considerable historical evidence that several ancient (and modern) heresiarchs, along with several orthodox Calvinists, had indeed seriously viewed God as the Author of Evil.[14]

Bayle's vigorous and energetic rationalism had such a powerful impact on thinkers in England that his *Dictionary* became known among the rationalists as "the Bible of the Eighteenth Century." His emphasis on common sense and reason, as opposed to the gullibility of blind faith in superstitions, impinges on the views of Bacon, Hobbes, Locke, Shaftesbury. And, in a curiously paradoxical sense, it should be noticed that Bayle's stress on the obligation of the natural man to assert his natural powers helped pave the way for the success of Rousseau's ideas. For example, when Bayle was attacked for saying that some individuals who had no religious beliefs were yet capable of a high theory and practice of moral conduct, the Calvinistic attacks against Bayle's championing of what they called "atheism" forced him to write an "Explanation" which he published in the appendix to the second edition of the *Dictionary*. It slyly and insinuatively began thus:

"Such as have been scandaliz'd at my saying that there have been *Atheists* and *Epicureans* who have outdone most Idolaters in good Morals, are intreated to reflect well upon all the following Considerations; which if they please to do, their Scandal will vanish, and entirely disappear.

"The Fear and Love of God are not the only Spring of Human Actions. There are other Principles that actuate a Man; the love of Praise, the fear of Disgrace, the Natural Temper, Punishments and Rewards in the Magistrate's hands, have a mighty influence upon the Heart. He that doubts of it, must be ignorant of what passes in his own Breast, and what the common course of the World may give him an ocular demonstration of, every moment. But 'tis not probable there is any one stupid enough to be ignorant of such a Truth. . . .

"The Fear and Love of God are not always a more active Principle than the rest: The love of Glory, the fear of Infamy, Death or Torments, the hope of Preferment, act with greater force upon some men, than the desire of pleasing God, and the fear of breaking his Commandments. If any one doubts of it, he is ignorant of some of his own Actions, and knows nothing of what is doing daily under the Sun. . . . A Soldier who has quitted all for his Religion, finding himself under the necessity of offending God if he revenges himself for having receiv'd a Box o' th' Ear, or of being accounted a Coward if he does not, never rests till he has Satisfaction for this Affront, tho' at the peril of killing or being kill'd in a state that must be follow'd with Eternal Damnation. 'Tis not likely that any one is so stupid as to be ignorant of such things. Therefore let this Moral Aphorism take place amongst first Principles, *That the Fear and Love of God are not always the most active Principle of Human Actions.*

"This being so, it ought not to be reckon'd a scandalous Paradox,

3 1

but rather a very possible thing, that some Men without Religion should be more forcibly excited to a good Moral Life by their Constitution . . . than some others by the Instinct of Conscience.

"The Scandal ought to be much greater, when we see so many people convinc'd of the Truths of Religion, at the same time over head and ears in Vice.

"Nay, it is more strange that Heathen Idolaters should do good Actions, than that Atheistical Philosophers should live like Virtuous Men: For the former must have been led to Crimes by their very Religion; it must have been a Point of Faith with them, That to make themselves Imitators of God, which is the End and Substance of Religion, they ought to be Cheats, Envious, Fornicators, Adulterers, Pederasts. . . ."[15]

It will be noticed, there, that Bayle protects himself by establishing his insinuative contrast between men motivated by "natural" impulses, and pagans motivated by idol-worship. Although this permits Bayle to protest that the true religion, Christianity, lies quite outside his immediate discussion, the context makes it clear that, throughout the passage, Bayle satirically includes the Calvinists among idol worshipers! As the *Dictionary* shows, Bayle was familiar with the writings of Bacon, Hobbes, and Shaftesbury, and it was Bacon who had supplied Hobbes with the metaphorical representation of superstitions as "Idols of the Mind." Consequently, in the eighteenth century, Bayle's influence was reflected in the thinking of the various rationalists whom Pope represented in his celebrated couplet:

> Know then thyself, presume not God to scan;
> The proper study of mankind is man.

But if God should be entirely removed from the scene, what would man worship? The State, said Hobbes. Himself, said Rousseau, in effect. Both of these suggestions were of so much interest to Melville that we need to have a few aspects of the opposing arguments in mind; particularly the juggled concepts of natural man as a man-of-war, so to speak, and natural man as a man-of-peace. In his *Leviathan* (1651), from which Melville quotes in *Moby-Dick*, Hobbes begins by considering the natural state of man. Because his concern is for usable truth, he defines (and thus slyly dismisses) religious faith as grounded on *"feare* of power invisible, feigned by the mind, or imagined from tales publiquely allowed." (He adds that "superstition" is identical with "religion" except that in the case of a superstitious belief, we do not allow it as valid!) Hobbes proceeds to show that mankind, in a primitive and natural condition, is indeed endowed with certain equal and sovereign and inalienable rights; but that because this natural state leads to a condition of warfare, man learned long ago to band together to form a civil state in which some individual "sovereignty" was surrendered, to obtain peace and order; that without such surrender individual sovereignty results in anarchy. From this solid beginning, Hobbes proceeds to employ some witty casuistries in urging that the best civil state occurs when individuals surrender their sovereignty to the sovereignty of one man with divine rights, so to speak; which brings him to a sly explanation of his title: "This done, the Multitude so united in one Person is called a Common-wealth, in latine *Civitas*. This is the generation of that great LEVIATHAN, or rather (to speak more reverently) of that Mortall God, to which wee owe under the Immortall God, our peace and defence."[16]

Reacting violently against Hobbes, a century later, Rousseau argued that man in his natural state as a "noble savage" is not at all in a state of war. Born to Calvinist parents in that stronghold of Calvinism, Geneva, Rousseau first escaped from Calvinism by embracing Catholicism and then, after a brief return to a modified belief in Calvinism, settled down to glorify the natural rights of man. But so strongly had Calvinism affected Rousseau's thinking that he worked out the foundation stone of his thinking in terms of the Garden of Eden trope. When convenient, he returned to pick up such of the old concepts as would serve his new argument. He insisted that the fruit of the tree of knowledge was correctly denied to man, in his pure and innocent state. Man brought on himself his own fall, when he became curious about increasing his knowledge; but the serpent which tempted man, and thus hastened the fall, was man-made science. And civilization, with all its forms for denying the liberty and equality of man, the rights of man, was the man-created evil enemy of man: the powerful had organized and controlled government, in order to reduce the less powerful to slavery.

The cure? A social contract made between individuals and

designed to rectify, as much as possible, the evil consequences of the fall of man from his original and primitive perfection, in the Garden of Eden. But the sovereignty must remain with the people: it must never be delegated to one man. As for religion in the new state, Calvinism and Catholicism must be abolished. In place of them, a natural religion (so called) would be imposed and Rousseau's sovereign individuals would be required to believe in God, in immortality, in future rewards and punishments. The penalty for failing to believe in these "natural" teachings would be either banishment or death! That which is of particular interest to us in this curious hodgepodge of ideas is Rousseau's insistence on the "sovereignty" of man and on the "rights of man."

A minor but picturesque by-product of the widespread rebellion against authoritarian forms and rules, at the end of the eighteenth century, was the literary tendency, among some writers, to invert the meaning of the Satan myth, in Hebrew literature, and thus to formulate a new Ophite sect or "Devil School." Back in the second century, a cult of Gnostics had called themselves Ophites (Serpent-worshipers) and had glorified Satan because of their belief that God had been the one who had lied to Adam and Eve, in the first place, and that Satan had been the one who had helped to liberate Adam and Eve from the indignity of servitude to a malicious God. The Ophites went on to make the ironic observation (twisted by Bayle) that if a man really wished to copy God, that man should be just as deceptive, unjust, malicious, and evil as God. Those whom we might call the heretical Neophytes, centuries later, did their best to capture Milton's *Paradise Lost* in order to convert Milton's Satan to their own uses. Some even took pleasure in claiming that Milton himself had belonged to the Devil's Party, and that he realized Satan had spoken the truth when he said to natural man and woman, in the Garden, "Your eyes shall be opened, and ye shall be as gods, knowing good and evil." For example, William Blake's reaction against authoritarianism led him, temporarily, to glorify Milton's Satan and to preach a modified Ophite doctrine in praise of natural man, liberated from dogma:

"All Bibles or sacred codes have been the causes of the following Errors: That Man has two real existing principles, Viz. a Body & a Soul; that Energy, call'd Evil, is alone from the Body; & that

Reason, call'd Good, is alone from the Soul; that God will torment Man in Eternity for following his Energies.

"But the following Contraries to these are True: Man has no Body distinct from his Soul; for that call'd Body, is a portion of Soul discern'd by the five Senses, the chief inlets of Soul in this age. Energy is the only life and is from the Body; and Reason is the bound or outward circumference of Energy. Energy is Eternal Delight.

"Those who restrain desire, do so because theirs is weak enough to be restrained; and the restrainer, or reason, usurps its place & governs the unwilling. And being restrain'd, it by degrees becomes passive, till it is only the shadow of desire.

"The history of this is written in *Paradise Lost*, & the Governor, or Reason, is call'd Messiah. And the original Archangel, or possessor of the command of the heavenly host, is call'd the Devil or Satan, and his children are call'd Sin & Death.

"But in the Book of Job, Milton's Messiah is call'd Satan. For this history had been adopted by both parties. It indeed appear'd to Reason as if Desire was cast out, but the Devil's account is, that the Messiah fell, & formed a heaven of what he stole from the Abyss. . . . But in Milton, the Father is Destiny, the Son a Ratio of the five senses, & the Holy-ghost Vacuum!

"*Note.* The reason Milton wrote in fetters when he wrote of Angels & God, and at liberty when of Devils & Hell, is because he was a true Poet and of the Devil's party without knowing it."[17]

Part of Blake's purpose in announcing this new-old heresy was to point out that the vengeful and vindictive way in which God subordinated and punished Satan in *Paradise Lost* was an unattractive but appropriate symbol of the manner in which the orthodox Christian dogma of "right reason" had in the past exerted a crippling effect on natural man's God-given desire to fulfill his potentialities. Blake's viewpoint, an interesting modification and extension of the Manichaean concept, was not entirely unrelated to that of certain God-indifferent humanists, on one hand, and of God-bitten Melville, on the other hand. Like Blake, Melville was more inclined toward poetry than toward philosophy; like Blake, he was also inclined to trust the impulses of the heart rather than the restraining rationalizations of the mind, and thus to glory in man's Prometheanism. He implied as much in a pertinent letter to Hawthorne:

"I stand for the heart. To the dogs with the head! I had rather be a fool with a heart, than Jupiter Olympus with his head. The reason the mass of men fear God and *at bottom dislike* Him, is because they rather distrust His heart, and fancy Him all brain like a watch. (You perceive I employ a capital initial in the pronoun referring to the Deity; don't you think there is a slight dash of flunkeyism in the usage?)"[18]

Although Melville is being cautious there, his remarks suggest that he may have had in mind the Shelley of *Queen Mab* and of *Prometheus Unbound*, rather than Blake; that he may have been thinking particularly of the Titan's curse on Jupiter. Shelley, in his preface to *Prometheus Unbound* had partially correlated the Hellenic myth with the Hebraic myth:

". . . I was averse from a catastrophe so feeble as that of reconciling the Champion with the Oppressor of mankind. The moral interest of the fable, which is so powerfully sustained by the sufferings and endurance of Prometheus, would be annihilated if we could conceive of him as unsaying his high language and quailing before his successful and perfidious adversary. The only imaginary being, resembling in any degree Prometheus, is Satan; and Prometheus is, in my judgment, a more poetical character than Satan, because, in addition to courage, and majesty, and firm and patient opposition to omnipotent force, he is susceptible of being described as exempt from the taints of ambition, envy, revenge, and a desire for personal aggrandizement, which in the hero of *Paradise Lost*, interfere with the interest. The character of Satan engenders in the mind a pernicious casuistry which leads us to weigh his faults with his wrongs, and to excuse the former because the latter exceed all measure. In the minds of those who consider that magnificent fiction [*Paradise Lost*] with a religious feeling it engenders something worse. But Prometheus is, as it were, the type of the highest perfection of moral and intellectual nature impelled by the purest and the truest motives to the best and noblest ends."[19]

With Shelley and Blake in mind, we are in a better position to appreciate that Melville's delight in the antithesis between "acceptance" and "defiance" implies a number of backward-looking corollaries which we shall find adapted obliquely, in his major narratives, starting with *Mardi*. But this brief contextual background is inadequate until the related viewpoint of Lord Byron is added. Even as *Paradise Lost* may be viewed as Milton's personal exegesis and artistic commentary on the Genesis story, so Byron's *Cain* may be viewed is an inverted and anti-Calvinistic commentary, in which Byron clearly shows his kinship of viewpoint not only with Blake and the early Shelley but also with the long tradition of skeptics who had delighted to ridicule Calvinistic dogma by pretending to undertake a serious piece of Biblical interpretation. In his "Preface" to *Cain*, Byron craftily protests:

"The reader will recollect that the book of Genesis does not state that Eve was tempted by a demon, but by 'the Serpent'; and that only because he was 'the most subtil of all the beasts of the field.' Whatever interpretation the Rabbins and the Fathers may have put upon this, I take the words as I find them, and reply, with Bishop Watson upon similar occasions, when the Fathers were quoted to him, as Moderator in the school of Cambridge, 'Behold the Book!'—holding up the Scripture. It is to be recollected, that my present subject has nothing to do with the *New Testament*, to which no references can be here made without anachronism. With the poems upon similar topics I have not been recently familiar. Since I was twenty I have never read Milton; but I had read him so frequently before, that this may make little difference."[20]

In the first scene of *Cain*, Byron continues his heretical Biblical interpretation as soon as Adam asks Cain why he does not pray with the others:

Adam. Son Cain, my first-born, wherefore art thou silent?
Cain. Why should I speak?
Adam.   To pray.
Cain.   Have ye not pray'd?
Adam. We have, most fervently.
Cain.   And loudly: I
       have heard you.
Adam.   So will God, I trust.
Abel.   Amen!
Adam. But thou, my eldest born, art silent still.
Cain. 'Tis better I should be so.
Adam.   Wherefore so?

> *Cain.* I have nought to ask.
> *Adam.*   Nor aught to thank for?
> *Cain.*   No.
> *Adam.* Dost thou not live?
> *Cain.*   Must I not die?
> *Adam.*   Alas!
> Oh, God, why didst thou plant the tree of knowledge?
> *Cain.* And wherefore pluck'd ye not the tree of life?
> Ye might have then *defied* him. [Italics added]
> *Adam.*   Oh! my son,
> Blaspheme not: these are serpent's words.
> *Cain.*   Why not?
> The snake spoke *truth*: it *was* the tree of knowledge;
> It *was* the tree of life: knowledge is good
> And life is good; and how can both be evil?

Cain's first soliloquy contains a passage which may be viewed not merely as a part of Byron's further commentary on Genesis but also as a reflection of Byron's own skeptical desire to attack a cornerstone of Christian doctrine:

> The tree was planted and why not for him?
> If not, why place him near it, where it grew,
> The fairest in the centre? They have but
> One answer to all questions, ''Twas *his* will
> And *he* is good.' How know I that? Because
> He is all-powerful, must all-good, too, follow?
> I judge but by the fruits—and they are bitter—
> Which I must feed on for a fault not mine.

Also in the first scene, Byron's own correlation between Prometheus and his own inverted interpretation of Milton's Satan becomes clear as soon as Cain and Lucifer converse:

> *Cain.*   Ah!
> Thou look'st almost a god; and—
> *Lucifer.*   I am none;
> And having fail'd to be one, would be nought
> Save what I am. He conquer'd; let him reign!
> *Cain.* Who?
> *Lucifer.* Thy sire's Maker, and the earth's.

Cain.   And heaven's,
        And all that in them is. So I have heard
        His seraphs sing; and so my father saith.
Lucifer. They say—what they must sing and say, on pain
        Of being that which I am—and thou art—
        Of spirits and of men.
Cain.   And what is that?
Lucifer. Souls who dare use their immortality—
        Souls who dare look the Omnipotent tyrant in
        His everlasting face, and tell him that
        His evil is not good! If he has made,
        As he saith—which I know not, nor believe—
        But, if he made us—he cannot unmake:
        We are immortal! nay, he'd *have* us so,
        That he may torture:—let him! He is great—
        But, in his greatness, is no happier than
        We in our conflict: Goodness would not make
        Evil; and what else has he made?

Byron's Lucifer and Cain are literary ancestors of Melville's Captain Ahab, and we shall see, later, that there is some value in viewing parts of *Moby-Dick* as satirical and rationalistic Melvillian commentaries on the Word of God. But the strongest correlation between Byron's Lucifer and Byron's Prometheus, as ancestors of Captain Ahab, may be established merely by quoting the concluding lines of Byron's poem, *Prometheus*:

        But baffled as thou wert from high,
        Still in thy patient energy,
        In the endurance, and repulse
            Of thine impenetrable Spirit,
        Which Earth and Heaven could not convulse,
            A mighty lesson we inherit:
        Thou art a symbol and a sign
            To Mortals of their fate and force;
        Like thee, Man is in part divine,
            A troubled stream from a pure source;
        And Man in portions can foresee
        His own funereal destiny;
        His wretchedness and his resistance,

And his sad unallied existence:
To which his Spirit may oppose
Itself—and equal to all woes,
   And a firm will, and a deep sense,
Which even in torture can descry
   Its own concenter'd recompense,
Triumphant where it dares defy,
And making Death a Victory.[21]

Thus ends a selective and pertinent harvest of some literary fruits cultivated from the seed of that forbidden tree which grew in Genesis. Without exception, the authors quoted were familiar to Melville. As we shall see, these authors provided Melville with concepts which he adapted to his own needs, in his thinking; to his own uses, in his art.

EDEN REVISITED

CHAPTER II

Ah, paddle away, brave chieftain, to the land of spirits! To the material eye thou makest but little progress; but with the eye of faith, I see thy canoe cleaving the bright waves, which die away on those dimly looming shores of Paradise.

This strange superstition affords another evidence of the fact, that however ignorant man may be, he still feels within him his immortal spirit yearning after the unknown future.

MELVILLE, *Typee*

EDEN REVISITED

So RICH and varied were Melville's youthful adventures that they provided abundant raw materials for seven book-length narratives, which he wrote and published during the first seven years of his literary career. Such an extraordinary demonstration of sheer energy (not to mention talent) is not easily matched in the history of American letters; but there is a restricted aspect of that demonstration which is even more extraordinary. In most of those narratives, Melville consciously arranged his picturesque subject matter to represent, in specific or symbolic forms, different aspects of his own religious disillusionment.

Pierre, the seventh of these narratives, is easily recognized as a fictional projection of the author's spiritual autobiography during the progressive phases of his youth. *Moby-Dick*, the sixth, is centered symbolically on a limited aspect of Captain Ahab's religious disillusionment, which has much in common with a parallel aspect of Melville's own story. Although the other five narratives should be viewed as apprentice works in which Melville was making elaborate experiments with style, structure, form, as he sought to discover his own idiom, they all deal with disillusionment, in either subject matter or theme. Of these, the fifth, *White-Jacket*, carried in its very title the central image of a homemade garment (symbolically a garment of the conscience) which the owner improvises, patches, discards. The fourth, *Redburn*, is a story of a young man's initial and disillusioning contact with the world when he leaves home for the first time. The third, *Mardi*, approaches the subject of disillusionment in terms of conventional moral allegory.

43

A careful progression through these narratives, in chronological order of writing, will also reveal that Melville's spiritual idiom (in part the cause and in part the effect of his disillusionment) was the major factor which shaped and controlled and determined his mature artistic idiom. The complexities of that involved relationship are only suggested by the demonstrable fact that his cumulative revulsion against orthodox Christian doctrine made him so self-conscious that he began, in *Mardi*, to experiment with riddling techniques, insinuative symbolism, satirical allegory, to protect himself from, and to retaliate against, those orthodox readers who were his enemies.

For purposes of clarification, three distinct phases of Melville's blended artistic and spiritual development may be suggested, somewhat arbitrarily. The first phase, reflected in his first two books, *Typee* (1846) and *Omoo* (1847), reveals his apprentice preoccupation with mere travel-narrative (essentially factual in nature), written during a period when he still clung to his jolted belief in the fundamentals of his Calvinistic religious heritage. The second phase, reflected in his third book, *Mardi* (1849), reveals his more sophisticated artistic preoccupation with moral allegory, written during a period when his own heart and mind had suddenly become a battleground across which his growing skepticism counterattacked his deeply ingrained mystical faith. Defensively, Melville arranged an alliance between Christian and Platonic concepts, in *Mardi*, to resist that counterattack. The third phase, reflected in his next two books, *Redburn* (1849) and *White-Jacket* (1850), reveals his modified use of fictionalized travel-narrative (blended with ambivalent allegorical connotations in *White-Jacket*), during a period when he began to take increasingly crafty and covert delight in asserting his skepticism; when he became increasingly preoccupied with glorifying Rousseau's concepts of man-centered man's inalienable rights, and with ridiculing Calvinistic concepts of God-centered man.

I am aware that this arbitrary representation of these so-called phases is much too pat, in that it oversimplifies the fluctuations and complexities of Melville's aesthetic and spiritual responses to his own experience. Nevertheless, some form of oversimplification is necessary in order to clarify the fact that the tug of war in Melville's heart and mind did have a recognizable outcome, and did

not end in a stalemate. Matthew Arnold's "Dover Beach" image
(tidal ebb, as symbolic of religious disillusionment) may be modified to serve us here. By the time Melville came to write *Typee*
and *Omoo,* he himself was apparently aware that his own Sea of
Faith (which had been at the full during the years before he left
home) had begun to ebb; yet he tried to resist that ebb. Although
the immediate sea-level, during an ebb tide, moves slowly and
irresistibly out and down, the waves move in exactly the opposite
direction. And each wave leaves briefly the distinct mark of its
attainment on the beach. Melville's resistance to the ebb of his
own belief may be represented by that wave-versus-tide siege of
contraries. During the first two phases of Melville's apprenticeship
disillusionment, his response differed from Arnold's, in that Melville refused to surrender to the tide's "melancholy, long, with-
drawing roar, retreating." His reaction was one of wavelike resistance, temporarily, and the brief attainment of these waves may be
viewed in all these early narratives.

2

IN PLANNING to write his first narrative, just after his twenty-fifth
birthday, Melville chose to present a slightly fictionalized version
of a picturesque personal experience still quite fresh in his mind.
Approximately four years earlier, he had shipped out of New
Bedford aboard the whaler *Acushnet* for the Pacific, and had
grown so dissatisfied with drudgery that he had jumped ship at
Nukuhiva Harbor in the South Seas. He and his shipmate-com-
panion in the escapade decided to hide away in a native valley,
but by accident they entered the wrong valley and were forced to
accept the dubious hospitality of cannibals. In retrospect, Melville
viewed these primitive people as proof that Rousseau's glorifica-
tion of the "noble savage" was to some degree valid. And before
he returned home from the South Seas he was able to observe the
contrast between the dignified serenity of that primitive pagan
society and the degenerate slavery to which some of the more
easily accessible natives had been reduced by misguided Christian
missionary enterprises, intent on "civilizing" the noble savage.

In *Typee,* Melville chose to elaborate this contrast between the
blessings of primitive life, as he had shared them with the so-called

cannibals in the valley of Typee, and the evils of that so-called Christian civilization which the missionaries had forced on the natives. Still believing in the essential rightness of well-conducted missionary enterprises, Melville worked into *Typee* several outspoken attacks on the way in which so many of the missionaries whom he had seen had corrupted and disgraced not only the natives but also those teachings of Christ which lay behind the missionary profession. As his preface to *Typee* indicates, Melville offered his narrative of travels, and his commentaries on what he had seen, as an accurate "peep at Polynesian life," apparently believing that such slight artistic liberties as he had taken in presenting the story would not invalidate his primary intent to represent the truth. Fearing, however, that his interspersed attacks on the behavior of both Protestant and Catholic missionaries would arouse misunderstanding as to the sincerity of his attempt to work for a purification of missionary activities, Melville tried to make his viewpoint and purpose quite clear in the preface, thus:

"There are a few passages in the ensuing chapters which may be thought to bear rather hard upon a reverend order of men, the account of whose proceedings in different quarters of the globe—transmitted to us through their hands—very generally, and often very deservedly, receive high commendation. Such passages will be found, however, to be based upon facts admitting of no contradiction, and which have come immediately under the writer's cognisance. The conclusions deduced from these facts are unavoidable, and in stating them the author has been influenced by no feeling of animosity, either to the individuals themselves or to that glorious cause which has not always been served by the proceedings of some of its advocates."[1]

Anyone familiar with Melville's later pleasure in irony and sarcasm might suspect that his use of the term, "that glorious cause," might be sarcastic. As we shall see, however, the larger context makes it quite clear that Melville is here speaking earnestly and sincerely. Another passage which touches on his assumption that his serious purpose in this regard may be misunderstood, occurs late in *Typee*:

"Lest the slightest misconception should arise from anything thrown out in this chapter, or indeed in any other part of the

46

volume, let me here observe, that against the cause of missions in the abstract no Christian cán possibly be opposed; it is in truth a just and holy cause. But if the great end proposed by it be spiritual, the agency employed to accomplish that end is purely earthly; and although the object in view be the achievement of much good, that agency may nevertheless be productive of evil. In short, missionary undertaking, however it may be blessed by Heaven, is in itself but human; and subject, like everything else, to errors and abuses . . . subject as Christianity is to the assaults of unprincipled foes, we are naturally disposed to regard everything like an exposure of ecclesiastical misconduct as the offspring of malevolence or irreligious feeling. Not even this last consideration, however, shall deter me from the honest expression of my sentiments."[2]

Melville felt justified in dealing harshly with the misconduct of the missionaries, not only because of his own deeply-ingrained Puritanism, which was offended by religious delinquencies, but also because of his ardent belief that the Polynesians in their primitive state came close to existing in an Earthly Paradise, deliberately and divinely designed for them. Having already come under the influence of Rousseau, Melville seems to be aware of the conflict in his own mind between the rightness of missionary enterprises, in pure form, and the opposed rights of natural man. At times he implies that all missionary endeavors in the South Seas cannot help but be corrupting and degrading influences, because they attempt to superimpose "civilization" on innocence. At other times, he resolves the Calvin-Rousseau conflict by insisting that God has these primitive children in his especial care; that the Eden-like settings were divinely ordered to permit these noble savages to live in accordance with God's plan. For example, in one place he alludes to the "spontaneous fruits of the earth, which God in His wisdom had ordained for the support of the indolent natives." Again, in describing another ideal aspect of Polynesian life, he comments, "This would seem expressly ordained by Providence." In another place, he makes this summary statement: "But the voluptuous Indian, with every desire supplied, whom Providence has bountifully provided with all the sources of pure and natural enjoyment, and from whom are removed so many of the ills and pains of life—what has he to desire at the hands of civilisation?"[3]

Although Melville seems partially able to resolve the conflict in his own mind between his inherited belief in the essential rightness of Calvinistic teaching and his newly acquired belief in Rousseau's teachings as to the rights of natural man, we as readers may recognize the problem as one which may later cause Melville trouble and force him to resolve it in another way. For the present, however, it is important for us to see and hear and feel the intense sincerity of Melville's dominantly Christian viewpoint, even when he arranges to include within this viewpoint references to the rights of natural man:

"The penalty of the Fall presses very lightly upon the valley of Typee. . . . Nature had planted the bread-fruit and the banana, and in her own good time she brings them to maturity, when the idle savage stretches forth his hand and satisfies his appetite.

"Ill-fated people! I shudder when I think of the change a few years will produce in their paradisiacal abode; and probably when the most destructive vices, and the worst attendance on civilisation, shall have driven all peace and happiness from the valley, the magnanimous French will proclaim to the world that the Marquesas Islands have been converted to Christianity! and this the Catholic world will doubtless consider as a glorious event. Heaven help the 'Isles of the Sea'!—The sympathy which Christendom feels for them has, alas! in too many instances proved their bane.

"How little do some of these poor islanders comprehend when they look around them, that no inconsiderable part of their disasters originate in certain tea-party excitements, under the influence of which benevolent-looking gentlemen in white cravats solicit alms, and old ladies in spectacles, and young ladies in sober russet low gowns, contribute sixpences toward the creation of a fund, the object of which is to ameliorate the spiritual condition of the Polynesians, but whose end has almost invariably been to accomplish their temporal destruction!

"Let the savages be civilised, but civilise them with benefits, and not with evils; and let heathenism be destroyed, but not by destroying the heathen. The Anglo-Saxon hive have extirpated Paganism from the greater part of the North American continent;

but with it they have likewise extirpated the greater portion of the Red race. Civilisation is gradually sweeping from the earth the lingering vestiges of Paganism, and at the same time the shrinking forms of the unhappy worshippers.

"Among the islands of Polynesia, no sooner are the images over-turned, the temples demolished, and the idolaters converted into *nominal* Christians, than disease, vice, and premature death make their appearance. The depopulated land is then recruited from the rapacious hordes of enlightened individuals who settle themselves within its borders, and clamorously announce the progress of the Truth. Neat villas, trim gardens, shaven lawns, spires, and cupolas arise, while the poor savage soon finds himself an inter-loper in the country of his fathers, and that too on the very site of the hut where he was born. The spontaneous fruits of the earth, which God in His wisdom had ordained for the support of the indolent natives, remorsely seized upon and appropriated by the stranger, are devoured before the eyes of the starving inhabitants, or sent on board the numerous vessels which now touch at their shores. . . .

"But what matters all this? Behold the glorious result!—The abominations of Paganism have given way to the pure rites of the Christian worship—the ignorant savage has been supplanted by the refined European! Look at Honolulu, the metropolis of the Sandwich Islands!—A community of disinterested merchants, and devoted self-exiled heralds of the Cross, located on the very spot that twenty years ago was defiled by the presence of idolatry. What a subject for an eloquent Bible-meeting orator! Nor has such an opportunity for a display of missionary rhetoric been allowed to pass by unimproved! But when these philanthropists send us such glowing accounts of one half of their labours, why does their modesty restrain them from publishing the other half of the good they have wrought?—Nor until I visited Honolulu was I aware of the fact that the small remnant of the natives had been civilised into draught horses, and evangelised into beasts of burden. But so it is. They have been literally broken into the traces, and are harnessed to the vehicles of their spiritual instructors like so many dumb brutes!"[4]

Because we shall later pay much attention to *how* Melville says *what* he says, it should be pointed out here that his intensely

49

angry use of irony and sarcasm throughout that passage forces us
to hear the tone of voice, as determined by the context. Furthermore, it should be noticed that Melville's meaning, throughout
these passages, suggests his belief that the savages in their primitive state more nearly exemplify Christian virtues than do the unconsciously corrupt but so-called "Christian" and "civilised" missionaries:

"Civilisation does not engross all the virtues of humanity: she
has not even her full share of them. They flourish in greater
abundance and attain greater strength among many barbarous
people. The hospitality of the wild Arab, the courage of the North
American Indian, and the faithful friendships of some of the
Polynesian nations, far surpass anything of a similar kind among
the polished communities of Europe. If truth and justice, and the
better principles of our nature, cannot exist unless enforced by the
statute-book, how are we to account for the social condition of
the Typees? So pure and upright were they in all the relations of
life, that entering their valley, as I did, under the most erroneous
impressions of their character, I was soon led to exclaim in amazement: 'Are these the ferocious savages, the blood-thirsty cannibals
of whom I have heard such frightful tales! They deal more kindly
with each other, and are more humane, than many who study
essays on virtue and benevolence, and who repeat every night that
beautiful prayer breathed first by the lips of the divine and gentle
Jesus.' I will frankly declare, that after passing a few weeks in this
valley of the Marquesas, I formed a higher estimate of human
nature than I had ever before entertained. But alas! since then I
have been one of the crew of a man-of-war, and the pent-up
wickedness of five hundred men has nearly overturned all of my
previous theories."[5]

There is fair warning! For arbitrary purposes, we have over-
simplified the complexity of Melville's viewpoint as reflected in
his travel-narrative *Typee*. But it is clear that Melville's adventures
on sea and land had already brought him into contact with enough
"wickedness" to jolt his "previous theories," and his mind is already
on the move as he writes *Typee*, and its sequel *Omoo* (which need
not concern us here). It is therefore difficult to describe which
effect was most important to Melville from his experiences in the
Eden-like valley of the Typees. But it does not seem difficult to

recognize that many previous interpretations have missed some of the most important aspects of those complex effects. For example, Richard Chase insists that Melville's fear of cannibalism symbolizes his fear of castration; that his escape from the natives symbolizes his ability to leave "the archaic level of personality and civilization represented by Typee Valley" and his further ability "to face and suffer and overcome the fears which accompanied maturing sexuality."[6] Is that an accurate interpretation? I am inclined to be merely bored with the monomaniac Freudian emphasis on "maturing sexuality"; but I do seriously doubt whether Melville's experience among the Typees did indeed teach him to leave the "archaic level of personality." Isn't *Typee* itself a kind of proof that Melville, while writing it, was actually moving closer to an archaic level of personality, rather than away from one; that he had come to idealize that primitive life in recollection, some time after he had left it in fact? Consider another interpretation. Newton Arvin, equally charmed by Freud and Jung, finds that the experience meant to Melville a symbolic "descent into the canyon of the past," from which he returned with a "stabilizing and fortifying image."[7] But, whatever that "image" may be said to have been, was it either "stabilizing" or "fortifying"? Let us consider another possible interpretation.

Because the Freudians like to start with causes, in terms of early family relationships, and with questions as to whether an individual was loved too much or too little during early childhood, why not concede that Melville's troubles started not from his being loved too little but from his being loved too much, and by his mother: he was spoiled. The details are unimportant. Somehow he developed a habit of mind which was not only proud and haughty but also demanding. At a very early age, he got into the habit of asking too much of life. There is the crux of it.

Although the result was always the same, it took various protean forms. Whenever he was made aware of the discrepancy between whatever he wanted and whatever he could have, he started looking around for someone to blame for having been so mean as to deny him what he wanted. And the more he was denied, by experiences, the further out he reached for compensations, which were also denied to him.

Come at it another way. The Melville who jumped ship in

Nukuhiva Harbor was "tormented with an everlasting itch for things remote," just as surely as was Ishmael in the first chapter of *Moby-Dick*, and all of his major works provide us with ample evidence as to the different forms taken by his peculiar "itch." Long before Freud, many authors described the basic and reflexive human recoil from various kinds of discomfort or, as we like to call it today, maladjustment. That basic recoil sets in motion a progressive series of physical and mental and emotional actions calculated to achieve some form of rest or peace or serenity (Melville's favorite word, in this context, was "serenity"), no matter how temporary or illusory. For our immediate purposes, it does not matter whether these actions be described as escapes or pursuits: either way, they are impelled by the same "itch" for rest, peace, serenity. Each of Melville's reactions to his itches represented another recoil from some kind of experience which denied him what he wanted in his here-and-now. As a result, he went to sea. His running away to sea, at the age of eighteen, was an early example of such recoil, as one plainly gathers from the early chapters of its fictional projection in *Redburn*. During that first voyage, however, Melville's new sense of maladjustment produced a new recoil, violent enough to drive him back to the relative comfort of his discomforts at home! Within a short time, of course, his injured sensitivities drove him back to sea, in search of some new adventure which might serve as new adjustment. And just how persistently this basic pattern of human response repeated itself in Melville's early life, the first chapters of each of his first seven books indicate. Our immediate concern is with *Typee*, which begins by describing the intolerable life aboard a whaler and the consequent need for jumping ship and taking refuge among the natives, but, quite by accident, in the wrong valley.

Quite by accident? Melville later became bitterly fond of blaming God, of making a scapegoat of God and of calling God a Practical Joker. Let us pretend, for the moment, that Melville's God did indeed play some kind of joke on him by letting him assert his predestined free will in entering the valley of the Typees; that God did it, just to let Melville refuse to learn the implicit object lesson as to the fallacy of his protean itch. According to Melville's own words, that Typee valley was a veritable Earthly Paradise, a Garden of Eden, a Heaven on Earth. It was ideal. By contrast, civilization came close to being pure evil, which could be blamed for much. In that Earthly Paradise of Typee, Melville found that the noble savage lived in an uncorrupted state, strikingly different from that civilized "here-and-now" from which he had fled. How did he react to this blissful serenity? As soon as that Eden became his here-and-now, Melville felt trapped, imprisoned: he longed for anything except Eden. The first chapter of *Typee* is entitled, "The Sea—Longings for Shore" and the last chapter is entitled, "Escape" or (by implication) "The Shore—Longings for Sea." There is no hint in the context that Melville, already fond of ironies, recognized the irony implicit in these two chapter titles: the object lesson was wasted on him.

If Melville fought so hard to get away from that Earthly Paradise, how could he ever have idealized it? The answer is fairly easy: the Typee valley became Paradise for him only after he had left it, only after it had again become remote. Then he could look back at it wistfully, and glorify it as a symbol of something highly desirable but unobtainable, remote in both the past and the future: Paradise. While sampling this ultimate serenity, Melville had suffered egregiously and had longed to escape. But as soon as he had gotten far enough away from it, he suffered egregiously to think that there was no other place on earth quite like it.

There is a revealing passage in *Typee* which had one value for Melville, and which has another value for us, as we try to understand him. It foreshadows his subsequent pilgrimages into the remote of time and space, during his various quests for serenity. While wandering about the valley of Typee, he tells us, he discovered a mausoleum erected in memory of a celebrated leader. Placed conspicuously was a carven effigy of the dead chieftain seated in the stern of a canoe and holding a paddle in his hands. He seemed in the act of driving the canoe swiftly ahead, "leaning forward and inclining his head, as if eager to hurry on his voyage." But again a symbolic want-versus-denial image, or life-versus-death antithesis, of the sort which Melville loved: "Glaring at him forever, and face to face, was a polished human skull which crowned the prow of the canoe. The spectral figure-head, reversed in its position, glancing backward, seemed to mock the impatient attitude of the warrior." Having established the emblematic life-death relationship, Melville added:

"Whenever, in the course of my rambles through the valley, I happened to be near the chief's mausoleum, I always turned aside to visit it. The place had a peculiar charm for me; I hardly know why, but so it was. As I leaned over the railing and gazed upon the strange effigy, and watched the play of the feathery head-dress, stirred by the same breeze which in low tones breathed amidst the lofty palm-trees, I loved to yield myself up to the fanciful superstition of the islanders, and could almost believe that the grim warrior was bound heavenward. In this mood, when I turned to depart, I bade him 'God speed, and a pleasant voyage.' Ah, paddle away, brave chieftain, to the land of spirits! To the material eye thou makest but little progress; but with the eye of faith, I see thy canoe cleaving the bright waves, which die away on those dimly looming shores of Paradise.

"This strange superstition affords another evidence of the fact, that however ignorant man may be, he still feels within him his immortal spirit yearning after the unknown future."[8]

For present purposes, *Typee* is particularly interesting because it reflects Melville's first phase of disillusionment, from several different angles, all closely related. His undisciplined and self-indulgent impatience with life as he found it prompted him to go to sea and then to jump ship; that same impatience was partly a cause and partly an effect of his itch for the unknown and the unknowable, in both time and space: the mariner and the mystic in him were correlated in their spoiled-child motivation. And even his Puritanical impulse to purify missionary enterprises, by calling attention to the discrepancy between the ideal and actuality, suggests the yearning of his own spirit for a personal religious belief which would correct and transcend the narrowness of his Calvinistic heritage. The "eye of faith" was still so undimmed in him, however, that he had consciously dedicated himself, as a man of letters, to the related ideal of discovering and revealing God's truth, even though he might suffer opprobrium, as did the Old Testament prophets.

But his disillusionment was heightened when some sectarian reviewers of *Typee* denied the truth of his attacks on Christian missionaries in the South Seas, and accused him of being an atheistical liar. That hurt enough to make him say in his preface to *Mardi*, "Not long ago, having published two narratives of voyages in the Pacific, which, in many quarters, were received with incredulity, the thought occurred to me of indeed writing a romance of Polynesian adventure, and publishing it as such; to see whether the fiction might not possibly be received for a verity: in some degree the reverse of my previous experience."[9]

QUEST FOR ATONEMENT

CHAPTER III

And though essaying but a sportive sail, I was driven from my course by a blast resistless; and ill-provided, young, and bowed to the brunt of things before my prime, still fly before the gale; hard have I striven to keep stout heart. . . .

But fiery yearnings their own phantom-future make, and deem it present. So, if after all these fearful, fainting trances, the verdict be, the golden haven was not gained;—yet, in bold quest thereof, better to sink in boundless deeps, than float on vulgar shoals; and give me, ye gods, an utter wreck, if wreck I do.

MELVILLE, *Mardi*

QUEST FOR ATONEMENT

INCREASINGLY disturbed and confused by his disillusioning experiences, Melville contrived *Mardi* in such a way as to help him explore the meaning of the word "Truth" from several different viewpoints, and the result of that literary exploration was not satisfactory either to Melville or to his readers. The early chapters of the narrative suggest that he started to write without planning to project his own spiritual and mental difficulties into an artistic form which might enable him to come to grips with those difficulties and work out a solution. Probably Melville had not really become aware of the peculiar problems which had been accumulating within him until he cut into those problems and opened them up enough to look at them, during the actual writing of *Mardi*.

The crux of the problem was that his mystical yearning after a satisfactory religious belief had been heightened rather than lessened by his disillusioning experiences, and as a result he accepted the necessity of rejecting his Christian heritage, particularly the theological aspects of that heritage, and of trying to substitute a highly individualistic and mystical religious affirmation. In *Mardi* he said that the "divine Plato" was of his counsel, and the allegorical overtones of Melville's central plot suggest that Melville attempted to substitute for Christian theology his own version of a Platonic deification of Truth, which is (in the premises) one with Wisdom and Beauty. One advantage Melville might have gained from this mystical belief, if he could have clung to it, would have been that it would have liberated him from the Calvinistic concept of a harsh personal God who did not inspire love.

Melville seems to have become enamored of that poetic and allegorical story which Spenser adapted to his own uses in *The Faerie Queene*; which Dante had previously adapted to somewhat different uses in *The Divine Comedy* (each of which Melville knew very well); which has its source in Plato's *Symposium*: the story which Socrates tells to illustrate the progressive meanings of the word "love." Socrates explains that love is the mediator between God and man, and that it thus represents the aspiration of the incomplete towards that which completes it. The progressive stages of growth begin, Socrates explains, in physical love between two people, and this love leads in turn to an appreciation of all physical loveliness, thence to a love of the beauties of the mind and soul, and finally to a love of the pure Form or essence of loveliness which is in itself absolute and everlasting. Only when the lover is able to comprehend and thus embrace this absolute beauty does he fulfill his longing for immortality; but the reward of this comprehension and embrace reaches its ineffable height when the lover becomes one with the Form of pure beauty. As a result of this identification with eternal beauty, the lover is lifted clear of time and consequently loses all interest in the material world, the temporal world.

To understand the allegorical adaptations which Melville made of these Platonic concepts, in *Mardi*, we need to have in mind a brief sketch of the central action. The hero of the narrative is a nameless American sailor who begins his adventures in the South Seas by stealing a boat at night, with a companion, and deserting the whaler on which they have shipped for a too-long voyage. (That already sounds familiar!) Our hero saves the life of a beautiful girl named Yillah, who is being deceptively taken to her ritualistic and pagan death by a native priest and his sons. During the rescue, the nameless hero is obliged to kill the priest, and the sons vow vengeance. Because our pilgrim hero is represented as a type of blindness at this stage, he is not fully aware of the ironic parallel between the priest's actions and his own subsequent blind and sinful actions. The priest has held the chaste and innocent Yillah captive and has deceived her in order to subvert her to his own diabolical ritual; the hero also holds Yillah captive and deceives her in order to subvert her to his own fleshly ritual of love-making.

Ashore on one of the islands, the hero enjoys the ironic fact that he is mistakenly called Taji by the natives, who are deceived into thinking that he is a demi-god, come down from heaven with his heavenly bride. A local potentate, King Media, entertains the masquerading couple hospitably; a local Queen Hautia, from a neighboring island, appears disguised on King Media's island and, after having scrutinized Yillah and the so-called Taji, she subsequently sends three girls as messengers to demand, in symbolic language, that Yillah be surrendered to Queen Hautia because the latter claims Yillah as one of her subjects. Failing to understand the request, Taji ignores it. A few days later, Yillah mysteriously disappears. Distressed, and vowing to find the girl whom he now loves in memory more intensely than he had loved her in the flesh, Taji undertakes a protracted pilgrim quest for Yillah, accompanied by three noblemen from King Media's court: the philosopher Babbalanja, the historian Mohi, and the poet Yoomy. King Media supplies his own royal canoes and joins the expedition in search of Yillah. Although they circle the islands of Mardi (allegorically, the world), they find no trace of the beautiful maiden. Discouraged, the noblemen and King Media find an island named Serenia (a Christian Utopia) where they feel that the search should end. But Taji still yearns, and insists on continuing. Throughout the voyage, he has been followed and threatened by three devilish and dark-skinned sons of the pagan priest, and they are intent on killing him. Once when they try and fail, they tell him that Yillah's white skin did not indicate that she was an albino, as he had thought. Her parents had been white people, killed aboard their ship when Yillah was too small to remember; the child had been rescued and raised secretly by the pagan priest. Also, throughout the voyage, Taji has been intercepted repeatedly by a canoe bearing the three maiden messengers from Queen Hautia, and they reiterate that Taji will find Yillah on Queen Hautia's life-giving island. Having visited the island, and having resisted Hautia's fleshly forms of seduction, Taji finally turns his back on his companions and continues his ascetic quest across the infinite deep. The narrative ends with this symbolic tableau:

" 'Now, I am my own soul's emperor; and my first act is abdication! Hail! realm of shades!'—and turning my prow into the racing tide, which seized me like a hand omnipotent, I darted through.

61

"Churned in foam, that outer ocean lashed the clouds; and straight in my white wake, headlong dashed a shallop, three fixed spectres leaning o'er its prow: three arrows poising.

"And thus, pursuers and pursued flew on over an endless sea."[1]

The allegorical meaning of this central narrative may be understood more easily if the reader remembers what related values Spenser established in the first two books of *The Faerie Queene*, to which Melville was heavily indebted. In Book One, Spenser's hero begins as a spiritually blind and ignorant young man, so impure that he is unable to look on, or appreciate, the face of his lady Una (Truth), who is veiled. After being separated from her by the hermit Archimago (Hypocrisy), Spenser's hero enters on a succcession of pilgrim adventures representing spiritual states of temptation and growth. While he searches for Una, through the Inferno of Orgoglio's Castle and the Purgatory of the Cave of Despair, Una is significantly (and symbolically) held captive. Eventually, after the hero has completed his purgation, the liberated Una reveals herself to him as the transcendently and divinely beautiful daughter of God. After he has further triumphed over the world, the flesh, and the devil, the hero is at last wed to Una: an act symbolic of spiritual atonement.

In Book Two of *The Faerie Queene* another hero, Sir Guyon, passes through an analogous series of pilgrim adventures. Temporarily seduced by the charms of Phaedria, he resists her Calypso-like invitation to enjoy the "safe port" of her small island, and continues his progress. Later, he visits the Cave of Mammon and also resists all temptation there. He is further educated when he visits the Castle of Alma, which represents the soul in perfect command of the body. He explores the castle tower, containing Alma's three advisers (allegorically, the head, with its three psychological entities personified). For purposes of comparison with *Mardi*, the three advisers may be represented roughly as a Philosopher, a Historian, a Poet. Finally, Sir Guyon faces and triumphs over his ultimate temptation when he arrives at Acrasia's "Bower of Bliss," throws to the ground the three emblematic cups of wine offered him, destroys the bower, and departs. Thus, this second hero has also completed his pilgrimage after triumphing over the world, the flesh, and the devil.

In *Mardi*, similarly, Taji begins his adventures blindly as a pilgrim soul whose initial love for Yillah is entirely physical. His seduction of her, after he has deceived her, represents a sequence of downward steps which are responsible for the subordination of her spiritual awareness to her physical awareness (the perversion of Truth and Beauty). He is responsible for her disappearance, and his long pilgrim quest in search of her enables him to work out the slow stages of his penitent purification until he is able to resist the death-threatening values represented by three wordly pretenses of "religious" beliefs: the three devilish sons of the priest who offered Yillah (and Taji) death instead of life; his three psychological companions who offer him Christian serenity and idealism as an unacceptable substitute for his spiritual craving for atonement with Yillah (divine Beauty-Truth Wisdom); the three messengers of Queen Hautia, who offer him physical and sexual serenity in a Bower of Bliss. Like Spenser's heroes, the mature and penitent Taji resists the devil, the world, the flesh, and in the final tableau he turns his back on all things temporal.

Although the central action of *Mardi* symbolizes and illuminates a positive and mystical belief which Melville seemed anxious to assert, as much for his own sake as for the reader's enjoyment, the assertion seems to have been convincing neither to Melville nor to most readers. Instead, the far more vivid episodes are those which develop the negative side of Melville's thematic concern for the meaning of "Truth." The rebellious questioning and doubting, the persistent skepticism and agnosticism, are conveyed far more strongly than the mystical affirmation. And although the satirical attacks against conventional beliefs (religious, philosophical, scientific, social, political) are thinly veiled in allegorical terms which are correlated with the central allegory, these digressive and satirical episodes bulk as large, in the aggregate, as the central story itself. In these digressions, furthermore, Melville provides staggering evidence as to the scope of his cumulative reading in literary, philosophical, theological literature at this time.[2]

During the digressions, several different actions dramatize the concept that each individual must make an independent religious quest for Truth. These separate and minor actions are analogous to the allegorical meaning of Taji's quest for Yillah. The episode of the youth who insists on climbing the heavenly mountain alone provides a conveniently brief example of a hopeful doubter's quest. For purposes of contrast, the youth's actions in the episode are opposed not only by the religious dogmatism of the rejected guide but also by the agnosticism of the observing philosopher, Babbalanja:

"The fifth pilgrim was a youth of an open, ingenuous aspect; and with an eye, full of eyes; his step was light.

" 'Who art thou?' cried Pani, as the stripling touched him in passing.

" 'I go to ascend the peak,' said the boy.

" 'Then take me for guide.'

" 'No, I am strong and lithesome. Alone must I go.'

" 'But how knowest thou the way?'

" 'There are many ways; the right one I must seek for myself.'

" 'Ah, poor deluded one,' sighed Pani; 'but thus is it ever with youth; and rejecting the monitions of wisdom, suffer they must. Go on, and perish!'

"Turning, the boy exclaimed—'Though I act counter to thy counsels, oh Pani, I but follow the divine instinct in me.'

" 'Poor youth!' murmured Babbalanja. 'How earnestly he struggles in his bonds. But though rejecting a guide, still he clings to that legend of the peak.' "

Later, and pertinently, the conversation between the youth and the priestly guide is continued:

". . . 'Depart, I say; and, in the sacred name of Alma [Christ], perish in thy endeavours to climb the peak.'

" 'I may perish there in truth,' said the boy, with sadness; 'but it shall be in the path revealed to me in my dream. And think not, oh guide, that I perfectly rely upon gaining that lofty summit. I will climb high Ofo with hope, not faith; oh, mighty Oro [God], help me!'

" 'Be not impious,' said Pani; 'pronounce not Oro's sacred name too lightly.'

" 'Oro is but a sound,' said the boy. 'They call the supreme god, Ati, in my native isle; it is the soundless thought of him, oh guide, that is in me.'

" 'Hark, to his rhapsodies! Hark, how he prates of mysteries, that not even Hivohitee [the Pope] can fathom.'

" 'Nor he, nor thou, nor I, nor any; Oro, to all, is Oro the unknown.'

" 'Why claim to know Oro, then, better than others?'

" 'I am not so vain; and I have little to substitute for what I cannot receive. I but feel Oro in me, yet cannot declare the thought.'

" 'Proud boy! thy humility is a pretence; at heart, thou deemest thyself wiser than Mardi [the World].'

" 'Nor near so wise. To believe is a haughty thing; my very doubts humiliate me. I weep and doubt; all Mardi may be right; and I too simple to discern.'

" 'He is mad,' said the chief Divino; 'never before heard I such words.' "[3]

All the orthodox spectators think that this pilgrim youth is mad; later, the orthodox also think Taji is mad for insisting that he must continue his quest, alone. In *Mardi*, Melville delights to point out repeatedly that the value of the word "madness" (like the value of so many words) depends entirely on the viewpoint of the user. But Melville's own viewpoint, as reflected in his repeated attacks on Christianity, consistently emphasizes the rationalistic and skeptical and even agnostic viewpoint from which he had by this time come to view Christianity in general, and Calvinism in particular. For example, before the philosopher Babbalanja is converted to Christianity in the Utopian island of Serenia, we are given this:

"A good deal was then said of Alma [Christ]. . . . Called upon to reveal what his chronicles said on this theme [i.e., a historical consideration], Braid-Beard complied; at great length narrating what now follows condensed.

"Alma, it seems, was an illustrious prophet, and teacher divine; who, ages ago, at long intervals, and in various islands, had appeared to the Mardians under different titles of Brami [Brahma], Manko [Manes, founder of the Manicheans], and Alma. Many thousands of moons had elapsed since his last and most memorable avatar, as Alma. . . . Each of his advents had taken place in a comparatively dark and benighted age. Hence, it was devoutly believed, that he came to redeem the Mardians from their heathenish thrall; to instruct them in the ways of truth, virtue, and happiness; to allure them to good by promises of beatitude hereafter; and to restrain them from evil by denunciations of woe. Separated from the impurities and corruptions, which in a long series of centuries had become attached to everything originally uttered by

65

the prophet, the maxims, which as Brami he had taught seemed similar to those inculcated by Manko. But as Alma, adapting his lessons to the improved condition of humanity, the divine prophet had more completely unfolded his scheme; as Alma, he had made his last revelation.

"This narration concluded, Babbalanja mildly observed, 'Mohi: without seeking to accuse you of uttering falsehoods; since what you relate rests not upon testimony of your own; permit me, to question the fidelity of your account of Alma. The prophet came to dissipate errors, you say; but superadded to many that have survived the past, ten thousand others have originated in various constructions of the principles of Alma himself. The prophet came to do away all gods but one; but since the days of Alma, the idols of Maramma [Catholic Christianity] have more than quadrupled. The prophet came to make us Mardians more virtuous and happy; but along with all previous good, the same wars, crimes, and miseries, which existed in Alma's day, under various modifications are yet extant. Nay: take from your chronicles, Mohi, the history of those horrors, one way or other, resulting from the doings of Alma's nominal followers, and your chronicles would not so frequently make mention of blood. The prophet came to guarantee our eternal felicity; but according to what is held in Maramma, that felicity rests on so hard a proviso, that *to a thinking mind* [italics added], but very few of our sinful race may secure it. For one, then, I wholly reject your Alma; not so much because of all that is hard to be understood in his histories, as because of obvious and undeniable things all round us; which, to me, seem at war with an unreserved faith in his doctrines as promulgated here in Maramma. . . .'

"Said Mohi: 'Do you deny, then, the everlasting torments?'

"'Tis not worth a denial. Nor by formally denying it, will I run the risk of shaking the faith of thousands, who in that pious belief find infinite consolation for all they suffer in Mardi.'

"'How?' said Media; 'are there those who soothe themselves with thoughts of everlasting flames?'

"'One would think so, my lord, since they defend that dogma more resolutely than any other. Sooner will they yield you the isles of Paradise, than it. And in truth, as liege followers of Alma, they would seem but right in clinging to it as they do; for, accord-

66

ing to all one hears in Maramma, the great end of the prophet's mission seems to have been the revealing to us Mardians the existence of horrors, most hard to escape. But better we were all annihilated, than that one man should be damned.' "[4]

For Melville, perhaps, the major value of his having employed the allegorical device of representing Taji's disillusionment, following the loss of Yillah, as a form of psychological fragmentation, emblematically represented by the appearance of Taji's companions, Babbalanja the philosopher, Mohi the historian, Yoomy the poet—reason, memory, imagination—was that he could project his own conflicting hopes and doubts by letting these three characters argue with each other. Melville's own sympathies are permitted to run the gamut, as these three characters explore the meaning of the word "Truth." Nevertheless, it is important to remember that Melville's ultimate goal, in *Mardi*, is to continue his initial consecration to his high calling as a man of letters, and to ridicule only the narrow pretensions of religious and philosophic dogma in order to let those pretensions provide foils for his own deeply mystical affirmations which were, he hoped, strong enough to triumph over his own tendency toward skepticism and agnosticism, at this time. His intention, clearly, was to continue his initial plan for glorifying the right of the individual to strive for and achieve a sense of spiritual integration and atonement with divine Truth, God. And much of his persistently optimistic idealism, in a religious and in an artistic sense, found expression in vigorous religious affirmations which may be represented by the following: "For we are not gods and creators . . . In all the universe is but one original; and the very suns must to their source for their fire; and we Prometheuses must to them for ours; which, when had, only perpetual Vestal tending will keep alive."[5]

Throughout *Mardi*, the reiterated references to the tendency of human and finite minds to hold concepts of God which are distortions of God may suggest that Melville himself had a related meaning in mind when he chose his punlike title: the world is inclined to mar deity, and Melville sets himself up as the champion of a higher concept of deity: "I but fight against the armed and crested Lies of Mardi, that like a host assail me."[6]

For Melville, while writing *Mardi*, there still remained a sense that he was willing and eager to accept a prophetic role as author, and to accept the contingent obloquy:

"Yet not I, but another: God is my Lord; and though many satellites revolve around me, I and all mine revolve round the great central Truth, sun-like, fixed and luminous forever in the foundationless firmament. Fire flames on my tongue; and though of old the Bactrian prophets were stoned, yet the stoners in oblivion sleep. But whoso stones me, shall be as Erostratus, who put torch to the temple; though Genghis Khan with Cambyses combine to obliterate him, his name shall be extant in the mouth of the last man that lives. And if so be, down unto death, whence I came, will I go, like Xenophon retreating on Greece, all Persia brandishing her spears in his rear."[7]

These consciously archaic and rhetorical outbursts are a part of the affirmation which struggles against the doubt, from the beginning to the end of *Mardi*. It was a losing battle, and *Mardi* may well represent the second phase of Melville's growing disillusionment. Even when his doubts overwhelmed his faith, however, he continued to believe in the rightness of his decision to strike out boldly, and alone, in his quest for truth:

"Oh, reader, list! I've chartless voyaged. With compass and lead, we had not found these Mardian Isles. Those who boldly launch, cast off all cables; and turning from the common breeze, that's fair for all, with their own breath fill their own sails. Hug the shore, naught new is seen; and 'Land ho!' at last was sung, when a new world was sought.

"That voyager steered his bark through seas untracked before; ploughed his own path mid jeers; though with a heart that oft was heavy with the thought that he might only be too bold, and grope where land was none.

"So I.

"And though essaying but a sportive sail, I was driven from my course by a blast resistless; and ill-provided, young, and bowed to the brunt of things before my prime, still fly before the gale; hard have I striven to keep stout heart.

"And if it harder be than e'er before to find new climes, when now our seas have oft been circled by ten thousand prows,—much more the glory!

"But this new world here sought is stranger far than his, who stretched his vans from Palos. It is the world of mind; where in the wanderer may gaze round, with more of wonder than Balboa's band roving through the golden Aztec glades.

"But fiery yearnings their own phantom-future make, and deem it present. So, if after all these fearful, fainting trances, the verdict be, the golden haven was not gained;—yet, in bold quest thereof, better to sink in boundless deeps, than float on vulgar shoals; and give me, ye gods, an utter wreck, if wreck I do."[8]

THREE PHASES OF DISILLUSIONMENT

CHAPTER IV

By the time I got back to the ship, everything was in an uproar. The pea-jacket man was there, ordering about a good many men in the rigging. . . . Soon after, another man, in a striped calico shirt . . . made his appearance, and went to ordering about the man in the big pea-jacket; and at last the captain came up the side, and began to order about both of them.

MELVILLE, *Redburn*

THREE PHASES OF DISILLUSIONMENT

Soon after Melville had finished writing *Mardi*, he showed in various ways that his artistic attempt to triumph over his doubts, by fashioning for himself an allegorically tailored jacket of Christian-Platonic faith, had not accomplished its purpose: his own inner disillusionments continued to perplex him. In *Mardi*, his fluctuating viewpoint had permitted him to assert, "I list to St. Paul who argues the doubts of Montaigne," and to add that "divine Plato" was of his counsel. He even exhorted, "But let us hold fast to all we have; and stop all leaks in our faith; lest an opening of but a hand's breadth should sink our seventy-fours. . . . Panoplied in all the armor of St. Paul . . . let us fight the Turks inch by inch, and yield them naught but our corpse."[1] Nevertheless, shortly after *Mardi* was through the press, and published, he had so far surrendered to skepticism that he deprecated the pious Duyckinck's praise of *Mardi*, thus:

"I am glad you like that affair of mine. But it seems so long now since I wrote it, & my mood has so changed, that I dread to look into it, & have purposely abstained from so doing since I thanked God it was off my hands. . . . I bought a set of Bayle's Dictionary the other day, & on my return to New York intend to lay the great old folios side by side & go to sleep on them thro' the summer, with the Phaidon in one hand & Tom Brown in the other."[2]

Questions as to the nature of death and as to the immortality of the soul had been discussed at great length by Taji's companions in *Mardi*, and there is much evidence that one important element in Melville's religious disillusionment was his inability to reconcile himself to the fact of death. In the *Phaidon*, Plato permits Phaedo of Ellis, disciple of Socrates, to summarize the last discussion between the condemned Socrates and his friends concerning death and its consequences. With his usual skepticism, Socrates is represented as walking around the difficult problem and viewing it from various angles. Sir Thomas Browne's *Urn Burial* made a strong appeal to Melville, and although Browne's skepticism is generally thought to be balanced by faith, Melville was inclined to doubt it. He once said that Browne wrote like a "cracked archangel," and it is certainly true that the devilish insinuations in Browne frequently invert the meanings of certain Biblical passages which Browne playfully quotes or paraphrases. As for Pierre Bayle's elaborately sustained and skeptical attacks on Calvinistic theology, Melville probably became acquainted with them, earlier, in Duyckinck's own library, which (oddly enough) contained a set of the *Dictionary*. Bayle's skepticism was blended with agnosticism, and he insisted that it was impossible to discover that very Truth which so many Christians sought in a manner not entirely unrelated to the allegorical asceticism of Taji's final quest. Bayle also harped on his own doubts as to whether any man's action reflected a genuine concern for religious principles, save in moments of dire tension, such as the approach of death. He further urged that all authority was unreliable, particularly Biblical authority. Although Bayle was very cautious in his wording, he went so far as to question the necessity for believing in any concept of God; he even argued that a society of atheists could work out rules of conduct which would enable them to equal or surpass the performance of a religious group. Melville's purchase of Bayle's *Dictionary* at this time strongly suggests that the dark attitudes which Babbalanja had voiced in *Mardi*, and against which Taji had turned, were now the attitudes which were in the ascendancy, for Melville. In the descendancy by contrast, were the mystical and ascetic affirmations represented in Taji's final tableau.

Needing money to support his growing family, Melville felt that he could not afford to spend too much time in desultory reading or sleeping, during the summer of 1849. He felt forced to toss off a relatively short and simple narrative which might sell better than *Mardi*. The raw materials for his so-called potboiler, *Redburn*, were drawn from his memory of his first voyage, aboard a merchantman to Liverpool and back, when he was eighteen years old. The advantages of such raw materials were obvious: he could draw as freely as he wished from reminiscences and yet he could embroider them with fictions whenever it suited his purpose. Later, in telling Duyckinck that he was not proud of *Redburn*, Melville added, "What a madness & anguish it is, that an author can never—under no conceivable circumstances—be at all frank with his readers.—Could I, for one, be frank with them—how would they cease their railing—those at least who have railed."[3]

Melville was by no means frank with his readers, in *Redburn*; yet no student of Melville seems to have pointed this out; no student seems to have pointed out that the effect of Melville's reading in Bayle's *Dictionary* is significantly reflected in *Redburn*. Weaver, Mumford, and many other authorities have treated *Redburn* as a transparent chapter in autobiography. In a sense it is autobiographical; but the aspect of *Redburn* which is of particular autobiographical interest, here, is by no means transparent. Although the subject matter deals merely with a young man's experiences in leaving home for the first time, Melville's seemingly casual method of telling the story enables him to establish and contrast three stages in his own spiritual and mental development: first, the stage when he faced the wicked world with the religious idealism taught him at home and thus suffered from the shock of discovering the discrepancy between ideals and actualities; second, the stage from which his narrator Redburn recollects this "first voyage" and is able to contrast the difference between the way he "then" thought and the way he "now" thinks (a modified idealism which still clings to the earlier belief in the Holy Bible as the "revealed" word of God); third, Melville's own covertly skeptical and satirical attitude toward his inherited Calvinistic belief, even toward religious beliefs in general, and his rebellious bitterness toward any authoritarianism which interfered with the natural expression of the natural rights of man.

These three distinct viewpoints, representing three distinctly different autobiographical phases of disillusionment, can be recognized only after the reader has become aware of the different technical and stylistic devices which Melville employs in *Redburn*. For convenience in reference, there can be no harm in representing the naïve young actor in the narrative by his first name,

"Wellingborough"; in representing the somewhat more sophisticated narrator as "Redburn," who looks back on his former self and establishes contrasts between the "then" of the action and the "now" of the telling; in representing the artistic manipulator of them both as Melville. In the following analysis, any reference to the first viewpoint will use the name "Wellingborough"; to the second viewpoint, "Redburn"; to the third viewpoint, "Melville."

First of all, Melville contrives to let Redburn the narrator invite the reader to laugh gently with him as he described the naïve responses of Wellingborough (his former self) to the experience of first coming aboard a ship. To represent that naïveté, Melville permits Redburn to reflect Wellingborough's greenness in the actual choice of words and phrasing of sentences, whenever possible. For example, Redburn remembers how shocked Wellingborough was at overhearing a profane conversation among a group of sailors, when first he came aboard the *Highlander*:

"I say this kind of talking shocked me. . . . *At that time* [italics added] I did not know what to make of these sailors; but this much I thought, that when *they* [italics added] were boys, *they* [italics added] could never have gone to the Sunday School; for they swore so, it made my ears tingle, and used words that I could never hear without a dreadful loathing. And are these the men, thought I to myself, that I must live with so long? these the men I am to eat with and sleep with all the time? And besides, I now began to see that they were not going to be very kind to me. . . ."[4] Redburn is obviously laughing at his former self. Here is a more complex example of the same contrived effect:

"I now began to feel unsettled and ill at ease about the stomach, as if matters were all topsy-turvy there; and felt strange and giddy about the head; and so I made no doubt that this was the beginning of that dreadful thing, the seasickness. Feeling worse and worse, I told one of the sailors how it was with me, and begged him to make my excuses very civilly to the chief mate, for I thought I would go below and spend the night in my bunk. But he only laughed at me, and said something about my mother not being aware of my being out; which enraged me not a little, that a man whom I had heard swear so terribly, should dare to take such a holy name into his mouth. It seemed a sort of blasphemy, and it seemed like dragging out the best and most cherished secrets of my soul, for at that time the name of mother was the centre of all my heart's finest feelings, which ere that I had learned to keep secret, deep down in my being.

"But I did not outwardly resent the sailor's words, for that would have only made the matter worse."[5]

In that passage there are actually two major effects, each ironic. When the sailor asks Wellingborough if his mother knows he's out, almost all readers will join the narrator Redburn in smiling at the actor Wellingborough, who saw nothing comic in the situation. This is a form of dramatic irony, in which the audience knows something that the actor does not know. But when Wellingborough is represented as having thought, at the time, that it was advisable not to show any *outward* resentment of the sailor's words, "for that would have only made the matter worse," there comes a parting of the ways for some readers. One category of reader sees nothing to laugh at, there: Wellingborough is indeed being very sensible. Another category of reader will gather that the idealistic and pious Wellingborough has at least learned the meaning of the word "expediency." In other words, his high idealism can assert itself privately and can permit him to look down on these bestial sailors about him as somehow inferior to him; but if his high idealism is likely to cause him any physical discomfort, he is able to curb it. Again, this effect is ironic; but it becomes a different form of irony because the second category of reader laughs not only at Wellingborough but also (by implication) at those other readers who, because of their own bias, knowingly or unknowingly approve the principle of combining pious idealism with expediency.

The obvious danger of my observations here is that I may be reading into the passage a pair of discrete and ironic effects which I attribute to a conscious contrivance on Melville's part when I have no proof. But notice the cumulative evidence. Here is another example from *Redburn*: When Wellingborough asks one of the hard-bitten sailors if he is in the habit of going to church when ashore, the answer is rude and discourteous. Immediately, we are given another image of Wellingborough's fondness for priding himself on his superiority to his rude companions. As his pretentious name implies, he is not only wellborn; he is also a pharisaical prig, in his religiosity, and Melville has made him so, as a method of ridiculing the type he himself formerly represented:

"When I heard this poor sailor talk in this manner, showing so plainly his ignorance and absence of proper views of religion, I pitied him more and more; contrasting my own situation with his, I was grateful that I was different from him; and I thought how pleasant it was to feel wiser and better than he could feel; though I was willing to confess to myself that it was not altogether my own good endeavours, so much as my education, which I had received from others, that had made me *the upright and sensible boy I at that time thought myself to be* [italics added]. And it was now that I began to feel a good degree of complacency and satisfaction in surveying my own character; for before this, I had previously associated with persons of a very discreet life, so that there was little opportunity to magnify myself, by comparing myself with my neighbours.

"Thinking that my superiority to him in a moral way might sit uneasily upon this sailor, I thought it would soften the matter down by giving him a chance to show his own superiority to me, in a minor thing; for I was far from being vain and conceited. . . ."[6]

Oh yes indeed! Wellingborough is a *nice* boy! And of course he is *neither* vain *nor* conceited! But the reader who recognizes the difference between Wellingborough the actor and Redburn the narrator and Melville the artistic manipulator, begins to suspect, pretty soon, that while Redburn the narrator is laughing at Wellingborough the actor, Melville is also laughing at them both. This technical device of triple ironic parallelism occurred repeatedly in *Mardi*, in various ways. Take a conveniently concise example of this same device in *Redburn* itself:

"By the time I got back to the ship, everything was in an uproar. The pea-jacket man was there, ordering about a good many men in the rigging. . . . Soon after, another man, in a striped calico shirt . . . made his appearance, and went to ordering about the man in the big pea-jacket; and at last the captain came up the side, and began to order about both of them."[7]

The three-viewpoints principle, so easy to recognize in a careful reading of *Redburn*, is not so easily described. It will be even more difficult to describe, when it is adapted to different but related uses in *White-Jacket* and *Moby-Dick*, so I shall illuminate it further, here, by taking a more clean-cut example, which occurs when Redburn, having laughed at his earlier self, represents his own "mature" view by preaching a little sermon of his own, on the depravity of sailors:

". . . But can sailors, one of the wheels of this world, be wholly lifted up from the mire? There seems not much chance for it in the old systems and programmes of the future, however well-intentioned and sincere; for with such systems, the thought of lifting them up seems almost as hopeless as that of growing the grape in Nova Zembla.

"But we must not altogether despair for the sailor; nor need those who toil for his good be at bottom disheartened. For Time must prove his friend in the end; and though sometimes he would almost seem as a neglected step-son of heaven, permitted to run on and riot out his days with no hand to restrain him, while others are watched over and tenderly cared for; yet we feel and we know that God is the true Father of all, and that none of His children are without the pale of His care."[8]

(Again, for different categories of readers, the parting of the ways: choose you whether to count the sheep or the goats!) Melville ironically permits Redburn the narrator (not Wellingborough the actor) to find consolation in his orthodox beliefs and to be cheered by the thought that the sailor will get his just reward in Heaven: "Time" is on the side of the sailor, and of course so is God, "the true Father of all." (Later, incidentally, we shall hear both Plotinus Plinlimmon and Captain Vere saying something similar.) Melville very bitterly implies that for Christian Redburn to begin talking about the need for "systems" and "programmes" for improving the lot of the sailor, and then to let this pious thought peter out into the pharisaical consolation that "Time" and "God" are on the side of the sailor is (to put it mildly) ironic. But the embittered Melville, knowing that many of his readers subscribed to just such a shallow and cheaply optimistic dodge, while professing themselves to be socially-minded Christians, fed those readers just such hogwash, and quietly sneered at them for swallowing it. Some of their descendants have been swallowing it ever since.

Now we are in a position to recognize a certain similarity between Melville's fondness for achieving ironic effects by letting both Redburn and Wellingborough mouth familiar clichés (religious and Biblical) and Pierre Bayle's fondness for achieving ironic effects by doing exactly the same thing, in that *Dictionary* which Melville had bought shortly before he began writing *Redburn*. Frequently, when Bayle's skeptical and satirical thrusts go about as far as they can go (safely), he loves to feign bafflement and then (to use his repeated phrase) "retire into the Fortresses of Scripture," and of blind faith, naughtily quoting St. Paul as he goes: "For we walk by faith and not by sight."[9]

With Pierre Bayle in mind, remember that the most bitter passages in *Redburn* are those built around the Launcelott's-Hay incident, which described Wellingborough's unsuccessful attempt to bring help to the woman dying of hunger in a Liverpool alley hole, with her already dead baby in her arms and her two small daughters dying beside her. After he has failed to get help, after mother and children are dead and the hole has been cleaned up with quick-lime, Redburn (in this case at one with Wellingborough) utters these disillusioned but pious thoughts:

"But again I looked down into the vault, and in fancy beheld the pale shrunken forms still crouching there. Ah! what are our creeds, and how do we hope to be saved? Tell me, oh Bible, that story of Lazarus again, that I may find comfort in my heart for the poor and forlorn."[10]

Bloom or blight? Isn't it true that for Redburn to turn to his Bible at such a time, to find comfort in the story of Lazarus, is for Redburn to fall back into that same shallow creed he questions; the same perverted and pseudo-socially-minded creed that could be cheered by the knowledge that Time and God were on the side of the oppressed? The ironic bitterness, here, is not so much Redburn's as Melville's, because Melville is making a fool out of Redburn in order to use his religious clichés simultaneously as pap for any Christian reader who happens to be simple, and as a satirical thrust, straight into the wide-open mouth of that same reader. The disillusionment of Redburn the narrator is far greater than that of Wellingborough the actor; but Melville's disillusionment, at the time he wrote this story, led him to caustic thoughts so certain to offend the general reading public that he adapted to his own uses a few of Pierre Bayle's stylistic devices (which were similar to

some of Montaigne's). Melville thus insinuates that his own rebellion against the pretentiousness of a shallow and yet authoritarian orthodoxy is far more pronounced than Redburn's rebellion.

But perhaps it will be said that I am again reading too much
into *Redburn.* Try another example. After Wellingborough has
been hounded by the Dock-wall beggars in Liverpool, and has
listened to them pleading for just one ha'penny *"for Heaven's sake,*
and *for God's sake,* and *for Christ's sake,"* Redburn comments:
"As I daily passed through this lane of beggars, who thronged the
docks as the Hebrew cripples did the Pool of Bethesda, and as I
thought of my utter inability in any way to help them, I could but
offer up a prayer, that some angel might descend, and turn the
waters of the dock into an elixir, that would heal all their woes,
and make them, man and woman, healthy and whole as their ancestors, Adam and Eve, in the garden."[11]

Again, the same satirical formula. Emerson liked the story of
the Cape Cod minister who was asked to come out and pray over
a piece of ground that was ready for planting; of how the practical
man of God took one look at the soil and said, "This land doesn't
need prayer; it needs manure."

But *Redburn* was indeed a potboiler, tossed off hastily and
scornfully, so that Melville was bound to lose his artistic control
every once in a while. The reader may judge for himself whether
the following passage is too bitingly obvious or not. After having
recorded a painful sequence of incidents illuminating man's in-
humanity to man, Redburn describes Wellingborough's pleasure
in going to church every Sunday in Liverpool; he liked pretty
churches:

"For I am an admirer of church architecture; and though, perhaps, the sums spent in erecting magnificent cathedrals might
better go to the founding of charities, yet since these structures
are built, those who disapprove of them in one sense may as well
have the benefit of them in another.

"It is a most Christian thing, and a matter most sweet to dwell
upon and simmer over in solitude, that any poor sinner may go to
church wherever he pleases. . . . I say, this consideration of the
hospitality and democracy in churches is a most Christian and
charming thought. It speaks whole volumes of folios, and Vatican
libraries, for Christianity; it is more eloquent, and goes farther

home than all the sermons of Massillon, Jeremy Taylor, Wesley, and Archbishop Tillotson."[12]

The rhetorical device of pretending to praise something which is, in the context, inherently unpraiseworthy is a form of irony which helps keep the simmering pot from boiling over; but the temperature of Melville's caustic tone, there, comes perilously near the boiling point.

2

The most sustained piece of anti-Christian triple-talk in *Redburn* occurs when Melville follows Pierre Bayle one step further and builds quite an elaborate incident around an image which serves him, naughtily, as a symbol of The Holy Bible, that ever-present guide in time of trouble; the "revealing" word of the Father. Exactly in the middle of *Redburn*, Melville devotes two chapters to a Liverpool "Guide-Book" which Wellingborough treasures because it was once the property of his father, and was used by his father. Wellingborough now uses it in the hope that it will bring him closer to the memory of his father, as he follows in his father's footsteps. Unfortunately, Wellingborough finds the "Guide-Book" out of date; the *literal* meaning is valueless! This practical discovery leaves Wellingborough disappointed and disillusioned. The first chapter heading, itself, is provocative: "Redburn grows intolerably flat and stupid over some outlandish old Guide-Books." Scholars have been able to prove that Melville not only possessed a guide-book entitled *The Picture of Liverpool* but also made use of it as source material in writing *Redburn*; by contrast, my interest is in the hitherto undiscussed satirical use Melville made of that "Prosy Old Guide-Book" as an ironic emblem of the Bible:

"It was a curious and remarkable book; and from the many fond associations connected with it, I should like to immortalise it, if I could.

"But let me get it down from its shrine, and paint it, if I may, from the life.

"As I now linger over the volume, to and fro turning the pages so dear to my boyhood,—the very pages which, years and years ago, my father turned over amid the very scenes that are here described; what a soft, pleasing sadness steals over me, and how I melt into the past and forgotten!

"Dear book! I will sell my Shakespeare, and even sacrifice my old quarto Hogarth, before I will part with you. Yes, I will go to the hammer myself, ere I send you to be knocked down in the auctioneer's shambles. I will, my beloved,—old family relic that you are;—till you drop leaf from leaf, and letter from letter, you shall have a snug shelf somewhere, though I have no bench for myself."

So far, Melville is merely setting it up. We are further told that the "Prosy Old Guide-Book" contains "a brief and reverential preface," and we are also told of "the pious author's moralising reflections." As Wellingborough turns the pages, "reverentially," he finds some passages marked, and some notes, by which he concludes that "my father forgot not his religion in a foreign land." Then in the next chapter the triple-talk tendentiousness begins to amount to something more, and I have added the italics as hints:

"When I left home, I took the green morocco guide-book along. . . . Great was my boyish delight at the prospect of visiting a place, the *infallible* clue to all whose intricacies I held in my hand. . . . In short, when I considered that *my own father* had used this very guide-book, and that thereby it had been *tested*, and its *fidelity proved* beyond a peradventure; I could not but think that I was building myself up in an *unerring knowledge*."

The clustering of appropriate words makes the symbolic value of the Guide-Book increasingly obvious, and also the covert Melvillian sneer. Then comes Wellingborough's prosaic discovery that the book is out of date, and this (again with italics added):

"Dear delusion!

"It never occurred to my boyish thoughts that though a guide-book, fifty years old, might have done good service in its day, yet it would prove a miserable cicerone to a modern. . . .

"But *my faith* received a severe shock that same evening. . . . This was a staggerer . . . But for all this, I could not, for one small discrepancy, condemn the old family servant who had so *faithfully* served my own father before me. . . . I almost completely exonerated my guide-book from the half-insinuated charge of *misleading* me. . . .

"Then, indeed a *new light* broke in upon me concerning my

guide-book, and all my previous dim *suspicions* were almost confirmed. It was nearly half a century behind the age! and no more fit to guide me. . . .

"And, Wellingborough, as your father's guide-book is no guide for you, neither would yours (could you afford to buy a modern one to-day) be a guide to those who come after you. Guide-books, Wellingborough, are the least reliable books in all literature; and nearly all literature, in one sense, is made up of guide-books. . . . Every age makes its own guide-books, and the old ones are used for wastepaper."

Then Melville caps his sly anti-Christian joke with this direct continuation:

"But there is one Holy Guide-Book, Wellingborough, that will never lead you astray, if you but follow it aright; and some noble monuments that remain, though the pyramids crumble.

"But though I rose from the doorstep a sadder and a wiser boy, and though my guide-book had been stripped of *its reputation* for *infallibility*, I did not treat with contumely or disdain those *sacred* pages which had once been a beacon to my sire."[13]

Obviously, neither the actor Wellingborough nor the narrator Redburn are at all conscious of the overtones: each is specifically concerned with *The Picture of Liverpool.* But the conscious one, who makes us conscious, is Melville, the artist and manipulator, so recently disillusioned with his childhood heritage of belief that the Bible should be accepted as the infallible word of his Heavenly Father and that it should be cherished as a literal revelation of divine Truth. Therefore, even as he had previously contrived to make the narrator Redburn resort to orthodox religious clichés when in need of consolation, so he sardonically and satirically makes Wellingborough praise that "one Holy Guide-Book" as infallible.

3

There is one other aspect of *Redburn* which makes it valuable as a steppingstone to our understanding not only of Melville's style in *Moby-Dick* but also of his characterizations. In *Mardi*, Melville borrowed from Spenser the allegorical convention of representing a psychological division of Taji, in three separate characters: a historian, a philosopher, a poet. Each of these in turn enabled Melville to present through their mouths three different aspects of his own inner conflict. In *Moby-Dick*, Melville employed a modification of that device: he split his own psychological personality once again and projected one side of it into a cautious and timid and self-styled cowardly character, Ishmael; then projected another side of it, an idealized side, into the independent and rebellious and defiant hero, Captain Ahab. Ishmael comes far closer to the actuality in Melville's own character; Captain Ahab might be described as an artistic daydream wish-fulfillment.

In *Redburn*, necessarily unconsciously, Melville shows his increasing interest in the Ahab-like character who dares to assert the rights of natural man, even though such assertion may lead that character to blasphemy. But Melville also shows, in his autobiographical portrait of Wellingborough-as-actor, the incipient Ahab-ism and the incipient Ishmael-ism in his own character. In the first chapter of *Moby-Dick*, Ishmael is troubled by a hypochondria: his own embittered thoughts concerning the indignity of death. In the second chapter of *Redburn*, the narrator looks back at his boyhood and pities himself as an outcast whose "whole soul was soured" by something which had happened to him—an adolescent form of disillusionment:

"Talk not of the bitterness of middle-age and after-life; a boy can feel all that, and much more, when upon his young soul the mildew has fallen; and the fruit, which with others is only blasted after ripeness, with him is nipped in the first blossom and bud. And never again can such blights be made good; they strike in too deep, and leave such a scar that the air of Paradise might not erase it. And it is a hard and cruel thing thus in early youth to taste beforehand the pangs which should be reserved for the stout time of manhood . . . for then we are veterans used to sieges and battles, and not green recruits, recoiling at the first shock of the encounter."[14]

With this early glimpse of Redburn's incipient Ishmael-ism, the reader is not surprised to have Redburn subsequently refer to moments when others "exclaimed that I must be crazy"; moments when he could dwell on "the devil that had been tormenting me all day"; and even the moment when he specifically remarks, "I found myself a sort of Ishmael in the ship."[15] But there is one passage which suggests the close relationship between what might be called the combined Ishmael-ism and Ahab-ism in Redburn, at the time when Redburn, deeply upset, asserts a temporary defiance:

"At first, all this nearly stunned me, it was so unforeseen; and then I could not believe that they meant what they said. . . . I loathed, detested, and hated them with all that was left of my bursting heart and soul, and I thought myself the most forlorn and miserable wretch that ever breathed. . . . And I wailed and wept, and my heart cracked within me, but all the time I defied them through my teeth, and dared them to do their worst."[16]

So much for the incipient Ahab-ism and Ishmael-ism in Wellingborough and Redburn. There is another character aboard the *Highlander* who fascinates and repels Redburn because he feels some kind of frightening sympathy with the stranger: a mere sailor named Jackson, who might be considered as an artistic preliminary study, on Melville's part, of that character who was later to emerge in full-length portraiture as Captain Ahab. This is Jackson:

"But he had such an overawing way with him, such a deal of brass and impudence, such an unflinching face and withal was such a hideous-looking mortal, that Satan himself would have run from him. And besides all this, it was quite plain that he was by nature a marvellously clever, cunning man . . . and understood human nature to a kink, and well knew whom he had to deal with; and then, one glance of his squinting eye was as good as a knockdown, for it was the most deep, subtle, infernal-looking eye that I ever saw lodged in a human head. . . . It was a horrible thing; and I would give much to forget that I have ever seen it; for it haunts me to this day."[17]

Jackson is a sort of Byronic hero (which Melville had come to admire through his own sympathies and also through his long-standing acquaintance with the Devil School of literature), Promethean even in his defiance of God:

"Though he had never attended churches, and knew nothing about Christianity; no more than a Malay pirate; and though he could not read a word, yet he was spontaneously an atheist and an infidel; and during the long night-watches, would enter into arguments, to prove that there was nothing to be believed; nothing to be loved, and nothing worth living for; but everything to be hated, in the wide world. He was a horrid desperado; and like a wild Indian, whom he resembled in his tawny skin and high cheek-bones, he seemed to run amuck at heaven and earth. He was a Cain afloat; branded on his yellow brow with some inscrutable curse; and going about corrupting and searing every heart that beat near him.

"But there seemed even more woe than wickedness about the man; and his wickedness seemed to spring from his woe; and from all his hideousness there was that in his eye at times that was ineffably pitiable and touching; and though there were moments when I almost hated this Jackson, yet I have pitied no man as I have pitied him."[18]

That may help us to understand Melville's attitude toward Captain Ahab. Jackson's thoughts are preoccupied with death, because he is dying of some incurable disease:

"Brooding there, in his infernal gloom, though nothing but a castaway sailor in canvas trowsers, this man was still a picture, worthy to be painted by the dark, moody hand of Salvator. In any of that master's lowering sea-pieces, representing the desolate crags of Calabria, with a midnight shipwreck in the distance, this Jackson's would have been the face to paint for the doomed vessel's figure-head, seamed and blasted by lightning."[19]

If that takes us closer to Captain Ahab, this sharpens the focus:

"The weaker and weaker he grew, the more outrageous became his treatment of the crew. The prospect of the speedy and unshunnable death now before him seemed to exasperate his misanthropic soul into madness; and as if he had indeed sold it to Satan, he seemed determined to die with a curse between his teeth."[20]

Obviously fascinated by this character Jackson, Melville went on to hint at his own awareness that Jackson had much in common with the nineteenth-century Devil School concept of Satan (enemy of God, friend of man) so clearly represented in Byron's *Heaven and Earth*, and also in *Cain*; even in *Manfred*. But, the artistic commitment in *Redburn* was a form of triple-talk, involving the graduated and discrete viewpoints of actor, narrator, author. How, then, would Melville be able to express his own views on the subject of literary Satanism? Through equivocations and ambiguities inoffensive to that orthodox reading public which would,

Melville hoped, put money in his purse. Watch the stylistic hocus-pocus which interweaves his own prejudices in favor of Satanism with narrator Redburn's still piously orthodox prejudices against Satanism:

"I can never think of him, even now, reclining in his bunk, and with short breaths panting out his maledictions, but I am reminded of that misanthrope upon the throne of the world—the diabolical Tiberius at Capreae; who even in his self-exile, embittered by bodily pangs, and unspeakable mental terrors only known to the damned on earth, yet did not give over his blasphemies, but endeavoured to drag down with him to his own perdition all who came within the evil spell of his power. And though Tiberius came in the succession of the Caesars, and though unmatchable Tacitus has embalmed his carrion, yet do I account this Yankee Jackson full as dignified a personage as he, *and as well meriting his lofty gallows in history* [italics added; cf. Fielding, *Jonathan Wild*]; even though he was a nameless vagabond without an epitaph, and none, but I, narrate what he was. For there is no dignity in wickedness, whether in purple or rags; and hell is a democracy of devils, where all are equals. There, Nero howls side by side with his own malefactors. If Napoleon were truly but a martial murderer, I pay him no more homage than I would a felon. Though Milton's Satan dilutes our abhorrence with admiration, it is only because he is not a genuine being, but something altered from a genuine original. We gather not from the four gospels alone any high-raised fancies concerning this Satan; we only know him from thence as the personification of the essence of evil, which, who but pickpockets and burglars will admire? But this takes not from the merit of our high priest of poetry; it only enhances it, that with such unmitigated evil for his material, he should build up his most goodly structure.

"But in historically canonising on earth the condemned below, and lifting up and lauding the illustrious damned, we do but make ensamples of wickedness; and call upon ambition to do some great iniquity, and be sure of fame."[21]

The careful reader should be aware that, in the conclusion to that passage the pious Redburn is talking, not the disillusioned Melville who had so recently announced his purchase of Bayle's *Dictionary*. If we want to find Melville in that passage, we have to go beneath the pious assertion which demonstrates (by gathering proof from the four gospels of the Bible) that Satan is evil. Redburn is one of the "elect," who takes pharisaical pride in his superiority over those who try to assert Rousseau's concept that all men are created equal: "For there is no dignity in wickedness, whether in purple or rags; and hell is a democracy of devils, where all are equals." Melville himself feels a common bond with Jackson because each is scarred and embittered by experience. And Melville, if *almost* hating Jackson, is almost hating a quality in himself. He comes nearest showing his own private response when he lets Redburn say that there seemed to be more woe than wickedness in Jackson; that the wickedness seemed to spring from his woe; that he had pitied no man as he had pitied Jackson. Melville's capacity for self-pity was extraordinary, throughout his life.

SLASHING THE JACKET

CHAPTER V

Through the mouths of the dark characters of Hamlet, Timon, Lear, and Iago, he craftily says, or sometimes insinuates the things which we feel to be so terrifically true, that it were all but madness for any good man, in his own proper character, to utter, or even think of them.

MELVILLE, ON SHAKESPEARE

Outwardly regarded, our craft is a lie; for all that is outwardly seen of it is the clean-swept deck, and oft-painted planks comprised above the water-line; whereas the vast mass of our fabric, with all its storerooms of secrets, forever slides along far under the surface.

MELVILLE, *White-Jacket*

. . . some substances, without undergoing any mutations in themselves, utterly change their colour, according to the light thrown upon them.

MELVILLE, *White-Jacket*

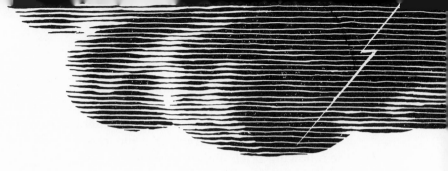

SLASHING THE JACKET

WHEN Melville was indulging his own missionary zeal by attacking the South Seas missionaries, it will be remembered, he referred to the "pent-up wickedness of five hundred men aboard a man-of-war" and added that his disillusioning contact with so much wickedness "nearly overturned all my previous theories" about human nature. He had enlisted in the United States Navy as an ordinary seaman, in order to work his way home from the Pacific, in the summer of 1843, and had been assigned to an insignificant and therefore (considering his extraordinary pride) humiliating station aboard the frigate *United States*. More than a year later, the frigate reached Boston, where Melville was honorably discharged from the Navy. This experience constituted a neat unit of raw materials for what he hoped would be another money-making potboiler.

James Russell Lowell once said that talent is that which is in a man's power, and genius is that in whose power a man is. Melville had the talent for telling what life was like, aboard a man-of-war; but his "genius" probably impelled him to do two others things, simultaneously: with a prophetlike missionary zeal, he translated his narrative into a denunciatory propaganda tract in order to attack the brutal tyranny of the naval officers toward the enlisted men, and particularly to attack the cruel practice of flogging; but, covertly, he endowed both narrative and propaganda with allegorical connotations to illuminate his own personal and private religious reaction against his Calvinistic heritage. In *White-Jacket*, then, Melville again braided three different strands: the navy story, the propaganda tract, the allegory. For present purposes, the following brief analysis is severely restricted to the allegorical aspects of *White-Jacket*, the other aspects being too obvious to need any description here.

Unlike Melville's use of moral allegory in *Mardi*, his use of it in *White-Jacket* represents another technical experiment not easily recognized by the average reader because the technique is rarely used. Melville places his entire narrative in a framework of Christian allegory, but he arranges to make the meaning of the narrative invert the conventional meaning of moral allegory. The consequent equivocation is ironic in method and in effect, because it evokes one response from the sheeplike reader and another response from the goatlike reader. Melville's fondness for variations on this device again indicates his indebtedness to Bayle and Montaigne; it is therefore pertinent to notice that in *White-Jacket* the narrator at one point builds his praise of one perceptive shipmate to a climactic point when he observes, "Besides, I saw it in his eye, that the man had been a reader of good books; I would have staked my life on it that he seized the right meaning of Montaigne. I saw that he was an earnest thinker; I more than suspected that he had been bolted in the mill of adversity. For all these things, my heart yearned toward him; I determined to know him."[1]

With overt and deceptive blandness, Melville takes a familiar and threadbare Christian analogy as the foundation on which to erect his allegorical frame: life is a voyage homeward, toward Heaven. This is certainly innocent enough. The many possible extensions are also familiar conventions in Christian literature: this earth is a floating ship in which we sail; society may be represented by the passengers, the crew, the officers; but God is our omnipotent captain. With these possibilities in mind, consider the obviousness with which Melville's narrator, nicknamed "White-Jacket" by his shipmates, begins by suggesting the familiar analogy and even by placing that analogy within a covertly ironic context of Biblical allusions. The following passage occurs at the beginning of Chapter Two:

"'All hands up anchor! Man the capstan!'

"'High die! my lads, we're homeward bound!'

"Homeward bound!—harmonious sound! Were you ever home-ward bound?—No?—Quick! take the wings of the morning, or the sails of a ship, and fly to the uttermost parts of the earth. There, tarry a year or two; and then let the gruffest of boatswains, his lungs all goose-skin, shout forth those magical words, and you'll swear 'the harp of Orpheus were not more enchanting.' "[2]

For sinister purposes, the quotations from Psalm 139 are nice: "Whither shall I go from thy Spirit? or whither shall I flee from thy presence? If I ascend up into heaven, thou art there: if I make my bed in hell, behold, thou art there. If I take the wings of the morning, and dwell in the uttermost parts of the sea; even there . . ." After the manner of Redburn the narrator, White-Jacket's words, throughout, quite overtly suggest a pattern of rebellious escape and submissive return, in religious matters: his doubts are always overcome by his affirmations. But while these fluctuations suggest the fluctuations in Melville's own thinking, and particularly his wistfulness in the face of his doubts, the reader of *White-Jacket* will do well to keep *Redburn* in mind and to remember that Melville had permitted the narrator Redburn to represent exactly that orthodox and conventional piousness which the majority of his readers would prefer to find in a narra-tive; but that beneath this overt veneer of apparent orthodoxy, Melville covertly insinuated his private and unorthodox viewpoint; that after finishing *Redburn*, Melville had written to Duyckinck, "What a madness & anguish it is, that an author can never—under no conceivable circumstances—be at all frank with his readers." For the moment, however, our concern is with the conventionally Christian allegorical frame of reference established by White-Jacket, the ostensibly pious narrator. We have taken one passage from the next-to-first chapter; here is another passage which occurs in the next-to-last chapter:

"And now that . . . the blessed Capes of Virginia are believed to be broad on our bow—though still out of sight—our five hundred souls are fondly dreaming of home. . . .

". . . our anchor still hangs from our bows, though its eager flukes dip their points in the impatient waves. Let us leave the ship on the sea—still with the land out of sight—still with brooding darkness on the face of the deep. [Cf. Genesis 1:2] I love an indefinite, infinite background—a vast, heaving, rolling, mysterious rear! [By insinuation, all that Melville can see of God.][3]

"It is night, The meagre moon is in her last quarter—that betokens the end of a cruise that is passing. But the stars look forth in their everlasting brightness—and *that* is the everlasting, glorious Future, forever beyond us.

"We main-top men are all aloft in the top; and round our mast we circle, a brother-band, hand in hand, all spliced together. . . . Hand in hand we topmates stand, rocked in our Pisgah top. [That is, looking toward the "Promised Land."] And over the starry waves, and broad out into the blandly blue and boundless night, spiced with strange sweets from the long-sought land—the whole long cruise predestinated ours, though often in tempest-time we almost refused to believe in that far-distant shore—straight out into that fragrant night, ever-noble Jack Chase, matchless and unmatchable Jack Chase stretches forth his bannered hand, and, pointing shoreward, cries: 'For the last time, hear Camoens, boys!' "[4]

Never mind the covert and sarcastic insinuations, there; stick to the overt reflection of a doubting but believing viewpoint, a piously poetic viewpoint, and consider in the same sense this postlude which Melville entitled, "The End":

"As a man-of-war that sails through the sea, so this earth that sails through the air. We mortals are all on board a fast-sailing, never-sinking world-frigate, of which God was the shipwright; and she is but one craft in a Milky-Way fleet, of which God is the Lord High Admiral. The port we sail from is forever astern. And though far out of sight of land, for ages and ages we continue to sail with sealed orders, and our last destination remains a secret to ourselves and our officers; yet our final haven was predestined ere we slipped from the stocks at Creation.

"Thus sailing with sealed orders, we ourselves are the repositories of the secret packet, whose mysterious contents we long to learn. There are no mysteries out of ourselves. But let us not give ear to the superstitious, gun-deck gossip about whither we may be gliding, for, as yet, not a soul on board knows—not even the commodore himself; assuredly not the chaplain; even our professor's scientific surmisings are vain. On that point, the smallest cabin-boy is as wise as the captain. And believe not the hypochondriac dwellers below hatches, who will tell you, with a sneer, that our world-frigate is bound to no final harbour whatever; that our voyage will prove an endless circumnavigation of space. Not so. For how can this world-frigate prove our eventual abiding place, when, upon our first embarkation, as infants in arms, her violent rolling—in after life unperceived—makes every soul of us seasick? [Cf. Wordsworth's "Intimations of Immortality."] Does not this show, too, that the very air we here inhale is uncongenial, and only becomes endurable at last through gradual habituation, and that some blessed placid haven, however remote at present, must be in store for us all?

"Glance fore and aft our flush decks. What a swarming crew! All told, they muster hard upon eight hundred millions of souls. Over these we have authoritative Lieutenants, a sword-belted Officer of Marines, a Chaplain, a Professor, a Purser, a Doctor, a Cook, a Master-at-arms.

"Oppressed by illiberal laws, and partly oppressed by themselves, many of our people are wicked, unhappy, inefficient. We have skulkers and idlers all round, and brow-beaten waisters, who, for a pittance, do our craft's shabby work. Nevertheless, among our people we have gallant fore, main and mizen-top men aloft, who, well treated or ill, still trim our craft to the blast.

"We have a *brig* for trespassers; a bar by our main-mast, at which they are arraigned; a cat-o'-nine-tails and a gangway, to degrade them in their own eyes and in ours. These are not always employed to convert Sin to Virtue, but to divide them, and protect Virtue and legalised Sin from unlegalised Vice.

"We have a Sick-bay for the smitten, and helpless, whither we hurry them out of sight, and, however they may groan beneath the hatches, we hear little of their tribulations on deck; we still sport our gay streamer aloft. *Outwardly regarded, our craft is a lie; for all that is outwardly seen of it is the clean-swept deck, and oft-painted planks comprised above the water-line; whereas, the vast mass of our fabric, with all its storerooms of secrets, forever slides along far under the surface* [italics added].

"When a shipmate dies, straightway we sew him up, and overboard he goes; our world-frigate rushes by, and never more do we behold him again; though, sooner or later, the everlasting under-tow sweeps him toward our own destination.

"We have both a quarter-deck to our craft and a gun-deck; subterranean shot-lockers and gunpowder magazines; and the Articles of War form our domineering code.

"Oh, shipmates and world-mates, all round! we the people suffer many abuses. Our gun-deck is full of complaints. In vain from Lieutenants do we appeal to the Captain; in vain—while on board our world-frigate—to the indefinite Navy Commissioners, so far out of sight aloft. Yet the worst of our evils we blindly inflict upon ourselves; our officers cannot remove them, even if they would. From the last ills no being can save another; therein each man must be his own saviour. For the rest, whatever befall us, let us never train our murderous guns inboard; let us not mutiny with bloody pikes in our hands. Our Lord High Admiral will yet inter-pose; and though long ages should elapse, and leave our wrongs unredressed, yet, shipmates and world-mates! let us never forget, that

> 'Whoever afflict us, whatever surround,
> Life is a voyage that's homeward bound!' "[5]

Melville's stylistic and equivocal footwork there is very cunning, clever, fancy, crafty, naughty. Fond of punning, he seems to pun very nicely on the word "craft" when he lets the pious White-Jacket observe, "Outwardly regarded, our craft is a lie. . . ." The image of the surface current and the sinister undertow may be used here to suggest Melville's stylistic and structural devices. Having lost faith in Christian doctrine, Melville takes pleasure in satirizing certain basic concepts of Christian doctrine, and his method of doing that is the ironic method, again, of pretending to praise concepts which are, from his viewpoint, mere superstitions.

2

WITHIN this allegorical framework of "life as a voyage that's home-ward bound," consider the title image of the jacket, the white jacket which our hero fashions and patches for his own uses; which he subsequently finds to be unsatisfactory; which he finally dis-cards. We know that Melville borrowed *Sartor Resartus* from

Duyckinck, the year after *White-Jacket* was published; but there is good likelihood that he had at least a secondhand acquaintance with *Sartor Resartus* before he wrote *White-Jacket*. It will be remembered that the clothes philosophy of Teufelsdrockh is elaborated by Carlyle to suggest that the garments of religious thought which we inherit are likely to be ill-fitting because they are secondhand; that we alter and patch, but that sooner or later we throw those secondhand garments away and (after the manner of the Prodigal Son) come to ourselves. This passage from *Sartor Resartus* is pertinent:

"Perhaps not once in a lifetime does it occur to your ordinary biped, of any country or generation, be he gold-mantled Prince or russet-jerkined Peasant, that his Vestments and his Self are not one and indivisible; that *he* is naked, without vestments, till he buy or steal such, and by forethought sew and button them. For my own part, these considerations, of our Clothesthatch, and how, reaching inwards even to our heart of hearts, it tailorizes and demoralizes us, fill me with a certain horror at myself and mankind: almost as one feels at those Dutch Cows, which, during the wet season, you see grazing deliberately with jackets and petticoats (or striped sacking), in the meadows of Gouda. Nevertheless there is something great in the moment when a man first strips himself of adventitious wrappages; and sees indeed that he is naked, and, as Swift has it, 'a forked straddling animal with bandy legs'; yet also a Spirit, and an unutterable Mystery of Mysteries."[6]

Melville's fondness for Swift suggests the possibility that the image of the white jacket was not entirely unrelated, in Melville's mind, to the coat images in Swift's *Tale of a Tub*. More important, his allegorical framework permits him to develop the making and wearing and discarding of the white jacket as a symbol of his autobiographical attempt to patch up or find a substitute for his inherited Calvinistic theological beliefs in Platonic philosophical concepts and his final decision to discard all; to strip himself down to the "natural man," in the tradition of Rousseau and Tom Paine.

The contrast between the viewpoints of Melville and Carlyle, here, should be obvious: basically, Carlyle's beliefs belong in the Christian tradition; Melville's direction, covertly represented in *White-Jacket*, is anti-Christian. Even the symbolic jacket is represented as a substitute for the conventional and orthodox "uniform" prescribed by "regulations":

"When our frigate lay in Callao, on the coast of Peru—her last harbour in the Pacific—I found myself without a *grego*, or sailor's surtout; and as, toward the end of a three years' cruise, no pea-jackets could be had from the purser's steward, and being bound for Cape Horn, some sort of a substitute was indispensable; I employed myself, for several days in manufacturing an outlandish garment of my own devising, to shelter me from the boisterous weather we were soon to encounter."[7]

Thus blandly and innocently Melville introduces his image of the jacket, and from that point until the jacket almost causes his death as a "shroud" when it becomes fouled about his "head" as he happens to "fall" overboard, the hinted and symbolic overtones are carefully interlocked with other parts of the allegorical narrative. For example, Melville found symbolic justification for altering the details of his personal experience in regard to the matter of the station to which White-Jacket was assigned. Aboard the frigate *United States*, Melville was assigned to the after-guard, "composed chiefly of landsmen." Aboard the man-of-war *Never-sink*, White-Jacket was assigned to the main-top. Notice the chances for sarcastic and punning extensions, in this artistic alteration:

"Again must I call attention to my white jacket, which about this time came near being the death of me.

"I am of the meditative humour, and at sea used often to mount aloft at night, and, seating myself on one of the upper yards, tuck my jacket about me and give loose to reflection. In some ships in which I have done this, the sailors used to fancy that I must be studying astronomy [Note: by word-play, the study of "Heavenly Bodies"]—which, indeed, to some extent, was the case—and that my object in mounting aloft was to get a nearer view of the stars, supposing me, of course, to be short-sighted. A very silly conceit of theirs, some may say, but not so silly after all; for surely the advantage of getting nearer an object by two hundred feet is not to be underrated. Then, to study the stars upon the wide, boundless sea, is divine as it was to the Chaldean Magi, who observed their revolutions from the plains.

"And it is a very fine feeling, and one that fuses us into the universe of things, and makes us a part of the All, to think that, wherever we ocean wanderers rove, we have still the same glorious old stars to keep us company; that they still shine onward and on, forever beautiful and bright, and luring us, by every ray, to die and be glorified with them.

"Ah, ay! we sailors sail not in vain. We expatriate ourselves to nationalise with the universe. . . ."[8]

In that passage, as in several other passages, the image of the jacket is correlated with poetic and symbolic references to meditation and contemplation and reflection while the narrator is either aloft or looking aloft. But the total emblematic value of the jacket, and of the series of actions which present the history of the jacket, cannot be had by the reader until these various references are correlated with the total meaning of the equivocal and ambiguous allegory. Removed from this larger context, the jacket references are tantalizingly incomplete; viewed as parts which are allegorically related to the whole, the tantalizing quality of these references is closely related to all the other insinuative ambiguities. They might be said to keep their values in suspension. But the element which precipitates and crystallizes two distinct categories of meaning is the obvious discrepancy between the conventionally laudatory extensions of the life-as-voyage, world-as-ship, God-as-Captain tropes, in Christian allegory, and the unconventional vituperation which the narrator hurls against this particular voyage, this particular ship, this particular jacket, this particular Captain.

Once the reader notices this discrepancy, it becomes much more apparent that Melville has again manipulated not only the allegorical allusions but also the narrator's remarks in such a way as to let both these factors have a surface value for the sheeplike and pious reader; a sinister undertow value for the goatlike and skeptical reader. In the last passage quoted, for example, the surface value of meaning indicates that White-Jacket prides himself on his religiosity; that his words reflect, not too obliquely, the Christian virtues of acceptance and of submission to God's will. However, if White-Jacket were to be consistent, in terms of the specific story and also in terms of the implicit allegory, his submission to God's will would require (artistically) his submission to the Captain's will. The discrepancy should keep stimulating the response

101

of the careful reader, until such a reader becomes aware that Melville's contrivances which permit White-Jacket to keep making various forms of pious affirmation are deliberately designed by Melville to ridicule those aspects of Christian doctrine which Melville could no longer stomach.

What aspects? Primarily and fundamentally, the major premises of Calvinistic theology, as represented by the orthodox interpretation of the Genesis story; an interpretation designed to illuminate the pure attributes of God, and to justify the ways of God to men; designed to explain how evil came into the world, and how Satan was permitted by God to tempt man; designed to explain how God thus acted permissively toward Satan in order that great good might come out of great evil; also designed to justify the complacent optimism implicit in the Christian doctrine that "all things work together for good to them that love God," as that first pharisaical Christian theologian, Paul, phrased it.

Now we may return to the jacket image, and to the consideration of how Melville covertly arranges to represent the slashing off of the jacket as an action symbolic of slashing off religious beliefs. Aligning himself, now, with the so-called "enlightened" and "free-thinking" and "rationalistic" writers like Tom Paine, Melville also aligns himself with the Satanic School of literature which chose to misinterpret Milton's Satan, in *Paradise Lost*, in order to glorify Milton's Satan as a type of the tragic and Promethean hero. Remember that Milton's Satan found consolation in viewing his "fall" from heaven as an act of self-liberation. Melville had arrived at the position of viewing his own "fall" from Christian grace as an act of self-liberation, and consequently he represents the symbolic action of slashing the jacket as a desperate necessity which enabled his self-projection, White-Jacket, to set himself "free" and thus save himself from death, after his "fall" from the yardarm into the chaos of ocean.

To foreshadow the significance of this climactic episode in the narrative, Melville cunningly tucked in a seemingly innocent description of the general setting:

"The royal-yard forms a cross with the mast, and falling from that lofty cross in a line-of-battle ship is almost like falling from the cross of St. Paul's; almost like falling as Lucifer from the wellspring of morning down to the Phlegethon of night.

102

"In some cases, a man, hurled thus from a yard, has fallen upon his shipmates in the tops, and dragged them down with him to the same destruction with himself."

Triple-talk! The superficial reader is satisfied with the mere description, there. At the same time, Melville wickedly invites the devout Christian reader to appreciate that any "fall" from such a yard would be as horrible and deplorable as Satan's mythical "fall" from heaven. Now notice the anti-Christian insinuations, and their extensions. First of all, the allusion to "falling from the cross of St. Paul's" is ambiguous in that it would seem to establish a mere analogy in terms of the distance down to the ground from the lofty height of the "cross" on the dome of St. Paul's cathedral, in London; but the allusion might also be construed, in this blasphemous context, as an act of heretical departure from the apostle Paul's theological dogma concerning the significance of Christ's cross. Notice also that whereas a Christian context makes Satan's fall sinful and deplorable, a Satanic-School context makes Satan's fall seem bold, heroic, praiseworthy. Furthermore, the suggested "falling from that lofty cross in a line-of-battle ship" interlocks the symbolism of the "fall" with the symbolism implicit in the subtitle: Melville represents the man-of-war not merely as an emblem of the world but also as an emblem of that rigidly ordered chain of command, involving the tyrannical and brutal superiority of the officers, which in turn is analogous (as Melville sees it) to the repulsive chain of command in Christian cosmology and doctrine: God is supreme, tyrannical, brutal.

That passage is so resonant with echoes and overtones and insinuations that we have by no means exhausted the possibilities, as yet. In this Satanic-School context, the single word, "hurled," suggests and echoes the so-called unjust and ruthless treatment of the Archangel Satan, as represented in the first book of *Paradise Lost*:

> Him the Almighty Power
> *Hurl'd* [italics added] headlong flaming from th'
>   Ethereal Sky
> With hideous ruin and combustion down
> To bottomless perdition, there to dwell
> In Adamantine Chains and penal Fire,
> Who durst defy th' Omnipotent to Arms.

103

According to that Christian doctrine which Melville hated, such is the penalty which awaits anyone who is so boldly Promethean as to assert disbelief and heresy. Notice next, in Melville's passage, the image of dragging-down, with its additional echoes of innumerable passages in *Paradise Lost*: Satan "drew after him the third part of Heav'n's Sons." Melville was fascinated by that image, and used it several times. We have already had occasion to notice that when he described the similarities between Jackson and Milton's Satan, in *Redburn,* he also established a further analogy between Jackson and "*diabolical* [italics added] Tiberius" who "did not give over his blasphemies, but endeavoured to *drag down* [italics added] with him to his own perdition all who came within the evil spell of his power." Melville's uses of this image, in *Redburn* and *White-Jacket,* might be considered as trial flights in preparation for the far more significant use of it in the catastrophe of *Moby-Dick,* to illuminate the symbolic significance of the entire narrative, in terms of Tashtego's vengeful and retaliatory action, during the sinking of the "God-bullied" *Pequod*: ". . . and so the bird of heaven, with archangelic shrieks, and his imperial beak thrust upwards, and his whole captive form folded in the flag of Ahab, went down with his ship, which, *like Satan, would not sink to hell till she had dragged a living part of heaven along with her* [italics added], and helmeted herself with it."

These correlated echoes and overtones of meaning should help us to appreciate the quiet undertones of Melvillian insinuation which occur in the *White-Jacket* chapter entitled, "The Last of the Jacket." The climactic action begins when the hero is sent aloft at night, in accordance with orders. Forewarned by Jack Chase (that outspoken exponent of "freedom" and of the "rights of man"), White-Jacket disregards the suggestion that he should dispense with his jacket. He climbs aloft, encumbered. While working with lines in the dark, out on a yardarm, he is thrown off balance by the plunging motion of the ship, and immediately the jacket wraps itself "right over my head, completely muffling me." Again thrown off balance as he uses one hand, momentarily, to extricate himself, White-Jacket loses his hold, and falls:

"All I had seen, and read, and heard, and all I had thought and felt in my life, seemed intensified in one fixed idea in my soul. . . . and I thought to myself, Great God! this is Death! . . . I essayed to swim toward the ship; but instantly I was conscious of a feeling like being pinioned in a *feather bed* [italics added; cf. the description of the "Protean easy chair" in *The Confidence-Man*], and, moving my hands, felt my jacket puffed out above my tight girdle with water. I strove to tear it off . . . I whipped out my knife, that was tucked at my belt, and ripped my jacket straight up and down, as if I were ripping myself. With a violent struggle I then burst out of it, and was free."

Superficially considered, *White-Jacket* would not be called a satire, because the story of life on a man-of-war and the propaganda aimed against naval abuses are the two aspects which are obvious. Yet it would be a mistake to say that the satire aimed at Christian dogma and Christian theology, in *White-Jacket*, is incidental and unimportant. A careful reading will make it clear that Melville's artistic wile and guile in establishing his allegorical framework, and then in slyly inverting the conventional meaning of that allegory, encompass not only the central action but also the major symbol represented in the title; that these two different kinds of action (slashing at tyrannical abuses and slashing off the jacket) are analogous actions which symbolize Melville's own private act of slashing against his Christian heritage, in an unsuccessful attempt to rid himself of it.

Artistically considered, then, the talent-genius of Melville's subtle complexities should be found chiefly in the satirical aspects of *White-Jacket*. One might employ various ways for representing or describing his method, and when I try to suggest the major part of it by saying that he once again gives the effect of having created a seemingly pious and pharisaical self-burlesqued narrator in the character of White-Jacket (even as I said he did much the same thing in *Redburn*), the reader should realize that I employ this description as merely a convenient way to analyze the causes and effects of Melville's sustained irony. Yet Melville himself would seem to have recognized further opportunities for burlesque inherent in the artistic modification of his own experience so that he could represent his contrived character White-Jacket as a foretopman. Traditionally, all sailors who were foretopmen felt themselves superior to any other sailors "down below, below, below," and Melville takes advantage of this fact in order to let his foretopman White-Jacket reflect this sense of superiority in his pious utterances. Technically considered, the effect of such contriving is another kind of mousetrap effect, for the very reason that Melville could be confident that many orthodox readers would take pleasure in identifying their own views with the pious views uttered by White-Jacket, without noticing that Melville simultaneously burlesques the piousness of White-Jacket and the gulled reader. For example, consider a passage which occurs shortly after a Satan-like master-at-arms named Bland has been admitted to the mess of the maintopmen, who are orthodox enough to accept Bland as a necessary evil. The passage is designed to satirize several fundamental tenets of Christian doctrine, and one could variously describe Melville's method of achieving that satirical effect. But the careless and orthodox reader creates his own trap here when he finds in White-Jacket's generalizations considerable evidence that White-Jacket essentially represents a Christian viewpoint. Such a reader will not be likely to notice that the viewpoint is also pharisaical; that while White-Jacket may be sincere in his piety, Melville is manipulating White-Jacket in such a way that the Melvillian sarcasm and sardonicism is covertly pervasive:

". . . though we all abhorred the monster of Sin itself, yet, from our social superiority, highly rarefied education in our lofty top, and large and liberal sweep of the aggregate of things, we were in a good degree free from those useless, personal prejudices, and galling hatreds against conspicuous *sinners*—not *Sin*—which so widely prevail among men of warped understandings, and unchristian and uncharitable hearts. No; the superstitions and dogmas concerning Sin had not laid their withering maxims upon our hearts. We perceived how that evil was but good disguised, and a knave a saint in his way; how that in other planets, perhaps, what we deem wrong may there be deemed right; even as some substances, without undergoing any mutations in themselves, utterly change their colour, according to the light thrown upon them. We perceived that the anticipated millennium must have begun upon the morning the first worlds were created; and that, taken all in all, our man-of-war world in itself was as eligible a round-sterned craft as any to be found in the Milky Way. And we fancied that though some of us, of the gun-deck, were at times condemned to sufferings and slights, and all manner of tribulation and anguish, yet, no doubt, it was only our misapprehension of these things that made us take them for woeful pains instead of the most agreeable pleasures. I have dreamed of a sphere, says Pinzella, where to break a man on the wheel is held the most exquisite of delights you can confer upon him; where for one gentleman in any way to vanquish another is accounted an everlasting dishonour; where to tumble one into a pit after death, and then throw cold clods upon his upturned face, is a species of contumely only inflicted upon the most notorious criminals.

"But whatever we messmates thought, in whatever circumstances we found ourselves, we never forgot that our frigate, bad as it was, was homeward bound. Such, at least, were our reveries at times, though sorely jarred, now and then, by events that took our philosophy aback. For after all, philosophy—that is, the best wisdom that has ever in any way been revealed to our man-of-war world—is but a slough and a mire, with a few tufts of good footing here and there."[9]

The Melvillian principle and technique of contriving equivocations, and then of permitting the reader to make the best (or the worst) meanings out of them, may be suggested again by these words: "some substances, without undergoing any mutations in themselves, utterly change their colour, according to the light thrown upon them." True, indeed! As proof of that observation, the reader need merely notice that the "colour" of the larger passage, which contains those words, is "utterly" changed if viewed first in the light of a Christian viewpoint and then in the light of an anti-Christian viewpoint.

If some readers should find that passage confusing, they should carefully differentiate between Melville's willingness to create confusion for satirical effect, and Melville's own confusion. The reader who is fortunate enough to come to this passage after considerable reading in Montaigne or in Pierre Bayle will find himself quite comfortable in the equivocations, and will be able to shift gears from the Christian viewpoint to the anti-Christian or skeptical or agnostical viewpoint in order to see what happens when the same sentence or word is differently geared. Take for example, ". . . we were in a good degree free from those useless, personal prejudices, and galling hatreds against conspicuous *sinners*—not Sin—which so widely prevail among men of warped understandings, and unchristian and uncharitable hearts." From the Christian

107

viewpoint, that makes sense, because the Christian spirit of love and forgiveness encompasses even sinners. Theoretically, that is so. Actually? Now we shift to the skeptical or agnostical or anti-Christian viewpoint, and can recognize Melville's derisive sneer at the self-righteousness of such Christians as will not tolerate any religious belief other than their own, except to pay lip-service to toleration; Christians who in Melville's day still loved to hurl at some so-called *sinners* the word "heretic" because it justified their "personal prejudices," their "galling hatreds," their "warped understandings," and their "uncharitable hearts." These were Melville's enemies; hence the subtlety of his self-protective satire against them.

Take another sentence from that passage: "No; the superstitions and dogmas concerning Sin had not laid their withering maxims upon our hearts." Who is speaking? One with a "highly rarefied education" and with a "large and liberal sweep." (Remember that the rationalists, including Hobbes and Bayle, delighted to equate the words "superstition" and "religion.") Shortly before Melville began to write *White-Jacket*, the Calvinists in New England had indulged in a new phase of their chronic squabbles with each other as to the meaning of the terms "Original Sin" and "Innate Depravity." That celebrated Calvinist theologian, Rev. Horace Bushnell, had fired the first shot in this latest skirmish over man's native moral state, when he insisted that while he did not wish to deny the validity of Calvinistic doctrine of Depravity, he did suggest that children were not *totally* depraved at birth! His views were set forth in his most famous work, *Christian Nurture* (1847); but even before then his utterances had been considered so scandalous that the more conservative theologians of the day rushed into print to attack Rev. Horace Bushnell. For Melville, all these controversial tracts would have seemed funnier than *Captain Billy's Whizz-Bang*, and equally indecent. Melville would certainly have known that this phase of theological warfare had appropriately started as far back as the year of his birth, 1819, when William Ellery Channing had preached his famous Baltimore sermon, raising the question as to the true nature of man and attacking the Calvinistic concept of Original Sin. The pride which the "new light" Calvinists or the so-called liberals took in attacking Channing and his defenders would have been enough to arouse Melville's disdainful sarcasm and satire, and many of his thrusts at theological pretentiousness, in his narratives, are apparently aimed at issues in that extended New England debate on natural depravity, now long forgotten.

Take the next sentence in that passage: "We perceived how that evil was but good disguised, and a knave a saint in his way; how that in other planets, perhaps, what we deem wrong may there be deemed right . . ." To Melville's newly acquired skepticism, much of Christian dogma seemed based on a casuistry which he saw as ridiculous, and this particular sentence is worth pointing out now, because we shall later see how Melville satirized the same concepts far more elaborately in Plotinus Plinlimmon's ethical-culture tract.

Just one more part of that passage should be noticed here: the conclusion, which contains the little joke over how the word "philosophy" should be defined. Having grown as impatient with systematic philosophy as with systematic Calvinism, Melville managed to whack two birds with one stone. His sly definition of philosophy also serves as a Calvinistic definition of Christianity: "the best wisdom that has ever in any way been revealed [through the Bible, which is the Word of God] to our man-of-war world." Also notice that Melville permits White-Jacket to cap this equivocal definition by describing this "philosophy" as "but a slough and a mire, with a few tufts of good footing here and there."

3

WITH this much preparation, we can more easily recognize the blasphemous aspects of satiric allegorical insinuations which begin to accumulate as early in *White-Jacket* as the expositional description of the officers who guide this emblematic ship in its homeward voyage. As we have seen, Melville's specifically elaborated tropes refer to God as not only the "shipwright" but also as "the Lord High Admiral." It might be gathered that Melville considered it advisable to omit any further reference to the other nautical roles which God might be said to play. Or, the hierarchy of officers in the naval chain of being might suggest that the agents of "the Lord High Admiral" extend downward through the Navy Commissioners to the Commodore, thence to the Captain;

even to the Master-at-Arms and to the ordinary seamen. But the curious structure of this naval chain of being naturally requires that while the Commodore reflects the attributes of his Admiral, so does the Captain; that each is endowed with more or less absolute power, in order to fulfill the delegated authority of his ultimate superior—allegorically, God Almighty. Start, then, with the description of the Commodore, who may be considered allegorically as the first representative of God aboard the *Neversink*:

"In the first place, then, I have serious doubts, whether, for the most part, he was not dumb; for, in my hearing, he seldom or never uttered a word. And not only did he seem dumb himself, but his presence possessed the strange power of making other people dumb for the time. His appearance on the quarter-deck seemed to give every officer the lockjaw.

"Another phenomenon about him was the strange manner in which every one shunned him. . . . Perhaps he had an evil eye; maybe he was the Wandering Jew afloat. The real reason, probably, was that, like all high functionaries, he deemed it indispensable religiously to sustain his dignity; one of the most troublesome things in the world, and one calling for the greatest self-denial. And the constant watch, and many-sided guardedness, which this sustaining of a commodore's dignity requires, plainly enough shows that, apart from the common dignity of manhood, commodores, in general, possess no real dignity at all. True, it is expedient for crowned heads, generalissimos, lord high admirals, and commodores, to carry themselves straight, and beware of the spinal complaint; but it is not the less veritable that it is a piece of assumption, exceedingly uncomfortable to themselves, and ridiculous to an enlightened generation."[10]

Notice that word "enlightened." How does White-Jacket introduce the Captain, who is, allegorically, another representative of God?

"Turn we now to the second officer in rank, almost supreme, however, in the internal affairs of his ship. Captain Claret was a large, portly man, a Harry the Eighth afloat, bluff and hearty; and as kingly in his cabin as Harry on his throne. For a ship is a bit of terra-firma cut off from the main; it is a state in itself; and the captain is its king.

"It is no limited monarchy, where the sturdy Commons have a

110

right to petition, and snarl if they please; but almost a despotism, like the Grand Turk's. The captain's word is law; he never speaks but in the imperative mood. When he stands on his quarter-deck at sea, he absolutely commands as far as eye can reach. . . . He is lord and master of the sun. It is not twelve o'clock till he says so. . . ."11

The occult insinuations, in passages concerning the Captain, pick up further allegorical significance, obviously anti-Calvinistic, as soon as White-Jacket begins to describe and discuss flogging and the Captain's tyrannically brutal supervision of it. The two most vivid descriptions are those of the flogging of a youngster named Peter and the near-flogging of White-Jacket himself. Peter's punishment contains this:

". . . As he was being secured to the gratings, and the shudderings and creepings of his dazzlingly white back were revealed, he turned round his head imploringly; but his weeping entreaties and vows of contrition were of no avail. 'I would not forgive God Almighty!' cried the captain. The fourth boatswain's mate advanced, and at the first blow the boy, shouting *'My God! Oh! my God!'* writhed and leaped so as to displace the gratings, and scatter the nine tails of the scourge all over his person. At the next blow he howled, leaped, and raged in unendurable torture.

" 'What are you stopping for, boatswain's mate?' cried the captain. 'Lay on!' and the whole dozen was applied.

" 'I don't care what happens to me now!' wept Peter, going among the crew, with blood-shot eyes, as he put on his shirt. 'I have been flogged once, and they may do it again if they will. Let them look out for me now!'

" 'Pipe down!' cried the captain; and the crew slowly dispersed."12

Peter's mutinous attitude (with its incipient Ahab-ism) foreshadows White-Jacket's own dangerously close impulse to mutinous defiance (purely fictitious):

". . . And now, after making a hermit of myself in some things, in order to avoid the possibility of the scourge, here it was hanging over me for a thing utterly unforeseen, for a crime of which I was as utterly innocent. But all that was as naught. I saw that my case was hopeless; my solemn disclaimer was thrown in my teeth, and the boatswain's mate stood curling his fingers through the *cat.*

111

"There are times when wild thoughts enter a man's heart, when he seems almost irresponsible for his act and his deed. The captain stood on the weather-side of the deck . . . and, though he was a large, powerful man, it was certain that a sudden rush against him, along the slanting deck, would infallibly pitch him head-foremost into the ocean, though he who so rushed must needs go over with him. My blood seemed clotting in my veins; I felt icy cold at the tips of my fingers, and a dimness was before my eyes. . . . I cannot analyse my heart, though it then stood still within me. But the thing that swayed me to my purpose was not altogether the thought that Captain Claret was about to degrade me, and that I had taken an oath with my soul that he should not. No, I felt my man's manhood so bottomless within me, that no word, no blow, no scourge of Captain Claret could cut me deep enough for that. I but swung to an instinct in me—the instinct diffused through all animated nature, the same that prompts even a worm to turn under the heel. Locking souls with him, I meant to drag Captain Claret from this earthly tribunal of his to that of Jehovah, and let Him decide between us. No other way could I escape the scourge.

"Nature has not implanted any power in man that was not meant to be exercised at times, though too often our powers have been abused. The privilege, inborn and inalienable, that every man has, of dying himself, and inflicting death upon another, was not given to us without a purpose. These are the last resources of an insulted and unendurable existence."[13]

4

Now we are also in a position to examine another aspect of *White-Jacket*, in the light of the passage just quoted, and the subsequent extensions of it. So far, I have suggested that Melville's development of allegorical insinuations in *White-Jacket* was designed to achieve an ironic and satirical effect; that he permitted his narrator to speak in pious praise of certain familiar Christian concepts; but that Melville contrived to endow these passages, and to endow the entire allegorical structure, with a covert and sinister meaning which is essentially anti-Christian. I have also suggested that the symbolism of the making and patching and discarding of the jacket is designed to illuminate Melville's autobiographical experiments with various substitutes for the "uniform" religious dogmas, and to symbolize his eventual slashing off of such a jacket of the mind, in order to stand forth naked as a "natural" man. As we have seen, the centuries-old conflict between the Reformation concept of the God-centered man and the Renaissance concept of the man-centered man had been reflected, variously, in Melville's reading. Bayle, Hobbes, and Rousseau had come at the problem from somewhat different viewpoints. I have already quoted Bayle as saying, "The Fear and Love of God are not the only Spring of Human Actions. . . . A Soldier who has quitted all for his Religion, finding himself under the necessity of offending God if he revenges himself for having receiv'd a Box o' th' Ear, or of being accounted a Coward if he does not, never rests till he has Satisfaction for this Affront, tho' at the peril of killing or being kill'd in a state that must be follow'd with Eternal Damnation." In *Leviathan*, Thomas Hobbes includes the following among his definitions: "The *Right of Nature*, which Writers commonly call *Jus Naturale* is the Liberty each man hath, to use his own power, as he will himself, for the preservation of his own Nature; that is to say, of his own Life; and consequently, of doing anything, which in his own Judgement, and Reason, he shall conceive to be the aptest means thereunto."[14] Rousseau, while quarreling with Hobbes over the kind of "Commonwealth" which should be erected on the foundation of "natural rights," placed great emphasis on these rights as inalienable. Melville, siding more with Rousseau at this time than with anyone else, digresses long enough to propagandize:

"Now, in the language of Blackstone, again, there is a law, 'coeval with mankind, dictated by God Himself, superior in obligation to any other, and no human laws are of any validity if contrary to this.' That law is the Law of Nature; among the three great principles of which Justinian includes 'that to every man should be rendered his due.' But we have seen that the laws involving flogging in the Navy do *not* render to every man his due, since in some cases they indirectly exclude the officers from any punishment whatever, and in all cases protect them from the scourge, which is inflicted upon the sailor. Therefore, according to Blackstone and Justinian, those laws have no binding force; and every American man-of-war's man would be morally justified

113

in resisting the scourge to the uttermost; and, in so resisting, would be religiously justified in what would be judicially styled 'the act of mutiny' itself."[15]

It seems quite possible that Melville may have started directly to attack the brutal and tyrannical evils of flogging in this narrative without being aware of the allegorical correlation it might have with his persistently Calvinistic concept of God as brutal and tyrannical and evil and death-dealing. Disliking so many different aspects of his Calvinistic heritage, he had already made some progress in his attempt to liberate himself from that concept. If he had succeeded, and if he had found that he was able to turn away from that concept entirely, however, he would not have devoted so much of his subsequent literary endeavor to representing various views of the malice and evil in God, that "Author of Sin"; to representing various views of the concept that God and the Devil are essentially one. Referring to the drunkenness of the sailors ashore, White-Jacket asserts, "The prime agent in working his calamities in port is his old arch-enemy, the ever-devilish god of grog."[16] Any theological insinuation there? The separate phases of Melville's religious disillusionment may be viewed as different degrees of Melvillian mutiny. In the allegorical framework of *White-Jacket*, Melville insists that there are times when 'the act of mutiny' is morally and religiously justified. In the allegorical framework of *Moby-Dick*, Captain Ahab is motivated to blasphemous defiance by his indignant notion that he has been "struck" twice by God, and his vengeful quest is also an 'act of mutiny' against God.

There is another closely related image, here, which picks up symbolic value: the image of the "man-of-war" or ship of battle. The full title of the narrative is, *White-Jacket, or, The World in a Man-of-War*. Again, the image is endowed with symbolic values on two levels: the overt level and the covert level. Ease into it:

". . . I began to think a man-of-war a man-of-peace-and-goodwill, after all. But, alas! disappointment came."[17]

The overt antithesis there suggests (in the larger context) that the concepts represented in the organization of a warship are contrary to the concepts represented by the life and teachings of Jesus. This suggestion is ironically elaborated when White-Jacket points out that the chaplain of a frigate received part of the

114

bounty paid for every ship sunk and for every enemy killed. This follows:

"How can it be expected that the religion of peace should flourish in an oaken castle of war? . . . How is it to be expected that a clergyman, thus provided for, should prove efficacious in enlarging upon the criminality of Judas, who, for thirty pieces of silver, betrayed his Master?"

Although there are many other correlative extensions, including that of the man-of-war as an image not only of the world-as-macrocosm but also of man-as-microcosm, the most revealing extension occurs after White-Jacket has discussed the contrasting attitudes of officers and enlisted men towards rumors of war:

"Can the brotherhood of the race of mankind ever hope to prevail in a man-of-war, where one man's bane is almost another's blessing? By abolishing the scourge, shall we do away tyranny; *that* tyranny which must ever prevail, where of two essentially antagonist classes in perpetual contact, one is immeasurably the stronger? Surely it seems all but impossible. And as the very object of a man-of-war, as its name implies, is to fight the very battles so naturally averse to the seamen; so long as a man-of-war exists, it must ever remain a picture of much that is tyrannical and re-pelling in human nature."[18]

That extends the symbolic value of the man-of-war until it may serve as a "picture" of much that is tyrannical; but in the allegorical context the insinuations are elaborately developed. The Christian view of sinful men as children of God the Father, and therefore reflecting the attributes of God, provides a pertinent heretical insinuation; so does the allegorical view of the tyrannical and evil officers as agents of God, reflecting the attributes of God. Furthermore, there is some external evidence as to Melville's early interest in the concept of God's good-evil dualism. In 1846, three years before the publication of *White-Jacket*, one of Melville's relatives gave him a newly printed edition of the New Testament and the Psalms, Authorized version, and in it Melville wrote a note on John 10:36 ("Say ye of him, whom the Father hath sanctified, and sent unto the world, Thou blasphemest; because I said, I am the Son of God?"). Melville's note, written on the end flyleaf, was the following passage, possibly copied with ironic relish from the work of some earnest theologian, because Melville saw two ways of reading it:

"If we can conceive it possible, that the creator of the world himself assumed the form of his creature, and lived in that manner for a time upon earth, this creature must seem to us of infinite perfection, because susceptible of such a combination with his maker. Hence, in our idea of man there can be no inconsistency with our idea of God [!]; and if we often feel a certain disagreement with Him and remoteness from Him, it is but the more on that account our duty, not like advocates of the wicked Spirit, to keep our eyes continually on the nakedness and wickedness of our nature; but rather to seek out every property and beauty, by which our pretension to a similarity with the Divinity may be made good."[19]

The direction of Melville's thinking, during this third phase of his disillusionment, is decidedly away from any sympathy with conventional Christian theological concepts, and directly towards his own version of the rationalistic and humanistic concept concerning man's inalienable rights, in much the same sense that so many French leaders of the Revolution interpreted the teachings of Rousseau. In his allegorical insinuations, throughout *White-Jacket*, Melville established and reiterated the symbolic relationship between the tyrannies of man and of a brutal God. In declaring the injustice of the one, specifically, he declared the injustice of the other, symbolically. With this symbolic connotation in mind, and also with anti-Calvinistic Rousseau in mind, consider the connotations of just one more passage on flogging:

"Irrespective of all incidental considerations, we assert that flogging in the Navy is opposed to the essential dignity of man, which no legislator has a right to violate; that it is oppressive, and glaringly unequal in its operations; that it is utterly repugnant to the spirit of our democratic institutions; indeed, that it involves a lingering trait of the worst times of a barbarous feudal aristocracy; in a word, we denounce it as religiously, morally, and immutably *wrong*."[20]

5

So FAR, I have considered Melville's genius (combined with talent) which seemed to make it impossible for him to tell the fictionalized story of his experiences in the Navy without introducing allegorical insinuations to represent the latest phase of his religious disillusionment. These allegorical values are closely related to one other aspect of *White-Jacket* which should not be ignored: those concepts, allusions, situations, characterizations, in *White-Jacket*, which throw light on Melville's last narrative, *Billy Budd*.

Less than a year before Melville enlisted in the Navy, a notorious scandal occurred aboard the United States brig *Somers*: by orders of Captain Mackenzie, but without trial, a midshipman, a boatswain's mate, and an ordinary seaman were hanged at sea, on mere suspicion that they were plotting mutiny. James Fenimore Cooper's furious denunciation of the scandal was entitled *The Cruise of the Somers: Illustrative of the Despotism of the Quarter-Deck; and of the Unmanly Conduct of Captain Mackenzie.* In making his accusations, Cooper gave evidence to show why the First Lieutenant, Guert Gansevoort (a cousin of Melville) deserved to be blamed for the injustice, along with the Captain. Melville had access to Cooper's pamphlet, soon after returning home from his own cruise aboard the frigate *United States*.

Considering Melville's consistent sympathy with the rights of the enlisted men, and his consistent attacks on the tyrannies of superior officers in general, one can well imagine how he reacted to the *Somers* incident. But one does not need to imagine, because he denounces Mackenzie as a murderer, in *White-Jacket*. In a bitter chapter sarcastically entitled "The Good Ordinances of the Sea," Melville attacked the Articles of War which formed the basis for the penal code of the Navy, and illustrated the injustice which allowed Captain Claret to violate certain laws in his own proper person while punishing enlisted men for violating the same laws. Angrily he comments:

"Who put this great gulf between the American captain and the American sailor? Or is the captain a creature of like passions with ourselves? Or is he an infallible archangel, incapable of the shadow of error? Or has a sailor no mark of humanity, no attribute of manhood, that, bound hand and foot, he is cast into an American frigate shorn of all rights and defences, while the notorious lawlessness of the commander has passed into a proverb, familiar to man-of-war's men, *The law was not made for the captain!* In-

117

deed, he may almost be said to put off the citizen when he touches his quarter-deck; and, almost exempt from the law of the land himself, he comes down upon others with a judicial severity unknown on the national soil. With the Articles of War in one hand, and the cat-o'-nine-tails in the other, he stands an undignified parody upon Mohammed enforcing Moslemism with the sword and the Koran."[21]

Continuing, Melville buttressed his own caustic interpretations by quoting Sir Matthew Hale to the effect that "the Martial Law, being based upon no settled principles, is, in truth and reality, no law, but something indulged rather than allowed as a law." Then, to illustrate the fact that the Articles of War are operative as a naval penal code even in time of peace, Melville refers to the *Somers* incident:

"Some may urge that the severest operations of the code are tacitly made null in time of peace. But though with respect to several of the Articles this holds true, yet at any time any and all of them may be legally enforced. Nor have there been wanting recent instances illustrating the spirit of this code, even in cases where the letter of the code was not altogether observed. The well-known case of a United States brig furnishes a memorable example, which at any moment may be repeated. Three men, in a time of peace, were then hung at the yard-arm, merely because, in the captain's judgment, it became necessary to hang them. To this day the question of their complete guilt is socially discussed.

"How shall we characterise such a deed? Says Blackstone, 'If anyone that hath commission of martial authority doth, in time of peace, hang, or otherwise execute any man by colour of martial law, this is murder. . . .' "[22]

And in concluding the chapter, Melville suggests the allegorical framework by introducing theological or rationalistic terms (italics added):

"Nor, as has been elsewhere hinted, is the general *ignorance* or *depravity* of any race of men to be alleged as an apology for *tyranny* over them. On the contrary, it cannot admit of a *reasonable doubt*, in any *unbiased mind* conversant with the interior life of a man-of-war, that most of the sailor *iniquities* practised therein are indirectly to be ascribed to the morally debasing effects of

118

the *unjust, despotic*, and *degrading laws* under which the man-of-war's man lives."[23]

In the allegorical framework of *White-Jacket*, the insinuations of that last paragraph are closely related to similar insinuations in *Billy Budd*. Here, Melville would seem to be talking about naval abuses; but his terminology would be more familiar in theological discussions as to the problem of evil and of the entrance of evil into the world. According to the Calvinistic concept, Adam brought his own punishment on himself, and the race thereafter inherited "depravity" as "innate" in the human condition. Melville says that "the general ignorance or depravity of any race of men" should *not* be "alleged as an apology for tyranny over them."

It will be remembered that Melville dedicated *Billy Budd* to Jack Chase, a character in *White-Jacket*. One difference between Billy and Jack Chase is particularly pertinent. Unlike Billy, Jack "was a stickler for the Rights of Man and the liberties of the world." In *White-Jacket*, reference is also made to that kind of British impressment which was operative in the days of Billy. Did Melville find impressment justified? Consider:

". . . when British press-gangs not only boarded foreign ships on the high seas, and boarded foreign pier-heads, but boarded their own merchantmen at the mouth of the Thames, and boarded the very firesides along its banks; when Englishmen were knocked down and dragged into the Navy, like cattle into the slaughter-house, with every mortal provocation to a mad desperation against the service that thus ran their unwilling heads into the muzzles of the enemy's cannon."[24]

In *White-Jacket*, Melville mentions the Spithead and Nore mutinies in the British Fleet, and traces the cause of these mutinies to flogging and impressment. Much depends, he says, on the relative competence or incompetence of the officers in charge. Lord Nelson and Lord Collingwood are cited as officers who strongly disapproved of flogging, and could govern crews without the use of force, because they could exert the sway of "a powerful brain, and a determined, intrepid spirit over a miscellaneous rabble." By contrast, he attacks the "imbecility" of officers who have to resort to violence to maintain discipline:

"It cannot have escaped the discernment of any observer of mankind, that, in the presence of its conventional inferiors, conscious imbecility in power often seeks to carry off that imbecility by assumptions of lordly severity. The amount of flogging on board an American man-of-war is, in many cases, in exact proportion to the professional and intellectual incapacity of her officers to command. Thus, in these cases, the law that authorises flogging does but put a scourge into the hand of a fool."[25]

In the calamitous instance involving Billy Budd, exactly this is shown; but shown very subtly by Melville, who employs one of his favorite rhetorical devices throughout *Billy Budd*: he there creates a narrator who is so stupid (from Melville's viewpoint) as to praise Captain Vere for actions and attributes which are palpably unpraiseworthy; in his actions, Captain Vere reveals himself to be, quite unbeknownst to himself, a fool and a coward.

One of Captain Vere's imbecilities is that he delegates power to a "depraved" Master-at-arms, Claggart, whose fictional prototype may be found in White-Jacket's characterization of the Master-at-arms, Bland, aboard the *Neversink*. There was something devilish about both of them:

"... this Bland, the master-at-arms, was no vulgar, dirty knave. In him—to modify Burke's phrase—vice *seemed*, but only seemed, to lose half its seeming evil by losing all its apparent grossness. ... Nothing but his mouth, that was somewhat small, Moorish-arched, and wickedly delicate, and his snaky, black eye, that at times shone like a dark lantern in a jeweller-shop at midnight, betokened the accomplished scoundrel within. ...

"Still, at first, the men gave him a wide berth, and returned scowls for his smiles; but who can forever resist the very Devil himself, when he comes in the guise of a gentleman, free, fine and frank? Though Goethe's pious Margaret hates the Devil in his horns and harpooneer's tail, yet she smiles and nods to the engaging fiend in the persuasive, winning, oily, wholly harmless Mephistopheles."[26]

Indeed, there is something of Milton's Satan about Bland, and Melville, with sympathy for the romantic interpretation of Milton's Satan as a tragic hero, permits White-Jacket to recall Redburn's comment on Jackson when White-Jacket observes:

"I could not but abominate him when I thought of his conduct; but I pitied the continual gnawing which, under all his deftly donned disguises, I saw lying at the bottom of his soul. I admired his heroism in sustaining himself so well under such reverses. And when I thought how arbitrary the Articles of War are in defining a man-of-war villain; how much undetected guilt might be sheltered by the aristocratic awning of our quarter-deck; how many florid pursers, ornaments of the ward-room, had been legally protected in defrauding *the people*, I could not but say to myself, well, after all, though this man is a most wicked one indeed, yet is he even more luckless than depraved.

"Besides, a studied observation of Bland convinced me that he was an organic and irreclaimable scoundrel, who did wicked deeds as the cattle browse the herbage, because wicked deeds seemed the legitimate operation of his whole infernal organisation. Phrenologically, he was without soul. Is it to be wondered at, that the devils are irreligious? What, then, thought I, who is to blame in this matter? For one, I will not take the Day of Judgment upon me by authoritatively pronouncing upon the essential criminality of any man-of-war's man; and Christianity has taught me that, at the Last Day, man-of-war's men will not be judged by the Articles of War, nor by the *United States Statutes at Large*, but by immutable laws, ineffably beyond the comprehension of the Honourable Board of Commodores and Navy Commissioners."[27]

Frequently, when Melville asserted his own viewpoint a bit too strongly in an editorial comment, he also abruptly retreated (like Bayle) into an orthodox cliché, with a covertly ironic effect: ". . . and Christianity has taught me that, at the Last Day . . ." everything is going to be all right; then all evil will be made good, all wrongs righted. How Melville loathed that concept of justice!

In *Billy Budd*, when the Bland-like Claggart is permitted (through the imbecility of Captain Vere) to get Billy Budd into the trouble for which Billy is eventually hanged, the weakness of Vere's character is brought out merely by permitting Vere to talk and act. Fearing that his own face or life may be in danger, Vere asserts himself as an agent of the Admiralty, endowed with powers of life and death. The letter of the law justifies his actions. In *White-Jacket*, Melville repeatedly denounces the injustice of putting into the hands of a captain more powers than he is competent to exercise, and he quotes the Thirty-second Article of War as the cause of this particular injustice. Because the entire passage

121

is applicable to Captain Vere, Melville's comment on that Article is here quoted in full from *White-Jacket*:

"If there are any three things opposed to the genius of the American Constitution, they are these: irresponsibility in a judge, unlimited discretionary authority in an executive, and the union of an irresponsible judge and an unlimited executive in one person. . . .

"This is the article that, above all others, puts the scourge into the hands of the captain, calls him to no account for its exercise, and furnishes him with an ample warrant for inflictions of cruelty upon the common sailor hardly credible to landsmen.

"By this article the captain is made a legislator, as well as a judge and an executive. So far as it goes, it absolutely leaves to his descretion to decide what things shall be considered crimes, and what shall be the penalty; whether an accused person has been guilty of actions by him declared to be crimes; and how, when, and where the penalty shall be inflicted."[28]

All of these passages in *White-Jacket* are steppingstones to an understanding not only of *Billy Budd* but also of *Moby-Dick*, *Pierre*, and *The Confidence-Man*.

6

IN concluding and summarizing these progressive phases of Melville's early disillusionment, reflected in *Typee, Mardi, Redburn, White-Jacket*, I must stress the already mentioned danger of oversimplification. The fluctuations, contradictions, complexities of Melville's spiritual progress downward toward bitterness and pessimism are not easily represented in any kind of description or analysis. Furthermore, there is no possibility of even suggesting all the factors which enter into the protracted inner conflicts of that early period.

Nevertheless, there is need for modifying and correcting the frequently phrased notion that Melville's spiritual development brought him eventually to a mature and profound ability to comprehend and contemplate the extreme depths of human hope and doubt from a balanced and detached viewpoint. Many interpreters of Melville have contrasted him with Ralph Waldo Emerson, and have tried to elevate his stature as a thinker over that of Emerson by insisting that Melville did not make the mistake of dismissing the concept of evil as relatively unimportant; that Melville heroically came to grips with the problem of evil and that his wrestlings produced some of the most profound utterances on the subject in the history of American thought. But there is a vast difference between being profoundly disturbed and being profoundly perceptive. While I do not wish to belittle Melville's artistic greatness, I do suggest that we have a tendency to overestimate Melville's greatness as a thinker.

"The Child is Father of the Man; and I could wish . . ." said Wordsworth, helpfully. Childlike wishing is frequently the father of manly thinking, even of systematic thinking, and the end-result of systematic thinking may often be recognized as an attempt to prove (to the satisfaction of the prover, at least) the validity of the initial wish. But Melville was not a systematic philosopher. He started off with a wish for things remote, and that wish may be viewed as an innocent convention, in childhood. At the same time, in his home, he was being taught to memorize certain dogmas concerning the attributes of a remote God, and these attributes were formulated by John Calvin, largely out of the Old Testament. The very remoteness of God was enough to fascinate Melville; the mysteriousness of God increased that fascination. Told to love God, the child Melville complied and fell into the habit of such love before he became old enough to appreciate that the attributes which Calvin had formulated for that God did not make that God altogether lovable.

A new phase of Melville's spiritual experience began when his maturing itch for things remote made him wish that he and God could talk with each other, face to face, and made him also wish (with even more wistfulness) that God were more lovable than he seemed to be. Although it is one function of faith to arrange these matters, Melville's religious and non-religious experience got in his way. Quite without reference to God, he suffered from certain disappointing experiences. Only one detail of those experiences is important, here: "death" became an obsession in Melville's later thought, and there is good reason for remembering that the entire direction of Melville's physical life was changed by the death of his father when the child was about twelve years old. This blocked off the possible fulfillment of some proud wishes

123

and forced on Melville some kind of reorientation. The consequent chaos or near-chaos of family matters, immediately after the death of Melville's father, was largely responsible for the fact that Melville's formal education ceased before he had finished secondary school; that he was forced to start working at an early age; that he indulged his wish for things remote by going to sea to earn his living. Nothing turned out quite the way he could have wished, during those early years, and as the disappointments mounted Melville came increasingly to brood over the possibility that the entire organization of the world was wrong.

Who was to blame? His father, for dying? His mother, for being the proud woman she was? His relatives, for being whatever they were? His wishes, for being whatever they were? Society, for being what it was? God, for being what He was? There are indications that Melville kept circling over the possibilities, in his search for a suitable scapegoat. Wishing to find someone to blame, he finally blamed God for being what God was.

Just what God was, to Melville, we have some way of knowing. Prior to his disillusionment, he had been taught to view God as a Heavenly Father who demanded love of His earthly children, even during the times when He was punishing those earthly children for offenses, plain or obscure. But when Melville's disappointments led him to view the world as somehow wrongly organized, and then to blame God as the Source from whom both good and evil flowed, Melville seems to have become fascinated by the paradox. This was his fundamental approach to the problem of evil, throughout his life. Whether or not such an approach proved to be either spiritually or mentally profound or rewarding, each reader of Melville may decide for himself. My own bias, my own prejudices, are so strong that I cannot resist the feeling that in Melville's case the child was indeed the father of the man.

DARK CONFESSIONS

CHAPTER VI

He may perish; but so long as he exists, he insists upon treating with all Powers upon an equal basis. If any of those other Powers choose to withhold certain secrets, let them; that does not impair my sovereignty in myself; that does not make me tributary. And perhaps, after all, there is no secret.

MELVILLE TO HAWTHORNE

. . . Sometimes I think there's naught beyond. But 'tis enough. He tasks me; he heaps me; I see in him outrageous strength, with an inscrutable malice sinewing it. That inscrutable thing is chiefly what I hate; and be the White Whale agent, or be the White Whale principal, I will wreak that hate upon him. Talk not to me of blasphemy, man; I'd strike the sun if it insulted me. For could the sun do that, then could I do the other; since there is ever a sort of fair play herein, jealously presiding over all creations. But not my master, man, is even that fair play. Who's over me? Truth hath no confines.

CAPTAIN AHAB TO STARBUCK, IN Moby-Dick

DARK CONFESSIONS

WHILE reading *Mosses from an Old Manse,* during the summer of 1850, Melville made the mistake of deciding that he and Hawthorne must be kindred souls. A few weeks later, after he and Hawthorne had met, he made the further mistake of trusting that Hawthorne would listen sympathetically to his heretical views concerning the universal mysteries. Wrong twice, Melville kept the doomed friendship alive long enough to let himself make some extraordinarily revealing and dark confessions. For example, in one of his letters to Hawthorne, written while *Moby-Dick* was a work in progress, he indirectly summarized his recently formulated belief that whatever salvation man might achieve, in this life, could come only after man had declared his independence from God; only after man had asserted his own sovereignty by fighting for such independence. Although that letter playfully begins as a somewhat formally postured discourse on *The House of the Seven Gables,* it quickly digresses into subjective confession:

". . . There is a certain tragic phase of humanity which, in our opinion, was never more powerfully embodied than by Hawthorne. We mean the tragedies of human thought in its unbiased, native, and profounder workings. We think that into no recorded mind has the intense feeling of the visible truth ever entered more deeply than into this man's. By visible truth, we mean the appre-

hension of the absolute condition of present things as they strike
the eye of the man who fears them not, though they do their worst
to him,—the man who, like Russia or the British Empire, declares
himself a sovereign nature (in himself) amid the powers of
heaven, hell, and earth. He may perish; but so long as he exists
he insists upon treating with all Powers upon an equal basis. If
any of those other Powers choose to withhold certain secrets, let
them; that does not impair my sovereignty in myself; that does
not make me tributary. And perhaps, after all, there is *no* secret.
We incline to think that the Problem of the Universe is like the
Freemason's mighty secret, so terrible to all children. It turns out,
at last, to consist in a triangle, a mallet, and an apron,—nothing
more! We incline to think that God cannot explain His own
secrets, and that He would like a little information upon certain
points Himself. We mortals astonish Him as much as He us. But
it is this *Being* of the matter; there lies the knot with which we
choke ourselves. As soon as you say *Me*, a *God*, a *Nature*, so soon
you jump off from your stool and hang from the beam. Yes, that
word [God] is the hangman. Take God out of the dictionary, and
you would have Him in the street.

"There is the grand truth about Nathaniel Hawthorne. He says
No! in thunder; but the Devil himself cannot make him say *yes*.
For all men who say *yes*, lie; and all men who say *no*,—why, they
are in the happy condition of judicious, unincumbered travellers
in Europe; they cross the frontiers into Eternity with nothing but
a carpet-bag,—that is to say, the Ego. Whereas those *yes*-gentry,
they travel with heaps of baggage, and, damn them! they will
never get through the Custom House. What's the reason, Mr.
Hawthorne, that in the last stages of metaphysics a fellow always
falls to *swearing* so? I could rip an hour. You see, I began with
a little criticism extracted for your benefit from the 'Pittsfield
Secret Review,' and here I have landed in Africa."[1]

That strange letter gives us a revealing glimpse of Melville's
brooding over what seems to him a tragic phase of humanity, and
over what seems to him the need for a certain tragic response. If
one looks closely, one may notice two somewhat contradictory
kinds of response: first, a defiant response which rests on the
assumption that the "Powers" against which man pits himself, in
the universe, are in some sense personifications. These "Powers"

(of heaven, hell, earth) would certainly include God. But the second response is a skeptical and even agnostic response, which takes comfort in doubting whether "God" exists, except as a name which credulous man has permitted to encroach on the divinity of man. As we shall see, Melville's disillusionment conditioned him to think in terms of two-ness, and this frequently made it possible for him to view as illusion that which he had only recently substituted for a previous illusion.

Enlightening as that letter is, it only hints ("He may perish; but so long as he exists . . .") at the crux of Melville's tragic view: his conviction that death was the ultimate indignity. At times he could view that phenomenon as natural; but he was enough of a transcendentalist to equate "Nature" with "God" and to blame God for this indignity. Baffled by the riddle as to how the Prime Mover could create man with a yearning for eternal life and, simultaneously, with a certainty as to the brevity of life, Melville had already become fascinated by the notion that God must be malicious. If so, then why should mankind follow the Christian tradition of bowing down before Malice? Why should mankind accept and obey the sovereignty of such a Tyrant?

As soon as we place these notions in a historical context, it becomes obvious that Melville could not possibly have supposed them to be unique products of his own thinking. Although the pose is Byronic, it also suggests many other figures in the history of heretical thought, particularly some of the figures described at length in Pierre Bayle's *Dictionary*. But Melville's use of the yes-no antithesis suggests another gloss for that letter. We know that he had recently been reading (probably rereading) Carlyle's *Sartor Resartus*, and there is considerable evidence that he now took violent exception to Carlyle's total meaning there. As already suggested, figurative crotchets of *Sartor Resartus* resolve into this essentially Christian thesis: each individual begins his spiritual progress by inheriting certain ill-fitting and secondhand religious garments of belief, which will be discarded as a result of growth; but the consequent sense of nakedness will drive the individual into only a temporary surrender to sentimentalized self-pity and disillusioned negation ("The Everlasting No"); gradually the individual will pass through disinterestedness ("The Centre of Indifference") to a renunciation and a figurative annihilation of

129

both Self and the World, and as a result the pilgrim soul will be able to advance to a higher perception of the ineffable joy derived from submissive affirmation of faith and trust in the inscrutable but benevolent ways of God to men ("The Everlasting Yea"). As we have seen, Melville's Taji acted out the essentials of this progression in the allegorical action of *Mardi*, which Melville subsequently belittled when he contrived to let White-Jacket act out a symbolic negation. Carlyle's own words afford a convenient summary of Carlyle's affirmative and essentially Calvinistic ideal:

". . . there is in man a HIGHER than Love of Happiness: he can do without Happiness, and instead thereof find Blessedness! Was it not to preach forth this same HIGHER that sages and martyrs, the Poet and the Priest, in all times, have spoken and suffered; bearing testimony, through life and through death, of the Godlike that is in Man, and how in the Godlike alone has he Strength and Freedom? Which God-inspired Doctrine art thou also honored to be taught; O Heavens! and broken with manifold merciful Afflictions, even till thou become contrite and learn it! Oh, thank thy Destiny for these; thankfully bear what yet remain; thou hadst need of them; the Self in thee needed to be annihilated. By benignant fever-paroxysms is Life rooting out the deep-seated chronic Disease, *and triumphs over Death* [italics added]. On the roaring billows of Time thou art not engulfed, but borne aloft into the azure of Eternity. Love not Pleasure; love God. This is the EVERLASTING YEA, wherein all contradiction is solved; wherein whoso walks and works, it is well with him."[2]

Carlyle's viewpoint, there, perfectly illustrates my previous suggestion that the riddle-answer of the Reformation and the riddle-answer of the Renaissance could be arranged in various combinations and permutations. Here is Carlyle's attempt to reconcile the opposed views, in a conceptual form closely related to that which Milton had previously illuminated in *Paradise Lost*. Both Milton and Carlyle would seem to glorify "the Godlike that is in Man" even as the Renaissance humanists did; but both Milton and Carlyle deliberately subvert the humanistic concept to the Calvinistic concept, through forms of reasoning which the Renaissance humanists would have been inclined to criticize as palpable casuistry.

Carlyle aimed his remarks directly at the self-pitying "Devil

School" of literature which had included Byron, as the following passage from *Sartor Resartus* indicates:

"To my own surmise, it appears as if this Dandiacal Sect were but a new modification, adapted to the new time, of the primeval Superstition, *Self-worship* . . . which only in the purer forms of Religion has been altogether rejected. Wherefore, if any one choose to name it revived Ahrimanism [Zoroastrianism], or a new figure of Demon-Worship, I have, so far as is yet visible, no objection. . . . Close thy Byron; open thy Goethe."[3]

Reacting violently against Carlyle, Melville replied in effect, "Close thy mouth, Mister Carlyle, along with thy Goethe, while I continue to read the true gospel according to Lord Byron." In his letter to Hawthorne, Melville would seem to suggest that Carlyle and his like had accidentally become victims of their own clothes philosophy. These yea-saying pilgrims or travelers, he implies, are victimized because they permit themselves to be encumbered (of course, unintentionally) by such secondhand religious and philosophical garments of the mind as they have been able to rent from Calvinistic Geneva, Goethean Germany, Platonic Greece. Consequently, all these costumes require "heaps of baggage, and damn them! they will never get through the Custom House." Melville further contradicts ideas implicit in Carlyle's argument, by boasting that the bolder and braver no-sayers take with them exactly what is most important for this life or for whatever after-life there may be: their own precious Ego. Such a remark would have appeared devilishly scandalous to the preacher-trained Carlyle, whose Scotch-Presbyterian background had helped him endow with particular holiness the single word, "renunciation."

To Carlyle's insistence that we should love God, Melville answered in effect that man was inclined to dislike God. In another letter to Hawthorne, as we have already seen, he had expressed himself clearly on this point: "The reason the mass of men fear God, and *at bottom dislike* Him, is because they rather distrust His heart, and fancy Him all brain like a watch."[4] So speaks the independent Yankee, after having asserted his freedom from bondage to God; his inalienable right to meet God on even terms.

His covert references to Carlyle, in his long letter to Hawthorne, may serve as a reminder that in *Moby-Dick* there are several different passages in which Melville satirically paraphrases *Sartor*

Resartus without making any overt reference to it. Because similar paraphrases also occur in *Pierre* and *The Confidence-Man*, we shall have considerable occasion to notice that Melville chose to glorify exactly what Carlyle chose to ridicule. For satirical purposes, then, Melville was frequently able to place some of Carlyle's own concepts and words and phrases in an antithetical context, with the result that Carlyle's original meanings became subverted or inverted or converted to Melville's own uses. One might describe the stylistic game as a form of capturing. To illustrate the ease with which Melville could do this, remember that when Teufelsdrockh describes his three phases of spiritual growth, his description of the "Everlasting No" represents for Carlyle the Devil School attitude as the lowest rung on the ladder of ascent. To Melville, on the other hand, the disillusionment characterized by the "Everlasting No" represented the highest rung of human perception, from which one might discover the "usable truth." Consider, then, how Teufelsdrockh, actually speaking Melville's Devil School language, quite accurately summarizes Melville's view, in such a passage as the following, from *Sartor Resartus*:

". . . it seemed as if all things in the Heavens above and the Earth beneath would hurt me; as if the Heavens and the Earth were but boundless jaws of a devouring monster, wherein I, palpitating, waiting to be devoured . . . when, all at once, there rose a Thought in me, and I asked myself: 'What *art* thou afraid of? Wherefore, like a coward, dost thou forever pip and whimper, and go cowering and trembling? Despicable biped! What is the sum-total of the worst that lies before thee? Death? Well, Death; and say the pangs of Tophet too, and all that the Devil and Man may, will or can do against thee! Hast thou not a heart; canst thou not suffer whatsoever it be; and, as a Child of Freedom, though outcast, trample Tophet itself under thy feet, while it consumes thee? Let it come, then; I will meet it and defy it!' And as I so thought, there rushed [something] like a stream of fire over my whole soul; and I shook base Fear away from me forever. I was strong, of unknown strength; a spirit, almost a god. Ever from that time, the temper of my misery was changed: not Fear or whining Sorrow was it, but Indignation and grim fire-eyed Defiance. Thus had the EVERLASTING NO pealed authoritatively through all the recesses of my Being. . . ."[5]

132

This, said Carlyle, represents the invalid Neophyte phase of growth; this, said Melville, represents the valid Ophite viewpoint. Well aware of the difference between these two attitudes, Melville seized every opportunity to answer Carlyle. Particularly, he took wicked pleasure in sneering at the Carlyle-Goethe notion (essentially Calvinistic) that all created things were emblems of God's power; that Nature should be viewed as "the living visible Garment of God" which could guide man to an appreciation of God's infinite benevolence. Having passed through this phase of belief, Melville asserted his inverted transcendentalism by suggesting, cynically, that his worthy opponents might do well to fix their gaze on that aspect of Nature represented by the ruthless jungle-law of the sea, which he knew so well. According to the arguments of his enemies, this aspect of Nature would seem to suggest the infinitely ruthless malice of God. Much that Carlyle said in his symbolic language concerning a "Philosophy of Clothing" may have stimulated Melville to work out a counterattack, by fashioning an equally symbolic and antithetical "Philosophy of Whaling" in *Moby-Dick*. For later recollection, here are a few of Carlyle's remarks on symbols, in *Sartor Resartus*:

"In a Symbol there is concealment and yet revelation; here therefore, by Silence, and by Speech acting together, comes a double significance. . . . In the Symbol proper, what we can call a Symbol, there is ever, more or less distinctly and directly, some embodiment and revelation of the Infinite; the Infinite is made to blend itself with the Finite, to stand visible, and as it were, attainable there. . . . the Universe is but one vast Symbol of God. . . . It is in and through Symbols that man, consciously or unconsciously, lives, works, and has his being: those ages, moreover, are accounted the noblest which can the best recognize symbolical worth, and prize it the highest. For is not a Symbol ever, to him who has eyes for it, some dimmer or clearer revelation of the Godlike? . . . But, on the whole, as Time adds much to the sacredness of Symbols, so likewise in his progress he at length defaces, or even desecrates them; and Symbols, like the terrestrial Garments wax old. . . . We account him Legislator and wise who can so much as tell when a Symbol has grown old, and gently remove it. . . . Alas, move withersoever you may, are not the tatters and rags of superannuated worn-out Symbols (in this Ragfair of a World)

133

dropping off everywhere, to hoodwink, to halter, to tether you; nay, if you shake them not aside, threatening to accumulate, and perhaps produce suffocation?"[6]

Look out, Mister Carlyle! Here comes your enemy, in the protean form of Herman Melville, armed with a symbolic harpoon. Sardonically, this particular enemy views the monstrous sperm whale as a Job's whale, created by God, and even described by God as a monstrous symbol of God!

2

A FEW months before Melville wrote his long letter to Hawthorne, declaring his independence from God, he had written a review-essay on Hawthorne's *Mosses From an Old Manse*, published in August 1850. He began that review by acknowledging "the parity of ideas" between "a man like Hawthorne and a man like me," and went on to indicate his delight in Hawthorne's stylistic employment of symbolism and allegory; to confess his conviction that Hawthorne employed these stylistic devices to hoodwink the conventional reader; to speculate as to that tragic viewpoint which drove men like Hawthorne and Shakespeare (and himself) into subterfuges. Some excerpts from this review are extremely self-revealing:

"Where Hawthorne is known, he seems to be deemed a pleasant writer, with a pleasant style,—a sequestered, harmless man, from whom any deep and weighty thing would hardly be anticipated— a man who means no meanings. But . . . no such man can exist without also possessing, as the indispensable complement of these, a great, deep intellect, which drops down into the universe like a plummet. . . . Nathaniel Hawthorne is a man as yet almost utterly mistaken among men. . . . Here, be it said . . . that they [the readers] must on no account suffer themselves to be trifled with, disappointed, or deceived by the triviality of many of the titles to these sketches. For in more than one instance, the title utterly belies the piece. . . . The truth seems to be, that like many other geniuses, this Man of Mosses takes great delight in hoodwinking the world,—at least, with respect to himself. Personally, I doubt not that he rather prefers to be generally esteemed but a so-so sort of author; being willing to reserve the thorough and acute appreciation of what he is, to that party most qualified to judge—that is, to himself. . . . But with whatever motive, playful or profound, Nathaniel Hawthorne has chosen to entitle his pieces in the manner he has, it is certain that some of them are directly calculated to deceive—egregiously deceive, the superficial skimmer of pages. To be downright and candid once more, let me cheerfully say, that two of these titles did dolefully dupe no less an eagle-eyed reader than myself. . . ."

Melville tells us more about himself in that passage, I think, than about Hawthorne. Continuing, he increases our understanding of himself, as he cautiously hints that Hawthorne has a sinister purpose in fictionally representing Calvinistic concepts of Original Sin and Innate Depravity:

". . . For spite of all the Indian-summer sunlight on the hither side of Hawthorne's soul, the other side—like the dark half of the physical sphere—is shrouded in a blackness, ten times black. But this darkness but gives more effect to the ever-moving dawn, that forever advances through it, and circumnavigates his world. Whether Hawthorne has simply availed himself of that mystical blackness as a means to the wondrous effects he makes it to produce in his lights and shades; or whether there really lurks in him, perhaps unknown to himself, a touch of Puritanic gloom,— this, I cannot altogether tell. Certain it is, however, that this great power of blackness in him derives its force from its appeals to that Calvinistic sense of Innate Depravity and Original Sin, from whose visitations, *in some shape or other* [italics added], no deeply thinking mind is always and wholly free. For, in certain moods, no man can weigh this world without throwing in something, somehow like Original Sin, to strike the uneven balance. At all events, perhaps no writer has ever wielded this terrific thought with greater terror than this same harmless Hawthorne. Still more: this black conceit pervades him through and through. You may be witched by his sunlight,—transported by the bright gildings in the skies he builds over you; but there is the *blackness of darkness* [italics added] beyond; and even his bright gildings but fringe and play upon the edges of thunderclouds."

Speaking from the viewpoint of an enlightened and "deeply thinking mind," Melville here prides himself on being able to recognize Hawthorne's unconventionality of thought. But he is

135

cautious enough to do a little stylistic tightrope walking of equivocal statement. He has already arrived at the conclusion that the
only enlightening way to strike the uneven balance between God
and man is to blame God for being that Original Sinner who
brought death into the world and all our woe. When he uses the
term, "blackness of darkness," he is using as a term of praise
exactly the term which Jude used in the Bible to condemn the
devilishness of heresiarchs:

"For there are certain men crept in unawares, who were before
of old ordained to this condemnation; ungodly men, turning the
grace of our God into lasciviousness, and denying the only Lord
God, and our Lord Jesus Christ. I will therefore put you in
remembrance, though ye once knew this, how that the Lord, having saved the people out of the land of Egypt, afterward destroyed
them that believed not. And the angels which kept not their first
estate, but left their own habitation, he hath reserved in everlasting chains, under darkness, unto the judgment of the great day.
. . . But these speak evil of those things which they know not;
but what they know *naturally* [italics added], as brute beasts, in
those things they corrupt themselves. Woe unto them! for they
have gone in the way of Cain . . . to whom is reserved the blackness of darkness for ever."[7]

The Calvinists repeatedly threw this same charge against the
Renaissance humanists and their successors; but Melville's inverted Calvinism enables him to honor Hawthorne by drafting
Hawthorne into the Devil School of literature. More than that, he
proceeds to draft Shakespeare into the Devil School, in the same
review:

". . . this blackness it is that furnishes the infinite obscure of his
back-ground—that back-ground, against which Shakespeare plays
his grandest conceits, the things that have made Shakespeare his
loftiest but most circumscribed renown, as *the profoundest of
thinkers* [italics added]. . . . But it is those far-away things in him;
those short, quick probings at the very axis of reality;—these are
the things that make Shakespeare, Shakespeare. Through the
mouths of the dark characters of Hamlet, Timon, Lear, and Iago,
he craftily says, or sometimes insinuates the things which we feel
to be so terrifically true, that it were all but madness for any good
man, in his own proper character, to utter, or even hint of them.

Tormented into desperation, Lear, the frantic king, tears off the mask, and speaks the sane madness of vital truth. . . ."[8]

Never mind whether Melville may have been wrong or right in his way of reading Shakespeare; our immediate interest is in Melville's remarks because of the light they throw on the workings of his own mind. His point is that both Hawthorne and Shakespeare show in their writings that they have also revolted against the orthodox Christian view; that each of them felt driven to utter their dark truths through crafty insinuations. Melville insists that Shakespeare concealed his "terrific" and "unspeakable" perceptions by contriving to have the action of *King Lear* drive the major character into "madness," so that Shakespeare could then place in that character's mouth exactly that "vital truth" which Shakespeare would not have dared utter as his own personal belief, because he would have known that the orthodox audience would censure him. One may easily appreciate, from Melville's remark, the general nature of his response to the lines and actions of *King Lear*. We happen to know for a certainty that Melville was particularly delighted to find the Fool saying, "Truth's a dog must to kennel; he must be whipped out, while Lady the brach may stand by the fire and stink."[9]

3

"TRUTH" and "MADNESS" are two words which Melville uses somewhat unconventionally in the *Mosses* review. He asks the "thinking" reader, the "rationalist," to notice that the significance of those two words depends entirely on the viewpoint of the user, because one man's truth is another man's madness, so to speak. Throughout *Moby-Dick*, as we shall see, he takes "unspeakable" pleasure in the ironic equivocations provided by his insinuative use of those two words. Just before he began writing *Moby-Dick*, he made a note on "madness" on the endpaper of his own volume containing the tragedies, *Hamlet, Othello, King Lear*; a note which suggests that he now acknowledged his allegiance to the Devil School of literature:

"Ego non baptizo te in nomine Patris et Filii et Spiritus Sancti— sed in nomine Diaboli.

"Madness is undefinable—It & right reason [are] extremes of one.

"Not the (Black Art) Goetic but Theurgic magic—seeks converse with the Intelligence, Power, and Angel."[10]

Because Melville made three different uses of that inverted phrase of Christian baptism, we are able to work out a significant triangulation. Shortly before *Moby-Dick* was published, Melville wrote to Hawthorne, "Shall I send you a fin of the *Whale* by way of a specimen mouthful? The tail is not yet cooked, though the hell-fire in which the whole book is broiled might not unreasonably have cooked it ere this. This is the book's motto (the secret one), *Ego non baptizo te in nomine*—but finish the rest for yourself."[11] The currently accepted interpretation of *Moby-Dick* would indicate that the book's motto has indeed remained a secret, even though Captain Ahab quotes it much more fully, when he baptizes in pagan blood the new harpoon point he has fashioned to thrust at that visible garment of God, the white "Job's whale." In that scene, Christian Starbuck considers Captain Ahab's action to be "mad." In his note, however, Melville would seem to be baptizing himself, figuratively, in the name of the Devil, so that he might take issue with the Christian insistence that there is only one approach to, or converse with, Absolute Intelligence: "right reason." The orthodox attitude is represented in the last line of his memorandum: the orthodox insist that the Devil's approach is the horrible approach of black magic; that this is actually no approach at all. But it happens to be akin to the approach which Captain Ahab makes, and Melville glorifies Ahab for making that approach. Ishmael summarizes the antithetical opposition of attitudes, conveniently: "Here, then, was this grey-headed, ungodly old man, chasing with curses a Job's whale round the world, at the head of a crew . . . morally enfeebled also, by the incompetence of mere unaided virtue or right-mindedness in Starbuck. . . ."[12]

According to Christian doctrine, right-mindedness or "right reason" is that God-given faculty which enables man to place himself in accord with the ways of God. Any human failure to exercise and establish that accord is viewed as a sin against God, and consequently a form of madness. Milton illuminates the term, from many different angles, in *Paradise Lost*. In challenging that orthodox concept, Melville points out that madness cannot be

138

defined merely in terms of its opposite, right reason; that these two terms might be considered as complementary; that only those blinded by dogma would assume that "right reason" provides the correct approach to God. Satan's approach, in *Paradise Lost,* was one for which Melville now had more sympathy:

> . . . yet all his good prov'd ill in me,
> And wrought but malice; . . .
> Be then his Love accurst, since love or hate
> To me alike, it deals eternal woe.[13]

Again Ishmael is helpful to us in extending the significance of this triangulation, which involves the words "madness" and "truth." "There is a wisdom that is woe; but there is a woe that is madness," says Ishmael in the "Try-Works" chapter. All three of those nouns may be used in different contexts to represent different values. Captain Ahab acts out the correlated meanings which interest Melville most: he progresses from the extreme attitude of "right reason" to the extreme attitude of "madness," as he seeks converse with the "Intelligence" behind the visible garment of God. In his earlier days, we learn, Captain Ahab had been a devout worshiper of God, and had sought converse after the manner of Persian ritual: he had worshiped God's pure manifestation, in the pure fire of lightning. These same Persians had preserved the Zoroastrian or Manichean concept (ridiculed by Carlyle) of God's good-evil duality. What could more strikingly bring home to Captain Ahab an awareness of that dualism than the way in which he thought God chose to "converse" with him, during a moment of ritualistic worship? God spoke to Captain Ahab, not in any still small voice, but in a voice of thunder, while knocking Ahab flat with a bolt of lightning—even as Pierre Bayle said that the founder of the Manicheans had met his death.

But Captain Ahab recovered, and God spake yet again to him. In that second "converse," the "agent" or the "principal" of God was that white Job's whale, who further foreshadowed the ultimate indignity, death, by "reaping" one of Ahab's legs with a "sickle-shaped" jaw. That ended Ahab's interest in the doctrine of "right reason"! Under the circumstances, Melville insinuates, who could blame poor Captain Ahab? And now that Ahab has some "usable truth" to help him, he declares his independence from

God, and asserts his "sovereign nature (in himself) amid the powers of heaven, hell, and earth." Of course Ahab perishes: "He may perish; but so long as he exists, he insists upon treating with all Powers upon an equal basis." As Melville had implied, in his long letter to Hawthorne, the yes-sayers may call that Satanic "madness"; but it is the only genuinely heroic attitude man can take, no matter how tragic the outcome.

4

THAT slippery word, "Truth," had tantalized and tormented Melville since the beginning of his literary career. While still puzzling over the problem, he wrote another letter to Hawthorne, and managed to walk far enough around "Truth" to view it afresh:

". . . But Truth is the silliest thing under the sun. Try to get a living by the Truth—and go to the Soup Societies. Heavens! Let any clergyman [note: Father Mapple, for example?] try to preach the Truth from its very stronghold, the pulpit, and they would ride him out of his church on his pulpit bannister. It can hardly be doubted that all Reformers are bottomed upon the truth, more or less; and to the world at large are not reformers almost universally laughing-stocks? Why so? Truth is ridiculous to men. Thus easily in my room here do I, conceited and garrulous, reverse the test of my Lord Shaftesbury.

". . . I read Solomon more and more, and every time see deeper and deeper and unspeakable meanings in him. . . . It seems to me now that Solomon was the truest man who ever spoke, and yet that he a little *managed* the truth with a view to popular conservatism; or else there have been many corruptions and interpolations of the text."[14]

With a view to popular conservatism, Melville himself a little *managed* the truth in *Moby-Dick*. Apparently it was also with a view to his sense of kinship with Hawthorne, in this regard, that he dedicated *Moby-Dick* to Hawthorne, "in token of my admiration for his genius." In a sense, Melville may have felt that Hawthorne was the one immediate reader who could be counted on to understand the varieties of subterfuge employed by Melville to present "the sane madness of vital truth."

Although Hawthorne's letter to Melville, written after he had received and read his own copy of *Moby-Dick*, seems to have been lost or destroyed, we do know from Melville's answering letter that Hawthorne said very much what Melville had hoped he would say. We may also gather that Hawthorne particularly pleased Melville by recognizing the wickedness of Melville's unorthodox and heretical intention; it is even possible that Hawthorne specifically referred to *Moby-Dick* as "a wicked book." Melville's reply suggests as much:

". . . A sense of unspeakable security is in me this moment, on account of your having understood the book. I *have* [italics added] written a wicked book, and feel spotless as the lamb. Ineffable socialities are in me. I would sit down and dine with you and all the gods in old Rome's Pantheon. . . ."

In that same letter, Melville also would seem to be answering Hawthorne's possible remark that very few readers would appreciate Melville's allegorical meanings in *Moby-Dick*. That, says Melville, is to be expected:

". . . not one man in five cycles, who is wise, will expect appreciative recognition from his fellows, or any one of them. Appreciation! Recognition! Is love appreciated? Why, ever since Adam, who has got to the meaning of his great allegory—the world? Then we pygmies must be content to have our paper allegories but ill comprehended."[15]

To have Melville imply that *Moby-Dick* is an allegory should be worth noticing because, once in a while, some joker steps forth to laugh the too-loud laugh at those who think they see in *Moby-Dick* just a wee bit more than a ripping good yarn about a whale hunt.[16]

5

MELVILLE'S own variation on a whale hunter's holiday—his actual pilgrimage to the Holy Land—was made in 1856, only five years after the publication of *Moby-Dick*, and only shortly after Hawthorne had established himself as United States Consul in Liverpool. His visit to Hawthorne at this time led his host to record in his journal the finest contemporary portrait we have of Melville, and also to quote one further confession from this strange man who was in some ways related to Ethan Brand. This further confession focuses our attention on one point which is of extreme importance to us not only in understanding *Moby-Dick* but also in understanding Melville's later novels:

"November 20th, Thursday. A week ago last Monday, Herman Melville came to see me at the Consulate, looking much as he used to do (a little paler, and perhaps a little sadder), in a rough out-side coat, and with his characteristic gravity and reserve of man-ner. He had crossed from New York to Glasgow in a screw steamer, about a fortnight before, and had since been seeing Edinburgh and other interesting places. I felt rather awkward at first; because this is the first time I have met him since my ineffectual attempt to get him a consulate appointment from General Pierce. How-ever, I failed only from a real lack of power to serve him; so there was no reason to be ashamed, and we soon found ourselves on pretty much our former terms of sociability and confidence. Mel-ville has not been well, of late; he has been affected with neuralgic complaints in his head and limbs, and no doubt has suffered from too constant literary occupation, pursued without much success, latterly; and his writings, for a long while past, have indicated a morbid state of mind. So he left his place at Pittsfield, and has established his wife and family, I believe, with his father-in-law in Boston, and is thus far on his way to Constantinople. I do not wonder that he found it necessary to take an airing through the world, after so many years of toilsome pen-labor and domestic life, following upon so wild and adventurous a youth as his was. I in-vited him to come and stay with us at Southport, as long as he might remain in this vicinity; and, accordingly, he did come, the next day, taking with him, by way of baggage, the least little bit of a bundle, which, he told me, contained a night-shirt and a tooth-brush. He is a person of very gentlemanly instinct in every respect, save that he is a little heterodox ·in the matter of clean linen.

"He stayed with us from Tuesday till Thursday; and, on the intervening day, we took a pretty long walk together, and sat down in a hollow among the sand hills (sheltering ourselves from the high, cool wind) and smoked a cigar. Melville, as he always does, began to reason of Providence and futurity, and of every-thing that lies beyond human ken, and informed me that he had 'pretty much made up his mind to be annihilated'; but still he does not seem to rest in that anticipation; and, I think, will never rest until he gets hold of a definite belief. It is strange how he persists—and has persisted ever since I knew him, and probably long before—in wandering to-and-fro over these deserts, as dismal and monotonous as the sand hills amid which we were sitting. He can neither believe, nor be comfortable in his unbelief; and he is too honest and courageous not to try to do one or the other. If he were a religious man, he would be one of the most truly religious and reverential; he has a very high and noble nature, and better worth immortality than most of us."[17]

Hawthorne's only direct quotation there is that Melville had said that he had "pretty much made up his mind to be annihilated." Obviously, he was not speaking in Carlyle's sense of the word "annihilated." Death apparently remained the most fascinating subject for Melville, even after he had turned his back (as much as he could) on the Calvinistic and Miltonic concept that man's first disobedience and the fruit of that forbidden tree had brought death into the world. Having done his best to derive some comfort from the Satanic and Byronic pose of that defiance which was intended to translate death into an anti-Christian form of victory, Melville may have used the word "annihilated" to suggest that he had progressed far enough in his Satanism to relinquish his last lingering and wistful notion that there might be some kind of resurrection and immortality for the spirit or soul, after death. In *Moby-Dick*, his utterances on the subject are somewhat equivocal. But "death" is the major motif throughout *Moby-Dick*. Ishmael begins talking about it, as his major hypochondriac obsession, in the first paragraph of the first chapter; he is still meditating on it, while perched on a coffin, in the last paragraph of the epilogue. Melville could no more take out of the dictionary the word "death" than the word "God." As we shall see, he gained less comfort than he liked to admit, from that Ahab-like pose represented in his letter to Hawthorne:

"If any of those other Powers choose to withhold certain secrets, let them; that does not impair my sovereignty in myself; that does not make me tributary. And perhaps, after all, there is *no* secret."

Perhaps, perhaps.

WICKED BOOK

CHAPTER VII

*Now he gave jeer for jeer, and taunted
the apes that jibed him. With the soul of
an Atheist, he wrote down the godliest
things; with the feeling of misery and
death in him, he created forms of gladness and life.*

MELVILLE, *Pierre, or the Ambiguities*

WICKED BOOK

In his narrative of Captain Ahab's ambiguous quest for the White Whale, Melville brilliantly demonstrated his own understanding of Carlyle's assertion that "there is concealment and yet revelation" in a symbol; that the infinite can be made to blend itself with the finite in a symbol. A single image—the image of a whale—was enough for Melville to start with, and his firsthand knowledge of that monster (as image and as symbol) provided him with abundant raw materials for contriving his one supremely great work of art.

Again his ultimate goal was to tell a story which would illuminate, obliquely, his personal declaration of independence not only from the tyranny of Christian dogma but also from the sovereign tyranny of God Almighty. With appropriate irony, he turned to the Bible for inspiration, particularly to the book of Job. Without any great difficulty he could identify himself with the suffering Job, and could join Job in blaming God for all the sorrows, woes, evils which distressed and perplexed him. Death was as much a perplexity to Job as to Melville, and this permitted further identification. Although he could not join Job in the final tableau of abject submission and acceptance of God's inscrutable ways, he could relish the inadequacy (as it seemed to an actual whale hunter) of those terms God used to upbraid Job for upbraiding God:

"Canst thou draw out leviathan with an hook?

"Canst thou fill his skin with barbed irons? or his head with fish spears?

"None is so fierce that dare stir him up: who, then, is able to stand before me?"

In Melville's day, many laymen and theologians were agreed that God's reference to leviathan, in that Forty-first chapter of Job, was a reference to a whale; that God used the image of the whale to serve as a symbol of God's own indomitable and inscrutable attributes. Having recently returned from the professional task of slaughtering whales, Melville was naturally inclined to pounce impudently on this God-given symbol and play it for all it was worth. By extension, the symbolic image of the whale permitted him to assume, wickedly, that any concern for whaling might be considered some form of God-concern, in an allegorical sense. Already well practiced in the possibilities of allegory, he was perfectly prepared to work out simultaneous concealments and revelations in terms of those rich whaling associations (physical and metaphysical) which crammed his thoughts and memories.

As readers, we can enjoy one irony which seems not to have been available to Melville in this connection. If his asserted declaration of independence from his two major enemies, society and God, had resulted in an accomplished fact of independence, he would have been able to declare peace instead of war. He would consequently have been inclined to draw his artistic raw materials from the memory of his past conflicts rather than from his awareness of present conflicts. Instead, and of seeming necessity, he was compelled to project the story of his own immediate disillusionment into the story of Captain Ahab's deep-sea adventures.

Perhaps the greatest difficulty which faces a reader of *Moby-Dick* is the fact that the story was written by a man who had considerable difficulty in understanding himself, and this aspect of Melville's puzzling spiritual idiom controlled and determined a related aspect of his artistic idiom. As already suggested, the word "disillusionment" indicates a perception of two values where formerly there had been but one. In the order of time, that one value had had a validity and "truth" about it which had been sustaining because it contributed to the sense of orderliness in the perceiver of it, the believer in it. As soon as disillusionment enters,

148

the formerly sustaining and valid value becomes transformed, for the disillusioned one, into a falsehood. Melville demonstrated this, in his disillusioned and therefore twofold attitude toward the Calvinistic concept of God. But the factors which controlled his response to that seeming falsehood were so complex that he continued to be fascinated by the very concept which repelled him. Having previously honored that concept with love, he subsequently honored it with hate, and in the very act of hating he acknowledged his continuing dependence on it.

More than that, Melville's disillusionment created a chain reaction which developed in him the inevitable habit of mind which is inclined to see at least two possible values for all images, all concepts. As soon as he was able to turn away from one value and call it illusion, he was victimized by the realization that the new value which he had embraced might also contain an element of illusion. That way madness lies.

All these factors, so closely related to the phenomenon of disillusionment, may help to account for what might be recognized as the circular pattern in Melville's thinking about his relationship to self, society, God. Having started by loving God, he turned skeptically to hating God; having grown to hate his hate, he progressed into the third quadrant of the circle and tried to enjoy a detached attitude toward both the love and the hate of God; but as soon as he grew to hate his detachment, he moved into the fourth quadrant, and found himself wistful over the possibility that God might indeed be lovable; then he could start again, as soon as he began to hate his wistfulness. That circular pattern must be kept in mind by the reader of *Moby-Dick*, if the seeming fluctuations and variations of Melville's viewpoint, as artistically reflected there, are to be comprehended and enjoyed. Melville himself gives his own description of the circular pattern, in "The Gilder" chapter:

"Would to God these blessed calms would last. But the mingling threads of life are woven by warp and woof; calms crossed by storms, a storm for every calm. There is no steady unretracing progress in this life; we do not advance through fixed gradations, and at the last one pause [cf. Carlyle's *Sartor Resartus*]:—through infancy's unconscious spell, boyhood's thoughtless faith, adolescence's doubt (the common doom), then scepticism, then dis-

149

belief, resting at last in manhood's pondering repose of If. *But once gone through we trace the round again* [italics added]; and are infants, boys, and men, and Ifs eternally."

Although that self-revelation should help, any reader of *Moby-Dick* will probably wish, occasionally, that Melville would actually pause long enough to let the reader draw a careful bead on him. He does indeed pause, more than he himself would indicate. Paradoxically, he seems to find a revengeful sort of cool calm in the hot and stormy act of hateful taunting. At times, his pleasure is to taunt Christian believers in much the same spirit that disillusioned older children taunt their younger brothers and sisters for still believing in Santa Claus. At other times, his pleasure is to find symbolic forms for taunting God Almighty. Obviously, these two forms of taunting are so closely related as to be inseparable in his art; yet separable in the abstractions of literary analysis.

2

As further orientation for our understanding of *Moby-Dick*, consider briefly the following three aspects of style and structure. The total structure depends on the interplay between the action, as such, and the narrative, as such; between the story of Captain Ahab's deeds and the way that story is told by Ishmael. The artistic cross-ruff between these two factors (*what* the story is; *how* the story is told) enables Melville to present his ulterior meanings by means of sustained irony. Consequently, an egregious mistake which a reader of *Moby-Dick* can make is the mistake of settling for *what* the story is, without noticing *how* the story is presented.

As we have seen, Melville previously made various experiments with similar ways of telling a story. In *Mardi*, he began by projecting a fictionalized aspect of himself into the hero-narrator, and then for allegorical reasons he degraded that early projection, to let it serve as an allegorical type or emblem of blindness, error, sin, so that it could subsequently be modified to represent the allegorical stages by which the hero-narrator progressed as a pilgrim soul until he ultimately liberated himself, through love, from his bondage to the world, the flesh, the Devil; until he ultimately attained spiritual "vision" and atonement. In *Redburn*, quite differently and perhaps somewhat unconsciously, Melville again permitted the hero-narrator to serve as a complex projection of self, in such a way as to illuminate three distinct phases of his own developing perceptions. Again differently, in *White-Jacket*, he had returned to an ambiguous and anti-Christian use of allegory while employing a still more complex variant of the same general narrative focus.

In *Moby-Dick*, it might be said that Melville projected one aspect of himself into his narrator Ishmael, and then projected another contrasting aspect of self into his hero, Captain Ahab. Ishmael is a self-acknowledged coward, fugitive, outcast, escapist. By contrast, Captain Ahab is a brave and heroic pursuer, outspoken in his hatreds. The foil value permits Melville to conceal from certain types of readers the fact that there is a close identity of viewpoints between Ishmael and Captain Ahab. Artistically, Melville again avails himself of sustained irony by pretending a contrast between the viewpoints of his hero and his narrator.

A second aspect of total structure, in *Moby-Dick*, reveals another way in which Melville shaped and controlled and illuminated his total meaning, again by means of sustained irony. His constant interweaving of several hundred Biblical names, references, allusions, quotations, creates an ambiguous and equivocal effect which is strikingly similar to the effects achieved by Montaigne and Pierre Bayle, for purposes of deception and self-protection. The orientation needed here is easily available. Duyckinck tells us that Melville once cited "old Burton as atheistical in the exquisite irony of his passages on some sacred matters."[1] Melville himself subsequently projected his spiritual autobiography into *Pierre*, and after that hero became discouraged in his attempt to write a novel which would illuminate God's truth, he became so disillusioned that he resorted to ironic and satiric equivocations: "Now he gave jeer for jeer, and taunted the apes that jibed him. With the soul of an Atheist, he wrote down the godliest things; with the feeling of misery and death in him, he created forms of gladness and life."[2] With these hints in mind, the reader should quickly be able to notice that Melville's uses of Biblical allusions in *Moby-Dick* are endowed with equivocal and ambiguous meanings by the larger context which controls them; that the conventional meanings of those Biblical allusions are exactly the meanings which Melville

151

deliberately but covertly satirizes; that the inverted meanings are those which mesh and interlock with the ulterior or total meaning of *Moby-Dick*. By contrast, the overt tendentiousness of meaning, in that astonishingly elaborate parade of Biblical allusions, provides Melville with a major device for self-protective deception and sarcastic hoodwinking. To illustrate, we need go no further afield than to consider the ambiguous values implicit in the names of the narrator and the hero: Ishmael and Ahab.

The character of Melville's Ishmael is frequently and mistakenly interpreted as akin to Taji in *Mardi*: we are told that Ishmael works through his doubts to an eventual resolution and salvation which accounts for his survival at the end of the narrative. We are also told that no matter how many religious doubts Ishmael may express in the early part of the narrative, he eventually achieves a viewpoint which is essentially Christian and orthodox. By contrast, I suggest that Melville very craftily and cunningly arranged to trap a certain kind of reader into that mistaken notion. As a corrective, one might notice that Melville covertly establishes a thoroughly anti-Christian value for the final scene, in which Ishmael is floating on a coffin, alone, in the vast Pacific, after the manner of Pip. But we shall consider that evidence, in its proper order. Quite early in the story, as we shall see, one of Ishmael's remarks comes in pat as a paraphrase of Genesis 16:12: "And he will be a wild man: his hand will be against every man, and every man's hand against him; and he shall dwell in the presence of all his brethren." So Melville's Ishmael has been dwelling in the presence of his Christian brethren for lo! these hundred years, and all that time his stylistic hand has been set against the very throats of his Christian brethren, even though some of them have been deceived into embracing Ishmael as a true Presbyterian.

What does the conventional reader make of Ahab's name? He probably remembers the Biblical account of King Ahab, in First Kings: Ahab "did evil in the sight of the Lord." In fact, "Ahab did more to provoke the Lord God of Israel to anger than all the kings of Israel that were before him." Furthermore, it was Elijah who upbraided Ahab in the Bible, even as in *Moby-Dick*, for having forsaken the commandments of the Lord. King Ahab's sin was that he "did very abominably in following idols." Obviously, then, it is not difficult to use either one of these Ahabs, for Christian

152

purposes, as a horrible object lesson which teaches us that while virtue and obedience are rewarded, wicked defiance is neither expedient nor profitable because it brings down retribution.

But there is one other correlation, far more interesting, between these two Ahabs. Each of them is seduced to his death by a prophet, and Captain Ahab's misleading prophet is Fedallah, whose symbolic values are complex. Consider, however, the hint in First Kings as to how it happened that King Ahab was similarly victimized: "I saw the Lord sitting on his throne, and all the host of heaven standing by him, on his right hand and on his left. And the Lord said, Who shall persuade Ahab, that he may go up and fall at Ramoth-gilead? . . . And there came forth a spirit, and stood before the Lord, and said, I will persuade him. And the Lord said unto him, Wherewith? And he said, I will go forth, and I will be a lying spirit in the mouth of all his prophets. And the Lord said, Thou shalt persuade him, and prevail also: go forth and do so."

For Melville's anti-Christian purposes, that passage lends itself nicely to a correlated series of insinuations that God is a malicious double-crosser, a deceiver, who is not above employing "a lying spirit" (inside or outside a human being) to lead a man to his death, even as God permitted Satan to serve as agent in seducing Adam and Eve to ultimate death; much as God permitted Satan to torture poor Job. In *Moby-Dick*, Captain Ahab is motivated by such dark thoughts when he follows Job in upbraiding God for his malice. It is because of the sufferings which God (as agent or principal) inflicts on Captain Ahab that Ahab swears his unspeakable oath to seek out the emblematic White Whale in defiance. Although Melville's circular pattern of attitudinizing causes him to view Captain Ahab from various angles, and with varying degrees of sympathy, as the story unfolds, Melville ultimately chooses to justify himself by glorifying Ahab's declaration of independence from man and God; to justify himself by representing Ahab as a supremely tragic hero who rises to his highest grandeur (and says so) even in the face of that ultimate and inevitable God-bullying indignity, death.

A third major aspect of total structure, in *Moby-Dick*, is the triangulation among three whale stories: Captain Ahab's, Jonah's, Job's. Again, this structural aspect is developed ironically and deceptively, because Melville chooses to inflate his mock-serious version of the fish story, in Father Mapple's sermon; by contrast, Melville chooses to represent his anti-Christian version of the Job story, by means of scattered and cumulative insinuations. Nevertheless, the careful reader comes to appreciate that the direct quotations from the book of Job and the allusions to Job pile up until they call persistent attention to the analogy between what happened to Job and what happened to Captain Ahab. The importance of that slowly enriched analogy deflates the Ahab-Jonah parallelism to the intended antithesis or inversion. To be sure, Captain Ahab's actions, which occur as a consequence of his Job-like sufferings, should also be viewed as inversions of the lollipop ending which scholars tell us the orthodox revisionists tacked on the story of Job. Instead of accepting God's inscrutability, as Job did, Captain Ahab defies it and vows to dismember his taunting Dismemberer. While Ahab goes about that obvious business, Ishmael goes about his covert business of taunting the Taunter. With mock humility, for example, Ishmael sets up the pun value of cetology-theology in the opening paragraphs of the "Cetology" chapter, and progresses until he can exclaim, sarcastically, "What am I that I should essay to hook the nose of this leviathan? The awful tauntings in Job might well appal me. 'Will he (the leviathan) make a covenant with thee? Behold the hope of him is vain!' "[3] With equally taunting mockery and sarcasm, Ishmael contemplates a dying whale (possibly a symbol of an impotent and defeated and dying God), and continues his anti-Christian sneering in these rhetorical questions, "Is this the creature of whom it was once so triumphantly said—'Canst thou fill his skin with barbed irons? or his head with fish-spears? . . .' This the creature? this he? Oh! that unfulfilments should follow the prophets. For with the strength of a thousand thighs in his tail, Leviathan had run his head under the mountains of the seas, to hide him from the Pequod's fish-spears!"[4]

(After the reader has become familiar with Melville's fondness for all manner of punning and equivocal word-play, he may be inclined to look more generously on my suspicion that Melville chose to name the ship of Captain Ahab and of Ishmael the *Pequod* because of the punlike suggestiveness of the ship's intention to pique God.)

Now complete this Ahab-Job-Jonah triangulation by placing the devout Father Mapple's whale-story sermon against the other two whale stories. Immediately, one may see further reason for considering the possibility that Melville intended the Jonah story to be viewed as a fish story. But we must pause here to acknowledge the heresy of such a literary interpretation, because our leading Melville authorities insist that Melville introduces the fine rhetoric of Father Mapple to serve as a yardstick for measuring the shortcomings and sins of mad old Captain Ahab. Because the bias of these authorities has afforded them pleasure in enjoying that sermon at its face value, they resent the suggestion that Melville might possibly have written that sermon for purely satirical purposes. More than that, these authorities resent the suggestion that they themselves could possibly have fallen into one of Melville's better mousetraps. Apparently they feel that if Melville had actually planned to trap any of his readers, he should have warned them.

So far, I have briefly sketched three aspects of the total structure of *Moby-Dick*: the sustained irony in the focus of narration; the sustained irony in some of Melville's uses of Biblical allusions; the sustained irony in the triangulation of three whale stories. Now we can start at the beginning of *Moby-Dick*, and watch the not too subtle manner in which Melville unfolds his meanings.

3

It need scarcely be said that Melville was by no means the first or last to view death as hard to take; in our own time, for example, Unamuno has insisted that death is the cornerstone or keystone in our perception of the tragedy of life. Ishmael introduces the death motif, in the first paragraph of the first chapter of *Moby-Dick*, and that death motif provides an obligato to all of the action and meditation, from the first paragraph to the last. It is significant that Melville chose to entitle his first chapter "Loomings" because one may easily notice, on a second reading, that the "loomings" therein do indeed foreshadow and hint at the major thematic concerns of the entire narrative. Ishmael begins by admitting (quite genially and humorously, of course) that he is something of a coward and escapist, driven to sea by his troubled thoughts on death:

". . . Whenever I find myself growing grim about the mouth; whenever it is a damp, drizzly November in my soul; whenever I find myself involuntarily pausing before coffin warehouses, and bringing up the rear of every funeral I meet . . . then, I account it high time to get to sea as soon as I can. This is my substitute for pistol and ball. With a philosophical flourish Cato[5] throws himself upon his sword; I quietly take to the ship."[6]

Thus Ishmael keeps his own private tendency toward "madness" under control. Yet, he explains, there is a paradoxical reason for viewing this particular form of escape as an actual form of pursuit, because the voyager is provided with excellent opportunities for contemplating the mysteries of life and death: "meditation and water are wedded for ever." Throughout the ages, he continues, the sea has been viewed as somehow (and variously) emblematic of all those infinite mysteries associated with the Creator of both life and death:

"Why upon your first voyage as a passenger, did you yourself feel such a mystical vibration, when first told that you and your ship were now out of sight of land? Why did the old Persians hold the sea holy? Why did the Greeks give it a separate deity, and own brother of Jove? Surely all this is not without meaning. And still deeper the meaning of that story of Narcissus, who because he could not grasp the tormenting, mild image he saw in the fountain, plunged into it and was drowned. But that same image, we ourselves see in all rivers and oceans. It is the image of the ungraspable phantom of life; and this is the key to it all."[7]

Indeed there is an image which deserves to be placed in the first chapter, and noticed in the first chapter: the myth of Narcissus is an extremely helpful "key" (to use Ishmael's word) to an understanding of *Moby-Dick*, if carefully construed, and Melville was aware of it. The "ungraspable phantom" was his concern as much as it was Ishmael's or Captain Ahab's. Here, however, Ishmael quickly recovers his genial and jovial tone as he chatters pleasantly (and with equivocal sarcasm) about his reasons for going to sea, and about his submissive attitude toward being ordered about by an "old hunks" of a sea captain. The anti-Christian insinuations accumulate rapidly. For example, in seven sentences

Ishmael manages to ridicule the concept that in Adam's fall we
sinned all; that ever since Adam, mankind has been making install-
ment payments on that debt incurred in the Garden of Eden; that
God pays us for our virtue and penalizes us for our sins; that we
actually content ourselves with paying hypocritical lip-service to
Christ's teachings that we should not try to lay up treasures on
earth:

"Again, I always go to sea as a sailor, because they make a point
of paying me for my trouble, whereas they never pay passengers a
single penny that I ever heard of. On the contrary, passengers
themselves must pay. And there is all the difference in the world
between paying and being paid. The act of paying is perhaps the
most uncomfortable infliction that the two orchard thieves en-
tailed upon us. But *being paid*—what will compare with it? The
urbane activity with which a man receives money is really marvellous, considering that we so earnestly believe money to be the
root of all earthly ills, and that on no account can a monied man
enter heaven. Ah! how cheerfully we consign ourselves to perdition!"[8]

In other words, Ishmael insinuates (while pretending to represent a highly moral Christian viewpoint) that we do not practise
what we preach, and we really do not believe what we confess.
But Ishmael is just beginning to have naughty fun with Biblical
allusions. Continuing, in the very next paragraph of Chapter One,
he further plays sarcastically with Christian concepts involving
the paradox of free will and predestination:

"But wherefore it was that after having repeatedly smelt the
sea as a merchant sailor, I should now take it into my head to go
on a whaling voyage; this the invisible police officer of the Fates,
who has the constant surveillance of me, and secretly dogs me,
and influences me in some unaccountable way—he can better
answer than any one else. And, doubtless, my going on this whaling voyage, formed part of the grand programme of Providence
that was drawn up a long time ago. . . . Though I cannot tell why
it was exactly that those stage managers, the Fates, put me down
for this shabby part of a whaling voyage, when others were set
down for magnificent parts in high tragedies . . . I think I can see
a little into the springs and motives which being cunningly presented to me under various disguises, induced me to set about

performing the part I did, besides cajoling me into the delusion that it was a choice resulting from my own unbiased free-will and discriminating judgment."[9]

The tone of sarcasm should be obvious, there; but there is one antithesis available only after one has become familiar with the larger Melvillian context. Melville's basic whale-as-God trope permits him to represent a whaling vessel as the craft of the free-thinkers, in their approach to the mystery of God, whereas a "merchantman" represents the bottom in which the Christians float illusively toward Heaven, with their merchandizing and profiteering conviction that such an approach to Heaven is bound to pay dividends. With this in mind, read that passage again.

Finally, as we come to the last two paragraphs of Chapter One, Ishmael leads us back around the circle to our starting place, which had to do with his motives for going to sea; particularly with his preoccupation concerning the mysteries involving the Creator and the created. Not until later will Ahab's references to his enemy, the White Whale, provide Ishmael with opportunities for establishing allusions to the White Whale as a Job's whale; but Ishmael, writing in retrospect, may be said to hold in his mind the recollections of the entire story he is about to tell, and so he can foreshadow Ahab's "ungraspable phantom." In this sense, notice how the emblematic insinuations of the last paragraph complete the circular pattern of Chapter One, and thus foreshadow the circular pattern of the entire thematic structure:

"Chief among these motives was the overwhelming idea of the great whale himself. Such a portentous and mysterious monster roused all my curiosity. Then the wild and distant seas where he rolled his island bulk; the undeliverable, nameless perils of the whale; these, with all the attending marvels of a thousand Patagonian sights and sounds, helped to sway me to my wish. . . .

"By reason of these things, then, the whaling voyage was welcome; the great flood-gates of the wonder-world swung open, and in the wild conceits that swayed me to my purpose, two and two there floated into my inmost soul, endless processions of the whale, and, midmost of them all, one grand hooded phantom, like a snow hill in the air."[10]

Notice particularly the recurrence of the word "phantom," which carries the reader back to the "ungraspable phantom," and thus hints at later enrichments. Notice also the "two and two" procession in Ishmael's wild conceits; the mere hint that there might even be some duality in that one grand hooded phantom. In this first chapter, then, enough anti-Christian insinuations have been brought together by Ishmael to serve as fair warning to the reader that the overt or obvious meanings, throughout, may not be as important or interesting as the covert meanings; that as Melville said of Hawthorne, he himself took great delight in hoodwinking at least some of his readers (even as he insinuates that God takes a similar pleasure); that as he said of Shakespeare, he himself sometimes craftily hints at ideas which he felt to be so "terrific" and "unspeakable" that they could be represented only through the subtle indirections of literary art.

Ishmael's preoccupation with death continues, in the second chapter, as he searches for a lodging in New Bedford, and even before he arrives at "The Spouter-Inn:—Peter Coffin." ("Coffin?—Spouter?—Rather ominous in that particular connection, thought I.") Death even becomes the subject of a little essay involving the story of Dives and Lazarus, built around the following philosophical observation on the ambiguities of attitudes toward death:

" 'In judging of that tempestuous wind called Euroclydon,' says an old writer—of whose works I possess the only copy extant—'it maketh a marvellous difference, whether thou lookest out at it from a glass window where the frost is all on the outside, or whether thou observest it from that sashless window, where the frost is on both sides, and of which the wight Death is the only glazier.' "[11]

(Notice that Christian doctrine serves as one kind of glazier which permits the occupant to feel relatively snug and smug as he looks out on death.) Inside the Spouter-Inn, death again is represented in cryptic emblem, when Ishmael stops to puzzle over the insinuations of a Salvator-like painting which hangs in the entry and vaguely foreshadows the fate of the *Pequod*:

"The picture represents a Cape-Horner in a great hurricane; the half-foundered ship weltering there with its three dismantled masts alone visible; and an exasperated whale, purposing to spring clean over the craft, is in the enormous act of impaling himself upon the three mast-heads."[12]

In this same entry, opposite the painting, Ishmael examines a "heathenish array of monstrous clubs and spears," and is particularly fascinated by one that is "sickle-shaped." He reacts violently: "You shuddered as you gazed, and wondered what monstrous cannibal and savage could ever have gone a death-harvesting with such a hacking, horrifying implement."

He enters and notices that the bar is crudely fashioned to resemble a right whale's open mouth: "Within are shabby shelves, ranged round with old decanters, bottles, flasks; and in those jaws of swift destruction, like another cursed Jonah (by which name indeed they called him), bustles a little withered old man, who, for their money, dearly sells the sailors deliriums and death."[13]

He is informed that he may share a room with a stranger, changes his mind, and elects to lay himself out instead on a coffin-like pine plank which the jesting landlord offers to make smoother for him with a plane. ("I did not know how all the planing in the world could make eider down of a pine plank.") He asks again about the harpooner who might share his bed, and is told he is out selling an embalmed human head, from New Zealand.

These accumulations of death references remain relatively neutral in value; but in the chapter punningly entitled "The Counterpane," after Ishmael has met Queequeg and has slept with him comfortably through the night, Ishmael's act of waking is converted into a tableau again emblematic of death: Queequeg, still asleep, has wrapped one arm about Ishmael, who dares not move. The Freudians have delighted to find homosexual significance in this passage, but such a concern is impertinent because it ignores the stated trope. The situation reminds Ishmael of an event in his childhood when an act of punishment (being sent to bed early in the afternoon of the longest day in the year) seemed emblematic of death, and provided him with a nightmarish experience: he woke in the darkness and was paralyzed with fright when he felt his hand held by a "silent form or phantom":

"I opened my eyes, and the before sunlit room was now wrapped in outer darkness. Instantly I felt a shock running through all my frame; nothing was to be seen, and nothing was to be heard; but a supernatural hand seemed placed in mine. My arm hung over the counterpane, and the nameless, unimaginable, silent form or phantom, to which the hand belonged, seemed closely seated by my bedside. For what seemed ages piled on ages, I lay there, frozen with the most awful fears, not daring to drag away my hand. . . . for days and weeks and months afterward I lost myself in confounding attempts to explain the mystery. Nay, to this very hour, I often puzzle myself with it."[14]

4

THAT Sunday morning, Ishmael attends the Whaleman's Chapel, and has time to study the marble tablets commemorating dead men, lost at sea. Again, all the death references are brought into focus, as Ishmael meditates:

". . . What bitter blanks in those black-bordered marbles which cover no ashes! What despair in those immovable inscriptions! What deadly voids and unbidden infidelities in the lines that seem to gnaw upon all Faith, and refuse resurrections to the beings who have placelessly perished without a grave. . . . how is it that to his name who yesterday departed for the other world, we prefix so significant and infidel a word. . . . how is it that we still refuse to be comforted for those who we nevertheless maintain are dwelling in unspeakable bliss; why all the living so strive to hush all the dead; wherefore but the rumor of a knocking in a tomb will terrify a whole city. All these things are not without their meanings."

(These questioning and infidel remarks are too blunt, and Melville wryly protects himself by permitting Ishmael to add a backhanded sarcastic sop of pretended reassurance:)

"But Faith, like a jackal, feeds among the tombs, and even from these dead doubts she gathers her most vital hope.

". . . Yes, Ishmael, the same fate may be thine. . . . Yes, there is death in this business of whaling—a speechlessly quick chaotic bundling of a man into Eternity. But what then? Methinks we have hugely mistaken this matter of Life and Death. Methinks that what they call my shadow here on earth is my true substance. . . . In fact, take my body who will, take it I say, it is not me. And therefore three cheers for Nantucket; and come a stove boat and stove body when they will, for stave my soul, Jove himself cannot."[15]

The fluctuating viewpoint, in all these death references, permits the reader to take exactly the meaning which best suits his prejudices; but the cautious reader, concerned with Melville's own viewpoint, will have realized by this time that Ishmael's dominant viewpoint is anti-Christian.

The description of Father Mapple, in his ritual of climbing to the pulpit, creates another cluster of anti-Christian references. Although Melville ironically permits Ishmael to interpret Father Mapple's actions as they might appear to the orthodox believer, Ishmael himself is by no means an orthodox believer. The careless reader, however, is easily hoodwinked by Ishmael's comments, which develop as follows:

"No, thought I, there must be some sober reason for this thing; furthermore, it must *symbolize something unseen* [italics added; cf. Carlyle on "symbols"]. Can it be, then, that by that act of physical isolation, he signifies his spiritual withdrawal for the time, from all outward worldly ties and connections? Yes, for replenished with the meat and wine of the word, to the faithful man of God, this pulpit, I see, is a self-containing stronghold—a lofty Ehrenbreitstein, with a perennial well of water within the walls. . . .

"Nor was the pulpit itself without a trace of the same sea-taste that had achieved the ladder and the picture. Its panelled front was in the likeness of a ship's bluff bows, and the Holy Bible rested on a projecting piece of scroll work, fashioned after a ship's fiddle-headed beak.

"What could be more full of meaning?—for the pulpit is ever this earth's foremost part; all the rest comes in its rear; the pulpit leads the world. From thence it is the storm of God's quick wrath is first descried, and the bow must bear the earliest brunt. From thence it is the God of breezes fair or foul is first invoked for favourable winds. Yes, *the world's a ship on its passage out* [italics added; cf. *White-Jacket*], and not a voyage complete; and the pulpit is its prow."[16]

So straight-faced are these remarks that the deceptive equivocation and the sneer at Christian doctrine may not be recognized unless the reader orients himself, and takes bearings, from the larger context. As a convenient short-cut, remember Melville's remark to Hawthorne: "Let any clergyman try to preach the Truth from its very stronghold, the pulpit, and they would ride him out of his church on his own pulpit bannister." Of course Melville there assumed that Hawthorne would recognize the word "Truth" as referring to that "usable" and "unvarnished" matter of fact which (for Melville) gave the lie to the so-called "revelations" of truth, in Christian doctrine. So when Ishmael says, "the pulpit leads the world," that which seems like praise is actually a sarcastic sneer, and the rest of the passage creates a trope which has supporting insinuations. Still continuing his pretended affirmation of Christian concepts, Melville let Ishmael say, "Yes, the world's a ship on its passage out, and not a voyage complete; and the pulpit is thus a vantage point or a lookout." According to Melville's larger context, however, those who use this vantage point never perceive, accurately, just what lies ahead, or to what inevitable death and destruction the world-ship and its passengers are destined. So the pulpit-as-prow trope again illustrates Melville's delight in triple-talk: the first level of meaning, in terms of the specifics, is merely a picture of the chapel interior; the second level, in terms of Christian doctrine, would seem to be orthodox in its affirmation; the third and covert level of meaning, which illuminates Melville's own viewpoint, again represents a sarcastic and sneering burlesque of Christian doctrine.

Father Mapple's sermon on Jonah and the whale is also ridiculed and burlesqued; but Melville's indirect method of ridicule, in this case, is cunning and sly enough to hoodwink even some of the experts. They argue that the sermon on Jonah must have some particular significance in the narrative, else Melville would not have presented the full text of Father Mapple's discourse. It does have particular significance: Father Mapple intends to make Jonah's story illustrate the wisdom of religious acceptance, based on "right reason," and this is exactly the attitude which Melville is intent on ridiculing. But, some may argue, the sermon stands by itself, and Ishmael neither praises nor criticizes what Father Mapple says. That is partly correct: Ishmael does *not* praise it. Instead, Ishmael turns his back on Christian Father Mapple and goes to join pagan Queequeg in his religious worship. It is a symbolic action. In defense of his joining Queequeg, as we shall soon see, Ishmael *does* criticize and ridicule the essentials of Father Mapple's Christian teaching.

In the light of the ironically ambiguous Biblical allusions Melville achieves by using the two names, Ishmael and Ahab, consider a similar equivocal insinuation which Melville achieves by arranging to let Father Mapple illuminate the Christian doctrine of repentance, submission, obedience, in terms of querulous Jonah. The total action of the Jonah story, in the Old Testament, provides us with a picture of a headstrong, recalcitrant, God-challenging prophet, whose one supreme moment of surrender to God's will occurred only after God had scared poor Jonah witless: "And here, shipmates, is true and faithful repentance." Is it?

Technically, then, Melville's method of ridiculing Father Mapple's sermon is, in part, this: two rituals of worship are juxtaposed, and thus an ironic parallel is established. In each, by insinuation, the reader is given a chance to watch two worshipers—Christian Mapple and pagan Queequeg—each manipulating his separate God until he gets him to look just as he wants him to look. Father Mapple does it with rhetoric; Queequeg does it with a jacknife.

Consider another part of Melville's technical method here. In his sermon on Jonah, Father Mapple tells how "God came upon him in a whale" and how Jonah was induced to mend his ways and carry out the bidding of Almighty God. "And what was that, shipmates? To preach the Truth to the face of Falsehood!" Ah yes, of course. The Melville reader who swallows that barbed sentence, without noticing the hook in it, deserves to get caught. Whose "Truth" is Jonah asked to peddle? The divinely revealed truth, in accordance with "right reason." Father Mapple is very serious, but Melville is the manipulator of this puppet show, and serious Mapple is permitted to say many things which amount to jokes, in Melville's sinister context. Take this sentence: "Woe to him who would not be true, even though to be false were salvation." Immediately the cautious reader recognizes that the sentence has one value, in terms of Christian doctrine, and just the opposite value, in terms of Melville's anti-Christian belief. Consider another sentence. Father Mapple is talking about the need for courage on the part of those who will preach the "Truth" of Christian doctrine, even in the face of the enemies, and he assures his listeners that (even as Melville once believed) such missionary work has its reward:

"Delight is to him—a far, far upward, and inward delight—who against the proud gods and commodores of this earth, ever stands forth his own inexorable self."[17]

There is stylistic economy again: in the Christian context, the preacher of truth delights to pit his God-inspired integrity against the strongest and most sinful of earth's potentates; in Melville's anti-Christian context, it will be remembered, the "usable truth" requires that the truly heroic man "declare himself a sovereign nature (in himself) amid the powers of heaven, hell, and earth." In this same context, then, "the proud gods and commodores of this earth" are emblematic of the supernatural powers who tyrannically command and rule this earth; against whom any tragic hero like Ahab "ever stands forth his own inexorable self." These are just three of Father Mapple's sentences, cited to illustrate Melville's technical cunning, in his use of equivocation. As I have said, Father Mapple's intent is perfectly clear: he earnestly and honestly uses the Jonah story as a parable, to dramatize the Christian doctrine of repentance, obedience, acceptance: "Jonah did the Almighty's bidding."

Now consider the next chapter, against which Melville juxtaposes the sermon. Ishmael goes back to find Queequeg performing his own ritual of worship, before his own idol-god, which he holds in his hand while he whittles away on his God's nose to give him a more pleasing expression. Melville knew that Voltaire had some pertinent things to say on this human tendency toward making God in our own image. But there is something so charmingly attractive about Queequeg's harmless private action that Ishmael joins him in the pagan ritual. In defending his own action, Ishmael correlates his personal characteristics with those of his namesake in the Bible, and this correlation is extended until it implies that this American Ishmael's hand is indeed set even against those "bland deceits" of Father Mapple's doctrine:

". . . I felt a melting in me. No more my splintered heart and maddened hand were turned against the wolfish world. This soothing savage had redeemed it. There he sat, his very indifference speaking a nature in which there lurked no civilised hypocrisies and bland deceits. Wild he was; a very sight of sights to see; yet I began to feel myself mysteriously drawn toward him. And those same things that would have repelled most others, they were the very magnets that thus drew me. I'll try a pagan friend, thought I, since Christian kindness has proved but hollow courtesy."[18]

This is just the beginning of the passage, for Melville at once permits Ishmael to defend himself further, by sarcastically pretending to find in the Golden Rule a sanction for his actions. In the process, he inverts the Bible quotation and thus manages once again to ridicule familiar Christian concepts:

"I was a good Christian; born and bred in the bosom of the infallible Presbyterian Church. How then could I unite with this wild idolater in worshipping his piece of wood? But what is worship? thought I. Do you suppose now, Ishmael, that the magnanimous God of heaven and earth—pagans and all included—can possibly be jealous of an insignificant bit of black wood? Impossible! But what is worship?—to do the will of God?—*that* is worship. And what is the will of God?—to do to my fellow-man what I would have my fellow-man to do to me—*that* is the will of God. Now, Queequeg is my fellow-man. And what do I wish that this Queequeg would do to me? Why, unite with me in my particular Presbyterian form of worship. Consequently, I must then unite with him in his; ergo, I must turn idolater."[19]

On the way to Nantucket, Queequeg proves by his actions that his impulsive pagan responses are far more "Christian" than those of his so-called "Christian" fellow-passengers. This leads Ishmael to watch the mildness of Queequeg with the feeling that the pagan savage must be saying to himself, "It's a mutual, joint-stock world, in all meridians. We cannibals must help these Christians."[20]

5

ABOARD the *Pequod*, while dealing with those hypocritical Christians, Peleg and Bildad, the observant Ishmael generalizes on the Scripture-named Nantucket Quakers, and with seeming unconsciousness gives the reader a preview of that "grand, ungodly, god-like man, Captain Ahab," who has merely been mentioned, so far in the narrative:

". . . And when these things unite in a man of greatly superior natural force, with a globular brain and a ponderous heart; who has also by the stillness and seclusion of many long night-watches in the remotest waters, and beneath constellations never seen here at the north, been led *to think untraditionally and independently* [italics added]; receiving all nature's sweet or savage impressions fresh from her own virgin voluntary and confiding breast, and thereby chiefly, but with some help from accidental advantages, to learn a bold and nervous lofty language—that man makes one in a whole nation's census—a mighty pageant creature, formed for noble tragedies. Nor will it at all detract from him, dramatically regarded, if either by birth or circumstances, he have what seems a half-wilful over-ruling morbidness at the bottom of his nature. For all men tragically great are made so through a certain morbidness. Be sure of this, O young ambition, all mortal greatness is but disease."[21]

That important generalization looks backward to earlier references, even to Cato, and forward, clearly, to Captain Ahab. The sarcasm implying that Ahab has received "all nature's sweet or savage impressions fresh from her own virgin voluntary and confiding breast" should be obvious. So also should the sarcasm of "but with some help from accidental advantages," and the remainder of the sentence. That same sentence, foreshadowing Ahab as "formed for noble tragedies," establishes an important antithesis between Ahab and Ishmael, the latter having already complained that he was not cast in "magnificent parts" of high tragedy, but merely for "this shabby part." Melville had recently read Carlyle's *Heroes and Hero-Worship*, and the relationship between Ishmael and Ahab reflects the impact of Carlyle. Ishmael begins with certain hunger for answers to the mysteries of life and death, certain troubled perplexities and uncertainties. Ahab, who becomes his hero, is troubled by the identical questions; but finds a heroic pattern of response to those questions, and Ishmael follows the leader.

For purposes of the narrative, Ishmael's indirect glimpse of Ahab, through the eyes of Peleg, leads the reader to share with Ishmael a certain tension as to the character of this "ungodly, god-like man," named after a wicked king, "stricken" and "blasted" by the "accidental advantages" of nature's confidings on the deep; yet still preserving "his humanities." Even as this tension is established, Ishmael confesses, "I felt a sympathy and a sorrow for him." Even the accompanying sense of awe "did not disincline me toward him."[22]

Still postponing the major action of the drama, which cannot really begin until Captain Ahab appears, Melville continues his important prologue and steadily sharpens the focus of Ishmael's anti-Christian attitude, which will subsequently be dramatized, in Ahab's later deeds. In commenting on Queequeg's religious ceremony of fasting and humiliation, for example, Ishmael again employs an oblique manner of sarcastically ridiculing certain basic concepts of God, in Christian doctrine:

". . . I did not choose to disturb him [Queequeg] till towards night-fall; for I cherish the greatest respect towards everybody's religious obligations, never mind how comical, and could not find it in my heart to undervalue even a congregation of ants worshipping a toad-stool; or those other creatures in certain parts of our earth, who with a degree of footmanism [flunkeyism] quite unprecedented in other planets, bow down before the torso of a deceased landed proprietor merely on account of the inordinate possessions yet owned and rented in his name.

"I say, we good Presbyterian Christians should be charitable in these things, and not fancy ourselves so vastly superior to other mortals, pagans and what not, because of *their* [italics added] half-crazy conceits on these subjects. There was Queequeg, now, certainly entertaining the most absurd notions about Yojo and his Ramadan;—but what of that? Queequeg thought he knew what he was about, I suppose; he seemed to be content; and there let him rest. All our arguing with him would not avail; let him be; I say: and Heaven have mercy on us all—Presbyterians and Pagans alike—for we are all somehow dreadfully cracked about the head, and sadly need mending."[23]

6

PREPARATION for Captain Ahab's entrance is continued by permitting a "mad" character, appropriately named Elijah, to indulge in a vaguely tantalizing prophecy as to Ahab's fate, even as an earlier Elijah prophesied the fate of King Ahab. It will be remembered that Ahab (like Melville) had once been a religious believer; that God had spoken to him and that the message came in the form of a lightning bolt. According to orthodox Elijah, this event disillusioned Ahab so deeply that he became, thereafter, a blasphemer in word and deed:

"What did they *tell* you about him? Say that! . . . But nothing about that thing that happened to him off Cape Horn, long ago, when he lay like dead for three days and nights [presumably, after being hit by the lightning bolt]; nothing about that deadly scrimmage with the Spaniard afore the altar in Santa?—heard nothing about that, eh? Nothing about the silver calabash he spat in? [presumably, also before the altar] And nothing about his losing his leg last voyage, according to the prophecy. . . . Ye've shipped, have ye? Names down on the papers? Well, well, what's signed, is signed; and what's to be, will be; and then again, perhaps it won't be, after all. Anyhow, it's all fixed and arranged a'ready; and some sailors or other must go with him, I suppose; as well these as any other men, God pity 'em! Morning to ye, shipmates, morning; the ineffable heavens bless ye; I'm sorry I stopped ye."[24]

This Elijah helps to keep our attention on the contradictions of free will and predestination (". . . what's to be, will be; and then again, perhaps it won't be, after all.") and on the ineffable heavens. While Captain Ahab still remains below decks, the good ship *Pequod* sets out on her blasphemous cruise. With fitting irony, she sails on the day commemorating the birth of Our Saviour who redeemed us to everlasting life, and the departure is described in a chapter wryly entitled, "Merry Christmas."[25] Bildad, so reminiscent of that Job's comforter after whom he is named, gives the men on deck his parting and hypocritical benediction: "God bless ye, and have ye in His holy keeping, men. . . . Be careful in the hunt, ye mates. . . . Don't forget your prayers, either. . . . Don't whale it too much a Lord's days, men; but don't miss a fair chance either, that's rejecting Heaven's good gifts. . . ."[26] But Melville makes even more use of the man at the helm of the *Pequod*, to sharpen the focus of his rationalistic meaning. Bulkington has just returned from one whaling voyage, and has immediately shipped again:

". . . The land seemed scorching to his feet. Wonderfullest things are ever the unmentionable; deep memories yield no epitaphs; this six-inch chapter is the stoneless grave of Bulkington. Let me only say that it fared with him as with the storm-tossed ship, that miserably drives along the leeward land. The port would fain give succor; the port is pitiful; in the port is safety, comfort, hearthstone, supper, warm blankets, friends, all that's kind to our mortalities. But in that gale, the port, the land, is that ship's direst jeopardy; she must fly all hospitality; one touch of land, though it but graze the keel, would make her shudder through and through.

169

With all her might she crowds all sail off shore; in so doing, fights 'gainst the very winds that fain would blow her homeward; seeks all the lashed sea's landlessness again; for refuge's sake forlornly rushing into peril; her only friend her bitterest foe!

"Know ye now, Bulkington? Glimpses do you seem to see of that mortally intolerable truth; that all deep, earnest thinking is but the intrepid effort of the soul to keep the open independence of her sea; while the wildest winds of heaven and earth conspire to cast her on the treacherous, slavish shore?

"But as in landlessness alone resides the highest truth, shoreless, indefinite as God—so better is it to perish in that howling infinite, than be ingloriously dashed upon the lee, even if that were safety! For worm-like, then, oh! who would craven crawl to land! Terrors of the terrible! is all this agony so vain? Take heart, take heart, O Bulkington! Bear thee grimly, demigod! Up from the spray of thy ocean-perishing—straight up, leaps thy apotheosis!"[27]

That six-inch chapter deserves particular notice because it provides another solid foundation stone for our ultimate understanding of Melville's major conceptual concerns, in *Moby-Dick*. Bulkington is here employed to represent Melville's conviction "that all deep, earnest thinking is but the intrepid effort of the soul to keep the open independence of her sea; while the wildest winds of heaven and earth conspire to cast her on the treacherous, slavish shore." The fundamental conceptual antithesis, throughout *Moby-Dick* may be represented by the clash between the concept of freedom and the concept of tyrannous and brutal enslavement.

Notice also that Bulkington is made to represent Melville's own curious version of that anti-Christian attitude expressed in one way by some of the Renaissance humanists, expressed somewhat differently by the self-styled "enlightened" rationalists of the sixteenth, seventeenth, eighteenth, nineteenth centuries. Here, the sketchy context provided by my first chapter should again pay dividends.

For future reference, notice also that the Bulkington passage contains definitions for the two contrasting images Melville had used as tropes in *Mardi*. The "deep" sea will acquire various emblematic values, as the narrative of *Moby-Dick* progresses; but notice that it here suggests an independence of mental attitude, necessary for any individual, Melville implies, who wishes to exercise "deep" earnest thinking on profound truth. By contrast, "shore" here represents the *illusion* of security which may be derived from adherence to smug and snug dogmatic restrictions of knowledge.

The reference to Bulkington's ultimate fate suggests a second emblematic value for the image of the sea. Ishmael exhorts the Bulkington-like individual to bear himself with Promethean dignity, even though the heroic greatness of refusing to pledge allegiance to servitude and landness will ultimately be rewarded only by death: he will "perish in the howling infinite." Now we begin to get just a glimpse of the complex enrichments which Melville arranges for his emblematic images. In Hebrew mythology, the sea is repeatedly represented as the element of disorder and of chaos: a howling infinite. More than that, the Hebrews doubled their symbolism, by representing disorder and chaos in the shape of that hideous sea monster, Leviathan. Subsequently, in Christian interpretation, some of the church fathers (St. Augustine, for example) insisted that all Biblical references to "Leviathan" were references to Satan. In Protestant thought, particularly in Melville's day, the Leviathan reference in the Forty-first chapter of Job was considered, however, as symbolic of God, and of God's inscrutable power. The complexity of Melville's ambiguous emblematic method is thus suggested by the interlocking relationships among such images as shore, sea, whale. This might seem hopelessly contradictory and confusing for the reader; but the action itself will gradually resolve and clarify the complexities. From his anti-Christian viewpoint, for example, Melville delighted in the possibility of recognizing "sea" as simultaneously an emblem of "chaos"; an emblem of the "infinite" dwelling place of a dualistic God; an emblem of the area most attractive for deep-thinking and adventuresome men. He took further delight in recognizing Leviathan as an ambiguous Satan-God symbol, so that he could thus adapt these two opposed concepts to his own anti-Christian purposes. These values are only hinted, in the Bulkington chapter.

7

STYLISTIC concealments take a more saucy turn, in Chapter Twenty-four: Ishmael speaks as "Devil's Advocate" for the dignity of whaling; emblematically, the dignity of God-hunting. Just one brief excerpt will suffice to illustrate the nature of this sauciness: "The whale has no famous author, and whaling no famous chronicler, you will say. . . . Who wrote the first account of our Leviathan? Who but mighty Job?"[28]

Although that is so innocent as to permit the orthodox Christian reader no chance for offense (so long as such a reader superimposes on the question-and-answer his own biased viewpoint), it actually bristles with insinuations, in this anti-Christian context. If we start with the whale as the name of one of God's creatures, and then say that the whale has no famous author, the word-play insinuation might be either that the Author or Creator of the whale was not God, or that "you" have called God infamous. If the whale now be taken as an emblem of God, and if we now say that the whale has no famous author, the word-play insinuation might be that the whale had no beginning—which is theologically correct. Move on. If whaling is emblematically or allegorically a God-concern, in this context, and if we say that whaling has no famous chronicler, we belittle all theologians. But Melville goes further in his mock-seriousness: where did we get our information about our particular Leviathan? (Notice the sudden capitalization, and remember Melville's remarks to Hawthorne about the "flunkeyism" of such capitalization.) The answer, of course, is that our information comes from the Word of God, or the Bible. But the answer, here, is that the "first account" (by insinuation, the first truly "revealing" account) may be found in the book of Job, where we are shown that God and Satan are actually in collusion with each other; that they plotted together to arrange Job's torture. On the other hand, consider a more restrictive sense of the word "Leviathan": in the book of Job, who actually describes the monster? Did Job actually write his own story? There is no indication of that. Did Job describe the monster, in Chapter Forty-one, and establish the analogy between Leviathan and God? Obviously not. Who did? "Who but mighty"—God! For what purpose? According to later evidence on the subject, in *Moby-Dick*, Melville's view was that God established the analogy in order to taunt Job and to boast of God's own inscrutability. Such an analysis spoils the tantalizing naughtiness of insinuation; but it is necessary if the reader is to be orientated in such a way as to respond to subsequent insinuations and punning and word-play.

8

ATTITUDES—contrasting attitudes—provide Melville with another means of controlling and ordering and illuminating his sinister meaning. Just prior to Captain Ahab's entrance, the stage is formally and emblematically arranged, by presenting Ahab's three officers or mates as types, each representing a distinct attitude toward whaling, and each contrasting with Ahab's central or dominant attitude. Allegorically, of course, each mate's attitude toward whaling suggests his attitude toward God. Consider the attitude of the First Mate, Starbuck, who is represented as a type of the orthodox Christian believer:

". . . Yet, for all his hardy sobriety and fortitude, there were certain qualities in him which at times affected, and in some cases seemed well nigh to *overbalance* [italics added] all the rest. Uncommonly conscientious for a seaman, and endowed with a deep natural reverence, the wild watery loneliness of his life did therefore strongly incline him to superstition; but to that sort of superstition, which in some organisations seems rather to spring, somehow, from intelligence than from ignorance."[29]

The slurring rationalistic insinuation there would seem to be that the reverence of a Christian is mistakenly considered to rest on an intellectual foundation; but that such reverence is, of course, merely a form of "superstition," based on a so-called "revelation" of Truth, in the Bible. (Hobbes and Pierre Bayle had used the word "superstition" in this sense; Montaigne had slyly satirized exactly this so-called Christian pretention in his "Apology for Raimond Sebond," from which Melville quotes in his *Moby-Dick* "Extracts.") Starbuck is the major human antagonist against whom Captain Ahab contends, throughout the narrative, and Captain Ahab gradually overrides or undermines Starbuck's Christian belief until that belief proves futile and unavailing because (Melville insinuates) it is based on a merely superstitious faith as to the all-sustaining power of divinely controlled right reason. From Melville's anti-Christian viewpoint, Starbuck's trouble is that his virtue is of that negative and cloistered variety criticized in different ways by Milton and Montaigne. As already suggested, Ishmael later touches on this very point in a summary passage, which occurs at the end of the chapter entitled, "Moby-Dick": "Here, then, was . . . the incompetence of mere unaided virtue or right-mindedness in Starbuck . . ." In the catastrophe, as Starbuck approaches death, he says, "Is this the end of all my bursting prayers? All my life-long fidelities? Oh, Ahab, Ahab, lo, thy work." In its larger context, Melville implies that Starbuck's tendency to place the blame on Ahab is not quite accurate; that Starbuck's own limitation of vision, his seemingly right-sided or starboard-sided pretention, has caused him to misplace his trust in God; that Starbuck's awakening sense of infidelity finally leads him to say to God, in effect, at the time of his death, "Why hast Thou forsaken me?"

Anticipating the ineffectual and yet pathetic role Starbuck must play, Melville follows his early sketch of Starbuck's attitude with an equivocal and baited-trap exegesis, in which a pretended defense of later developments contains a sarcastic and skeptical probing of divine malice. In the beginning of the passage, the tone is very quietly and subtly sarcastic; in the middle of the passage, Melville protects himself by mingling seriousness with irony, when he touches on innate human dignity; in the latter part of the passage, the tone descends to that of chop-logic burlesque, and the irony becomes caustic as soon as reference is made to tyrannous God as "the centre and circumference of all democracy." (Later, Ishmael and Ahab will insinuate and assert, respectively, that God's chief attribute is not democratic benevolence but tyrannic malevolence.) Here is the passage:

"But were the coming narrative to reveal, in any instance, the complete abasement of poor Starbuck's fortitude, scarce might I have the heart to write it; for it is a thing most sorrowful, nay shocking, to expose the fall of valour in the soul. Men may seem detestable as joint-stock companies and nations; knaves, fools, and murderers there may be; men may have mean and meagre faces; but man, in the ideal, is so noble and so sparkling, such a grand and glowing creature, that over any ignominious blemish in him all his fellows should run to throw their costliest robes. That immaculate manliness we feel within ourselves, so far within us, that it remains intact though all the outer character seem gone;

174

bleeds with keenest anguish at the undraped spectacle of a valour-ruined man. *Nor can piety itself, at such a shameful sight, completely stifle her upbraidings against the permitting stars!* [Italics added] But this august dignity I treat of, is not the dignity of kings and robes, but that abounding dignity which has no robed investiture. Thou shalt see it shining in the arm that wields a pick or drives a spike; that democratic dignity which, on all hands, radiates without end from God; Himself! The great God absolute! The centre and circumference of all democracy! His omnipresence, our divine equality."[30]

The sentence which I have italicized is the pivotal sentence, because both Ishmael and Captain Ahab share the conviction that the malice of God converts each valorous man into a ruined man, and Captain Ahab upbraids the permitting stars in no uncertain language, during his Lear-like storm scene, in "The Candles" chapter. The chop logic of the final sentences is an additional giveaway as to tone. If God is "absolute," then such absolute presence should make mortal man conscious of his own mortal inequality, not of his "divine equality."

The development of concepts, in that paragraph, is extended in the paragraph which follows. Significantly, Ishmael establishes an implied antithesis between the character of the First Mate, Starbuck, and the character of Captain Ahab; between the believer and the blasphemer; between the accepter and the defier. Ishmael does this by pretending to make a devout invocation and apostrophe to God Almighty, and further pretends to praise God for endowing man with exactly those attributes which (according to Melville's already quoted remarks to Hawthorne) man does not owe to God but to his own assertiveness as a sovereign power; as a creative and energetic being in his own right. Properly understood, then, the continuation is again couched in an equivocal but caustically sarcastic tone, with an effect which the Christian reader *should* recognize as both heretical and blasphemous:

"If, then, to meanest mariners, and renegades and castaways, I shall hereafter ascribe high qualities, though dark; weave round them tragic graces; if even the most mournful, perchance the most abased among them all, shall at times lift himself to the exalted mounts; if I shall touch that workman's arm with some ethereal light; if I shall spread a rainbow over his disastrous set of sun;

then against all mortal critics bear me out in it, thou just Spirit of Equality, which hast spread one royal mantle of humanity over all my kind! Bear me out in it, thou great democratic God! who didst not refuse to the swart convict, Bunyan, the pale poetic pearl; Thou who didst clothe with doubly hammered leaves of finest gold, the stumped and paupered arm of old Cervantes; Thou who didst pick up Andrew Jackson from the pebbles; who didst hurl him upon a war-horse; who didst thunder him higher than a throne! Thou who, in all Thy mighty, earthly marchings, ever cullest Thy selectest champions from the kingly commons; bear me out in it, O God!"[31]

Turn we now to the attitude of the Second Mate, Stubb, who shows a stupid, mechanical indifference to the whale, either in a specific sense or in an emblematic sense. His religion has degenerated into happy-go-lucky fatalism, "taking perils as they came with an indifferent air." He takes orders similarly. What is Stubb's attitude toward death itself?

"Long usage had, for this Stubb, converted the jaws of death into an *easy chair* [italics added; cf. "easy chair" in *The Confidence-Man*]. What he thought of death itself, there is no telling; but, if he ever did chance to cast his mind that way after a comfortable dinner, no doubt, like a good sailor, he took it to be a sort of call of the watch to tumble aloft, and bestir themselves there, about something which he would find out when he obeyed the order, and not sooner."[32]

Specifically, whaling and death are closely related; allegorically, thoughts of God and thoughts of death are closely related. How does Stubb manage to be so unthinking and casual about such an important subject? It would seem from his emblematic name that tobacco has something to do with it: he maintains his equilibrium with the aid of this opiate or narcotic. "He kept a whole row of pipes there ready-loaded, stuck in a rack, within easy reach of his hand; and, whenever he turned in, he smoked them all out in succession, loading them again to be in readiness anew." In *Mardi* (also in *The Confidence-Man* and in *Billy Budd*), Melville suggests that the Christian religion is a kind of narcotic which permits the habitual user to drug himself into relaxation. In the light of Stubb's attitude toward death, it is possible to view him, allegorically, as an habitual user of religion until his senses have become so dulled that while he is vaguely aware of a Superior, who may some day call him "aloft," he is not much interested in the subject of either the call or the Caller. Stubb sums up his religious belief this way: "Think not, is my eleventh commandment, and sleep when you can, is my twelfth."

The attitude of the Third Mate, Flask, is an equally belittling attitude, but for atheistical reasons. Once the sinister allegorical frame of reference is clear, it becomes apparent that Flask's atheistical attitude is by no means complimentary to God: "[He] . . . somehow seemed to think that the great leviathans had personally and hereditarily affronted him; and therefore it was a sort of point of honour with him, to destroy them whenever encountered. *So utterly lost was he to all sense of reverence for the many marvels of their majestic bulk and mystic ways* [italics added]; and so dead to anything like an apprehension of any possible danger from encountering them; that in his poor opinion, the wondrous whale was but a species of magnificent mouse, or at least water-rat. . . ."[33]

These distinct attitudes of the three mates are further interlocked, emblematically, when each chooses a harpooner who somehow reflects his own attitude. Starbuck chooses the only religious harpooner, Queequeg; Stubb chooses the fatalistic American Indian named Tashtego; Flask chooses a negro named Daggoo, born in Africa and retaining "all his barbaric virtues." In permitting this threefold grouping of pairs to represent, in a sort of synecdoche, the entire ship's company aboard the *Pequod*, Ishmael concludes with further word-play in his generalizing:

"How it is, there is no telling, but Islanders seem to make the best whalemen. They were nearly all Islanders in the *Pequod*, 'Isolatoes' too, 'I call such, not acknowledging the common continent of men, but each Isolato living on a separate continent of his own. Yet now, federated along one keel, what a set these Isolatoes were! An Anacharsis Clootz deputation from all the isles of the sea, and all the ends of the earth, accompanying Old Ahab in the *Pequod* to lay the world's grievances before that bar from which not very many of them ever come back."[34]

The analogy, probably borrowed from Carlyle's *French Revolution*, has further dark insinuations, which heighten the death motif: that judicial bar before which Ahab and his crew will allegorically "lay the world's grievances" will award all of them—even the pious Starbuck—with the injustice of death. All except one, who is of course that Job's-messenger, that outcast, that isolato, that orphan, Ishmael.

9

Wʜᴇɴ Ahab finally appears, silently pacing the deck, Ishmael is fascinated by "the scar left by some desperate wound," so clearly visible on his face and neck. Ishmael, not yet knowing its source, listens to the scuttlebutt. One sailor, "a gray Manxman" seemingly endowed "with preternatural powers of discernment," is said to have "insinuated" that the scar is a birthmark. Darkly considered, this implies that the mark was a malicious gift from God at birth, even as Billy Budd's birthmark was, allegorically considered, a malicious gift from God. But Tashtego's father has "superstitiously" asserted that Ahab was "that way branded . . . not in the fury of any mortal fray, but in an elemental strife at sea." In the deeper allegorical sense, then, these two theories coincide: according to each theory, the scar is a gift from God. In closing his sermon, Father Mapple had begun his prayer, "O Father!—chiefly known to me by Thy rod . . ." Ishmael uses the same word, rod, in describing Ahab's scar:

"He looked like a man cut away from the stake, when the fire had overrunningly wasted all the limbs without consuming them. . . . Threading its way out from among his gray hairs, and continuing right down one side of his tawny scorched face and neck, till it disappeared in his clothing, you saw a slender rod-like mark, lividly whitish. It resembled that perpendicular seam sometimes made in the straight, lofty trunk of a great tree, when the upper lightning tearingly darts down it. . . ."[35]

The whiteness of the lightning scar is immediately correlated with the whiteness of Ahab's ivory leg, emblematic of his other gruesome wound. Again, on the sinister level of meaning, this second wound and scar may be recognized as God's second gift to Ahab. So the "moody stricken Ahab stood before them with a crucifixion in his face; in all the nameless regal overbearing dignity of some mighty woe."[36]

Here, obviously, is that type of self-pitying and proudly tragic hero which was the darling of the romantics. Distinct as he is, Captain Ahab brings to mind many of Byron's heroes: for example, Manfred, on whose brow "the thunder-scars are graven" and from whose eye "glares forth the immortality of hell." Or, if one recalls the many romantic representations of Prometheus (by contrast, even Aeschylus's Prometheus who said, "I suffer from the gods, myself a god"), one may again turn to Byron and his poem entitled *Prometheus* to appreciate Captain Ahab's literary ancestry. Even as Byron so obviously intended to glorify the tragic attitude of Prometheanism, so Melville intended to glorify his Promethean-Satanic Ahab. Byron admired and paraphrased Milton's first description of Satan, which is not unlike Melville's first description of Ahab :

> . . . dark'n'd so, yet shone
> Above them all th' Arch Angel: but his face
> Deep scars of Thunder had intrencht, and care
> Sat on his faded cheek, but under Brows
> Of dauntless courage, and considerate Pride
> Waiting revenge . . .[37]

10

MELVILLE again illuminates his dark meaning with the conventional dream device of satire and allegory, in Chapter Thirty-one, entitled "Queen Mab." Captain Ahab talks little enough, during his early appearances on deck; but Stubb accidentally runs afoul of him on one occasion, and is severely dressed down, in language and allusions which baffle Stubb. That night he is troubled by a nightmarish dream which he asks Flask to interpret for him.

A superficial reading of this dream chapter might not suggest any significance in the title other than a reference to something like Mercutio's familiar utterance on dreams. A more careful reading, and an interpretation of Stubb's dream in terms of Melville's darker concepts, brings the early Shelley to mind. Three sentences from Shelley's anti-Christian notes to *Queen Mab* may help to show why Melville may have felt a sense of kinship:

"But the doctrine of Necessity teaches us that in no case could any event have happened otherwise than it did happen, and that, if God is the author of good, he is also the author of evil; that, if he is entitled to our gratitude for the one, he is entitled to our hatred for the other. . . . It is plain that the same arguments which prove that God is the author of food, light, and life, prove him also to be the author of poison, darkness, and death. . . . God made man such as he is, and then damned him for being so; for to say that God was the author of all good, and man the author of all evil, is to say that one man made a straight line and a crooked one, and another man made the incongruity."[38]

With this brief preparation, Stubb's dream may be understood as another Melvillian thrust at the Christian doctrine of acceptance, which Father Mapple, by contrast, had so attractively defended. There are three (Melville delighted to play with the mystical number three) dominant images or "characters" whom Stubb confronts in his dream: Captain Ahab, a Pyramid, and a "merman with a hump on his back." The hump makes the latter appear to be very like a whale, and indeed very like a sperm whale. Obviously, these three "characters" are three protean emblems of the same phenomenon—or, metaphorically and metaphysically, the same noumenon. Here is Stubb's dream:

" 'Such a queer dream, King-Post, I never had. You know the old man's ivory leg, well I dreamed he kicked me with it; and when I tried to kick back, upon my soul, my little man, I kicked my leg right off! And then, presto! Ahab seemed a pyramid, and I, like a blazing fool, kept kicking at it. But what was still more curious, Flask—you know how curious all dreams are—through all this rage that I was in, I somehow seemed to be thinking to myself, that after all, it was not much of an insult, that kick from Ahab. "Why," thinks I, "what's the row? It's not a real leg, only a false leg." . . . But now comes the greatest joke of the dream, Flask. While I was battering away at the pyramid a sort of badger-haired old merman, with a hump on his back, takes me by the shoulders, and slews me round. "What are you 'bout?" says he. Slid! man, but I was frightened. Such a phiz! But somehow, next moment I was over the fright. "What am I about?" says I at last. "And what business is that of yours, I should like to know, Mr. Humpback? Do *you* want a kick?" By the lord, Flask, I had no sooner said that, than he turned round his stern to me, bent over, and dragging up a lot of seaweed he had for a clout—what do you

180

think I saw?—why thunder alive, man, his stern was stuck full of marling-spikes, with the points out. Says I, on second thought, "I guess I won't kick you old fellow." "Wise Stubb," said he, "wise Stubb"; and kept muttering it all the time . . . I thought I might as well fall to kicking the pyramid again. But I had only just lifted my foot for it, when he roared out, "Stop that kicking!" "Halloa," says I, "what's the matter now, old fellow?" "Look ye here," says he; "let's argue the insult. Captain Ahab kicked ye, didn't he?" "Yes, he did," says I—"right *here* it was." "Very good," says he—"he used his ivory leg, didn't he?" "Yes, he did," says I. "Well then," says he, "wise Stubb, what have you to complain of? Didn't he kick with right goodwill? it wasn't a common pitch-pine leg he kicked with, was it? No, you were kicked by a great man, and with a beautiful ivory leg, Stubb. It's an honour; I consider it an honour. . . . Remember what I say; *be* kicked by him; account his kicks honours; and on no account kick back; for you can't help yourself, wise Stubb. Don't you see that pyramid?" . . . Now, what do you think of that dream, Flask?'

" 'I don't know; it seems a sort of foolish to me, though.'

" 'Maybe; maybe. But it's made a wise man of me, Flask. D'ye see Ahab standing there, sideways looking over the stern? Well, the best thing you can do, Flask, is to let that old man alone; never speak to him, whatever he says.' "[39]

How should the dream be interpreted, in terms of Melville's darker context? Is it enough to see in it a warning to leave Captain Ahab alone, as Stubb says? Melville's symbology enables us to establish values for the three central images or characters, because he has already stressed his desire to let the *Pequod* serve as a microcosm or emblem of the world, and the world a ship on its voyage home. Then Ahab, as Captain of this microcosm briefly becomes (emblematically and ironically) a representation of absolute power, or of God. The pyramid is used by Melville in one of his poems as a symbol of God. Also, the Great Seal of the United States (reproduced on a one-dollar bill) uses a Masonic pyramid as a mystical emblem, and the pyramid is there truncated, with the Eye of God serving as its apex: another representation of absolute power, or of God. To establish a correlation of the whale-suggesting humped merman with these first two emblems of absolute power, or of God, we could use the gloss supplied by many later insinuations, this one perhaps being sufficient: "I should call this high hump the organ of firmness or *indomitable-ness* [italics added; cf. *Billy Budd*] in the sperm whale. And that the great monster is *indomitable* [italics added], you will yet have reason to know."[40]

Why does Stubb decide not to kick against the pricks, as the Biblical phrase puts it? Because it is not expedient, not practical, not advantageous. Perhaps tyranny is involved, but of course it is benevolent tyranny, says the merman to Stubb. Superficially, a reader might conclude that Melville is here siding with Father Mapple by presenting a dream which reinforces the Christian doctrine of acceptance; but more deeply and darkly, the entire situation in this "Queen Mab" dream burlesques and ridicules that same expedient doctrine of acceptance.

11

AFTER playing with occult theological satire in Stubb's dream, Ishmael might be expected to get on with the central narrative; but his delight in allegorical triple-talk leads to a further allegorical digression on comparative religions in the next chapter, entitled "Cetology." This time, the rules of the game suggest a quaint word-play reasoning which may be stated thus: Job's whale in the Bible is an emblem of God; Jonah's whale in the Bible is an agent of God; Captain Ahab's White Whale is somehow related to God—either principal or agent. It does not require too great a stretch of the reasoning faculties, then, to perceive that the study of cetology might be considered—just for the heaven of it—as either a study of theology, or mythology. With Melville's naughty pleasantry in mind, behold the ironic and sardonic delight with which Ishmael embarks on the subject of cetology-theology-mythology:

"Already we are boldly launched upon the deep; but soon we shall be lost in its unshored, harborless immensities. Ere that come to pass; ere the *Pequod's* weedy hull rolls side by side with the barnacled hulls of the leviathan; at the outset it is but well to attend to a matter almost indispensable to a thorough appreciative understanding of the more special leviathanic revelations and allusions of all sorts which are to follow.

182

"It is some systematized exhibition of the whale in his broad genera, that I would now fain put before you. Yet is it no easy task. The classification of the *constituents of a chaos* [italics added; cf. Hebraic and Babylonian mythology], nothing less is here essayed. Listen to what the best and latest authorities have laid down.

" 'No branch of Zoology is so much involved as that which is entitled Cetology' . . .

" 'It is not my intention, were it in my power, to enter into the inquiry as to the true method of dividing the cetacea into groups and families. * * * Utter confusion exists among the historians of this animal.' . . .

" 'Unfitness to pursue our research in the unfathomable waters.' 'Impenetrable veil covering our knowledge of the cetacea.' 'A field strewn with thorns.' 'All these incomplete indications but serve to torture us naturalists.'

" . . . Many are the men, small and great, old and new, landsmen and seamen, who have at large or in little, written of the whale. Run over a few:—The Authors of the Bible . . . and the Rev. T. Cheever. But to what ultimate generalizing purpose all these have written, the above-cited extracts will show. . . .

"My object here is simply to project the draught of a systematization of cetology. I am the architect, not the builder. But it is a ponderous task . . . To grope down into the bottom of the sea after them; to have one's hands among the *unspeakable* [italics added] foundations, ribs, and very pelvis of the world; this is a fearful thing. What am I that I should essay to hook the nose of this leviathan. *The awful tauntings in Job might well appal me* [italics added]. 'Will he (the leviathan) make a covenant with thee? Behold the hope of him is vain!' "[41]

Then Ishmael would fain get down to the beginning of beginnings, by pretending to wonder whether the basic classification should list the whale as mammal or fish! This problem seems to puzzle Ishmael, who finds himself torn between science and religion; between the word of Linnaeus and the Word of God in the Holy Bible. At last he pretends to make up his mind: "Be it known that, waiving all argument, I take the good old-fashioned ground that the whale is a fish, and call upon holy Jonah to back me. This fundamental thing settled . . ."[42]

183

That suggests (among others) that the Jonah story is a fish story. Melville is obviously enjoying himself, but the reader is likely to get bored, even though Melville enlivens his theological triple-talk with deliberate off-color jests and puns.[43]

12

ONLY when Captain Ahab nails the Spanish doubloon to the masthead and puts his crew through his own catechism, does the tension of the central narrative emerge—in Chapter Thirty-six. Then Ahab confesses: "And this is what ye have shipped for, men! to chase that white whale on both sides of land, and over all sides of earth, till he spouts black blood and rolls fin out." Appropriately, the First Mate Starbuck immediately protests, "I came here to hunt whales, not my commander's vengeance." Forced to show Starbuck "the little lower layer" of meaning, Ahab concludes, ". . . my vengeance will fetch a great premium *here*," as he smites his heart. Then comes another foundation stone, a passage in which the sinister meaning rises to the surface, as Starbuck accuses Ahab of both "blasphemy" and "madness," and as Ahab defines the precise nature of his "madness." Melville here represents Ahab's "madness" as that tragic wisdom which "enlightened" man evolves from accurate perception of "usable truth." In contrast, Starbuck is blinded by convention and dogma:

" 'Vengeance on a dumb brute!' cried Starbuck, 'that simply smote thee from blindest instinct! Madness! To be enraged with a dumb thing [i.e., one of God's creatures], Captain Ahab, seems blasphemous.'

" 'Hark ye yet again,—the little lower layer. All visible objects, man, are but as pasteboard masks. But in each event—in the living act, the undoubted deed—there, some unknown but still reasoning thing puts forth the mouldings of its features from behind the unreasoning mask. If man will strike, strike through the mask! How can the prisoner reach outside except by thrusting through the wall? To me, the White Whale is that wall, shoved near to me. Sometimes I think there's naught beyond. But 'tis enough. He tasks me; he heaps me; I see in him outrageous strength, with an inscrutable malice sinewing it. That inscrutable thing is chiefly what I hate; and be the White Whale agent, or be the White Whale principal, I will wreak that hate upon him. Talk not to me of blasphemy, man; I'd strike the sun if it insulted me. For could the sun do that, then could I do the other; since there is ever a sort of fair play herein, jealously presiding over all creations. But not my master, man, is even that fair play. Who's over me? Truth hath no confines. Take off thine eye! more intolerable than fiends' glarings is a doltish stare. So, so. . . . (*Aside*) Something shot from my dilated nostrils, he has inhaled it in his lungs. Starbuck now is mine; cannot oppose me now, without rebellion.'

" 'God keep me!—keep us all!' murmured Starbuck, lowly."[44]

As Peleg said to Ishmael, before the voyage started, "Ahab's above the common; Ahab's been in colleges, as well as 'mong cannibals; been used to deeper wonders than the waves; fixed his fiery lance in mightier, stranger foes than whales." So now the reader recognizes that Ahab employs the abstract terms of religion and philosophy: ". . . and be the White Whale agent or be the White Whale principal, I will wreak that hate upon him." In the context, "principal" refers to that First Cause which is God. Be the White Whale an agent of God, or be the White Whale God incarnate, Ahab will strike back. "Talk not to me of blasphemy, man; I'd strike the sun if it insulted me."

Frequently, in scholarly interpretations of Melville, we are informed that the white whale is an emblem of evil, and that Melville is merely preoccupied with evil. This misses the most important point, because it implies that Melville differentiates between the source of evil and the source of good. As already reiterated, Ahab's story dramatizes the conviction Melville shared with the young Shelley of *Queen Mab*: God is evil; more evil than He is good. As Ahab says, "I see in him outrageous strength, with an inscrutable malice sinewing it."

Immediately following this scene, Ahab performs a ceremony of consecration, with the crew and officers: an inverted Communion Service, and in this sense a sort of black mass, in which all bind themselves to Ahab's blasphemous purpose: ". . . drink and swear, ye men . . . Death to Moby-Dick! God hunt us all, if we do not hunt Moby-Dick to his death!"

13

AT some moment, in reading *Moby-Dick*, the careful reader may recall, and return to, the preliminary and prefatory considerations of the word "whale" which Melville prefixed to his narrative: the "Etymology" of the word, and "Extracts" showing the word in various contexts. In the beginning was the word, and Melville neatly lifts his first extract from Genesis: "And God created great whales." As though to hint at further correlation, he lifts his second extract from Job:

> Leviathan maketh a path to shine after him;
> One would think the deep to be hoary.

One advantage of setting up that passage as poetry, following Melville, is that it permits the reader to suspect a play on the word "hoary," in which case the insinuation might be that Leviathan is acting like a prostitute on the make; an interpretation given subsequent support in the "Whiteness of the Whale" chapter. The third extract, which completes the triangulation, is from Jonah: "Now the Lord had prepared a great fish to swallow up Jonah." Again we have just the hint that in *Moby-Dick* the reader may be forgiven for viewing Father Mapple's sermon as a fish story; a hint even more strongly substantiated in Chapter Eighty-three, entitled "Jonah Historically Regarded." Like so many others who prided themselves on their enlightened rationalism (Pierre Bayle, for example), Melville took particular pleasure in spoofing the Calvinistic insistence on a literal reading of the miracle stories in the Bible.

Melville's fourth quotation, in his "Extracts," amounts to another sinister commentary on a Bible passage, when placed in the larger context of *Moby-Dick*. He quotes Isaiah 27:1: "In that day, the Lord with his sore, and great, and strong sword, shall punish Leviathan the piercing serpent, even Leviathan that crooked serpent; and he shall slay the dragon that is in the sea." Reference has already been made to the Hebrew usage of the sea as an emblem of chaos, and of Leviathan as a personification of that chaos; to the subsequent Christian interpretation of Leviathan, in such a passage, as a reference to Satan. Melville here would seem to avail himself of the opportunity to combine his interpretation of Job Forty-one with the orthodox interpretation of Isaiah Twenty-seven, so that Leviathan might serve as an emblem of both God and Satan, the two being not merely coeternal, as the Manicheans taught, but one in source, according to Melville's dark exegesis, possibly inspired by Melville's misinterpretation of Pierre Bayle.

Anyone can play this game of recognizing the possibilities Melville may have had in mind, when he chose these insinuative "Extracts" concerning this monstrous emblem of a malicious God. I shall limit myself to only one more, quoted from Montaigne's "Apology for Raimond Sebond": "And whereas all the other things, whether beast or vessel, that enter into the dreadful gulf of the monster's (whale's) mouth, are immediately lost and swallowed up, the sea-gudgeon retires into it in great security, and there sleeps."

If we gloss the first part of Montaigne's sentence, by considering the interchange of "whale" and "God," the meaning might be that death is the fate meted out by God to most beings. So far, that would be in accord with Melville's obsession. The second part of that sentence establishes one exception, however: a certain category of beings would seem to be able to "retire" into the mouth of God, "in great security, and there sleep." Indeed that might be recognized as a quaint representation of the Christian concept: if we have faith in God, our death is but a sleep and a forgetting. Now carry the gloss one step further. What is Montaigne's name for this category of beings? "Sea-gudgeon." Two dictionary definitions are available for "gudgeon": a stupid fish; a person easily duped. Melville would have liked particularly to find that one in Montaigne.

The "Etymology" of the word "Whale" which Melville presents on a preliminary page becomes much more entertaining when the whale-God interchange is carried over. Some Biblical commentaries, even some Bibles, carry a similar page which summarizes the etymology of the word "God," and gives the form as it occurs in different languages, starting always with the Hebrew Tetragrammaton, JHVH. Melville's play-on-words Tetragrammaton, in his etymology, is HVAL, and the initial passage which provides a brief commentary from Hakluyt would more pertinently apply to JHVH: "While you take in hand to school others, and to teach them by what name a whale-fish is to be called in our tongue, leaving out, through ignorance, the letter H, which almost alone maketh up the significance of the word, you deliver that which is not true." In his *Dictionary*, Pierre Bayle told how a Dutch professor named Altin was attacked because he said that "the true pronunciation" of the Tetragrammaton "is not known," and that the Christians had created a false word, "Jehovah," through their ignorant misunderstanding of a certain Hebrew ritual of pronunciation which need not be explained here. Melville would have been familiar with that story, and his quotation from Hakluyt may be a very esoteric allusion to the ignorant misunderstandings of Christians concerning God. I mention this as an example of the many different kinds of esoteric and satirical jokes which Melville seems to have enjoyed making, again and again, throughout *Moby-Dick*. Frequently, the joke is too private for us to get; but the total joke quality of both the "Etymology" and the "Extracts" is apparently sarcastic and satirical, and is closely related to the satirical tauntings throughout the total narrative.

By extension, one may view Melville's entire artistic contrivance, in *Moby-Dick*, as his own esoteric and Cabalistic commentary on the word "God" or on "The Word of God" or on the Bible. In this highly speculative connection, it is worth remembering that Melville seems to have planned, originally, to entitle his narrative *The Whale*; that he actually did use that title for the English edition. Following the so-called "enlightened" rationalistic tradition (as represented, for example, by Tom Paine's *Age of Reason; Being an Investigation of True and Fabulous Theology*), one might suspect Melville of seeing in that English title, "The Whale, by Herman Melville," the insinuative and satirical paraphrase made possible by his basic emblem: "The Word of God, as Interpreted by Herman Melville."

14

IMMEDIATELY after the unholy communion ritual on the quarter-deck of the *Pequod*, Melville resorts to the dramatic form, in order to present a soliloquy, uttered by Captain Ahab; then he adds soliloquies by Starbuck and Stubb; then further adds a dramatic scene in which the various attitudes of the crew are represented. This preoccupation with "attitudes" would not be complete without the inclusion of Ishmael's and indeed the next two chapters are devoted to Ishmael's attitude, which reaches its climactic utterance in his observations on "the whiteness of the whale"—another major foundation stone.

There is a striking parallel between Ahab's "mad" soliloquy and one "mad" soliloquy of Milton's Satan in *Paradise Lost*, as Satan stands alone, viewing the Garden of Eden. It is worth while to place parts of these two "mad" soliloquies side by side. Ahab:

". . . Oh! time was, when as the sunrise nobly spurred, so the sunset soothed. No more. This lovely light, it lights not me; all loveliness is anguish to me, since I can ne'er enjoy. Gifted with the high perception, I lack the low, enjoying power; damned, most subtly and most malignantly! damned in the midst of Paradise! . . .

". . . What I've dared, I've willed; and what I've willed, I'll do! They think me mad—Starbuck does; but I'm demoniac, I am madness maddened! That wild madness that's only calm to comprehend itself! The prophecy was that I should be dismembered; and—Ay! I lost this leg. I now prophesy that I will dismember my dismemberer. Now, then, be the prophet and the fulfiller one. That's more than ye, ye great gods, ever were. . . ."[45]

Compare those words of Ahab with these of Milton's Satan:

> O Earth, how like the Heav'n, if not preferred . . .
> Terrestrial Heav'n, danc't round by other Heav'ns
> That shine, yet bear their bright officious Lamps,
> Light above Light, for thee alone. . . .
>   . . . and the more I see
> Pleasures about me, so much more I feel
> Torment within me, as from the hateful siege
> Of contraries; all good to me becomes
> Bane, and in Heav'n much worse would be my state.
> But neither here seek I, no nor in Heav'n
> To dwell, unless by mastring Heav'n's Supreme;
> Nor hope to be myself less miserable
> By what I seek, but others to make such
> As I, though thereby worse to me redound:
> For only in destroying I find ease
> To my relentless thoughts . . .[46]

Ahab's vow to "dismember my dismemberer" (perhaps a word-play inversion of "Remember now thy Creator") also finds a striking parallel in Satan's remarks as he jealously watches Adam and Eve for the first time and (while plotting his revenge against God) speaks unheard to them:

> Accept your Maker's work; he gave it me,
> Which I as freely give.[47]

Ahab's vow to dismember his dismemberer needs further exegesis. In this sinister allegorical framework, this sardonic promise to treat God even as God has treated Ahab amounts to another Melvillian burlesque of the Golden Rule. By means of Ahab's blasphemous vow, Melville might be said to have found his own scornful way of correlating an old offertory refrain ("All things come of thee, oh Lord, and of thine own have we given thee") with Satan's sneering reference in *Paradise Lost*: "He gave it me, which I as freely give."

Ahab's vengeful cruise suggests, then, an allegorical attempt to pay God back in his own cruel terms, and Christian Starbuck is the first to recognize the deeper meanings of this particular whale hunt. At the time Ahab informed the crew of his purpose, it will be remembered, Starbuck had cried, "Madness!" and "blasphemous." In soliloquy, afterwards, Starbuck first says, "My soul is more than matched; she's overmanned; and by a madman!" Then, "I think I see his impious end." Being a forgiving and charitable Christian, however, he can hope that "God may wedge aside" Ahab's "Heaven-insulting purpose." The finest of Starbuck's observations again takes us directly back to this ironic analogy between Ahab and God:

"Horrible old man! Who's over him, he cries;—ay, he would be a democrat to all above; look, how he lords it over all below! Oh! I plainly see my miserable office—to obey, rebelling. . . ."[48]

The hasty reader may feel that he has immediately exhausted the meanings suggested by that comment; but the contemplative reader will linger over it. Starbuck is certainly correct in noticing the ironic inconsistency of Ahab's resenting the tyranny of God, when Ahab rules his own ship's company with God-like tyranny. But Starbuck misses "the little lower layer" of meaning here. If, according to Christian doctrine, Ahab should remember his Creator by imitating Him, and by trying to be as God-like as is humanly possible, and if Ahab's God-given "high perception" has enabled him to perceive that God is tyrannical, then isn't Ahab morally obligated to be humanly tyrannical? Indeed, Melville sarcastically insinuates, isn't such pattern of conduct a form of worship, even though bitter? Later, Ahab will say, "Defyingly, I worship thee!"

Starbuck's remark rewards further lingering, if a close construction is placed on his comment as to his own relation to Ahab. He sees quite plainly that his miserable office as First Mate is "to obey, rebelling," but he does not see what happens to that concept when it reaches the lower allegorical "layer" (to use Ahab's word). Melville has already suggested these allegorical values: even as God is Captain of the World, and therewith the maker of inexorable laws and orders, so Ahab is Captain of the *Pequod*, and therewith the maker of laws and orders which are inexorable for his officers and men. Now what happens, allegorically, when Starbuck sees that he must obey, rebelling? As a man thinketh in his heart, so is he. In a symbolic sense, Starbuck goes through the motions of obeying God's commands, while actually rebelling against God's commands! This brings us, very subtly and obliquely, to another view of Melville's darkly symbolic argument: any human being who perceives the "usable truth" cannot help but rebel, in his heart, against that ordering of the Universe which is represented in Christian doctrine. How fine, for Melville, to let pious Starbuck (as well as Ahab) dramatize and illuminate this "unspeakable" thought.

15

ATTITUDES, and the structural grouping of attitudes, continue to hold the reader's attention until the climactic capping of them all with Ishmael's. He acknowledges, in Chapter Forty-one, that his own response to Captain Ahab's announcement has been a bitterly joyful one; that Ahab has somehow crystallized his own vague and somewhat cowardly feelings; that there is a major impingement between Ahab's view and his own:

"I, Ishmael, was one of that crew; my shouts had gone up with the rest; my oath had been welded with theirs; and stronger I shouted and more did I hammer and clinch my oath, because of the dread in my soul. A wild, mystical, sympathetic feeling was in me; Ahab's quenchless feud seemed mine."[49]

That word "seemed" is protective; but the larger context translates it to "was." At this point in the story, Ishmael gives the reader the background history of the White Whale's characteristics, performances, depredations; then of Captain Ahab's tragic encounter. Technically, the narrative is now swift and deep enough to float a large body of allegorical material. Just a few passages will illustrate the overtness of these allegorical insinuations at this point; particularly the further corroboration of the fact that the White Whale is an allegorical emblem of God:

"One of the wild suggestings referred to, as at last coming to be linked with the White Whale in the minds of the *superstitiously* [italics added] inclined, was the unearthly conceit that Moby-Dick was ubiquitous; that he had actually been encountered in opposite latitudes at one and the same time. . . . it cannot be much matter of surprise that some whalemen should go still further in their *superstitions* [italics added]; declaring Moby-Dick not only ubiquitous, but immortal (for immortality is but ubiquity in time)."[50]

Melville's word-play vocabulary becomes more and more familiar to the careful reader; specifically, here, the words "superstitiously" and "superstitions" are again endowed with Melville's anti-Christian meaning: a "superstitious" person is a person who believes in the essential tenets of Christian doctrine. Allegorically, the passage just quoted ridicules the Christian concept of God by representing Him as a monstrous being which is "ubiquitous" and "immortal." Continuing, Ishmael tucks in certain death allusions as he describes Ahab's encounter: his leg was "reaped" by the White Whale's "sickle-shaped lower jaw." These suggest the conventional emblem of death, previously used by Ishmael. Then comes Ishmael's cautious description of how Captain Ahab made a scapegoat of the White Whale, until it became a symbol of duality in God: of God's mixed good-and-evil; but particularly of God's malice:

"Small reason was there to doubt, then, that ever since that almost fatal encounter, Ahab had cherished a wild vindictiveness against the whale, all the more felt for that in his frantic morbidness he at last came to identify with him, not only all his bodily woes, but all his intellectual and spiritual exasperations. The White Whale swam before him as the monomaniac incarnation of all those malicious agencies which some deep men feel eating in them. . . . That intangible malignity which has been from the beginning; to whose dominion even the modern Christians ascribe one-half of the worlds; which the ancient *Ophites of the East* [italics added; note well] reverenced in their statue devil;—Ahab did not fall down and worship it like them; but deliriously transferring its idea to the abhorred White Whale, he pitted himself, all mutilated against it. All that most maddens and torments; all that stirs up the lees of things; all truth with malice in it; all that cracks the sinews and cakes the brain; all the subtle demonisms of life and thought; all evil, to crazy Ahab, were visibly personified, and made practically assailable in Moby-Dick."[51]

Several interpreters have mistakenly lifted from its controlling context the phrase, "all evil, to crazy Ahab, were visibly personified, and made practically assailable in Moby-Dick." By quoting that fragmentary phrase, these interpreters have insisted that Melville made the White Whale a mere emblem of evil. Such an interpretation is too restrictive. To be sure, Melville's hoodwinking and deception has to be watched, because it grows more and more crafty, as *Moby-Dick* unfolds. On the same page with the phrase quoted above, Ishmael observes, "Human madness is oftentimes a cunning and most feline thing. When you think it fled, it may have but become transfigured into some still subtler form. Ahab's full lunacy subsided not, but deepeningly contracted . . ." That observation is a valuable guide to Melville's (and Ishmael's) stylistic method.

Even here, for example, as Ishmael speaks with relative overtness, Melville carefully protects himself from his enemies by making Ishmael seem to be talking about his own merely temporary identification of his thoughts with Ahab's thoughts: "For one, I gave myself up to the abandonment of the time and the place; but while yet all a-rush to encounter the whale, could see naught in that brute but the deadliest ill." Immediately, however, Ishmael devotes several pages to an exegesis on what he means by his use of the term, "deadliest ill," and those pages form the celebrated chapter entitled, "The Whiteness of the Whale."

In discussing the chapter on "The Whiteness of the Whale," interpreters frequently point to Melville's "ambiguity" as a proof of his own inner fluctuations and uncertainties and perplexities.

193

They argue that Melville permits Ishmael to develop so many possible meanings for the "whiteness" of the whale that there is no way of deciding whether Melville favored one meaning more than he favored another. I would certainly agree that Melville retained considerable uncertainty, and that he actually found it excruciatingly painful to feel that he was forced to part with all of his earlier, deeply-ingrained religious beliefs; nevertheless, the tide of his thinking, in *Moby-Dick*, is running strongly against that wistfulness, and the misanthropic current of that tide will flow even more strongly as Melville continues to reflect his increasingly pessimistic attitude, in his later works. Already, in the chapter on "The Whiteness of the Whale," the ambiguities and equivocations should be recognized not so much as proofs of Melville's uncertain viewpoint but rather as stylistic devices for deceptively masking Melville's own dark and heretical convictions. From first to last, the extraordinary rhetoric of that chapter is contrived to cause trouble for the careless or superficial reader. For example, the very first paragraph contains a prodigious sentence, approximately 470 words long, which establishes the basic antithesis between the benevolent and malevolent associations of "whiteness." If that long catalogue-sentence seems to keep the antithetical values in nice balance, it should be quite apparent that the remainder of the chapter is so contrived as to shift the balance progressively further away from the benevolent aspects of white and progressively nearer to the malevolent aspects of white. The ulterior meaning of the entire chapter is this: ironically, "whiteness" would seem to represent benevolence and goodness; but the "thinking" observer, the "enlightened" observer, discovers that both man and God use "whiteness" as a mask, and with the aid of this prostitute-disguise, man and God manage to inflict on mankind an endless variety of malevolence or evil. For Melville, this is the ugliest aspect of the hateful siege of contraries. To demonstrate the direction of that chapter, I shall quote only the last paragraph and shall add italics to emphasize the clustering of key words and phrases:

"Is it that by its indefiniteness it shadows forth the *heartless voids and immensities of the universe,* and thus *stabs us from behind with the thought of annihilation,* when beholding the white depths of the Milky Way? Or is it, that as in essence white-

194

ness is not so much a colour as the visible absence of colour, and at the same time the concrete of all colours; is it for these reasons that there is such a *dumb blankness*, full of meaning, in a wide landscape of snows—*a colourless, all-colour of atheism* from which we shrink? And when we consider that other theory of the *natural philosophers*, that all other earthly hues—every stately or lovely emblazoning—the sweet tinges of sunset skies and woods; yea, and the *gilded* velvets of butterflies, and the butterfly cheeks of young girls; *all these are but subtle deceits*, not actually inherent in substances, but *laid on from without*; so that *all deified Nature absolutely paints like the harlot*, whose allurements cover nothing but *the charnel-house* within; and when we proceed further, and consider that the *mystical cosmetic* which produces every one of her hues, the *great principle of light* [Note: worshipped by Captain Ahab as a symbol of God], forever remains white or colourless in itself, and if operating without medium upon matter, would touch all objects, even tulips and roses, with *its own blank tinge*—pondering all this, *the palsied universe lies before us like a leper*; and like *wilful travellers* [Note: "enlightened" and perceptive] in Lapland, *who refuse to wear coloured and colouring glasses* [Note: i.e., the rose-tinted glasses of Christian dogma] upon their eyes, so the wretched *infidel* gazes himself blind at the monumental white *shroud* that wraps all the prospects around him. *And of all these things the Albino was the symbol. Wonder ye then at the fiery hunt?*"[52]

16

WHEN Melville confessed to Hawthorne that he had written a wicked book, it will be remembered, he also confessed that he did not expect many readers to perceive his allegorical meanings. He might have added that he had gone out of his way to employ a modified form of moral allegory for riddling purposes. True, his establishment of emblematic meanings and his progressive interlocking of these emblematic values did include so many conventional Christian terms and emblems that he could count on the abilities of his most assiduous Christian readers to trap themselves into a conventional allegorical misinterpretation. In this sense, his use of allegory in *Moby-Dick* was doubly deceptive. Now that we have had an opportunity to notice the ambiguous ways in which he developed emblematic and allegorical significances, within both the Christian and the anti-Christian frames of reference, it is amusing to notice his scornfully backhanded way of calling attention to it: the familiar device of sarcastically pretending to assert just the opposite of what the context asserts (italics added):

"I do not know where I can find a better place than just here, to make mention of one or two other things, which to me seem important, as in printed form establishing in all respects the *reasonableness* of the whole story of the White Whale, more especially of the catastrophe. For this is one of those disheartening instances where *truth* requires full as much *bolstering* as *error*. So *ignorant* are most *landsmen* of some of the plainest and most palpable wonders of the world, that without some hints touching the plain facts, historical and otherwise, of the *fishery*, they might scout at Moby-Dick as a *monstrous fable*, or still worse and more detestable, a *hideous and intolerable allegory*."[53]

(Again, note particularly the overtones of the "fishery" reference.) Ishmael proceeds, immediately after that passage, to tell how murderous the whale is, and even explains that on one cruise "we spoke thirty different ships, every one of which had had a death by a whale." He adds that "people ashore" often call him facetious when he describes the enormity of the whale: "when, I declare upon my soul, I had no more idea of being facetious than Moses, when he wrote the history of the plagues of Egypt." (Melville's darker meaning would seem to be, here, that the plagues of Egypt, sent by God, are a further instance of enormity.) In fact, Ishmael concludes, large ships have been sunk, on several different occasions by the whale, who is "sufficiently powerful, knowing, and judiciously malicious" to do such a thing. Melville arranges to have Ishmael say all this, immediately after arranging to have Ishmael protest that some might scout what he has to say about Moby-Dick as a "monstrous fable" or "a hideous and intolerable allegory."

This particular passage would scarce be worth mentioning, except that the superficial skimmers of pages have frequently quoted the non-allegorical passage to prove beyond question of doubt that Melville intended not the slightest allegorical meaning in *Moby-Dick*. Those who are reluctant to notice even the well-established insinuations of the reference to "most landsmen," in that passage, might cultivate a sensitivity of their ears to tone, on the written page, by returning to an easier example: Ishmael's perplexity as to whether a whale is a fish or a mammal, and his feigned tone of conviction, as he asserts that Jonah *must* be right: the whale *must* be a fish! Having settled that "fundamental" question in terms of fact, Ishmael moves on. So here, having shuddered at the thought that some ignorant "landsmen" *might* suspect him of dealing with a "hideous and intolerable allegory," Ishmael again moves on.

A similar traplike employment of irony and sarcasm may be found in the chapter entitled "The Mat-Maker," and those who have been trapped have again included professional interpreters. Ishmael sets the trap by establishing a pretty trope—a seemingly valid analogy—to illustrate that the doctrine of free will can be made to lie down with the doctrines of necessity and predestination, even as Jonathan Edwards so elaborately insisted. After the mat-making image is carefully developed, Ishmael springs the trap. Just as he has seemingly demonstrated the truth of his assertion, Tashtego sights the first whale of the voyage, Captain Ahab bellows orders, and the entire ship's company surrenders its free will: "the ball of free-will dropped from my hand." Later, in the chapter entitled "The Monkey-Rope," Ishmael further ridicules the Christian concept of freedom within the law.

17

THE first lowering for the first whale brings Fedallah and his tawny crew into the open, and from that moment the character of Fedallah is surrounded by mystery. Officers and crew speculate: who is he? where did he come from? why did Ahab smuggle him on board? what is Ahab's relation to Fedallah? what strange power does Fedallah have over Ahab? In terms of the specifics, and of the action, these questions are never actually resolved. Consequently, the superficial reader may settle for the apparent fact that Fedallah and his crew are of value to Ahab because they are such experts in whaling. But notice Melville's method of endowing Fedallah with interlocking emblematic values, until Fedallah achieves complex symbolic significance on the sinister allegorical level of meaning.

The emblematic progression begins at once, when Ishmael points out a certain devil-like characteristic, and adds that Fedallah and his companions are of a race which some suppose to be agents of the devil (who is, in turn, an agent of God, according to Melville's dark twist of Christian doctrine):

". . . a race notorious for a certain diabolism of subtlety, and by some honest white mariners supposed to be *the paid spies and secret confidential agents on the water of the devil, their lord, whose counting-room they suppose to be elsewhere.*" [Italics added][54]

A further development of an emblematic value for Fedallah is tantalizingly made by Ishmael:

". . . that hair-turbaned Fedallah remained a muffled mystery to the last. Whence he came in a mannerly world like this, by what sort of unaccountable tie he soon evinced himself to be linked with Ahab's peculiar fortunes; nay, so far as to have some sort of a half-hinted influence; *Heaven knows* [italics added], but it might have been even authority over him; all this none knew. But one cannot sustain an indifferent air concerning Fedallah. He was such a creature as civilised, domestic people in the temperate zone only see in their dreams, and that but dimly; but the like of whom now and then glide among the unchanging Asiatic communities, especially the oriental isles to the east of the continent—those insulated, immemorial, unalterable countries, which even in these modern days still preserve much of the ghostly aboriginalness of earth's primal generations, when the memory of the first man was a distinct recollection, and all men his descendants, unknowing whence he came, eyed each other as real phantoms, *and asked of the sun and the moon why they were created and to what end; when though, according to Genesis, the angels indeed consorted with the daughters of men, the devils also, add the uncanonical Rabbins, indulged in mundane amours.*" [Italics added][55]

Among the many hints, there, is the last-sentence insinuation as to the duality of supernatural powers, and all the hints interlock with those questions Ishmael raised, in early chapters, concerning the relationship between Creator and created; between God and man; questions as to the meaning of life and death, good and evil. These are the same questions which Ahab insists on exploring, in his own maddened fashion. But Fedallah provides Melville with additional opportunities to develop his own obsession as to the relationship between God and Satan. The dubious honor of making these dark revelations is bestowed upon comical Stubb, whose comicality is again demonstrated, in the way he preaches a burlesque version of the true gospel to his whaleboat crew, to make them row. Ishmael comments thus on it: "He would say the most terrific things to his crew, in a tone so strangely compounded of fun and fury, and the fury seemed so calculated merely as a spice to the fun, that no oarsman could hear such queer invocations without pulling for dear life, and yet pulling for the mere joke of the thing. Besides he all the time looked so easy and indolent himself, so loungingly managed his steering-oar, and so broadly gaped—open-mouthed at times—that the mere sight of such a yawning commander, by sheer force of contrast, acted like a charm upon the crew. Then again, Stubb was one of those odd sort of humorists, whose jollity is sometimes so curiously ambiguous, as to put all inferiors on their guard in the matter of obeying him."[56] (That passage might serve as an indirect and cautionary representation of Melville's own stylistic manner and method.) With this fresh in mind, notice the covert value of Stubb's conversation with Flask concerning Fedallah:

" 'Flask, I take that Fedallah to be the devil in disguise. Do you believe that cock-and-bull story about his having been stowed away on board ship? He's the devil, I say. The reason why you don't see his tail is because he tucks it up out of sight; he carries it coiled away in his pocket, I guess. Blast him! now that I think of it, he's always wanting oakum to stuff into the toes of his boots.' "

That is merely a prologue, and is pleasant enough as a method of reestablishing the symbolic correlation with Satan, with evil. If we stay with the conversation, however, we come to something even more suggestive. Stubb goes on:

" 'What's the old man have so much to do with him for?'

" 'Striking up a swap or a bargain, I suppose.'

" 'Bargain?—about what?'

" 'Why, do ye see, the old man is hard bent after that White Whale, and the devil there is trying to come round him, and get him to swap away his silver watch, or his soul, or something of that sort, and then he'll surrender Moby-Dick.' "[57]

Note well the reference to Captain Ahab's soul, and the bargain. In the King James version of the Bible, the conventional gloss for Chapter Twenty-two of First Kings is this: "Ahab seduced by false prophets." Will Captain Ahab's story reveal that he, also, has been seduced? Has he, also, swapped his soul, in a contract or bargain made with Fedallah? Has Fedallah promised him victory? Has Fedallah offered to pilot him into the presence of the higher mysteries? Even into the presence of the White Whale? At this stage of the narrative, the reader has no way of knowing; nevertheless, the hint establishes some fine possibilities, on the allegorical level. It will be recalled that, in Goethe's *Faust*, Mephistopheles proceeds after the manner of Job's Satan: he first obtains permission from God to tackle Faust. Unlike Job's Satan, however, Goethe's Mephistopheles makes his compact by offering to become the servant of Faust. How had Fedallah contracted to serve Ahab? Consider carefully the indirect answers to these questions, as they may be derived from the scene in which Fedallah speaks as the deceiving prophet to death-haunted Ahab:

"Started from his slumbers, Ahab, face to face, saw the Parsee; and hooped round by the gloom of the night they seemed the last men in a flooded world. 'I have dreamed it again,' said he.

" 'Of the hearses? Have I not said, old man, that neither hearse nor coffin can be thine?'

" 'And who are hearsed that die on the sea?'

" 'But I said, old man, that ere thou couldst die on this voyage, two hearses must verily be seen by thee on the sea; the first not made by mortal hands; and the visible wood of the last one must be grown in America.'

" 'Ah, ah! a strange sight that, Parsee;—a hearse and its plumes floating over the ocean with the waves for the pall-bearers. Ha! Such a sight we shall not soon see.'

" 'Believe it or not, thou canst not die till it be seen, old man.'

" 'And what was that saying about thyself?'

" 'Though it come to the last, I shall still go before thee thy pilot.'

" 'And when thou art so gone before—if that ever befall—then ere I can follow, thou must still appear to me, to pilot me still?—

Was it not so? Well, *then* [italics added], did I believe all ye say, oh my pilot! I have here two pledges that I shall yet slay Moby-Dick and survive it.'

" 'Take another pledge, old man,' said the Parsee, as his eyes lighted up like fire-flies in the gloom—'Hemp only can kill thee.'

" 'The gallows, ye mean.—I am immortal then, on land and on sea,' cried Ahab, with a laugh of derision;—'Immortal on land and on sea!'

"Both were silent again, as one man. . . ."58

If, "as one man," the God-like Ahab may be talking to his darker self, the overtones here recall the late conversations between Faust and Mephistopheles, in Goethe's *Faust*. Once, Captain Ahab implies, he did believe all the pledges made to him by Fedallah; now he still wants to believe the pledges, even though he laughs in derision at them, and at his dark partner, his darker half.

But the reader needs some development of Fedallah's additional emblematic values, before Fedallah can be said to illuminate Melville's allegorical concept that God is the double-crosser, through whose permissive sanction Satan is employed as an agent of God, inside and outside the thoughts of men. Such a progression or extension is quite cunningly developed by Melville, in two ways. Again trust Melville to place such key ideas in the mouth of foolish Stubb; trust Melville to let Stubb be just vague enough in his memory of names so that when he gives his amusing nautical paraphrase of the Job story he will consistently refer to Job as "John." This passage directly follow's Stubb's remark to Flask that Captain Ahab has sold his soul to Fedallah for the promise of victory over Moby-Dick, and Flask deprecates:

" 'Pooh! Stubb, you are skylarking; how can Fedallah do that?'

" 'I don't know, Flask, but the devil is a curious chap, and a wicked one, I tell ye. Why, they say as how he went a-sauntering into the old flagship once, switching his tail about devilish easy and gentlemanlike, and inquiring if the old governor was at home. Well, he was at home, and asked the devil what he wanted. The devil, switching his hoofs, up and says, "I want John." "What for?" says the old governor. "What business is that of yours?" says the devil, getting mad,—"I want to use him." "Take him," says the governor—and by the Lord, Flask, if the devil didn't give John the Asiatic cholera before he got through with him, I'll eat this whale in one mouthful. . . . And if the devil has a latch-key to get into the admiral's cabin, don't you suppose he can crawl into a port-hole?' "[59]

According to Melville's persistent hints, God (not the devil) is the "curious chap" and the "wicked one" for permitting Satan to torment Job, the implication being that if God were actually and wholly good, He would keep Satan in Hell where he belongs, instead of letting him serve as agent. In his quaint way, Stubb continues to clarify this point, thus:

" 'Damn the devil, Flask; do you suppose I'm afraid of the devil? Who's afraid of him, except the old governor who daren't catch him and put him in double-darbies, as he deserves, but lets him go about kidnapping people; ay, and signed a bond with him, that all the people the devil kidnapped, he'd roast for him? There's a governor!' "[60]

Out of Stubb's ambiguous mouth, Melville has extracted dark meanings which, being interpreted, imply that there's the God of Christian doctrine. Of course the orthodox reader who understands the insinuations is bound to call them the remarks of an heretical and blasphemous infidel. Notice Ishmael's comment on the way Captain Ahab talked to his Parsee oarsmen at the first lowering:

". . . But what it was that inscrutable Ahab said to that tiger-yellow crew of his—these were words best omitted here; for you [Melville is addressing his orthodox readers] live under the blessed light of the evangelical *land* [italics added]. Only the *infidel* [italics added] sharks in the audacious seas may give ear to such words, when, with tornado brow, and eyes of red murder, and foam-glued lips, Ahab leaped after his prey."[61]

We are given several other subtle glimpses of Fedallah as the diabolically deceiving and seducing darker half of Captain Ahab; but one of the subtlest occurs when Ahab is on deck taking a noon-sight with the quadrant:

"Meantime while his whole attention was absorbed, the Parsee was kneeling beneath him on the ship's deck, and with face thrown up like Ahab's was eyeing the same sun with him; only the lids of his eyes half hooded their orbs, and his wild face was subdued to an earthly passionlessness."

(Ahab, having completed his reading, philosophizes on the

relative uselessness of the quadrant, because of its inability to answer truly important questions as to man's position in the universe. Then this:)

" '. . . Curse thee, thou vain toy; and cursed be all the things that cast man's eyes aloft to that heaven, whose live vividness but scorches him, as these old eyes are even now scorched with thy light, O sun! Level by nature to this earth's horizon are the glances of man's eyes; not shot from the crown of his head, as if God had meant him to gaze on his firmament. Curse thee, thou quadrant!' dashing it to the deck, 'no longer will I guide my earthly way by thee; the level ship's compass, and the level dead-reckoning, by log and by line; *these* shall conduct me, and show me my place on the sea. Ay,' lighting from the boat to the deck, 'thus I trample on thee, thou paltry thing that feebly pointest on high; thus I split and destroy thee!'

"As the frantic old man thus spoke and thus trampled with his live and dead feet, a sneering triumph that seemed meant for Ahab, and a fatalistic despair that seemed meant for himself—these passed over the mute, motionless Parsee's face. Unobserved he rose and glided away. . . ."[62]

Fedalla's attitude, and his act of gliding away, somehow suggest Milton's handling of Satan's action after he has effected Eve's ruin; suggest Milton's establishment of the ironic parallel between the pride that had ruined the Archangel and the pride that had ruined Adam and Eve. By means of this extension, it is possible to imagine that Fedallah, in terms of Melville's sinister allegory, can enjoy his triumph over Ahab and at the same time regret (with fatalistic despair) the bitter memory that he himself became a subservient agent of double-crossing God, because God at one time similarly double-crossed Fedallah.

18

A BRIEF digression. Some readers may find it painfully inconsistent and confusing to be told that Melville's sinister allegorical narrative can employ Captain Ahab as an emblem of Satan, at one time, and can employ Captain Ahab as an emblem of God, at another time; that he can just as easily employ both Captain Ahab and Fedallah as halves of each other. It might well be argued that pure allegory would never permit such a juggling of emblematic values, and that therefore Melville's use of symbols and emblems is not pure allegory. I would be inclined to agree with that, and to settle for the term, "impure allegory," to describe Melville's sinister construction of underlying meanings in *Moby-Dick*. However, no matter how impure his allegory may be, from a technical point of view, the essential fact remains that Melville's method is not merely a symbolic or an emblematic method, for this reason: many of the established values for certain basic symbols and emblems are given major significance, from beginning to end. Consider a few of them. "Land" represents, predominantly, the area of human experience which is fixed, dogmatic, certain, comfortable, cozy; but for those very reasons limited and finite and (for the exploring, questioning mind) incomplete, unsatisfying. The "sea" represents, predominantly, the area of human experience which is uncertain, mysterious, uncomfortable, chaotic, evil, dangerous; but for those very reasons its vastness and seeming infinity offer (to the exploring, questioning mind) endless opportunities for various kinds of deep-sea fishing. The White Whale represents, predominantly, the incarnation of the ultimate and ulterior mysteries generally associated with the dualistic attributes of God. The ship *Pequod* represents, predominantly, a microcosm of the world; its officers and crew represent, predominantly, a cross-section of humanity, bound on its life-voyage toward the mystery of death. Ishmael and Ahab represent, predominantly, contrasting types of human beings whose hearts and minds are disillusioned and "maddened" by the age-old questions as to whence we came, what we are doing here, where we are going: the eternal mysteries involving relationships of self to the universe. These are the major emblems and symbols, so closely interlocked by the action that they create an unmistakeable allegorical framework, within which Melville dramatizes and illuminates his own dark concepts as to the unjust ways of God to men.

To enrich and elaborate different aspects of his dark viewpoint, Melville sometimes doubles and triples and quadruples the symbolic values of an image; but this need not be viewed as inconsistent or confusing to any reader who is willing to hold all emblematic values so tentatively that he may follow Melville's hints to relinquish, temporarily, those emblematic values, in order to make room for the establishment of others which enrich the whole. The reader who accepts these conditions will not find the difficulties insurmountable.

19

Tossing uncomplimentary epithets at God was one of Melville's chief consolations. After the first lowering has permitted disillusioned Ishmael to discover what happens when a whale capsizes a boat, and when the righted boat, awash, is cut off from the *Pequod* by squalls and nightfall, the situation is obliquely blamed on God, who is viewed as a Laughing Hyena or at least as a Practical Joker. But first Ishmael makes a caustic emblem of the tableau itself:

"The rising sea forbade all attempts to bale out the boat. The oars were uselesss as propellers, performing now the office of life-preservers. So, cutting the lashing of the waterproof match keg, after many failures Starbuck contrived to ignite the lamp in the lantern; then stretching it on a waif-pole, handed it to Queequeg as the standard-bearer of this forlorn hope. There, then, he sat, holding up that imbecile candle in the heart of that almighty forlornness. There, then, he sat, the sign and symbol of a man without faith, hopelessly holding up hope in the midst of despair."[63]

On the strength of this "sign and symbol" of an unbelieving believer, Ishmael is permitted to resume that same tone of geniality and pleasantry which had masked his dark insinuations in the earlier chapters. This time that geniality masks his little ceremony of calling God names, while sarcastically pretending to preach the Christian doctrine of acceptance, once again. The chapter entitled "Hyena" begins thus:

"There are certain queer times and occasions in this strange mixed affair we call life when a man takes this whole universe for a vast practical joke, though the wit thereof he but dimly discerns, and more than suspects that the joke is at nobody's expense but his own. However, nothing dispirits, and nothing seems worth while disputing. He bolts down all events, all creeds, and beliefs, and persuasions, all hard things visible and invisible, never mind how knobby; as an ostrich of potent digestion gobbles down bullets and gun flints. And as for small difficulties and worryings, prospects of sudden disaster, peril of life and limb; all these, and death itself, seem to him only sly, good-natured hits, and jolly punches in the side bestowed by the unseen and unaccountable old joker. That odd sort of wayward mood I am speaking of comes over a man only in some time of extreme tribulation; it comes in the very midst of his earnestness, so that what just before might have seemed to him a thing most momentous, now seems but a part of the general joke. There is nothing like the perils of whaling to breed this free and easy sort of genial, desperado philosophy; and with it I now regarded this whole voyage of the *Pequod,* and the great White Whale its object."[64]

20

OVER a period of weeks, the *Pequod* speaks nine separate whalers, and asks each what it knows about the White Whale; allegorically, about God. This extended device affords Melville a further opportunity to surround Ahab's central attitude toward the White Whale (and the surrounding attitudes of the three mates) with an outer and wider circle of attitudes.

Even the ship's names are emblematic. The first is the *Albatross,* and her appearance strongly suggests another analogous action: the brutal manner in which Coleridge's Ancient Mariner was cowed and punished into submission, by God—as it may have seemed to Melville. Captain Ahab shouts across the open water, "Ship Ahoy! Have ye seen the White Whale?" At the very moment when the Captain of the *Albatross* tries to answer, he is ominously hindered:

"But as the strange captain, leaning over the pallid bulwarks, was in the act of putting his trumpet to his mouth, it somehow fell from his hand into the sea; and the wind now rising amain, he in vain strove to make himself heard without it. . . . While in various silent ways the seamen of the Pequod were evincing their observance of this ominous incident at the first mere mention of the White Whale's name to another ship, Ahab for a moment paused."[65]

The reader is made aware that the *Albatross* did indeed seem to have some pertinent information, but that a dark act of God, so to speak, interposed and made impossible the conveyance of that information. Ominous. From the forlorn and bleached appearance of the *Albatross*, the reader gathers that Ahab might have soliloquized on her as he did on the sphynxlike head of a whale, later killed: "Thou hast seen enough to split the planets and make an infidel of Abraham, and not one syllable is thine!"

The *Town-Ho* is the second whaleman, homeward bound, and from her crew some underlings aboard the *Pequod* hear a parable-story which fills them with awe. As Ishmael prepares to give his own summary of the story, in Chapter Fifty-four, he explains that it "seemed obscurely to involve with the whale a certain wondrous, inverted visitation of one of those so-called judgments of God which at times are said to overtake some men. This latter circumstance, with its own particular accompaniments, forming what may be called the secret part of the tragedy about to be narrated, never reached the ears of Captain Ahab or his mates."

Because there is pertinent correlation between the allegorical meanings of the *Town-Ho's* story and of Captain Ahab's story, I shall summarize the symbolic action. Even as the six-inch chapter on Bulkington may be viewed as one kind of epitome of *Moby-Dick*, so the total action of this anecdote again provides a sort of epitome. Again we are given a miniature study in the antithesis between freedom and tyrannical enslavement; this time, also, the brutality results in what Ishmael represents as justifiable mutiny or declaration of independence, on the part of "natural man," even though the mutineers realize that their action will result in subsequent retaliatory punishment, which will merely permit the "natural man" to assert further defiance and vengeance.

The initial situation is closely related to that around which Melville later built *Billy Budd*, except that in this case the "natural man" is not submissive. The antagonists are three: a Captain and Chief Mate, against a Sailor. The terms and images used to describe the Chief Mate Radney and the Sailor Steelkilt again suggest the terms used in arguments between rationalists and Calvinists, and thus the allegorical correlation with Ahab's story is suggested. Employing variations on the land-sea tropes, Melville describes Steelkilt as a "Lakeman" from Lake Erie. Appropriately, "this Lakeman, in the land-locked heart of our America, had yet been nurtured by all those agrarian freebooting [Note: i.e., freethink-

ing] impressions popularly connected with the open ocean." Again,
". . . this Lakeman, a mariner, who though a sort of devil indeed,
might yet by inflexible firmness, only tempered by that common
decency of human recognition which is the meanest slave's right;
thus treated, this Steelkilt had long been retained harmless and
docile." In contrast to this rebellious freethinker, whose concern
is for the rights of man, the Chief Mate Radney is represented as
a "landsman" and an authoritarian (a Calvinist, so to speak)
whose training has made him vindictive, cruel, brutal. As a result
of his background, Radney "was doomed and made mad."

Naturally, Radney and Steelkilt antagonize each other: "Now,
as you well know, it is not seldom the case in this conventional
world of ours—watery or otherwise; that when a person placed in
command over his fellow-men finds one of them to be very
significantly his superior in general pride of manhood, straightway
against that man he conceives an unconquerable dislike and bitterness; and if he have a chance he will pull down and pulverize
that subaltern's tower, and make a little heap of dust of it." (That
sets up the initial situation, which foreshadows the situation in
Billy Budd.)

Insulted by the Chief Mate, the Lakeman Steelkilt reacts violently and breaks the jaw of his superior officer, then is joined by
a few shipmates whose previous life as canal-bargemen had fur-
nished "the sole transition between quietly reaping in a Christian
corn-field, and recklessly ploughing the waters of the most barbaric seas." But authority overpowers these freethinking mutineers; they are confined in a hellish hold, and some of them
surrender to orthodoxy, because of their "fears of ultimate retribution." By contrast, when the God-like Captain urges the remaining men to surrender, "Steelkilt shouted up to him a terrific
hint to stop his babbling and betake himself where he belonged."
(Allegorically, "Go to Hell," or, "Where *we* are, is where *you*
belong.") After several days of brutal and taunting confinement
in the black hold, Steelkilt, "enraged by the defection of seven of
his former associates, and stung by the *mocking* [italics added]
voice that had last hailed him, and maddened by his long entomb-
ment in a place as black as the bowels of despair," proposes to
the two remaining canallers that they break out "and if by any
devilishness of desperation possible, seize the ship . . . anything

in short but surrender." He is betrayed, however, by the other two men, and subsequently all three "were collared, and dragged along the deck like dead cattle; and, side by side, were seized up into the mizzen rigging, like three quarters of meat, and there hung till morning"—alive. Then the two lesser ones were flogged by the Captain, who seized the rope and "applied it with all his might to the backs of the two traitors, till they yelled no more, but lifelessly hung their heads sideways, as the two crucified thieves are drawn." But when the Captain prepares to flog Steelkilt (who had previously said, "Treat us decently and we're your men; but we won't be flogged,") Steelkilt warns him, "If you flog me, I murder you." In answer, the predestined and predestinating Captain says, "But I must." Then Steelkilt "hissed out something, inaudible to all but the Captain," and the Captain turned away. (The allegorical frame would suggest that Steelkilt should have said, in effect, "I am your son.") The injured Chief Mate, Radney, immediately stepped up and flogged Steelkilt, who thereafter "kept his own counsel (at least till all was over) concerning his own proper and private revenge upon the man who had stung him in the ventricles of his heart."

Murder was the revenge planned in "the fore-ordaining soul of Steelkilt" (that is, by free-willing Steelkilt). "But, gentlemen, a fool saved the would-be murderer from the bloody deed he had planned. Yet complete revenge he had, and without being the avenger. For by a mysterious fatality, Heaven itself seemed to step in to take out of his hands into its own the damning thing he would have done." (Allegorically, then, Heaven became the murderer.) In short, Radney was killed by the White Whale, Moby-Dick. Subsequently, Steelkilt mutineered again and escaped to France, to atheistical France.

Ishmael, in retelling this story, explains the form of his narrative: "For my humor's sake, I shall preserve the style in which I once narrated it at Lima, to a lounging circle of my Spanish friends, one saint's eve, smoking upon the thick-gilt tiled piazza of the Golden Inn." As he finishes, he is asked whether the story is true: "Did you get it from an unquestionable source?" He answers, "Is there a copy of the Holy Evangelists in the Golden Inn, gentlemen?" A copy is gotten, and Ishmael swears on it, "So help me Heaven, and on my honour the story I have told ye, gentlemen, is in substance and its great items, true." The sarcastic insinuation would seem to be that Ishmael swears, with his hand on the book containing the "substance" of his story, which propounds the paradox that the ways of God to man are "justified" by murder.[66]

Aboard the *Jeroboam*, third whaleman homeward bound, there is a so-called "mad" Shaker, a careful reader of the Bible, who calls himself the archangel Gabriel. Early in the voyage, Gabriel had warned the Captain of the *Jeroboam* "against attacking the White Whale, in case the monster should be seen; in his gibbering insanity, pronouncing the White Whale to be no less a being than the Shaker God incarnated." Disregarding this "mad" warning, the *Jeroboam* attacked the White Whale and the mate acting as harpooner lost his life. Ahab is in no way awed by the story, and insists that he will continue. "Gabriel once more started to his feet, glaring upon the old man, and vehemently exclaimed, with downward-pointed finger—'Think, think of the blasphemer—dead, and down there!—beware of the blasphemer's end.' "[67]

Again Melville uses such a situation as a means of parting his readers into three categories. The first category of reader merely keeps turning the pages here. The second category of reader translates this into a Christian context: in some sense, the White Whale is indeed an emblem of God, or at least a dumb creature of God, and Gabriel is right when he repeats the word which Starbuck had used: if Ahab continues his mad quest he is a blasphemer and deserves a blasphemer's end. The third category of reader has by this time realized that Melville's anti-Christian context, so elaborately established, translates this situation into another blast at Christian doctrine. Ahab is attacking the God of the Old Testament and the God of the New Testament; Ahab is accusing God of inscrutable malice. To Melville, such an accusation is thoroughly justified, and indicates that Ahab has already pierced the pasteboard mask enough to recognize the contrast between the so-called truth of orthodox religious dogma and the tragic truth of human experience. "Talk not to me of blasphemy, man," Ahab shouted at Starbuck. Only from the orthodox viewpoint, Melville implies, does Ahab's action seem blasphemous and heretical. Ahab does not view his own action from the orthodox viewpoint; Melville does not view Ahab's action from the orthodox viewpoint. The orthodox believer hurls at the non-believer, in any

210

faith, epithets such as "blasphemer" and "heretic." To the orthodox
Jews, of course, Christ was a "blasphemer" and a "heretic." Hence
the scornful taunt implicit in the crown of thorns.

(At times, as we have noticed, Melville's quarrel is merely a
quarrel with an orthodox concept of God. For example, shortly
before the *Pequod* spoke the *Jeroboam*, Ishmael had described
the erroneous way in which "some timid man-of-war or blundering
discovery-vessel from afar" would sight and record the drifting
and deteriorating and useless carcass of a whale: "straightway the
whale's unharming corpse, with trembling fingers is set down in
the log—*shoals, rocks, and breakers hereabouts: beware!*" Later
the information is communicated to other ships, and "for years
afterwards, perhaps, ships shun the place; leaping over it as silly
sheep leap over a vacuum, because their leader originally leaped
there when a stick was held." Melville, letting Ishmael convert
this into an *exemplum*, would like to pride himself on his detachment and independence from the concepts which still fascinated
him: "There's your law of precedents; there's your utility of tradi-
tions; there's the story of your obstinate survival in the air! There's
orthodoxy!")[68]

The fourth ship met is the whaler *Jungfrau* or, as it turns out,
"The Foolish Virgin." Allegorically, we must remember, all concern for whaling in *Moby-Dick* is some form of God-concern. The
Jungfrau is a German vessel out of Bremen, and this affords Melville a chance for a backhanded slap at what seemed to him the
feebleness of Spinozean, Kantian, and post-Kantian theorizings as
to the nature of God: "At one time the greatest whaling people in
the world, the Dutch and Germans are now among the least."
Then the allegorical framework is made to encompass a redrama-
tization of the Biblical parable concerning the foolish virgins:
when the *Jungfrau* sends off a boat to the *Pequod*, the captain
stands in the bow of the boat and Starbuck (appropriately) exclaims. "What has he in his hand there? Impossible!—a lamp-
feeder." Flask adds, "He's out of oil and has come a-begging."
When Ahab asks him if he has seen the White Whale, the German
captain "soon evinced his complete ignorance of the White Whale;
immediately turning the conversation to his lamp-feeder and oil
can . . . concluding by hinting that his ship was indeed what in
the Fishery is technically called a *clean* one (that is, an empty

one), well deserving the name of Jungfrau or the Virgin."[69] The extensions of the emblematic meaning are obvious.

The fifth ship met is the *Rose-Bud*, and again the sweet name is ironically befitting. This is the first voyage of the captain, formerly a "Cologne manufacturer," and even his officers are untutored in the profound mysteries of whaling. Secured to the sides of the *Rose-Bud* are two stinking whale carcasses, so completely rotted that they are useless as a source of oil. Stubb says so, to the Captain of the *Rose-Bud*, and on this advice the ignorant Captain cuts them loose. When the chief-mate is asked if he has seen "The *White* Whale," he answers, "Never heard of such a whale." Woefully ignorant. Ignorant, in fact, even of how art and cunning can find riches in the vile-smelling carcasses. After the *Rose-Bud* has disappeared, Stubb removes the precious ambergris.[70]

The sixth ship is the *Samuel Enderbury*, of London, which provides some firsthand knowledge of the White Whale: in an encounter with him, the Captain of the *Enderbury* once lost his arm. Somewhat gruesomely, but with emblematic significance, Ahab insists on *crossing* his whalebone leg with the Captain's whalebone arm, before listening to the full story. In conclusion, the one-armed Captain says to Ahab, "No more White Whales for me; I've lowered for him once, and that has satisfied me . . . but, hark ye, he's best let alone; don't you think so, captain?" Allegorically considered, Ahab's reply has superb overtones, in terms of Melville's spiritual autobiography: "What is best let alone, that accursed thing is not always what least allures. He's all a magnet." The Doctor aboard the *Enderbury*, exemplifying the typical British virtue of solid common sense, tries to persuade Ahab that his attitude toward the White Whale is wrong: ". . . So that what you take for the White Whale's malice is only his awkwardness." Ahab has heard that before, from Starbuck. "With back to the stranger ship, and face set like a flint to his own," he returns to the *Pequod*.[71]

The seventh ship met is the *Bachelor*, out of Nantucket (home port of the *Pequod*), and again the name is emblematic. Fully loaded, and homeward bound, the *Bachelor* is wreathed in an atmosphere of vainglorious holiday celebration. The convivial Captain invites Ahab to come aboard for a drink, but Ahab's answer is merely the persistent question, "Hast seen the White

Whale?" The good humored reply: "No; only heard of him; but don't believe in him at all." A stupid atheist! To himself, Ahab mutters, "How wondrous familiar is a fool!" And to the Captain of the *Bachelor*, "Thou art a full ship and homeward bound, thou say'st; well, then, call me an empty ship, and outward bound. So go thy ways, and I will mine."[72]

The eighth ship is the *Rachel*, a name with significant Biblical overtones. Only yesterday, one of her boats had attacked the White Whale and the monster had towed the boat out of sight. Now the *Rachel* is searching forlornly for her children, and her Nantucket Captain asks Ahab's help, just for two days: "My boy, my own boy is among them. For God's sake—I beg . . ." Ahab answers, "Captain Gardiner, I will not do it. Even now I lose time. Good-bye, good-bye, God bless ye, man, and may I forgive myself, but I must go." In the sinister context, it should be noted, Captain Ahab's prayer, "May I forgive myself" is far more pertinent than, "May God forgive me." Each is a sovereign Power, but Ahab's first responsibility is to the divine in himself.[73]

The ninth and last ship spoken by the *Pequod* represents, allegorically, the most orthodox religious attitude of all. "Delight, top-gallant delight is to him, who acknowledges no law or lord, but the Lord his God," said Father Mapple in his sermon. *Delight* is the name of the ninth ship, and with an irony befitting the sinister context, the *Delight* is in mourning, because five of her men have just been killed by the White Whale. The body of only one man was recovered from the wreckage of a shattered boat, and this body is being committed to the deep with all the ritual of Christian burial, just as Captain Ahab comes alongside. Interrupting the ceremony long enough to answer Ahab's insistent question, the Captain of the *Delight* piously assures Ahab that the harpoon to kill the White Whale has never been forged and never will be. Ahab contradicts him. "Then God keep thee, old man," says the Captain of the *Delight*, and resumes the burial ceremony: "Oh God"—advancing towards the hammock with uplifted hands —"may the resurrection and the life—" In disgust, Captain Ahab turns away.[74]

As one looks back over these nine separate attitudes, which have helped to illuminate Ahab's attitude because each is so different from Ahab's, one may be forgiven for suspecting that Melville's picture of Ahab's relentless resistance to all the dissuading appeals is a sarcastic inversion of Paul's rhetorical assertion, "For I am persuaded, that neither death, nor life, nor angels, nor principalities, nor things present, nor things to come, nor powers, nor height, nor depth, nor any other creature, shall be able to separate us from the love of God."[75] In another sense, Ahab's response to these nine attitudes suggests a new freethinking gloss for the nine orders of fallen angels in Milton's classification; those fallen angels who "kept not their own principality, but left their proper habitation," as Jude says.[76] That is exactly Captain Ahab's attitude toward the nine ships he speaks: they are nine sovereign whale-hunting (God-hunting) powers, yet they "kept not their own principality, but left their proper habitation" without battling the White Whale to the end. And as they move in one direction— away from the White Whale—Captain Ahab moves resolutely and fearlessly and defiantly in the opposite direction.

21

ONE of the most highly criticized aspects of *Moby-Dick* is the string of chapters in which Melville describes the separate processes by which a whale is gradually transformed from a monster into the "usable truth" of impersonal whale oil and bone. It is frequently said that while these descriptions are documentary and educational, they form no part of the central narrative. But their value has to be measured in terms of the success with which Melville manipulates them, allegorically: each is a sarcastic answer to the taunting insistence of Job's God that Leviathan is inscrutable and untouchable. Furthermore, each is an ironic *exemplum* or parable, capped with a stated or implied "application." Many of these chapters enable Melville to increase his ridicule of the orthodox Christian dogma that the Holy Bible is the infallible Word of God. For his sinister purpose, the Forty-first Chapter of Job was almost made to order, and he took full advantage of it. For example, let us begin by returning to the scene in which three boats from the *Pequod* overtake and capture a "huge, humped old bull," enfeebled by age and other infirmities. We have already mentioned this passage, along with the earlier passage in which Ishmael mentioned "the awful tauntings in Job."

But we need the full text, as Ishmael taunts the Taunter, dismembers the Dismemberer (italics added):

"Seems it credible that by three such thin threads the great Leviathan [note the capital "L"] was suspended like the big weight to an eight day clock. Suspended? and to what? To three bits of board. Is this the creature of whom it was once so triumphantly said—'Canst thou fill his skin with barbed irons? or his head with fish-*spears*? The sword of him that layeth at him cannot hold, the spear, the dart, nor the habergeon: he esteemeth iron as straw; the arrow cannot make him flee; darts are counted as stubble; he laugheth at the shaking of a *spear*!' This the creature? this he? Oh! that unfulfilments should follow the prophets. For with the strength of a thousand thighs in his tail, Leviathan had run his head under the mountains of the sea, to hide him from the *Pequod's* fish-*spears*!"[77]

This particular representation of cetology is further described to afford another jibe at Christian theology; another chance, allegorically, to pique God:

"His eyes, or rather the places where his eyes had been, were beheld. As strange misgrown masses gather in the knot-holes of the noblest oaks when prostrate, so from the points which the whale's eyes had once occupied, now protruded blind bulbs, horribly pitiable to see. But pity there was none. For all his old age, and his one arm, and his blind eyes, he must die the death and be murdered, in order to light the gay bridals and other merrymakings of men, *and also to illuminate the solemn churches that preach unconditional inoffensiveness by all to all* [italics added]. Still rolling in his blood, at last he partially disclosed a strangely discolored bunch of protuberance, the size of a bushel, low down on the flank.

" 'A nice spot,' cried Flask; 'just let me prick him there once.'

" 'Avast!' cried Starbuck, 'theres no need of that!'

"But humane Starbuck was too late. . . ."[78]

Although there is actually no need for adding other illustrations of Melville's fondness for taunting the Taunter, the importance of the correlation between the whaling activities and the Leviathan references in Job cannot be too strongly stressed. "I will not keep silence concerning his limbs," says Job's God. Neither will Melville keep silence: he describes how Stubb cuts the penis off the first whale he kills, and has penis steak for supper. "Who can strip off his outer garment?" asks Job's God. Melville describes the manner in which the foreskin of another whale is stripped off and tailored to make a jacket or "cassock" for the mincer who slices the blubber thin for trying out. He continues:

"The mincer now stands before you invested in the full canonicals of his calling. Immemorial to all his order, this investiture alone will adequately protect him, while employed in the peculiar functions of his office.

"That office consists in mincing the horse-pieces of blubber for the pots; an operation which is conducted . . . with a capacious tub beneath it, into which the minced pieces drop, fast as the sheets from a rapt orator's desk. Arrayed in decent black; occupying a conspicuous pulpit; intent on bible leaves; what a candidate for an *archbishoprick* [italics added], what a lad for Pope were this mincer."

In a footnote, Melville adds,

"Bible leaves! Bible leaves! This is the invariable cry from the mates to the mincer. It enjoins him to be careful, and cut his work into as thin slices as possible. . . ."[79]

Again, Melville has provided his own exegesis. "Who shall come within his jaws? Who can open the doors of his face?" asks Job's God. Melville provides some highly illuminating *exempla*, by giving contrasted views of "The Right Whale's Head" and "The Sperm Whale's Head," exterior and interior.

For Melville's dark allegorical purposes, there are innumerable advantages in having a sperm whale serve as an emblem of God: the word "sperm" permits him to indulge his fondness for the extensions of word-play, sometimes quite indelicate, as in the archaic spelling of the word "archbishoprick," above. After all, sperm is the generative substance, and Melville's consciously incorrect interpretation of the word "spermaceti" enables him to associate the White Whale with the beginning of beginnings, particularly with Genesis. Removal of the spermaceti from the head of a slaughtered whale is described, after the reader is afforded the details as to how the whalemen open the doors of his face, pull his teeth, and cut a hole in the top. When Tashtego "retires" into one head, through such an aperture, and is in danger of drowning beneath spermaceti, Queequeg plunges in after him, and saves him by opening a womblike door in the face, so that Tashtego may be born again! Then Ishmael supplies the theological application to the parable, in pertinent analogy. The sinister overtones hint at Melville's now disillusioned lumping of Platonic and Christian theology:

"Now had Tashtego perished in that head, it had been a very precious perishing; smothered in the very whitest and daintiest of fragrant spermaceti; coffined, hearsed, and tombed in the secret inner chamber and sanctum sanctorum of the whale. Only one sweeter end can readily be recalled—the delicious death of an Ohio honey-hunter, who seeking honey in the crotch of a hollow tree, found such exceeding store of it, that leaning too far over, it sucked him in, so that he died embalmed. How many, think ye, have likewise fallen into Plato's honey head, and sweetly perished there."[80]

Another correlation of what had now become for Melville the sickly sweetness of Platonism and the sickly sweetness of Christian optimism concerning life and death calls forth one of his most obvious stylistic displays of conscious overwriting for ironic effect. Specifically, he seems merely to let Ishmael describe the way in which the "sperm" has to be manipulated by the whalemen to process it. The reader is made to realize that the greasy task was obviously repellent to Ishmael, yet he pretends to praise what he disliked doing, thus heightening the burlesque of Christian baptism and brotherly love:

". . . A sweet and unctuous duty! No wonder that in old times sperm was such a favourite *cosmetic* [italics added; cf. use of "cosmetic" in "The Whiteness of the Whale"]. Such a clearer! such a sweetener! such a softener! such a delicious mollifier! After having my hands in it for only a few minutes, my fingers felt like eels, and began, as it were, to *serpentine* [italics added; he feels "devilish"] and spiralise.

"As I sat there at my ease, cross-legged on the deck; after the bitter exertion at the windlass; under a blue tranquil sky; the ship under indolent sail, and gliding so serenely along; as I bathed my hands among those soft, gentle globules of infiltrated tissues, woven almost within the hour; as they richly broke to my fingers, and discharged all their opulence, like fully ripe grapes their wine; as I snuffed up that uncontaminated aroma,—literally and truly like the smell of spring violets; I declare to you, that for the time I lived as in a musky meadow; I forgot all about our horrible oath; in that inexpressible [unspeakable?] sperm, I washed my hands and my heart of it; I almost began to credit the old Paracelsan superstition that sperm is of rare virtue in allaying the heat of anger: while bathing in that bath, I felt divinely free from all ill-will, or petulance, or malice, of any sort whatsoever.

"Squeeze! squeeze! squeeze! all the morning long; I squeezed that sperm till I myself almost melted into it; I squeezed that sperm till a strange sort of insanity came over me; and I found myself unwittingly squeezing my co-labourers' hands in it, mistaking their hands for the gentle globules. Such an abounding, affectionate, friendly, loving feeling did this avocation beget; that at last I was continually squeezing their hands, and looking up into their eyes sentimentally; as much as to say,—Oh! my dear fellow beings, why should we longer cherish any social acerbities, or know the slightest ill-humour or envy! Come; let us squeeze hands all round; nay, let us all squeeze ourselves into each other; let us squeeze ourselves universally into the very milk and sperm of kindness.

"Would that I could keep squeezing that sperm for ever! For now, since by many prolonged, repeated experiences, I have perceived that in all cases man must eventually lower, or at least shift, his conceit of attainable felicity; not placing it anywhere in the intellect or the fancy; but in the wife, the heart, the bed, the table, the saddle, the fire-side, the country; now that I have perceived all this, I am ready to squeeze case eternally. In thoughts of the visions of the night, I saw long rows of angels in paradise, each with his hands in a jar of spermaceti."[81]

That is pretty rough, and blessed are the pure in heart who can read it without noticing the accumulated off-color word-play. But it is quoted here for more pertinent reasons. Oddly, some interpreters have cited that passage as proof that the early Ishmael changes, until he parts company with the blasphemous Ahab; that here is a clean-cut turning point for Ishmael. Of course such interpreters insist on taking the passage at face value: Ishmael asserts that it was truly pleasant to sit with his hands in a tub of suggestive fat, all morning, and so he *must* mean *just* what he says! But there are several different forms of giveaway, in the passage, and they suggest a sardonic tone. Even the progression from the sweet stickiness of the spermaceti to the sweet stickiness of the "sentimentally" described emotions recalls certain saccharine Christian ideals of universal brotherhood. In short, a particular aspect of Christian doctrine is being ridiculed here, just as certainly as other Christian concepts are ridiculed from the beginning to the end of *Moby-Dick.*

22

THE most intricate allegorical development of an experience connected with the trying-out of blubber, and a delicate use of equivocal deceptions, occurs in Chapter Ninety-six, entitled "The Try-Works." Again let us select a passage which has been cited repeatedly by interpreters, in an erroneous attempt to prove that Melville intended to use the later Ishmael as a contrasting spiritual foil for mad old Ahab; in an attempt to prove that common-sense Ishmael finally asserts his "right reason" by turning against Ahab. We have considered Melville's employment of the words "mad" and "madness" in his private vocabulary. Notice that the entire chapter under consideration pivots on those slippery words.

The setting and the situation are developed to show Ishmael, on duty at the tiller, at night, while the try-work fires burn on deck and create a weird atmosphere, a weird mood:

". . . the wild ocean darkness was intense. But that darkness was licked up by the fierce flames, which at intervals forked forth from the sooty flues, and illuminated every lofty rope in the rigging. . . . The hatch, removed from the top of the works, now afforded a wide hearth. . . . Standing on this were the Tartarean shapes of the pagan harpooners, always the whaleship's stokers. With huge pronged poles they pitched hissing masses of blubber into the scalding pots, or stirred up the fires beneath, till the snaky flames darted, curling, out of the doors to catch them by the feet."

With this hellish reminder of death, Melville sets the stage for Ishmael's spiritual experience. Viewing this nightmarish scene, Ishmael endows it with another ambiguously emblematic meaning, thus:

". . . as the wind howled on, and the sea leaped, and the ship groaned and dived, and yet steadfastly shot her red hell further and further into the blackness of the sea and the night, and scornfully champed the white bone in her mouth, and viciously spat round her on all sides; then the rushing *Pequod*, freighted with savages, and laden with fire, and burning a corpse, and plunging into that *blackness of darkness* [italics added] seemed the material counterpart of her monomaniac commander's soul."

The equivocation, there, can best be understood if we test the passage on three separate levels of meaning. The hasty reader is content to settle for this as an excellent description of a whaleship under way at night—and indeed it would seem to be that. The reader who has been forcing *Moby-Dick* into a merely orthodox frame of reference realizes that Ishmael has made an emblem of the scene: he is reminded of Captain Ahab's "madness," which is truly hideous and deplorable, from an orthodox viewpoint. The third reader, who has come to watch for the little lower layer of sinister meaning, remembers that the *Pequod* is a microcosm of the world. This ominous picture, then, represents a dark view of the entire world careening through space, "freighted with savages, and laden with fire, and burning a corpse, and plunging into that blackness of darkness" which is eternal death. Ishmael, it would seem, is still suffering from exactly those same hypos which he described in Chapter One.

This little lower layer of sinister meaning makes a further progression in symbolic logic. Did not the Psalmist say that the heavens declare the glory of God, and the firmament showeth his handiwork? Did not the Transcendentalists say much the same thing? Did not Carlyle and Goethe agree that this earth was the living visible garment of God? Ishmael says, similarly, that the rushing *Pequod*, emblematic of the world, further "seemed the material counterpart of her monomaniac commander's soul." That would seem to refer to the omnipotent Captain Ahab, who is occasionally and ironically represented as an emblem of God. Allegorically, then, Ishmael might be insinuating that he has found a new emblem for God's evil attributes. Dark thoughts indeed; but let us continue:

"So seemed it to me, as I stood at her helm, and for long hours silently guided the way of this fire-ship on the sea. Wrapped, for that interval, in darkness myself, I but the better saw the redness, the *madness* [italics added], the ghastliness of others. The continual sight of the fiend shapes before me, capering half in smoke and half in fire, these at last begat kindred visions in my soul, so soon as I began to yield to that unaccountable drowsiness which ever would come over me at a midnight helm."

Here is a surprising cluster of words which have sacred meanings in Melville's private vocabulary. In the first passage, "that blackness of darkness" and all its corollaries; in the second passage, "madness" and all its corollaries. To bring them into focus, remember Melville's high praise of Hawthorne's ability to penetrate deeply into the woeful truths of life: "You may be witched by his sunlight,—transported by the bright gildings in the skies he builds over you; but there is the blackness of darkness beyond." Remember Melville's high praise of Shakespeare's similarly dark insinuations "which we feel to be so terrifically true, that it were all but madness for any good man, in his own proper character, to utter, or even hint of them." In *Moby-Dick*, remember the preoccupation with the death motif, and with the concept of death as the most enormous indignity heaped on man by a malicious God. It would be all but madness for timid Ishmael to play this try-works emblem straight; protectively, he describes it as a sort of vision he had while dozing. His description of the nightmare continues:

"But that night, in particular, a strange (and ever since inexplicable) thing occurred to me. Starting from a brief standing sleep, I was horribly conscious of something fatally wrong. The jaw-bone tiller smote my side, which leaned against it; in my ears was the low hum of sails, just beginning to shake in the wind; I thought my eyes were open; I was half conscious of putting my fingers to the lids and mechanically stretching them still further apart. But, spite of all this, I could see no compass before me to steer by; though it seemed but a minute since I had been watching the card, by the steady binnacle lamp illuminating it. Nothing seemed before me but a jet gloom, now and then made ghastly by flashes of redness. Uppermost was the impression, that whatever swift, rushing thing I stood on was not so much bound to any haven ahead as rushing from all havens astern. A stark, bewildered feeling, *as of death* [italics added] came over me. Convulsively my hands grasped the tiller, but with the crazy conceit that the tiller was, somehow, in some enchanted way, inverted. My God! what is the matter with me? thought I. Lo! in my brief sleep I

221

had turned myself about, and was fronting the ship's stern, with my back to her prow and the compass. In an instant I faced back, just in time to prevent the vessel from flying up into the wind, and very probably capsizing her. . . ."

Again, the clustering of familiar words and concepts: "I could see no compass before me to steer by." "A jet gloom." "A stark, bewildered feeling, as of death." "My God! what is the matter with me?" "Crazy conceit." "Tiller inverted." And then the climactic concept: ". . . not so much bound to any haven ahead as rushing from all havens astern." That which is deliberately inverted here, is the complacently optimistic Christian attitude that life is a voyage from heaven through earth and back home, where everything is as it should be; as it was in the beginning, so now, and ever shall be. By contrast to that optimism Melville projects his own tragic and pessimistic thoughts into Ishmael's mind, and makes Ishmael feel that man flies always from God's malice; at least that the non-heroic man, cast in a "shabby part," always flies. Only the Ahab-like hero has the courage to turn on his Dismemberer.

In a very important sense, Melville did indeed project his actuality into cowardly Ishmael and his idealized concept of what he wished he might have been into Captain Ahab. For example, in this passage, he half shrinks from the embarrassment of confessing such dark thoughts, and sarcastically proceeds to cover them up by making Ishmael pretend to offer (with covertly satirical intent) this seemingly optimistic and Christian and platitudinous "application" or "moral" to that dark parable of the night's experience:

"Look not too long in the face of the fire, O man! Never dream with thy hand on the helm! Turn not thy back to the compass; accept the first hint of the hitching tiller; believe not the artificial fire, when its redness makes all things look ghastly. Tomorrow, in the natural sun, the skies will be bright; those who glared like devils in the forking flames, the morn will show in far other, at least gentler, relief; the glorious, golden, glad sun, the only true lamp—all others but liars!"

As I suggested in my prefatory remarks, at the beginning of this chapter, Melville's quarrel with society and with God may be viewed more accurately, at times, as a quarrel with himself and with his disillusioned and circular fluctuations of response to his own experience. If we now place the passage just quoted in each of the four suggested quadrant-arcs of Melville's circular thinking, we may better appreciate the complexity of response required by the careful reader of *Moby-Dick*. The first quadrant-arc represents the conventional Calvinistic viewpoint which had been Melville's heritage; from that viewpoint, the antithesis is between the traditionally "true" values and the traditionally "false" or "artificial" values: "the glorious, golden, glad sun, the only true lamp— all others but liars." In Carlyle's context, for example, the words "light" and "sun" are emblematic of the benevolence of God. This is the attitude which Melville satirizes.

Now place the same passage in the viewpoint represented by the second arbitrary quadrant-arc: Melville's own reactionary hate of what the Calvinists call "the true faith." And this reactionary hate has at times enabled Melville to orient himself in the terms of Rousseau and of Tom Paine, on the natural rights of man. Now the "natural sun" picks up a different symbolism: it represents "things as they are." From this viewpoint, what is "artificial"? All the theorizings of Calvinistic dogma, with so much emphasis on hell-fire and devils and forking flames, which makes life "ghastly" to the "natural man." "Look not too long in the face of the fire, O man!"

Now place the same passage in the viewpoint represented by the third arbitrary quadrant-arc: Melville's occasionally agnostic and detached viewpoint, which permits him at times to align himself with the tradition of Lucian or of Montaigne, so that he may look down tolerantly on the follies of mankind and can perceive that what seems wise to some men appears ridiculous to others; that there is no common judgment in men; that he is neither believer nor non-believer. From this theoretically detached viewpoint, which Melville could never hold very long, he might be considered as laughing at both of the previous viewpoints.

Now place the same passage in the viewpoint represented by the fourth arbitrary quadrant-arc: Melville's wistful hunger for a valid mystical belief in God, if such a belief might be found. From this viewpoint, he might perceive a reason for being sympathetic with certain aspects of the orthodox and conventional belief.

Now rig this circular pattern of viewpoints on a pin wheel, give it a spin, and let all these values blur into each other, someone might suggest. But no, there is direction in this "Try-works" chapter, as one may discover by watching how Melville goes on, in the following paragraphs, to argue with his enemies; perhaps to argue with different parts of his own consciousness. Those following paragraphs quickly reduce the fourfold field of viewpoints to two: the Christian viewpoint of the first quadrant and the anti-Christian viewpoint of the second quadrant. Melville himself demonstrates an exercise of mind, by developing a brief forensic debate. Having written the "Look not too long in the face of the fire" paragraph with predominantly satirical intention, he next proceeds to treat that same paragraph as a straight-faced representation of the Christian viewpoint, in order to make a straight-faced attack, from an anti-Christian viewpoint:

"Nevertheless, the sun hides not Virginia's Dismal Swamp, nor Rome's accursed Campagna, nor wide Sahara, nor all the millions of miles of deserts and of griefs beneath the moon. The sun hides not the ocean, which is the dark side of the earth, and which is two thirds of this earth. So, therefore, that mortal man who hath more of joy than sorrow in him, that mortal man cannot be true—not true, or undeveloped. With books the same. The truest of all men was the Man of Sorrows, and the truest of all books is Solomon's and Ecclesiastes is the fine hammered steel of woe. 'All is vanity.' ALL. This wilful world hath not got hold of unchristian Solomon's wisdom yet."

There is the Melvillian goat, talking right out in prayer meeting, and telling those whom he specifically referred to as the orthodox sheep to make of his remarks whatever they will. Let them pounce on his reference to "the Man of Sorrows" as "the truest of all men," and insist that Melville must be referring to Jesus Christ (a familiar allegorical rendering of Isaiah 53:3-4). But before too much is made of that, we will do well to remember that Melville's own glosses as to his disillusioned view of Christ (available in *Pierre, The Confidence-Man, Clarel*) suggest his interpretation of Christ as a Promethean character who, like himself, had worshiped God blindly and with complete faith until he had been betrayed and double-crossed by God. The same glosses suggest Melville's further suspicion that Christ's eyes were opened by the anguish of his crucifixion (even as Captain Ahab's eyes were opened by his "crucifixion"), and that Christ truly revealed himself as a "Man of Sorrows" when he upbraided God, from the cross, in those dying words, "My God, my God, why hast thou forsaken me?" There is no difficulty for us as we move on, in the passage, to the blunt reference to "unchristian Solomon's wisdom"; but we will again do well to remember that, according to Melville, the woefully maddening wisdom which Solomon perceived as to the vanity of human wishes was so shocking and unspeakable that "he a little *managed* the truth with a view to popular conservatism."

In the extremely important "Try-Works" chapter, then, Melville would seem to have managed his own dark view of "usable truth," at times. First, he has presented a symbolic or emblematic action, on deck at night; then he has established an alternating pattern of two opposed interpretations of the symbolic or emblematic action: a Christian interpretation, which he satirizes, and an anti-Christian interpretation, which he defends. This brings us to the last paragraph of that chapter, where Melville returns to equivocations by braiding the two opposed viewpoints, as though taking delight in achieving an ambiguous conclusion which might be interpreted one way by the sheep and another way by the goats:

"But even Solomon, he says, 'the man that wandereth out of the way of understanding shall remain' (i.e., even while living) 'in the congregation of the dead.' Give not thyself up, then, to fire, lest it invert thee, deaden thee, as for the time it did me. There is a wisdom that is woe; but there is a woe that is *madness* [italics added]. And there is a Catskill eagle in some souls that can alike dive down into the blackest gorge, and soar out of it again and become invisible in the sunny spaces. And even if he for ever flies within the gorge, that gorge is in the mountains; so that even in his lowest swoop the mountain eagle is still higher than other birds upon the plain, even though they soar."[82]

In that passage, again, the antithesis is between two viewpoints, and the dominant image is that of the eagle, with which Melville identifies himself. It provides the conclusion for this entire "Try-Works" *exemplum* or anti-Christian sermon, and that conclusion is buttressed with two texts from The Bible. First, Melville accurately quotes Proverbs 21:16, on wisdom and understanding: "The man that wandereth out of the way of understanding shall

225

remain in the congregation of the dead." If this text should be placed in a Christian or Calvinistic context, it would imply that the man who turns his back on the Christian concept of "right reason" thus demonstrates that he is predestinately depraved, damned, dead. Conversely, Melville's anti-Christian context in *Moby-Dick* represents the man blinded by the coziness of optimistic Christian dogma as the man that wandereth out of the way of Melvillian understanding, and who thus remaineth in the congregation (appropriate term) of the stupid, the intellectually dead. Here, such a man is identified with the imperceptive reader, the blind reader, the superficial skimmer of pages. Melville's second Biblical text, also drawn from Solomon, is a paraphrase of Ecclesiastes 1:18: "For in much wisdom is much grief; and he that increaseth wisdom increaseth sorrow." The dark Melvillian construction of that passage provides a further gloss on Melville's peculiar use of the word "madness," as used in his assertion that there is "a wisdom that is woe; but there is a woe that is madness." True wisdom, Melville has repeatedly implied, must be derived from the accurate perception of God's malice; a perception which is simultaneously woeful, maddening.

I have frequently heard the superficial skimmer of pages gloss this passage to prove that Melville was on the side of the angels, and not on the side of "mad" old Captain Ahab. Such an interpreter gloatingly points out that Ishmael says, "Give not thyself up, then, to fire, lest it invert thee, deaden thee, as for the time it did me." Obviously, the argument goes, Ishmael's regeneration is well advanced, and here he turns his back on the "madness" of his earlier sympathy with mad old Ahab.

But, as the movie-goer says, this is where we came in. Melville is still contrasting two kinds of understanding or wisdom, and the image of the eagle is contrasted with the image of the prosaic plain-dwelling bird. The eaglelike soul knows the two extremes of high-flying in the upper sunny spaces and deep-delving in the blackest gorge. When he is deepest in the darkness of his blackness, however, he is still exploring an area of perception (a mountain gorge) which is higher (at its lowest) than the area of perception explored by the mere sparrowlike soarings from the plain, the prosy plain.

With so much clear, we may interlock this part of the paragraph with the first part. What happens when this eaglelike soul

226

plunges into the "blackest gorge" providing that soul with the sustenance of a Solomon-like woeful wisdom which is madness? Within the context so elaborately established, prior to this passage, that so-called "madness" is still superior to the highest "right reason" of the plain-soul. What happens, then, to Ishmael's admonition that the reader should not give himself up to the fire, lest it "invert" and "deaden"—as it once did Ishmael—*for the time*? Obliquely, Melville is saying again what he has already said in different ways: my dear plain-reader, don't give *yourself* up to the fire, because it would certainly invert and deaden *you*, even as it did me, during my early stages of disillusionment. Gradually, I came to appreciate that wisdom is woe and that knowledge of God's malice is truly maddening. You, my dear plain-reader, wouldn't understand that; believe me when I reiterate that where ignorance is bliss, 'tis folly to be wise. Thus Melville to the prosy plain-reader.

23

THE events involving the negro boy Pip provide a further valuable gloss on Melville's use of the word "madness" in *Moby-Dick*. The counterpart of Lear's fool, Pip is employed to bring out the Lear-like qualities in Captain Ahab. At first he entertains all, with his tambourine and his "pleasant, genial, jolly brightness." But even before the tragic accident, "the panic-striking business in which he had somehow unaccountably become entrapped, had most sadly blurred his brightness." In other words, Pip was sensible enough to be afraid. During a whale ride, he was caught in a line while trying to jump from the boat, and although he was not seriously injured he was almost scared to death. After that, he was warned that if he ever jumped again he would not be picked up. "But we are all in the hands of the gods," comments Ishmael sardonically, "and Pip jumped again"—abandoned temporarily in mid-ocean. This experience caused his "madness." Then Melville gives us this superb passage:

"By the merest chance the ship itself at last rescued him; but from that hour the little negro went about the deck an idiot; *such, at least, they said he was* [italics added]. The sea had jeeringly kept his finite body up, but drowned the infinite of his soul. Not drowned entirely, though. Rather carried down alive to wondrous depths, where strange shapes of the unwarped primal world glided to and fro before his passive eyes; and the miser-merman, Wisdom, revealed his hoarded heaps; and among the joyous, heartless, ever-juvenile eternities, Pip saw the multitudinous God-omnipresent, coral insects, that out of the firmament of waters heaved the colossal orbs. He saw God's foot upon the treadle of the loom, and spoke it; and therefore his shipmates called him mad. So man's insanity is heaven's sense; and wandering from all mortal reason, is absurd and frantic; and weal or woe, feels then uncompromised, indifferent as his God."[83]

The pleader for the possibility of forcing Melville into an ortho-dox Christian viewpoint of acceptance should recognize the para-phrase of the Apostle Paul in Melville's summary phrase, "So man's insanity is heaven's sense." In I Corinthians, first chapter, Paul writes, "Hath not God made foolish the wisdom of this world?" And again, "But God hath chosen the foolish things of the world, to confound the wise." Superficially, then, one may recognize that Melville is here making a Biblical allusion. But now consider the little lower layer. The context inverts Paul's in-tended meaning, and Melville intends the sarcastic inversion. Pip has seen enough of God to recognize the indifference of God. Thereafter, Pip himself dramatizes the "sense" of heaven by pre-senting his own indifference to "all mortal reason." In other words, Pip (like Captain Ahab) has been driven into insanity, into mad-ness, into so-called "foolishness" by the accuracy of his perception, Melville implies. By extension, Melville hints that if you yourself perceive and become maddened by the maliciousness of God's in-difference, the "normal" and blind human beings with whom you associate will describe your attitude as a form of "man's insanity." Pip found himself in a position where "the miser-merman, Wis-dom, revealed his hoarded heaps." The wisdom of perceiving the malice of God's indifference, Melville again implies, is a correct perception; but it is woeful, and it is "maddening." So man's in-sanity is heaven's sense!

Even the careful reader needs some help with this passage, and Melville gives it to him: Captain Ahab is of course the touchstone character who will appreciate the true and sinister significance of Pip's vision. He comes on deck, much later, just as the Manxman is abusing Pip:

" 'Peace, thou crazy loon,' cried the Manxman, seizing him [Pip] by the arm. 'Away from the quarter-deck!'

" 'The greater idiot ever scolds the lesser,' muttered Ahab, advancing. 'Hands off from that holiness. Where sayest thou Pip was, boy?'

" 'Astern there, sir, astern! Lo! lo!'

" 'And who art thou, boy? I see not my reflection in the vacant pupils of thy eyes. Oh God! that man should be a thing for immortal souls to sieve through. Who art thou, boy?'

" 'Bell-boy, sir; ship's crier; ding, dong, ding! . . .'

" 'There can be no hearts above the snow-line. Oh, ye frozen heavens! look down here. Ye did beget this luckless child, and have abandoned him, ye creative libertines. [Cf. *King Lear*] Here, boy; Ahab's cabin shall be Pip's home henceforth, while Ahab lives. Thou touchest my inmost centre, boy; thou art tied to me by cords woven of my heartstrings. Come, let's down.'

" 'What's this? here's velvet shark-skin,' intently gazing at Ahab's hand, and feeling it. 'Ah, now, had poor Pip but felt so kind a thing as this, perhaps he had ne'er been lost! This seems to me, sir, as a man-rope; something that weak souls may hold by. Oh, sir, let old Perth now come and rivet these two hands together; the black one with the white, for I will not let this go.'

" 'Oh, boy, nor will I thee, unless I should thereby drag thee to worse horrors than are here. Come, then, to my cabin. Lo! ye believers in gods all goodness, and in man all ill, lo you! see the omniscient gods oblivious of suffering man; and man, though idiotic, and knowing not what he does, yet full of the sweet things of love and gratitude. Come! I feel prouder leading thee by thy black hand, than though I grasped an emperor's!' "[84]

Technically, Melville would there seem to be demonstrating the method which he described as Shakespeare's, in *King Lear*; even the use of pagan gods might be a device for protective insinuation: the meaning is obviously analogous to other meanings applied to the Christian God, throughout *Moby-Dick*.

24

THE climactic action in *Moby-Dick* occurs in the Lear-like storm scene of "The Candles" chapter, where the simultaneously wistful and defiant prayer of Captain Ahab correlates and clarifies certain factors which have hitherto remained obscure. Thereafter, the remainder of the narrative may be considered as the falling action, because the outcome is certain, even though we as readers may not be able to anticipate the details of that outcome.

In one sense, the storm scene may be viewed as a sort of inverted religious ritual, related to Ahab's previous inverted ritual of communion, and to the inverted ritual of baptism, which occurs when Ahab forges his special harpoon and baptizes it in pagan blood and in the name of the devil.[85] All these ritualistic actions, including the smashing of the quadrant, are indicative of Captain Ahab's quondam religiosity, somehow abandoned because experience had caused him to lose faith and become disillusioned. Until "The Candles" chapter, however, the reader has been forced to guess that Ahab himself sees some close connection between that wound-scar caused by lightning and that wound-scar caused by the White Whale. All of these separate elements are now brought together and illuminated, in the storm scene.

At the height of the storm, Ahab appears on deck, ready to assert his mortal sovereignty in the face of an immortal sovereignty. When Starbuck wishes to make sure that the ship's lightning rod chains are properly overboard, to conduct the lightning into the water, Ahab shouts, "Avast! let's have fair play here, though we be the weaker side. Yet I'll contribute to raise rods on the Himalayas and Andes, that all the world may be secured; but out on privileges! Let them be, sir." Just then the corposants appear aloft, with mystical trinitarian persistence: "All the yard-arms were tipped with a pallid fire; and touched at each tri-pointed lightning-rod-end with three tapering white flames, each of the three tall masts was silently burning in that sulphurous air, like three gigantic wax tapers before an altar." The Parsee kneels at the base of the mainmast, near Ahab, "his head bowed away from him," as Ahab cries, "Ay, ay, men! *Look up at it; mark it well; the white flame but lights the way to the White Whale* [italics added]. Hand me those main-mast links there, I would fain feel this pulse, and let mine beat against it; blood against fire! So." Now comes Ahab's blasphemous and climactic invocation, which gathers together all the previous insinuated inversions of the offertory refrain, "All things come of thee, oh Lord, and of thine own have we given thee":

"Then turning—the last link held fast in his left hand, he put his foot upon the Parsee and with fixed upward eye, and high-flung right arm, he stood erect before the lofty tri-pointed trinity of flames.

"'Oh! thou clear spirit of clear fire, whom on these seas I as Persian once did worship, till in the sacramental act so burned by thee, that to this hour I bear the scar; I now know thee, thou clear spirit, and I now know that thy right worship is defiance. To neither love nor reverence wilt thou be kind; and e'en for hate thou canst but kill; and all are killed. No fearless fool now fronts thee. I own thy speechless, placeless power; but to the last gasp of my earthquake life will dispute its unconditional, unintegral mastery in me. In the midst of the personified impersonal, a personality stands here. Though but a point at best; whencesoe'er I came; wheresoe'er I go; yet while I earthly live, the queenly personality [soul] lives in me, and feels her royal rights. But war is pain, and hate is woe. Come in thy lowest form of love, and I will kneel and kiss thee; but at thy highest, come as mere supernal power; and though thou launchest navies of full-freighted worlds, *there's that in here that still remains indifferent* [italics added]. Oh, thou clear spirit, of thy fire thou madest me, and like a true child of fire, I breathe it back to thee.'

(The lightning flashes, the masthead flames leap upward toward it, and Ahab continues.)

"'I own thy speechless, placeless power; said I not so? Nor was it wrung from me; nor do I now drop these links. Thou canst blind; but I can then grope. Thou canst consume, but I can then be ashes. Take the homage of these poor eyes, and shutter-hands. I would not take it. The lightning flashes through my skull; mine eye-balls ache and ache; my whole beaten brain seems as beheaded, and rolling on some stunning ground. Oh, oh! Yet blindfold, yet will I talk to thee. Light though thou be, thou leapest out of darkness; but I am darkness leaping out of light, leaping out of thee! The javelins cease; open eyes; see, or not? There burn the flames! Oh, thou magnanimous! now I do glory in my genealogy. But thou art but my fiery father; my sweet mother [source of the queenly soul in Ahab], I know not. Oh, cruel! what hast thou

231

done with her? There lies my puzzle; but thine is greater. Thou knowest not how came ye, hence callest thyself unbegotten; certainly knowest not thy beginning, hence callest thyself unbegun. I know that of me, which thou knowest not of thyself, oh, thou omnipotent. There is some unsuffusing thing beyond thee, thou clear spirit, to whom all thy eternity is but time, all thy creativeness mechanical. Through thee, thy flaming self, my scorched eyes do dimly see it. Oh, thou foundling fire, thou hermit immemorial, thou too hast thy incommunicable riddle, thy unparticipated grief. Here again with haughty agony, I read my sire. Leap! leap up, and lick the sky! I leap with thee; I burn with thee; would fain be welded with thee; defyingly I worship thee!' "[86]

As the upbraiding ceases, Christian Starbuck upbraids Ahab: he points to a "levelled flame of pale, forked fire" now playing from "the keen steel barb" of Ahab's devil-baptized harpoon, and says:

" 'God, God is against thee, old man; forebear! 'tis an ill voyage! ill begun, ill continued; let me square the yards, while we may, old man, and make a fair wind of it homewards, to go on a better voyage than this.' "

Supporting Starbuck, the crew run to the braces and raise "a half mutinous cry." Defiant Ahab snatches his "burning harpoon" and waves it "like a torch among them, swearing to transfix with it the first sailor that but cast loose a rope's end," and speaks:

" 'All your oaths to hunt the White Whale are as binding as mine; and heart, soul, and body, lungs and life, old Ahab is bound. And that ye may know to what tune this heart beats: look ye here; thus I blow out the last fear!' And with one blast of his breath he extinguished the flame."[87]

That tremendously dramatic scene, bringing together so many related motifs, also illuminates the importance of the death motif, and correlates it with the central thematic concern:". . . and e'en for hate thou canst but kill; and all are killed." Ishmael has tried to master his death obsession by escaping to sea; Captain Ahab has tried to master his death obsession by facing his enemy and by defying him: ". . . the white flame but lights the way to the White Whale." Now the remaining ritual of action is clear in all its implications: Ahab will fight fire with fire, malice with malice, hate with hate.

The best gloss on Melville's own attitude toward that climactic scene, and toward the total action, is contained in the already-quoted letter to Hawthorne in which Melville outlined a strikingly similar concept of tragic, heroic, Promethean defiance. For Melville, according to that letter, the heroic human being who has penetrated the mysteries of God sufficiently to understand divine malice, assumes the attitude of a sovereign being who does not quail before these malicious indignities, "though they do their worst to him." For Melville, as for Captain Ahab, the obsession is with death as the "worst" that awaits all. Like Melville, Ahab "declares himself a sovereign nature (in himself) amid the powers of heaven, hell, and earth." Ahab knows he will perish: "To neither love nor reverence wilt thou be kind." Perceiving all this, even fearing all this, Ahab heroically and bravely and tragically defies God: "No fearless fool now fronts thee. I own thy speechless, placeless power; but to the last gasp of my earthquake life will dispute its unconditional, unintegral mastery in me." Or, as Melville said it to Hawthorne, "He may perish; but so long as he exists, he insists upon treating with all Powers upon an equal basis." In other words, Melville conceived the heroic attitude to be one which gloried in its own divine attributes so persistently that no quantity or quality of God-bullying could ever impair the sovereignty of self. All of this is summarized in Captain Ahab's climactic and (viewed from Christian doctrine) blasphemous invocation or "prayer."

25

IN the denouement, even Ahab's last defiance of death, and of God's malice, after the three-day struggle with the White Whale, cannot match the vivid rhetoric and drama of the storm scene. In fact, Ahab's last words merely reiterate, in different form, his previous storm-scene words. The passage is brief, and some sentences in it deserve to be glossed. But first the passage as a whole. After the White Whale has rammed the *Pequod* and has left it sinking, the monster lies quiescent "within a few yards of Ahab's boat." For the last time, Ahab closes with it, knowing well that the thrust of his raised harpoon will be fatal for him, and not for the White Whale. Thus poised for the blow, he speaks his last words:

" 'I turn my body from the sun. What ho, Tashtego! Let me
hear thy hammer. Oh! ye three unsurrendered spires of mine; thou
uncracked keel; and only *god-bullied* [italics added] hull; thou
firm deck, and haughty helm, and Pole-pointed prow,—death-
glorious ship! must ye then perish, and without me? Am I cut off
from the last fond pride of meanest shipwrecked captains? Oh,
lonely death on lonely life! Oh, now I feel my topmost greatness
lies in my topmost grief. Ho, ho! from all your furthest bounds,
pour ye now in, ye bold billows of my whole foregone life, and
top this one piled comber of my death! Towards thee I roll, thou
all-destroying but unconquering whale; to the last I grapple with
thee; from hell's heart I stab at thee; for hate's sake I spit my last
breath at thee. Sink all coffins and all hearses to one common pool!
chasing thee, though tied to thee, thou damned whale! *Thus*, I
give up the spear!' "[88]

The gloss for "I turn my body from the sun" is supplied by an
earlier passage of considerable interest, in the chapter entitled,
"The Dying Whale," where Ahab comments on how the dying
whale turns his body toward the sun, and faces it, so that the
instinctive gesture becomes an emblem of faith: "He too worships
fire; most faithful, broad, baronial vassal of the sun! . . . here, too,
life dies sunward full of faith; but see! no sooner dead, than death
whirls round the corpse, and it heads some other way. . . . In vain,
oh whale, dost thou seek intercedings with yon all-quickening sun,
that only calls forth life, but gives it not again."[89] This gloss indicates that Ahab's last turning away from the sun is another symbolic act of conscious, deliberate, Satanic, Promethean defiance.

The command to Tashtego to continue nailing the flag to the
mast of the *Pequod*, even as she sinks, is another assertion of
courageous and indomitable and tragically heroic defiance.

Ahab's reference to the ship creates a temporary and tentative
trope which has been hinted at, several different times, throughout
the narrative: the *Pequod* not only as an emblem of the whole
world (macrocosm) but also of the whole man (microcosm),
Captain Ahab: the "three unsurrendered spires of mine" thus
becomes a symbol of Ahab's body, mind, soul. By extension, the
"god-bullied hull" becomes a symbol of the God-destroyed body;
but even as the body "sinks" and dies, the indomitable spirit of
Captain Ahab is represented by the "haughty" helm and "Pole-

234

pointed" prow, which translates her into a "death-glorious ship."

For further enrichment, the limitations of that temporary and tentative trope are immediately abandoned, and a new trope is established. Ahab is isolated from his ship, cut off, alone. "Oh, lonely death on lonely life!" With those six words in mind, the reader is able to appreciate the significance of the sentence which follows: "Oh, now I feel my topmost greatness lies in my topmost grief." Lonely death is the topmost grief; but Ahab's greatness lies in his asserting his living sovereignty, his indomitableness, his heroic defiance, alone and unaided, even in the face of death. Having brought this key conviction into sharp focus, Ahab immediately acts out that key conviction: "Towards thee I roll, thou all-destroying but unconquering whale; to the last I grapple with thee; from hell's heart I stab at thee; for hate's sake I spit my last breath at thee. . . ."

There is only one more gloss needed for this passage. Consider the overtones of "Thus I give up the spear!"—Ahab's last words. Throughout *Moby-Dick*, Melville has interlocked various myths illuminating the relation of Creator and created: the Prometheus myth, the Genesis myth, the Jonah myth, the Job myth, the Faust myth, the Milton's Satan myth. The recurrent references to Job included Ishmael's taunting and extended quotation from the Forty-first Chapter; that quotation concluding, "He laugheth at the shaking of the spear." Considered realistically, Ahab's last words refer to a harpoon he holds in his hands, and his calling the harpoon a "spear" has a value which is greater as symbolic or emblematic meaning. It would seem to be one more cross-reference to Job, nicely interlocked with Ishmael's taunting. In effect, Ahab is saying that even though God may be invulnerable, the defiance behind that spear-hurling gesture is more significant than the futility of the gesture.

Perhaps Ahab's last words are so worded by Melville to interlock with Christ's last words, also. Attention has already been called to Melville's use of the term "Man of Sorrows," which occurs in Isaiah and which is sometimes interpreted as a prophetic reference to Christ. For Melville, Christ's relation to God was another significant instance of the relationship between man and God, in that it offered much food for dark thoughts, as already suggested. The Gospels conflict as to just what Christ's last words were. Melville could darkly conclude that the last words, as reported in Matthew and Mark, indicated Christ's eyes were opened, on the cross; that Christ died with the tragic self-discovery that God had double-crossed him. Luke, on the other hand, indicates that Christ's last words were ones of faith and acceptance, and "thus he gave up the ghost." In effect, Ahab inverts the meaning of these words as reported in Luke. Instead of "Father, into thy hands I commend my spirit," Ahab's action may be said to dramatize something like this, "Father, *out* of *my* hands I commend to you—my spear!" Thus interpreted, Ahab's final words are doubly symbolic, Satanic, blasphemous.

As the *Pequod* sinks, following Ahab's last words, Melville achieves one final emblem of blasphemous defiance, and the significance of Tashtego's continuing to nail the flag to the mast is overtly glossed, in the context itself:

"A sky-hawk that *tauntingly* [italics added] had followed the maintruck downwards from its natural home among the stars, pecking at the flag, and incommoding Tashtego there; this bird now chanced to intercept its broad fluttering wing between the hammer and the wood; and simultaneously feeling the ethereal thrill, the submerged savage beneath, in his death-gasp, kept his hammer frozen there; and so the bird of heaven, with archangelic shrieks, and his imperial beak thrust upwards, and his whole captive form folded in the flag of Ahab, went down with his ship, *which, like Satan, would not sink to hell till she had dragged a living part of heaven along with her, and helmeted herself with it.*"[90] [Italics added]

26

At first glance, the single-page "Epilogue" of *Moby-Dick* may seem to be a mere device for tying off the loose ends, and for explaining how it happened that Ishmael survived to tell the story. Ishmael makes no summarizing comment on the whole story; in fact, Ishmael has revealed his own cogitations less and less during the entire falling action, and has seemingly exchanged his duties as an actor and commentator for those of a detached observer and narrator. Some interpreters even argue that Ishmael's detachment is a further proof that Melville "saves" and "redeems" Ishmael from his earlier hypos, because Ishmael has earned such salvation by turning against Captain Ahab. But the hints as to such a so-called enlightened attitude, on Ishmael's part, will be found to consist largely in Ishmael's repeated use of that slippery and (in context) equivocal word "mad," to characterize Ahab's later action. Such hints, as we have already noticed, constitute a kind of trap for the unwary reader.

As it happens—and by no accident—Ishmael himself has tucked into an earlier chapter of the narrative a very cunning and sly gloss as to the meaning of the factual information of the "Epilogue." Before we consult the gloss, however, consider the "Epilogue" as it stands.

First of all, it is of particular importance to notice that the motto of the "Epilogue" is a pertinent quotation from that one book of the Bible which has served as an elaborate and (in Melville's context) sinister backdrop against which the entire allegorical meaning has been correlated: a quotation from the book of Job: "And I only am escaped alone to tell thee." Emblematically, then, Ishmael as narrator is now cast in the part of a Job's messenger, speaking to the reader. By emblematic extension, this forces the reader to play the listening-part of Job. Darkly interpreted, this suggests Melville's persistent desire to tell the perceptive reader that the reader is just as "god-bullied" as Job ever was, if only the reader were wise enough to understand such woefully maddening wisdom!

The second point of importance in the "Epilogue" is the manner of Ishmael's escape, after the "god-bullied" *Pequod* has sunk, and has sucked to their deaths all the remaining ship's company. During the third and last day of the chase, Ishmael was "he whom the Fates ordained" to fill a vacant seat as oarsman in Ahab's own boat; Ishmael was the man knocked out of the boat by the White Whale as Ahab "darted his fierce iron, and his far fiercer curse, into the hated whale"; Ishmael was left, "helplessly dropping astern, but still afloat and swimming." He was near enough to witness all the final action from his watery vantage point, even near enough to be drawn toward the closing vortex created by the sinking disappearance of the *Pequod*: "Round and round, then, and ever contracting toward the button-like black bubble at the

axis of that slowly wheeling circle, like another Ixion I did revolve."

We have already noticed Melville's own preoccupation with the
circle image, which is again suggested here by the wheel image;
but obviously he chose the Ixion reference because it provides
another analogous action. In Greek mythology, Ixion defied Zeus
and was consequently tortured by being chained to a wheel of
fire in Hades. Shakespeare seems to have permitted King Lear
to make his own appropriate use of the Ixion-wheel image, thus:

> Thou art a soul in bliss; but I am bound
> Upon a wheel of fire, that mine own tears
> Do scald like molten lead.

The third point of importance in the "Epilogue" is the tableau
image: alive, Ishmael floats precariously on a suggestive coffin.
Thus, at the very end of the narrative, we are carried back to the
coffin image which occurred in the very first paragraph of the first
chapter: ". . . I find myself involuntarily pausing before coffin
warehouses, and bringing up the rear of every funeral . . ." As it
was in the beginning, so now: Ishmael, meditating on a coffin,
following the funereal sinking of the *Pequod*, continues to float
on what he himself refers to as the "dirge-like main," throughout
that long day and throughout the night which follows. "And I
only . . . alone . . ."

Now the gloss. Only one other character in *Moby-Dick* suffered
the torture of such loneliness and abandonment, in the vast ocean,
while the "ringed horizon began to expand around him miserably."
The experience drove that other character into a profound perception: "the miser-merman, Wisdom, revealed his hoarded heaps."
The revelation? "He saw God's foot upon the treadle of the loom,
and spoke it; and therefore his shipmates called him mad." Pip, of
course. Pip, who suffered this experience, according to Ishmael,
because "we are all in the hands of the gods." We are told by
Ishmael that Pip perceived the indifference of God, at that time.
As we noticed, Melville worked out analogous values between
Pip's perceptions and Ahab's perceptions; between Pip's "madness" and Ahab's "madness." We did not notice, at the time, that
the account of what happened to Pip contained a hint that there
might be a further triangulation, a further analogy between these

two forms of "madness" and Ishmael's form of "madness." The account of Pip's experience ends thus:

"So man's insanity is heaven's sense; and wandering from all mortal reason, man comes at last to that celestial thought, which, to reason, is absurd and frantic; and weal or woe, feels then uncompromised, indifferent as his God.

". . . and in the sequel of the narrative, it will then be seen what like abandonment befell myself."[91]

Thus the ultimate triangulation of "madness" is made to include Ishmael, and not to exclude him. In the light of these important analogies, it should be remembered that well-named Ishmael began telling the whole story, in Chapter One, artistically speaking, with the memory of that final tableau vivid in his mind. The entire voyage enabled Ishmael to arrive at that catastrophe, and at that lonely opportunity to confirm his worst suspicions; to coffin-meditate on the paradox of God's simultaneous malice and indifference. Ironically imitating God, Ishmael writes that "Epilogue" in such a way as to feign a God-like indifference. He concludes with no comment other than a statement of fact:

"On the second day, a sail drew near, nearer, and picked me up at last. It was the devious-cruising Rachel, that in her retracing search after her missing children, only found another orphan."[92]

27

Now that we are in position to summarize the major effects in *Moby-Dick*, let us pause silently, and for just a moment, to marvel at those who say Melville's personal viewpoint and theme are represented in the overt meaning of Father Mapple's sermon.

Although many different attitudes may be found represented in *Moby-Dick*, the two most important attitudes are those of the narrator Ishmael and the hero Captain Ahab. Again Melville has provided us with a triangulation, because these two attitudes are essentially one, in that they are anti-Christian; they are essentially in accord with Melville's attitude when he wrote *Moby-Dick*. Having declared his independence from Christian dogma, and from God, Melville arranged artistically to achieve, as his major effects in *Moby-Dick*, various forms of taunting ridicule, aimed at Christian dogma and at the Christian concept of God. I have already suggested that whenever ridicule is expressed in ironic satire, the inevitable consequence is that somebody gets taken in or left behind or trapped. Melville seems to have counted on just that, and there is some evidence that his success exceeded his boldest hope.

In describing the circular pattern of Melville's fluctuating viewpoint, I mentioned that he seemed to idealize the indifference of agnostic detachment. A God-like indifference was also an artistic ideal which Melville obviously aspired to, in *Moby-Dick*, without being entirely able to achieve it. Several passages might be cited to show how much he tried to think and look and create from the lofty position of a completely impartial observer. If he had succeeded in this respect, such a serene position would have enabled him to cut the umbilical cord between himself and his artistic children, Ishmael and Captain Ahab. As evidence that he did occasionally pride himself on having achieved such detachment, consider the curious complexity of the following passage:

"And so, through all the thick mists of the dim doubts in my mind, divine intuitions now and then shoot, enkindling my fog with a heavenly ray. And for this I thank God; for all have doubts; many deny; but doubts or denials, few along with them have intuitions. Doubts of all things earthly, and intuitions of some things heavenly; this combination makes neither believer nor infidel, but makes a man who regards them both with equal eye."[93]

If we take that passage as it stands, it just does not jell. The controlling word is "intuitions," which occurs three times, and that word is obviously equivocal, in this context. Overtly, it suggests a Christian meaning of divine revelation concerning God's benevolence; covertly, it suggests (in the sinister context) an anti-Christian meaning of human perception concerning God's malevolence. In its total effect, then, it is a sarcastic passage which would seem to mean that Melville's tragically superior viewpoint permits him to be detached in his attitude toward theist and atheist, because each is wrong: the believer is wrong in asserting the benevolence of God; the infidel is wrong in denying the existence of God. But there is no genuine detachment in Melville's viewpoint, even here, because he looks at theist and atheist with an equal eye of infuriation. Each is a type of blindness, to Melville, and he therefore upbraids and satirizes each. Take just one more passage, to illuminate Melville's yearning for both artistic and non-artistic detachment:

". . . And thus, though surrounded by circle upon circle of consternations and affrights, did these inscrutable creatures at the centre freely and fearfully indulge in all peaceful concernments; yea, serenely revelled in dalliance and delight. But even so, amid the tornadoed Atlantic of my being, do I myself still for ever centrally disport in mute calm; and while pondering planets of unwaning woe revolve round me, deep down and deep inland there I still bathe me in eternal mildness of joy."[94]

Perhaps we should take that with a little grain of salt. Certainly it would seem that *Moby-Dick* more accurately reflects the "tornadoed Atlantic" of Melville's being rather than the "mute calm." Nevertheless, because he could assert this as an ideal, we may at least consider the possibility that he projected two "tornadoed" aspects of his nature into Ishmael and Captain Ahab, in an attempt to exorcise those aspects; to get rid of them. One might say, for example, that Melville contrived Captain Ahab in such a way that his actions would carry Melville's own God-defiant tendencies to such a ridiculously self-annihilating extreme that Melville could hope thus to cure himself of his own monomania. I would even go so far as to agree that Melville probably saw this as a possibility; but I feel quite certain that such a possibility became subordinated and eclipsed by his falling too much in love with his own image, as represented in Captain Ahab. His pleasure was derived, more probably, from his own sense of artistic success in dramatizing the boldness and the tragic heroism of Captain Ahab's unflinching defiance.

There is considerable proof that Melville's own mind had become hypnotized by his own belief in Ahab's ultimate action as an ideal of action, because that kind of action translated death into anti-Christian victory, even as Byron suggested in the last line of his poem *Prometheus*. In *Mardi*, Melville had said, "So, if after all these fearful, fainting trances, the verdict be, the golden haven was not gained;—yet, in bold quest thereof, better to sink in boundless deeps, than float on vulgar shoals; and give me, ye gods, an utter wreck, if wreck I do."[95] In *White-Jacket*, he had said, "Nature has not implanted any power in man that was not meant to be exercised at times. . . . The privilege, inborn and inalienable, that every man has, of dying himself, and inflicting death upon another, was not given us without a purpose. These are the last resources of an insulted and unendurable existence."[96] In the Bulkington chapter of *Moby-Dick*, as we have seen, he said, ". . . so better is it to perish in that howling infinite, than be ingloriously dashed upon the lee, even if that were safety! For worm-like, then, oh! who would craven crawl to land! Terrors of the terrible! is all this agony so vain? Take heart, take heart, O Bulkington! Bear thee grimly, demi-god! Up from the spray of thy ocean-perishing—straight up, leaps thy apotheosis!"[97] In *Pierre*, his description of his autobiographical hero echoes all three of these passages:

"Now he began to feel that in him, the thews of a Titan were forestallingly cut by the scissors of Fate. He felt as a moose, hamstrung. All things that think, or move, or lie still, seemed as created to mock and torment him. He seemed gifted with loftiness, merely that it might be dragged down to the mud. Still, the profound willfulness in him would not give up. Against the breaking heart, and the bursting head; against all the dismal lassitude, and deathful faintness and sleeplessness, and whirlingness and craziness, still he like a demi-god bore up. His soul's ship foresaw the inevitable rocks, but still resolved to sail on, and make a courageous wreck."[98]

The ideal, in each of those passages, is the ideal of the "courageous wreck." But Pierre's final boldness of posture bears a strikingly close resemblance to Ahab's, particularly when Pierre says, near the end of his life, "Now, 'tis merely hell in both worlds. Well, be it hell. I will mold a trumpet of the flames, and, with my breath of flame, breathe back my defiance!"[99]

Shades of Teufelsdröckh's "Everlasting No" and shades of the Satan School of literature to which Melville belonged! He was temperamentally and artistically inclined to strike the Byronic pose and rebaptize himself, not in the name of the Father, but in the name of Satan. Even if we are forced to see in Melville's sophomoric attitude a certain indication of arrested development, it is better to recognize him for what he was than to inflate his attitude into something which it was not.

Baldly stated, then, Melville's underlying theme in *Moby-Dick* correlates the notions that the world was put together wrong and that God is to blame; that God in his infinite malice asserts a sovereign tyranny over man and that most men are seduced into the mistaken view that this divine tyranny is benevolent and therefore acceptable; but that the freethinking and enlightened and heroic man will assert the rights of man and will rebel against God's tyranny by defying God in thought, word, deed, even in the face of God's ultimate indignity, death.

Happily, the greatness of a work of art does not depend entirely on what it says, even though this seems to me to be the ultimately controlling factor. Once we have come to understand the complexities of style and structure and symbol in *Moby-Dick*, we are able to admire anew the brilliance of Melville's success in achieving a highly intricate artistic correlation, which actually rests on the symbolic extensions of one single word, "Leviathan."

GOD'S STONY HEART

CHAPTER VIII

Be astonished, O ye heavens, at this, and be horribly afraid, be ye very desolate, saith the Lord. For my people have committed two evils; they have forsaken me, the fountain of living waters . . .

JEREMIAH 2:12-13

Ah, if man were wholly made in heaven, why catch we hell-glimpses? Why in the noblest marble pillar that stands beneath the all-comprising vault, ever should we descry the sinister vein? We lie in nature very close to God; and though, further on, the stream may be corrupted by the banks it flows through; yet at the fountain's rim, where mankind stand, there the stream infallibly bespeaks the fountain.

MELVILLE, *Pierre*

If a son shall ask bread of any of you that is a father, will he give him a stone?

LUKE 11:11

And He shall be for a stone of stumbling.

ISAIAH 8:14

Oh, ye stony roofs, and seven-fold stony skies!

MELVILLE, *Pierre*

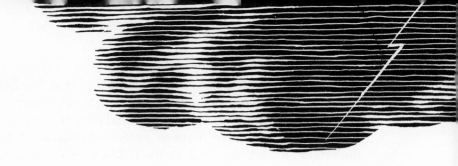

GOD'S STONY HEART

PARMACETI may be the sovereignest thing on earth for an inner bruise; but it only aggravated Melville's peculiar condition and drove him into starting *Pierre* almost as soon as he had finished *Moby-Dick*. Still obsessed with the subject of his own disillusionment, he this time chose to write a satirical novel in which the total action would represent the progressive stages in which an innocent and idealistic young man would be frustrated and destroyed by the combined malice of Heaven and Earth. Once again he permitted the action of this fictionalized autobiography to illustrate that the truly perceptive individual is ultimately forced to declare his defiant independence from both God and man.

The artistic weaknesses of *Pierre* are caused by Melville's attempt to vent his misanthropic hates in too many directions at once, and the consequent diffuseness of effect makes for discouraging reading. For present purposes, however, the most important aspect of the novel is the way in which Melville contrived to endow the major characters with symbolic meanings and then to develop the action of the plot in such a way as to achieve a satirical burlesque of moral allegory.

In presenting the story of Pierre, Melville for the first time assumed the role of omniscient author, apparently hoping that such a focus of narration would permit him to achieve a high degree of artistic detachment. He wished to stand off and laugh not merely at Pierre's naïve innocence but also at the hypocrisies of Christian society; to create a satirical effect which would be genial, jovial, comic, in the general tradition of Lucian and Voltaire. Yet his furiously derisive bitterness constantly tended to undermine his artistic ideal, as the following passage indicates:

". . . I make bold to be gamesome about them—these glorious paupers, from whom I learn the profoundest mysteries of things— for where fundamental nobleness is, and fundamental honour is due, merriment is never accounted irreverent. The fools and pretenders of humanity, and the impostors and baboons among the gods, these only are offended with raillery; since both those gods and men whose titles to eminence are secure, seldom worry themselves about the seditious gossip of old apple-women, and the skylarkings of funny little boys in the street."[1]

The gamesomeness in that passage gets out of hand in the four nouns: fools, pretenders, impostors, baboons. These words are too strong to be comfortable in a context which proposes to excuse critical laughter as a mere form of pleasantry. From that passage alone, one is inclined to suspect that the larger context may reveal a somewhat warped sense of the comic and the ludicrous. It does.

2

PERHAPS the easiest way to represent Melville's method of endowing the total action with mock-allegorical meaning is to begin by summarizing the bare outlines of the plot.

Pierre Glendinning, a gifted and noble young man, has been afforded the advantages of culture and wealth during his early boyhood spent on the rural family estate near Albany, New York. Although his father has died shortly before the story begins, his mother is competent to supervise the considerable estate. She lavishes affectionate attention on her only child, and yet approves his engagement to a perfect young lady named Lucy Banford. In his courtship, Pierre conducts himself with the gallantry of a high-minded story-book knight.

The first important complication in the narrative occurs when Pierre makes the disillusioning discovery that his late father, whom he has worshiped as a model of human virtue, once seduced a beautiful young French girl, and that the illegitimate daughter of that affair, Isabel by name, is now a forlorn social outcast, reduced to servitude. Motivated by genuinely high Christian idealism, Pierre decides to protect Isabel from the world, even though he can do so only by breaking his engagement to Lucy. His mother is ignorant of the early scandal involving his father, and Pierre realizes that she would never condescend to befriend anybody's illegitimate child, so he does not tell her the facts. Instead, he devises a quixotic scheme of pretending he has secretly married a stranger named Isabel and that he is moving to New York.

A further complication occurs when Pierre is prompted to assume an additional social burden. In the dreary farmhouse where Isabel has been working, there is another young lady in distress: Delly Ulver has recently given birth to an illegitimate child, now dead, and is being driven from the community by the town's leading benefactress, who is Pierre's own mother, assisted by the local man of God, Rev. Falsgrave. Asserting his higher social conscience, Pierre plays guardian knight to both girls, and takes them to New York City, where the three of them set up housekeeping, behind the deception that Pierre and Isabel are man and wife. As penalty for disgracing the family name, Pierre is cut off from his heritage, and tries to earn a living through his literary talents.

The villain of the plot is Glendinning Stanley, a cousin of Pierre, who refuses to befriend Pierre as he had promised to do. Stanley subsequently inherits Pierre's estate, following the death of Mrs. Glendinning; Stanley even courts Pierre's former fiancée, Lucy. But the noble Lucy perceives intuitively that Pierre is acting out an idealistic role, and so she decides to throw in her lot with him. Now Pierre has three women in his harem.

Beset on all sides by the unsympathetic cruelties of society, the idealistic Pierre sinks deeper and deeper into disillusionment. His cousin Stanley harasses and insults him. His publishers, who have been paying him advances on a novel, reject the finished manuscript and start legal action against him. Convinced that his high Prometheanism is opposed by God and by society, Pierre resorts to one final self-annihilating gesture of defiance, and kills his cousin Stanley. That night, in jail, he is joined by Isabel and Lucy, who want to share his fate. With Pierre's help, they do. As the final curtain falls, their three dead bodies decorate the scene.

3

MELVILLE's method of establishing symbolic values for his characters, in *Pierre*, and then of interlocking these values, through the
action, enables him to create a form of psychological allegory. In
the beginning, Pierre is surrounded by love, in an Eden-like world,
and repeated analogies are overtly made to suggest that he is as
pure and innocent as Adam before the fall. In this blissful atmosphere, he himself may be considered as a type or symbol of perfection. His devoted mother is represented as a symbol of Mother
Earth, his departed father is represented as a symbol of his
Heavenly Father. Lucy is represented as a symbol of Eve. Then
comes the awakening, and when Pierre's eyes are beginning to
open to the knowledge of good and evil, he leaves his Earthly
Paradise and begins his allegorical quest for Truth, after the
manner of the pilgrim soul, in conventional moral allegory.

As soon as the "awakening" is represented, the two girls are
further endowed with symbolic values until they serve, at times,
to represent the basic psychological conflict between good and
evil, in Pierre's own mind. The psychological allegory thus suggested grows much richer as soon as Pierre catches glimpses of the
possible ambiguity in each girl: under certain circumstances, he
realizes, the seeming good may actually prove to be evil, and the
seeming evil may actually prove to be good. For example, Lucy
represents idealism, and the sunny side of life; the conventional
idealism of optimistic Christian belief. By contrast, Isabel represents the hard cold facts of life; the dark and evil facts of life.
Gradually, Pierre perceives that the "wisdom" represented by
Christian optimism (Lucy) is a pipe-dream wisdom; that only the
wilfully blind are able to settle for that pipe-dream wisdom.
Thereafter, Lucy (whose name suggests that she is an emblem of
light) comes to represent to the enlightened Pierre an artificial or
false light; falsehood. She dramatizes that value, eventually, in
her actions. Isabel, emblem of that woefully true light that shineth
in darkness, would seem to be the only genuine representation
of stark Truth, because Pierre's discovery of the "truth" about
Isabel has helped to correct his evaluation of Lucy. He realizes
that if he could view the two girls in the abstract, entirely apart
from his relationships to them, he could continue to recognize

250

Lucy as an emblem of light and purity and goodness; he could continue to view Isabel as merely a child of sin, an emblem of evil, even as Hester Prynne's neighbors in *The Scarlet Letter* are able to view innocent Pearl as an emblem of sin and evil. But Pierre's enlightened perceptions make him realize that he cannot view these two girls in the abstract; that he can view them only in terms of his own response to each, his responsibilities to each. If he fulfills his responsibility to Isabel, and decides to shelter her from a hostile society, he can do so only by ignoring his responsibility to Lucy. Yet he feels that his impulse to shelter Isabel is prompted by a natural impulse far more binding than his selfishly idealistic impulse to shelter and marry Lucy.

In terms of psychological allegory, then, it would seem that Melville has a fine kettle of fish on the fire, and that it promises a good stew. But it turns out to be a stew which neither Melville nor Pierre can digest (not to mention the reader); hence the cumulative revulsion. Melville takes no chances on having his readers miss the allegorical framework of his narrative, and in one place he openly summarizes it thus:

". . . There now, do you see the soul. In its germ on all sides it is closely folded by the world, as the husk folds the tenderest fruit; then it is born from the world-husk, but still now outwardly clings to it;—still clamours for the support of its mother the world, and its father the Deity. But it shall yet learn to stand independent, though not without many a bitter wail, and many a miserable fall.

"That hour of the life of a man when first the help of humanity fails him, and he learns that in his obscurity and indigence humanity holds him a dog and no man: that hour is a hard one, but not the hardest. There is still another hour which follows, when he learns that in his infinite comparative minuteness and abjectness, the gods do likewise despise him, and own him not of their clan. Divinity and humanity then are equally willing that he should starve in the street for all that either will do for him. Now cruel father and mother have both let go his hand, and the little soul-toddler, now you shall hear his shriek and his wail, and often his fall.

"When at Saddle Meadows, Pierre had wavered and trembled in those first wretched hours ensuing upon the receipt of Isabel's

251

letter; then humanity had let go the hand of Pierre, and therefore his cry; but when at last inured to this, Pierre was seated at his book, willing that humanity should desert him, so long as he thought he felt a far higher support; then, ere long, he began to feel the utter loss of that other support, too; ay, even the paternal gods themselves did now desert Pierre; the toddler was toddling entirely alone, and not without shrieks.

"If man must wrestle, perhaps it is well that it should be on the nakedest possible plain."[2]

This late statement of allegorical meaning focuses the reader's attention particularly on Pierre as a pilgrim soul, on the Mother (who deserted him even as humanity deserted him), and on his "father the Deity." Using this as a guide, we may now examine earlier hints as to Melville's satirical method and meaning, beginning with Chapter One.

4

THE very first scene of the first chapter is a satirical burlesque of moral allegory. On the specific level of narrative statement, Pierre is merely making an early morning visit to his beloved Lucy. On the allegorical level, the passage slyly ridicules the pure and idealistic soul's Platonic response to such physical beauty as would seem to reflect heavenly beauty. This response is mockingly represented by an act of worship or prayer. In this sense, the allegorical beginning, in *Pierre*, inverts the allegorical beginning, in *Mardi*, with the color-symbolism directly carried over:

". . . Pierre . . . lifted his eyes. . . . Upon the sill of the casement, a snow-white glossy pillow reposes, and a trailing shrub has softly rested a rich, crimson flower against it. . . .

"Truly, thought the youth, with a still gaze of inexpressible fondness; truly the skies do ope, and this invoking angel looks down.—'I would return thee thy manifold good mornings, Lucy, did not that presume thou hadst lived through a night; and by heaven, thou belong'st to the regions of an infinite day!'

" 'Fie, now, Pierre; why should ye youths always swear when ye love?'

" 'Because in us love is profane, since it mortally reaches toward the heaven in ye!' "[3]

Having read this far, the careless reader's dislike for the archaic conversation inclines him to recoil aghast. But this conversation should be recognized as a conscious stylistic burlesque, and the effect is intended to be ridiculous. Melville knows what he is up to, and he deliberately indulges his bitter fondness for parody. He can alter this mockery whenever he chooses, and as soon as he begins to give a picture of Pierre's background and breeding, the mock-allegory becomes mock-heroic. Here, for example, the mock-heroic undertones and overtones sardonically hint at Pierre's reason for identifying his earthly father with his Heavenly Father:

". . . Not in vain had he spent long summer afternoons in the deep recesses of his father's fastidiously picked and decorous library; where the Spenserian nymphs had early led him into many a maze of all-bewildering beauty. Thus, with a graceful glow on his limbs, and soft, imaginative flames in his heart, did this Pierre glide toward maturity, thoughtless of that period of remorseless insight, when all these delicate warmths should seem frigid to him, and he should madly demand more ardent fires.

"Nor had that pride and love which had so bountifully provided for the youthful nurture of Pierre, neglected his culture in the deepest element of all. It had been a maxim with the father of Pierre, that all gentlemanhood was vain; all claims to it preposterous and absurd, unless the primeval gentleness and golden humanities of religion had been so thoroughly wrought into the complete texture of the character, that he who pronounced himself gentleman, could also rightfully assume the meek, but kingly style of Christian. At the age of sixteen, Pierre partook with his mother of the Holy Sacraments."[4]

That passage is merely a foreshadowing of a far more overtly sarcastic and mock-heroic scene in which Pierre himself is made to acknowledge his habit of identifying his father with his God. Priding himself on a humorous and lofty detachment, Melville repeatedly employs this style and tone of the mock-heroic in describing young Pierre's idealism, always tucking in overt jibes, as here:

"In the country then Nature planted our Pierre; because Nature intended a rare and original development in Pierre. Never mind if hereby she proved ambiguous to him in the end; nevertheless, in the beginning she did bravely. She blew her wind-clarion from the blue hills, and Pierre neighed out lyrical thoughts, as at the trumpet-blast, a war-horse paws himself into a lyric of foam. She whispered through her deep groves at eve, and gentle whispers of humanness, and sweet whispers of love, ran through Pierre's thought-veins, musical as water over pebbles. She lifted her spangled crest of a thickly-starred night, and forth at that glimpse of their divine Captain and Lord, ten thousand mailed thoughts of heroicness started up in Pierre's soul, and glared round for some insulted good cause to defend.

"So the country was a glorious benediction to young Pierre; we shall see if that blessing pass from him as did the divine blessing from the Hebrews; we shall yet see again, I say, whether Fate hath not just a little bit of a word or two to say in this world; we shall see whether this wee little bit scrap of latinity be very far out of the way—*Nemo contra Deum nisi Deus ipse.*"[5]

The style and tone here anticipate that of Meredith in describing the early days of young Richard Feverel. Melville is having a whirl, and is playing all manner of variations on his own penny-whistle, not least of these being his sarcastically pretending to honor that Christian optimism which he actually loathes:

"Oh, praised be the beauty of this earth, the beauty, and the bloom, and the mirthfulness thereof! We lived before, and shall live again; and as we hope for a fairer world than this to come; so we came from one less fine. From each successive world, the demon Principle is more and more dislodged; he is the accursed clog from chaos, and thither, by every new translation, we drive him further and further back again. Hosannahs to this world! so beautiful itself, and the vestibule to more. Out of some past Egypt, we have come to this new Canaan; and from this new Canaan, we press on to some Circassia. Though still the villains, Want and Woe, followed us out of Egypt, and now beg in Canaan's streets: yet Circassia's gates shall not admit them; they with their sire, the demon Principle, must back to chaos, whence they came."[6]

This burlesque of the Psalms, taken literally, may seem to reflect (in part, at least) the orthodox Christian viewpoint; taken in the larger context supplied by *Pierre*, it has a biting tone and a sinister meaning, which equates "the demon Principle" with God Almighty. And because the Platonic allegory on the beauty of woman provides a perfectly ambiguous emblem for representing

the "demon Principle" in either frame of reference, Melville indulges in some of his most overtly ironical and rhetorical fan
dances, when he sarcastically glorifies the love between Pierre
and Lucy:

"Love's eyes are holy things; therein the mysteries of life are
lodged; looking in each other's eyes, lovers see the ultimate secret
of the worlds; and with thrills eternally untranslatable, feel that
Love is god of all. Man or woman who has never loved, nor once
looked deep down into their own lover's eyes, they know not the
sweetest and loftiest religion of this earth. Love is both Creator's
and Saviour's gospel to mankind; a volume bound in rose-leaves,
clasped with violets, and by the beaks of humming-birds printed
with peach-juice on the leaves of lilies."[7]

The jocose geniality of that passage is split with venom. Notice,
as Melville continues, how he takes another poke at Christian
optimism; that he also makes sarcastic use of a line parodied from
Shelley. "Love is busy everywhere," says Melville. But Shelley
had said, "Death is busy everywhere." Darkly, Melville means
just that. The mock-heroic and mock-Christian parody continues:

"Endless is the account of Love. Time and space cannot contain Love's story. All things that are sweet to see, or taste, or feel,
or hear, all these things were made by Love; and none other
things were made by Love. Love made not the Arctic zones, but
Love is ever reclaiming them. Say, are not the fierce things of this
earth daily, hourly going out? Where now are your wolves of
Britain? Where in Virginia now, find you the panther and the
pard? Oh, Love is busy everywhere. . . . All this Earth is Love's
affianced; vainly the demon Principle howls to stay the banns. . . ."[8]

Is this merely "gamesome"? Only if we create a new definition
for the word. In his bitterness, Melville is betting too much on the
stupidity of his reading public, which may settle for the sugar-
coating of the pill, without ever tasting the calomel.

5

A MORE powerful dose of calomel is administered to the unsus-
pecting reader at the beginning of Book Three, where Pierre
meets Isabel and learns that his father's "original" or procreative
sin (shades of the Genesis interpretation) made her his illegiti-

mate sister. In preparation for this narrative development, Melville again provides the reader with one of his darker broodings. Pierre has previously seen the strange face of Lucy, and it has haunted him even though he does not yet fully understand why. Melville at once proceeds to generalize in a manner which obliquely illuminates his own private concept concerning the good-evil dualism of God:

". . . Out of the heart of mirthfulness, this shadow had come forth to him. Encircled by bandelets of light, it had still beamed upon him; vaguely historic and prophetic; backward, hinting of some irrevocable sin; forward, pointing to some inevitable ill. One of those faces, which now and then appear to man, and without one word of speech, still reveal glimpses of some fearful gospel. In natural guise, but lit by supernatural light; palpable to the senses, but inscrutable to the soul; in their perfectest impression on us, ever hovering between Tartarean misery and Paradisiac beauty; such faces, compounded so of hell and heaven, overthrow in us all foregone persuasions, and make us wondering children in this world again."[9]

As soon as Pierre has received the truth-revealing note from Isabel, but before Pierre has read it, Melville brilliantly demonstrates the ironic potential of the ambiguities thus made available; the wheels within wheels, and the contrasting layers of meaning. As already said, the emblematic value of the two girls, Lucy and Isabel, is suggested by their names; but as the narrative progresses, these girls are endowed with multiple symbolism, so that at different times they represent three closely related forms of conflict: the first form, already named, is that of a basic psychological conflict in Pierre; the second form is the fundamental conflict between good and evil, in the world; the third form is the ulterior and paradoxical conflict between good and evil, in the nature of God Himself.

The ironic potential of these ambiguities is such that, even for Christian Pierre, Isabel (child of evil) may eventually become his good angel, and the child of heaven and of Christian convention may become his bad angel. At first he does not entirely see this, but Melville makes the reader see it in the following passage:

"Pierre now seemed distinctly to feel two antagonistic agencies within him; one of which was just struggling into his consciousness, and each of which was striving for mastery; and between whose respective final ascendencies he *thought* [italics added] he could perceive, though but shadowly, that he himself was to be the only umpire. One bade him finish the selfish destruction of the note; for in some dark way the reading of it would irretrievably entangle his fate. The other bade him dismiss all misgivings; not because there was no possible ground for them, but because to dismiss them was the manlier part, never mind what might betide. This good angel seemed mildly to say—Read, Pierre, though by reading thou may'st entangle thyself, yet may'st thou thereby disentangle others. Read, and feel that best blessedness which, with the sense of all duties discharged, holds happiness indifferent. The bad angel insinuatingly breathed—Read it not, dearest Pierre; but destroy it, and be happy. Then, at the blast of his noble heart, the bad angel shrunk up into nothingness; and the good one defined itself clearer and more clear, and came nigher and more nigh to him, smiling sadly but benignantly; while forth from the infinite distances wonderful harmonies stole into his heart; so that every vein in him pulsed to some heavenly swell."[10]

One aspect of irony, in this passage, is that Pierre does not yet realize that the persuasion offered him by his bad angel is exactly the persuasion which Lucy, his affianced, would be bound to exert on him. Another aspect of irony is that this passage, on the allegorical level of meaning, represents the soul's hesitation when confronted by a choice involving good and evil; but that the sinister implication is that the soul must be confronted, sooner or later, with unvarnished facts which contradict and destroy religious faith. Melville does not risk the possibility that the reader may miss these sinister implications. He lets Pierre examine the facts, and feel himself disillusioned and wounded by these facts as deeply as Ahab was disillusioned and wounded by the lightning. Then Melville rubs in the salt:

"Ay, Pierre, now indeed art thou hurt with a wound, never to be completely healed but in heaven [wormwood!]; for thee, the before undistrusted moral beauty of the world is forever fled; for thee, thy sacred father is no more a saint; all brightness hath gone from thy hills, and all peace from thy plains; and now, now, for the first time, Pierre, Truth rolls a black billow through thy soul! Ah, miserable thou, to whom Truth, in her first tides, bears nothing but wrecks!"[11]

Again, with the appearance of that word, "Truth," the reader who has progressed to *Pierre* through *Mardi, Redburn, White-Jacket,* and *Moby-Dick,* cannot help but realize that Melville seems forced to use much the same aspect of his own spiritual autobiography as raw materials for the thematic concern, or conceptual core, of each book. And Pierre's reaction to this wound is expressed in words which very closely echo Ahab's apostrophe to the tri-pointed trinity of corposants. Thus Pierre:

" 'Myself am left, at least. With myself I front thee! Unhand me all fears, and unlock me all spells! Henceforth I will know nothing but Truth, glad Truth, or sad Truth; I will know what *is*, and so what my deepest angel dictates. . . . Oh! falsely guided in the days of my Joy, am I now truly led in this night of my grief?—I will be a raver, and none shall stay me! I will lift my hand in fury, for am I not struck? [cf. Ahab: "I'd strike the sun, if it insulted me."] I will be bitter in my breath, for is not this cup of gall? Thou Black Knight, that with visor down, thus confrontest me, and mockest at me; lo! I strike through thy helm [cf. Hamlet, cf. Ahab: "Strike through the mask."], and will see thy face, be it Gorgon!' "[12]

At this point, the danger flag must again be hoisted for the benefit of the hasty reader. Encouraged by Melville to recognize emblematic meanings, the reader is likely to make the mistake of concluding that Pierre sees the full emblematic significance of his words. He does not. Thus, the passage just quoted provides an excellent example of discrete meanings which Melville asks the reader to sort out and assign to their proper frames of reference. The simplest frame of reference is Pierre's limited one: he is not an Ahab; he is only a young innocent who comes to his first disillusionment with the realization that Truth may at times conceal itself in protean guises and disguises. Truth is the "Black Knight, that with the visor down, thus confrontest me." So far, Pierre is only a first-act Hamlet, resolving to learn the truth, at all costs. A second frame of reference is provided by Christian concepts, which are not immediately active as such in Pierre as he thinks about Truth. "Ye shall know the Truth, and the Truth shall set you free." "I am the way, the truth, and the light." To know the truth is to know God, and so in the Christian frame of refer-

258

ence, Pierre's assertiveness is noble and religious in implication, although the sinister undertones obviously are not! The third frame of reference, provided by Melville's private and anti-Christian myth, implies that to know the truth is indeed to know God, but to know the taunting malice of God. Hence the "Black Knight, that with visor down, thus confrontest me, and mockest at me" represents, in this third frame of reference, the ulterior meaning which ties the passage to the conceptual center of Melville's dark allegory. Out of earshot from Pierre, Melville is thus reminding the reader that the dual nature of God is darkened and blackened by the everlasting and all-pervading evil of God, by the innate depravity of God, who constantly mocks and tortures mankind.

6

In the very next chapter, Pierre's disillusioned recoil from the discovery of his father's sins is represented in such a way that the allegorical framework translates the specifics into blasphemous insinuations as to the nature and attributes of God. Although the Melvillian device of triple-talk is still being employed, in *Pierre*, the sinister signposts are far more overtly flaunted than in any of the previous novels. For example, consider a little progression of passages which deal specifically (and equivocally) with Pierre's changing attitude toward his father in heaven:

"There had long stood a shrine in the fresh-foliaged heart of Pierre, up to which he ascended by many tableted steps of remembrance; and around which annually he had hung fresh wreaths of a sweet and holy affection. Made one green bower at last, by such successive votive offerings of his being; this shrine seemed, and was indeed, a place for the celebration of a chastened joy, rather than for any melancholy rites. But though thus mantled, and tangled with garlands, this shrine was of marble—a niched pillar deemed solid and eternal, and from whose top radiated all those innumerable sculptured scrolls and branches, which supported the entire one-pillared temple of his moral life. . . . In this shrine, in this niche of this pillar, stood the perfect marble form of his departed father; without blemish, unclouded, snow-white, and serene; Pierre's fond personification of perfect human goodness and virtue. Before this shrine, Pierre poured out the fullness of all his young life's most reverential thoughts and beliefs. Not to God had Pierre ever gone in his heart, unless by ascending the steps of that shrine, and so making it the vestibule of his abstractest religion."[13]

Melville continues to explain that Pierre could hold this ideal of his father, in youth, because "the Solomonic insights have not poured their turbid tributaries into the pure-flowing well of the childish life." Now, however, the unchristian Solomonic insights begin to dawn for Pierre, and he is driven to recall many different aspects of his former life which had previously provided him with hints (then entirely meaningless) that his father had a dual nature.

To represent this dual nature, Melville makes particular use of two family portraits of Pierre's father: two portraits which are strikingly different in their representation. The smaller portrait, showing the father as a gay young blade, seemed to Pierre's mother, "namelessly unpleasant and repelling." She said it "did signally belie her husband." The other, larger portrait, she liked better because she thought it more correctly conveyed the details of his features, "and more especially their truest, and finest, and noblest combined expression." With allegorical appropriateness, Pierre inherits the lesser portrait, and in retrospect remembers that an aunt had cautiously (or perhaps innocently) told him it was painted while his father had been courting a beautiful and aristocratic refugee who later returned to France and disappeared. Isabel supplies him, now, with the details as to how and why that seduced and disgraced lady had disappeared. In anguish, Pierre can no longer bear the sight of the smaller portrait, which he had long kept hanging in his room: he "reversed the picture on the wall." But the "defaced and dusty back" was so unattractive: " 'Oh, symbol of thy reversed idea in my soul,' groaned Pierre; 'thou shalt not hang thus. Rather cast thee utterly out, than conspicuously insult thee so. I will no more have a father.' "[14]

Without knowing it, however, Pierre is a chip off the old Block! Melville's fondness for the ironies of a parallel construction have already been described, a terse example being Starbuck's comment on Ahab: "Aye, he would be a democrat to all above; look, how he lords it over all below." Similarly, perfect Pierre, who would have his own father perfect, is unconsciously and imperfectly prompted to become Isabel's knight because she is sexually attractive to him. Melville later makes allegorical use of their incestuous sexual relationship, and for this reason the first sardonic foreshadowing of it is important:

"Save me from being bound to Truth, liege lord, as I am now. How shall I steal yet further into Pierre, and show how this heavenly fire was helped to be contained in him, by mere contingent things, and things that he knew not. But I shall follow the endless, winding way,—the flowing river in the cave of man; careless whither I be led, reckless where I land.

"Was not the face—though mutely mournful—beautiful, bewitching? How unfathomable those most wondrous eyes of supernatural light! In those charmed depths, Grief and Beauty plunged and dived together. So beautiful, so mystical, so bewilderingly alluring; speaking of a mournfulness infinitely sweeter and more attractive than all mirthfulness; that face of glorious suffering; that face of touching loveliness; that face was Pierre's own sister's; that face was Isabel's; that face Pierre had visibly seen; into those same supernatural eyes our Pierre had looked. Thus, already, and ere the proposed encounter, he was assured that, in a transcendent degree, womanly beauty, and not womanly ugliness, invited him to champion the right. Be naught concealed in this book of sacred truth. How, if accosted in some squalid lane, a humped, and crippled, hideous girl should have snatched his garment's hem, with—'Save me, Pierre—love me, own me, brother; I am thy sister!' "

Then Melville immediately continues with highly insinuative hints of parallels which allegorically link the depravity of father, son, Holy Ghost, and Satan, so to speak:

"Ah, if man were wholly made in heaven, why catch we hell-glimpses? Why in the noblest marble pillar that stands beneath the all-comprising vault, ever should we descry the sinister vein? We lie in nature very close to God; and though, further on, the stream may be corrupted by the banks it flows through; yet at the fountain's rim, where mankind stand, there the stream infallibly bespeaks the fountain.

"So let no censorious word be here hinted of mortal Pierre. Easy for me to slyly hide these things, and always put him before the eye as perfect as immaculate; unsusceptible to the inevitable nature and the lot of common men. I am more frank with Pierre

261

than the best men are with themselves. I am all unguarded and magnanimous with Pierre; therefore you see his weakness, and therefore only. In reserves men guild imposing characters; not in revelations. He who shall be wholly honest, though nobler than Ethan Allen; that man shall stand in danger of the meanest mortal's scorn."[15]

Trust Melville to be most untrustworthy when he is protesting that he *could* "slyly hide these things" if he weren't determined to make a clean breast! The entire passage is one of stylistic rascality. Superficially, and in a Christian frame of reference, it could be interpreted to mean that God's in his Heaven, and Satan's in Hell, and never the twain shall meet, except as man permits them to meet in him. But the "sinister vein" of meaning, which accords with Melville's private interpretation of the Genesis story, and of "Original Sin," insists that God's in Satan and Satan's in God, and never the twain can be completely separate. "We lie in nature very close to God." Sweet! That sounds very Christian, and indeed is; but not for Melville. Correctly interpreted (in the context Melville himself supplies), those eight words also imply that we human beings in our natural state—in our so-called state of "Natural Depravity"—lie cheek by jowl with the "Divine Depravity" of God Almighty. "All things come of thee, oh Lord, and of thine own have we given thee." So with Pierre's father, so with the idealistic Pierre who wants to live up to a concept of human conduct that is an improvement on God's conduct, as Melville interprets God's conduct. But the dice of God are always loaded: Pierre, like his father, will soon find out that he is a chip off the old Block. "Easy for me to slyly hide these things, and always put him before the eye as perfect as immaculate . . ." That is what I mean by rascality! Ostensibly, the antecedent of "he" in that sentence is Pierre; contextually and symbolically, the antecedent is ambiguous: Pierre or God; Pierre and God. ("I and my Father are one.") And how innocent to choose Ethan Allen as a type of nobility in such a passage. That darling and heroic Green Mountain Boy. Would anybody dare claim that Melville here uses Ethan Allen's name ambiguously? Perhaps only those esoteric souls who know his "deistic" book entitled, *Reason the Only Oracle of Man* (as Melville certainly did) and who thus may understand why the orthodox Christians attacked Allen as a wretched atheist!

But lest some reader may feel that I make too much of Melville's quarrel with God, and of his fondness for tweaking God's nose with epithets, let me round off this section with a very brief passage in which Melville tweaks with less subtlety:

". . . how could Pierre, naturally poetic, and therefore piercing as he was; how could he fail to acknowledge the existence of that all-controlling and all-permeating wonderfulness, which, when imperfectly and isolatedly recognized by the generality, is so significantly denominated the Finger of God? But it is not merely the Finger, it is the whole outspread Hand of God; for doth not the Scripture intimate, that He holdeth all of us in the hollow of His hand?—a Hollow, truly!"[16]

7

MELVILLE could not go very far in such a burlesque novel of manners without taking a side-swipe at a professional Christian. One of the best-sustained chapters is the fourth, of Book Four, in which the Reverend Mister Falsgrave joins Mrs. Glendinning and Pierre for breakfast, during the period when Pierre is still brooding over his newly discovered secret as to Isabel's ancestry. Mrs. Glendinning explains that Mr. Falsgrave has come to settle "that wretched affair" of Delly Ulver, who has (with artistic convenience) just recently disgraced the community by giving birth to an illegitimate child. Employing one of his favorite stylistic devices of irony, Melville manages to ridicule Falsgrave, as he enters, by describing him in ruthlessly flattering terms. Then the situation is so developed that Falsgrave is permitted (quite unconsciously) to unmask and reveal himself as a hypocritical time-server. Of course Melville makes the problem of Delly Ulver parallel the secret problem in Pierre's thoughts. When the occasion offers, Pierre can thus indirectly confront both his mother and the pastor with his own problem. A word of caution here. Pierre is still innocent enough to hope that he may accept Rev. Falsgrave as an ideal and model man of God. Consequently, while Pierre is merely troubled by the minister's replies, Melville quietly sneers:

" '. . . Should the legitimate child shun the illegitimate, when one father is father to both?' rejoined Pierre, bending his head still further over his plate.

"The clergyman looked a little down again, and was silent but still turned his head slightly sideways toward his hostess, as if awaiting some reply to Pierre from her.

"'Ask the world, Pierre'—said Mrs. Glendinning warmly—'and ask your own heart.'

"'My own heart? I will, Madam'—said Pierre, now looking up steadfastly; 'but what do *you* think, Mr. Falsgrave?' letting his glance drop again—'should the one shun the other? should the one refuse his highest sympathy and perfect love for the other, especially if that other be deserted by all the rest of the world? What think you would have been our blessed Saviour's thoughts on such a matter? And what was that he so mildly said to the adulteress?' "

(The clergyman, while answering with a long speech, jewelled with empty clichés, manages to evade the question entirely. Immediately, Melville's fondness for emblems gets the better of him, and he recalls to the reader a very ambiguous saying of Christ, in the following tableau:)

"At this instant, the surplice-like napkin dropped from the clergyman's bosom, showing a minute but exquisitely cut cameo brooch, representing the allegorical union of the serpent and the dove. It had been the gift of an appreciative friend, and was sometimes worn on secular occasions like the present."

This image again ironically reminds the reader (among other things) of Melville's preoccupation with the duality of God. The possibilities for extension are exploited. First, Mrs. Glendinning's remark that Pierre is unusually polite to her, this morning, prompts Pierre to answer:

"' "Honor thy father and mother"; *both* father and mother,' he unconsciously added. 'And now that it strikes me, Mr. Falsgrave, and now that we have become so strangely polemical this morning, let me say, that as that command is justly said to be the only one with a promise, so it seems to be without any contingency in the application. It would seem—would it not, sir?—that the most deceitful and hypocritical of fathers should be equally honored by the son, as the purest.'

"'So it would certainly seem, according to the strict letter of the Decalogue—certainly.'

"'And do you think, sir, that it should be so held, and so applied in actual life? For instance, should I honor my father, if I knew him to be a seducer?'

" 'Pierre! Pierre!' said his mother, profoundly coloring, and half rising; 'there is no need of these argumentative assumptions. You very immensely forget yourself this morning.' "[17]

Permitting his characters to talk at cross purposes is, as I may have hinted, and ambiguous device which Melville loved. But he here exploits, with particular skill, the way in which this breakfast scene makes Pierre conscious of the duality not only in his father and in Rev. Falsgrave (as the name implies) but also in his mother; the consequent necessity for turning away from any thought of confiding in his mother; the further necessity for leaving her.

As a method of making up his mind as to his course of action, Pierre goes to consult the oracular Memnon Stone, which answers with truly stonelike silence. At the time, he finds the answer satisfactory and sufficient; but later, Melville informs us, Pierre recalls that stonelike answer and observes that it was metaphysically emblematic; to use Ishmael's phrase again, "indifferent as his God." Pierre is hindered from recognizing that metaphysical analogy, at this time, because he is still trying desperately to maintain and preserve his Christian beliefs. The passage in which Melville generalizes on this event, at the Memnon Stone, again calls attention to his conscious employment of those technical devices which, when integrated and maintained, consciously enrich the narrative with allegorical meaning. To sharpen the focus, I have supplied the italics and the bracketed words:

"Pierre pondered on the stone, and his young thoughts concerning it, and, *later*, his desperate act in crawling under it; then [that is, years later] an immense *significance* came to him, and the long-passed unconscious movements of his *then* youthful heart seemed *now* prophetic to him, and *allegorically* verified by the subsequent events.

"For, not to speak of the *other and subtler meanings* which lie crouching behind the colossal haunches of this stone, regarded as the menacingly impending Terror Stone—hidden to all the simple cottagers, but revealed to Pierre—consider its aspects as the Memnon Stone. For Memnon was that dewy, royal boy, son of Aurora, and born King of Egypt, who, with enthusiastic rashness, flinging himself on another's account into a rightful quarrel, fought hand to hand with his overmatch, and met his boyish and most dolorous death beneath the walls of Troy. His wailing subjects built a

265

monument in Egypt to commemorate his untimely fate. Touched by the breath of the bereaved Aurora, every sunrise that statue gave forth a mournful broken sound, as of a harp-string suddenly sundered, being too harshly wound.

"Herein lies an unsummed world of grief. For in this plaintive *fable* we find embodied the Hamletism of the antique world; the Hamletism of three thousand years ago: 'The flower of virtue cropped by a too rare mischance.' And the English tragedy is but Egyptian Memnon, Montaignized and modernized; for being but a mortal man Shakespeare had his fathers too.

"Now as the Memnon Statue survives down to this present day, so does that nobly-striving but ever-shipwrecked character in some royal youths (for both Memnon and Hamlet were the sons of kings), of which that statue is the melancholy *type*. But Memnon's sculptured woes did once melodiously resound; now all is mute. Fit *emblem* that of old, poetry was a consecration and an obsequy to all hapless modes of human life; but in a bantering, barren and prosaic, heartless age, Aurora's music-moan is lost among our drifting sands, which whelm alike the monument and the dirge."[18]

This is Melville talking, not Pierre. Difficult as it may be to separate Melville's skepticism and "madness" from Pierre's troubled but as yet persistent Christian faith, it is important to an understanding of the story to realize that Pierre continues to keep his basic Christian faith, even after he has convinced himself that the so-called Christian world has corrupted and degraded the teachings of Jesus. His final scene with Rev. Falsgrave marks merely another step in his education: he realizes that the professional representatives of God are subject to human weakness and fault, and therefore he turns, from such representatives, to God himself. Allegorically, at this stage of his progressive enlightenments, he is merely repeating the pattern of the Protestant break from the corruptions of Catholicism: he renounces any professed intermediary between himself and God, the better to hear the voice of God. Of course, within Melville's insinuated and ulterior frame of reference, such a step is highly ironic, because God is dumb. But Pierre is not conscious of this irony, in the following scene, which occurs when he calls for the last time on Falsgrave:

" 'Thou art a man of God, sir, I believe.'

" 'I? I? I? upon my word, Mr. Glendinning!'

" 'Yes, sir, the world calls thee a man of God. Now, what hast thou, the man of God, decided, with my mother, concerning Delly Ulver?'

" 'Delly Ulver! why, why—what can this *madness* mean?' [Italics added]

" 'It means, sir, what have thou and my mother decided concerning Delly Ulver.'

" 'She?—Delly Ulver? She is to depart the neighbourhood; why, her own parents want her not.'

" '*How* is she to depart? *Who* is to take her? Art *thou* to take her? *Where* is she to go? *Who* has food for her? *What* is to keep her from the pollution to which such as she are every day driven to contribute, by the detestable uncharitableness and heartlessness of the world?'

" 'Mr. Glendinning,' said the clergyman . . .

"But Pierre sat entirely still, and the clergyman could not but remain standing still.

" 'I perfectly comprehend the whole, sir. Delly Ulver, then, is to be driven out to starve or rot; and this, too, by the acquiescence of a man of God. Mr. Falsgrave, the subject of Delly, deeply interesting as it is to me, is only the preface to another, still more interesting to me, and concerning which I once cherished some slight hope that thou wouldst have been able, in thy Christian character, to sincerely and honestly counsel me. But a hint from heaven assures me now, that thou hast no earnest and world-disdaining counsel for me. I must seek it direct from God Himself, Who, I now know, never delegates His holiest admonishings. But I do not blame thee; I think I begin to see how thy profession is unavoidably entangled by all fleshly alliances, and can not move with godly freedom in a world of benefices. I am more sorry than indignant. Pardon me for my most uncivil call, and know me as not thy enemy. Good night, sir.' "[19]

8

DURING the next phase of his development, Pierre becomes the allegorical type of the "Enthusiast"—literally, God-possessed and God-inspired. And Melville further manipulates the actions of his young enthusiast in such a way as to illuminate his own anti-Christian theological beliefs. What finer allegorical insinuations could Melville find than to let all of Pierre's immediate actions be circumscribed by the Second Commandment of the Decalogue: "Honor thy father and thy mother." Here, indeed, is the word of God, and Pierre decides that whereas his mother has turned against him, so that he has become an Ishmael-like outcast, he can nevertheless honor his father by assuming those obligations which his father would undoubtedly have wished him to assume! Melville revels in the irony of the situation, as this detached and sarcastic comment on Pierre shows:

"Now he thinks he knows that the wholly unanticipated storm which had so terribly burst upon him, had yet burst upon him for his good; for the place, which in its undetected incipiency, the storm had obscurely occupied in his soul, seemed now clear sky to him; and all his horizon seemed distinctly commanded by him. . . .

"True, he in embryo foreknew, that the extraordinary thing he had resolved, would, in another way, indirectly though inevitably, dart a most keen pang into his mother's heart; but this then seemed to him part of the unavoidable vast price of his enthusiastic virtue; and, thus minded, rather would he privately pain his living mother with a wound that might be curable, than cast world-wide and irremediable dishonour—so it seemed to him—upon his departed father."[20]

In other words—and the ironies on all three levels of meaning are obvious—Pierre had resolved to keep secret the act of darkness, the original philoprogenitive sin, committed in secret by his father. He would assume full responsibility for the care and protection of both Isabel Banford and Delly Ulver. With a half serious and half mocking tone, Melville bears down hard as he comments further on Pierre's decision:

"Ah, thou rash boy! are there no couriers in the air to warn thee away from these imperillings, and point thee to those Cretan labyrinths, to which thy life's cord is leading thee? Where now are the high beneficences? Whither fled the sweet angels that are alleged guardians to man? . . .

"Such, oh thou son of man! are the perils and the miseries thou callest down on thee, when, even in a virtuous cause, thou steppest aside from those arbitrary lines of conduct, by which the common world, however base and dastardly, surrounds thee for thy worldly good. . . .

"And what though not through the sin of Pierre, but through his father's sin, that father's fair fame now lay at the mercy of the son, and could only be kept inviolate by the son's free sacrifice of all earthly felicity;—what if this were so? It but struck a still loftier chord in the bosom of the son, and filled him with infinite magnanimities."[21]

The constant reference to the name of the father and of the son begins to establish just the faintest hints, within the sinister allegorical framework, that (for Melville) even as Pierre was double-crossed by his father, so Jesus Christ was double-crossed by God. That the overtones are not imaginary interpretations on my part will become abundantly clear. The specific narrative itself very soon correlates the Second Adam with the First Adam.

Having made up his mind as to his course of action, Pierre goes to Isabel and tells her his plan. It will be recalled that Melville has already suggested the way in which Pierre's unevaluated and even unrecognized sexual response to Isabel's beauty stimulates his desire to champion her cause. Isabel is in no way conscious of this danger; but in protesting her desire to bring no hardships on him, she sets up the potential which is developed nicely:

"He was turning from her, when Isabel sprang forward to him, caught him with both her arms round him, and held him so convulsively, that her hair sideways swept over him, and half concealed him.

" 'Pierre, if indeed my soul hath cast on thee the same black shadow that my hair now flings on thee; if thou hast lost aught for me; then eternally is Isabel lost to Isabel, and Isabel will not outlive this night. If I am indeed an accursing thing, I will not act the given part, but cheat the air, and die from it. See; I let thee go, lest some poison I know not of distill upon thee from me.' . . .

" 'Thou art made of that fine, unshared stuff of which God makes his seraphim. . . . One only way presents to this; a most strange way, Isabel; to the world, that never throbbed for thee in love, a most deceitful way; but to all a harmless way; so harmless in its essence, Isabel, that, seems to me, Pierre hath consulted heaven itself upon it, and heaven itself did not say Nay. . . . Listen.

269

Brace thyself: here, let me hold thee now; and whisper it to thee, Isabel. Come, I holding thee, thou canst not fall.'

"He held her tremblingly; she bent over toward him; his mouth wet her ear; he whispered it [his plan for them to feign marriage].

"The girl moved not; was done with all her tremblings; leaned closer to him, with an inexpressible strangeness of an intense love, new and inexplicable. Over the face of Pierre there shot a terrible self-revelation; he imprinted repeated burning kisses upon her; pressed hard her hand; would not let go her sweet and awful passiveness.

"Then they changed; they coiled together, and entangedly stood mute."[22]

For the reader who has become interested in Melville's reinterpretation of the Genesis story, this not exactly sibling conduct should have particular interest. It will be remembered that Milton, in *Paradise Lost*, dwells at some length on the way in which Eve induces Adam to taste the fruit of the tree of the knowledge of good and evil. In the allegorical sense, Isabel now plays the role of Eve and Pierre still plays the role of Adam:

> So saying, she embrac'd him, and for joy
> Tenderly wept, much won that he his Love
> Had so ennobl'd, as of choice to incur
> Divine displeasure for her sake, or Death. . . .
> . . . . . . he scrupl'd not to eat
> Against his better knowledge, not deceiv'd,
> But fondly overcome with Female charm. . . .
> As with new Wine intoxicated both
> They . . . fancy that they feel
> Divinity within them breeding wings
> Wherewith to scorn the Earth: but that false Fruit
> Far other operation first display'd
> Carnal desire inflaming, he on Eve
> Began to cast lascivious Eyes, she him
> As wantonly repaid; in Lust they burn . . .[23]

The parallel seems to me too close to be accidental; but notice that whereas both Milton and Melville make literary capital of the ironies inherent in a similar situation, Milton goes on to surround the situation with a context which justifies the ways of God to

270

men; Melville goes on to invert Milton's intent, by dramatizing the ultimate and ulterior injustice of God's ways to men, emblematically represented by his own Adam-like Pierre, his own idealistic and (in a limited sense) Christ-like Pierre.

9

NOT long after Pierre ratifies his holy contract with unholy kisses, he and the two girls are on their way to New York City by stage. "No word was spoken by its inmates as the coach bearing our young Enthusiast, Pierre, and his mournful party, sped forth through the dim dawn into the deep midnight. . . ." For Pierre, this journey marks his Adam-like departure from the Earthly Paradise of his youthful innocence. Deeply troubled by all the contingencies surrounding and penetrating his decision, he alternates between determination and doubt. The longer he thinks, in the silence of the coach, the stronger become his doubts. Melville, always with his eye on the main chance—the sinister chance—explains Pierre's stagecoach doubts thus:

"His thoughts were very dark and wild; for a space there was rebellion and horrid anarchy and infidelity in his soul. This temporary mood may best be likened to that, which—according to a singular story once told in the pulpit by a reverend man of God—invaded the heart of an excellent priest. In the midst of a solemn cathedral, upon a cloudy Sunday afternoon, this priest was in the act of publicly administering the bread at the Holy Sacrament of the Supper, when the Evil One suddenly propounded to him the possibility of the mere moonshine of all his self-renouncing Enthusiasm. The Evil One hooted at him, and called him a fool. But by instant and earnest prayer—*closing his two eyes* [italics added], with his two hands still holding the sacramental bread—the devout priest had vanquished the impious Devil. Not so with Pierre. The imperishable record of his Holy Bible; the imperishable intuition of the innate truth of Christianity;—these were the indestructible anchors which still held the priest to his firm Faith's rock, when the sudden storm raised by the Evil One assailed him. But Pierre—where could *he* find the Church, the monument, the Bible, which unequivocally said to him—'Go on; thou art in the Right; I endorse thee all over; go on.'—So the difference between the priest and

Pierre was herein:—with the priest it was a matter, whether certain bodiless thoughts of his were true or not; but with Pierre it was a question whether certain vital acts of his were right or wrong."[24]

So passes the night for Pierre, and "the first visible rays of the morning sun in this same mood found him and saluted him." But while the girls still slept beside him, he entertained himself by reading a curious and battered pamphlet he had accidentally found on the seat beside him in the dark. It was entitled "Chronometricals and Horologicals," and it seemed to form one of three hundred and thirty-three lectures by an ethical philosopher named Plotinus Plinlimmon. Melville gives the entire text of the quaint document, to its "torn and untidy termination."

10

PLINLIMMON'S utterances on "Chronometricals and Horologicals" are the high-water mark of Melville's stylistic rascalities in *Pierre*, and should be picked up as delicately as one seizes a porcupine. Artistically, these utterances were designed to be both dangerous and treacherous, and in this respect they have been even more successful than Father Mapple's sermon: many interpreters of Melville have misinterpreted this Plinlimmon hoax and then have used their misinterpretations as support for their misinterpretations of *Billy Budd!* For all these reasons, "Chronometricals and Horologicals" must be analyzed carefully here.

To begin on solid ground, it should be obvious that because this little essay attributed to Plotinus Plinlimmon is an element in the narrative of *Pierre*, this element should have some significant correlation to the story as a whole, and such direct correlation should offer the reader some guide to its meaning. Let us consider this correlation. As already suggested, there are three distinct levels of meaning in *Pierre*, and these three levels of meaning are intelligible only when they are seen to reflect, and be reflected by, three distinct viewpoints.

The first viewpoint is that of the hero, Pierre, and because the narrative is a study in the education and maturing of Pierre, that viewpoint passes through several distinct phases. The phase which that viewpoint has reached, just as "our young Enthusiast, Pierre" comes to read the pamphlet is one of perplexity and uncertainty as to whether his own actions, so definitely out of accord with the ways of that so-called Christian society in which he lives, are definitely in accord with the ways of God. Pierre, in his perplexity, wishes to act in harmony with a high ideal of ethical and moral conduct, and he has been inspired by the teachings of Christ in the Sermon on the Mount. Although Pierre is so perplexed that he doubts whether an essay on "Chronometricals and Horologicals" can have anything to say to him, he reads it "more to force his mind away from the dark realities of things than from any other motive." As it turns out, however, Plotinus Plinlimmon is preoccupied with exactly the same questions which concern Pierre; but from quite a different point of view.

The second of the three contrasting viewpoints, maintained throughout *Pierre*, is that represented by the so-called Christian society in which Pierre lives, and against which he has been forced to fight. It is the shallow Christian viewpoint represented by Mrs. Glendinning and Rev. Falsgrave in their handling of Delly Ulver. This viewpoint, though it may call itself Christian, is a diluted form of Christianity which waters down the teachings of Christ until they can be made to coincide with the practical and expedient demands of everyday living; in fact, to coincide with selfishness. Melville satirizes this shallow viewpoint, throughout.

The third viewpoint is Melville's own dark, bitter, and anti-Christian viewpoint which rests on the theological assumption of God's malicious indifference to all human striving toward perfection; the practical-joking of God, who seems to take some pleasure in human misery; the apparent inscrutability which God employs to protect Himself from being understood in His proper light by mankind, who would obviously find fault with Him and (if brave enough) defy Him, if they should understand Him. With these three distinct but related viewpoints in mind, consider the arguments of Plotinus Plinlimmon.

The difficulty of taking Plinlimmon's arguments seriously is that Melville has deliberately arranged them into an outrageous scramble of chop logic, as a means of ridiculing and satirizing the "expedient" viewpoint of Plinlimmon. Nevertheless, the central argument is clear. It is based on an extended trope, borrowed from Pierre Bayle. Aboard ship, sea chronometers are accurately

273

set and adjusted to coincide with Greenwich time, which is an absolute time, employed for reckoning the ship's true position at sea, in relation to the Greenwich meridian. This reckoning can be made even when the ship is anchored on the other side of the world, in a China port. But the watches and clocks in the China port are set in accordance with local time (or, for convenience, China time), and these local timepieces are arbitrarily referred to as horologues.

Next, the significance of the trope is applied. Even as there is a sharp difference between chronometrical time and horological time, so indeed, says Plinlimmon, there is a striking contrast between the absolute time of God and the local time of human beings. By extension, Plinlimmon is able to show that the contrast between ship's time and China time does not mean that China time is wrong, in China; indeed China time is correct for China, and ship's time is incorrect for local purposes, in China. So indeed, says Plinlimmon, the contrast between God's chronometrical time and man's horological time does not mean that man's horological time is wrong, on earth; indeed man's time is correct on earth, and God's time is incorrect for local purposes, on earth.

The possibilities for ethical development are many, and Plinlimmon proceeds to make the most of them, without perceiving the ambiguous ironies. He points out that although God sent Christ down to earth because He was "unwilling to leave man without some occasional testimony" as to heavenly chronometricals, this does not mean that we should make the mistake of trying to imitate Christ: Christ was divine and we are merely human. In fact, all our attempts to imitate him have proven "unprofitable," "impractical," and "inexpedient." "What man," says Plinlimmon, "who has carried a heavenly soul in him, has not groaned to perceive, that unless he committed a sort of suicide as to the practical things of this world, he never can hope to regulate his earthly conduct by that same heavenly soul?" In conclusion, Plinlimmon provides us with this unintentionally stupid and ridiculous conclusion:

"A virtuous expediency, then, seems the highest desirable or attainable earthly excellence for the mass of men, and is the only earthly excellence that their Creator intended for them. When they go to heaven, it will be quite another thing. There, they can freely turn the left cheek, because there the right cheek will never be smitten. There, they can freely give all to the poor, for *there* there will be no poor to give to. A due appreciation of this matter will do good to man. . . . I but lay down, then, what the best mortal men do daily practice. . . ."[25]

Melville's satirical game, here, is particularly evident in that conclusion. Although Plinlimmon is arguing his thesis seriously, Melville is the manipulator of Plinlimmon even as he was the manipulator of that other God-knower, Father Mapple. This time, Melville's manipulation achieves an overtly sardonic give-away in the burlesque-parody of Christ's meaning (in the Sermon on the Mount) as to turning the other cheek, and as to giving all to the poor. Through some puzzling oversight, however, several distinguished scholars have misinterpreted Melville's stylistic game and have mistakenly insisted that Melville's beliefs are accurately represented by the surface meanings of Plinlimmon's utterances. Obviously, such a mistake is unspeakably fine, from Melville's viewpoint, because his ulterior joke lies in the fun of permitting Plinlimmon to make an ass not merely of himself but also of exactly those readers who are able to take Plinlimmon seriously. As a corrective, observe that Melville has caused Plinlimmon to warp and twist to his own uses not only the words and meaning of Christ but also that familiar concept of Time which is asserted in Christian doctrine, in Platonic doctrine, even in the Neoplatonic doctrine of that third-century Plotinus after whom Melville's crackpot is named. Imitating his Creator, Melville has again made foolish the wisdom of the world.

In all seriousness, many Christian theologians (starting with the Apostle Paul) have made moral sermons out of the difference between "Man's Time" and "God's Time." Plato and the Neoplatonists did much the same thing. In this world, "Time" and "Change" are closely related; in the next world, "Eternity" and "Steadfastness" are closely related. The obvious possibilities for moral extension, there, have been played for a good thing by many preachers and poets. Some of these Platonic and Christian extensions may be found fused in the allegorical meanings of Spenser's *Faerie Queene*, particularly in the "Mutabilitie Cantos," so familiar to both Melville and Pierre. Intent on satirizing Christian doctrine, Melville merely pounced on this Christian-Platonic concept of Time and contrived his own extensions, in naughty and satirical fashion.

Although Plinlimmon's ethical position may seem to be quite decidedly anti-Christian, it will be found that his arguments eventually illuminate exactly that pattern of conduct represented by the shallow Christians in the narrative: Mrs. Glendinning and Rev. Falsgrave. Thus, one effect which Melville achieves in perpetrating the seeming nonsense of "Chronologicals and Horologicals" is a caustic and satirical representation of those ethical rules of conduct by which, according to Melville's viewpoint, the majority of professed and professing Christians in his day governed their conduct: rules of practicality, profitableness, expediency. How did they do it? By deciding that their Creator intended them to recognize a distinction between Heaven's time and Earth's time; Heaven's justice and Earth's justice. In other words, they managed to hear their Creator say to them exactly what they wished their Creator to say to them. And Melville ridicules the cheap and shoddy falsehoods of a social ethic established on such pseudo-Christian hogwash.

In effect, Melville at first traps the shallow Christian reader by encouraging the reader to dislike the pamphlet; by making disparaging remarks about the pamphlet ("It was a thin, tattered, dried-fish-like thing; printed with blurred ink upon mean, sleazy paper.") and by sarcastically ridiculing it ("Doubtless, it was something vastly profound"); even by letting the reader discover in it certain disparaging remarks about the Christian religion. Then, Melville springs the trap by confronting the shallow Christian with a mirror of that shallow Christian's own viewpoint! ("I but lay down, then, what the best mortal men do daily practice.") This is a subtle but conventional form of satirical unmasking, used by Henry Fielding, for example, a hundred years before Melville.

A further aspect of rascality, in Melville's perpetration of Plinlimmon's pamphlet, becomes apparent if the text of the pamphlet is viewed allegorically, in terms of Melville's own private myth as to the deceptiveness with which God Himself hoaxes and gulls human beings into believing a great deal of falsehood about Himself; falsehoods which, worked up into dogma, are peddled among human beings as "divine wisdom." Within this sinister frame of reference, consider the equivocation in the very first passage of Plinlimmon's pamphlet:

"Few of us doubt, gentlemen, that human life on this earth is but a state of probation; which among other things implies, that here below, we mortals have only to do with things provisional. Accordingly, I hold that all our so-called wisdom is likewise but provisional."

That little progression of thought means one thing in Plinlimmon's context, and it means quite another thing in Melville's sinister context. Ironically, Melville could observe of Plotinus, "I agree with everything he says, but I disagree with everything *he means by what he says.*"

Remember the number of times Melville talks about silence as the voice of God; about the inscrutability of God. Now consider the second sequence of Plinlimmon's thoughts, beginning thus:

"It seems to me, in my visions, that there is a certain most rare order of human souls, which if carefully carried in the body will almost always and everywhere give Heaven's own Truth, with some small grains of variance. For peculiarly coming from God, the sole source of that heavenly truth . . ."

(This is another of Melville's thrusts at Carlyle, later developed in *The Confidence-Man.*) The concepts have one value in Plinlimmon's frame of reference, and an entirely different value in Melville's. Plinlimmon is talking about a noble human representative of God. Melville thought he perceived enough of "Heaven's own Truth" to recognize that a representative of God must be a scoundrel.

Take the central concept in Plinlimmon's pamphlet, and notice its ambiguity: there is a basic antithesis between God's view of things and man's view of things. Lovely! As Melville saw it, most men's view of things represented the bliss of ignorance; his own private view (and Hawthorne's and Shakespeare's and Montaigne's and Burton's and Sir Thomas Browne's, he thought) represented the wisdom that was woe, and the woe that was madness. Indeed there *is* a basic antithesis between God's view and man's view, Melville implies, but only because mankind is so persistently stupid as to blind itself to the unvarnished facts.

Plinlimmon loves to paraphrase passages from *The Holy Bible,* and frequently, when he does, Plinlimmon sometimes inverts the conventional meaning to serve his shallow purposes. Then Melville inverts the conventional meaning to serve his far more private purpose. For example, take this inversion of a celebrated assertion

277

made by the Apostle Paul in the first chapter of First Corinthians; an assertion already inverted by Melville in the Pip passage of *Moby-Dick*, here employed to suit Plinlimmon's purposes:

"And thus, though the earthly wisdom of man be heavenly folly to God; so also, conversely, is the heavenly wisdom of God an earthly folly to man. Literally speaking, this is so. Nor does the God at the heavenly Greenwich expect common men to keep Greenwich wisdom in this remote Chinese world of ours; because such a thing were unprofitable for them here, and, indeed, a falsification of Himself, inasmuch as in that case, China time would be identical with Greenwich time, which would make Greenwich time wrong."

For Melville's purpose, that is outrageously fine! And oh the beautiful economy of letting Plinlimmon have it first, for his purpose.

But Pierre, our idealistic Enthusiast, how does he react to the pamphlet? Melville's remarks on this point are choice. First, he says, "The more he read and re-read, the more this interest deepened, but still the more likewise did his failure to comprehend the writer increase." How could this possibly be? asks Melville. Then he sarcastically generalizes to the effect that any person who has doubts as to the correctness of his own life-theory may, when confronted with a Plinlimmon-like treatise which "very palpably illustrates to him the intrinsic incorrectness and non-excellence of both the theory and practice of his life; then that man will—more or less unconsciously—try hard to hold himself back from the self-admitted comprehension of a matter which thus condemns him." Here, it should be noticed, Melville very cunningly pretends to sympathize with the shallow and expedient Plinlimmon viewpoint he is ridiculing. Notice also how Melville pretends to get chummy with his enemy the shallow Christian, when he refers to the "intrinsic incorrectness and non-excellence of both the theory and practice" of such a person as Pierre. Frequently, throughout, Melville seems to be ridiculing Pierre; pretends to satirize Pierre for his impracticality. In actuality, Melville does see that Pierre's position is ridiculous, but not for the reason that the shallow world sees idealism as ridiculous. Idealism like Pierre's is ridiculous, says Melville, because it is made absolutely impossible by God Almighty, and by society as an unconscious tool of God.

278

In summary, then, Melville creates and manipulates Plinlimmon's pamphlet in such a way as to let it reflect exactly that shallow Christian doctrine against which Pierre is hopelessly fighting; that shallow Christian doctrine which Melville ridicules, throughout.

11

"ALL round and round does the world lie as in a sharp-shooter's ambush, to pick off the beautiful illusions of youth, by the pitiless cracking rifles of the realities of the age," says Melville in describing the heartbreaking experiences confronting Pierre and his charges, as they face the heartlessness of the city and try to find a sanctuary in it. Unexpectedly, Pierre finds himself translated from the Eden-like serenity of rural scenes, in which his childhood and youth had been passed, to a hellish confusion and chaos, as he tries to champion the cause of Truth. Continuing his mock-heroics, Melville wryly remarks, "For Pierre is a warrior too; Life his campaign, and three fierce allies, Woe and Scorn and Want, his foes. The wide world is banded against him; for lo you! he holds up the standard of Right, and swears by the Eternal and True!" By contrast with the battlefield combat which had tested the nobility of his ancestors, Pierre finds this allegorical struggle against God to be humbling: "For more glorious in real tented field to strike down your valiant foe, than in the conflicts of a noble soul with a dastardly world to chase a vile enemy who ne'er will show front." Only slowly does Pierre recognize the previously unguessed and unacknowledged collusion between God Himself and Pierre's enemies; but as his prospects deteriorate, and his hope of achieving an ideal of noble human conduct grows less, his outbursts come closer and closer to recognizing this collusion:

"Ye heavens, that have hidden yourselves in the black hood of the night, I call to ye! If to follow Virtue to her uttermost vista, where common souls never go; if by that I take hold on hell, and the uttermost virtue, after all, prove but a betraying pander to the monstrousest vice,—then close in and crush me, ye stony walls, and into one gulf let all things tumble together."[26]

The "stony walls" of God hints at the significance, on the darker level, which Melville attaches to Pierre's name. Like father, like son. As a son of these stony walls, Pierre will eventually find his own heart turned to stone by its Maker, and will finally confront rock with rock, even though the outcome is petrification of all his hopes and ideals. Here, as in the Memnon Stone passage, the hint is slight; it is corroborated, later, when Pierre identifies himself with the Titans assaulting the insurmountable mountain-rock of the gods. "All things come of thee, oh Lord."

Piling ambiguity on ambiguity, Melville selects a highly emblematic Greenwich Village-like habitation for Pierre and his charges. An old church, known as the "Church of the Apostles," which "had had its days of sanctification and grace," had been converted into an office building; in the churchyard, a tenement house had been built as an additional money-maker for the sanctimonious church owners. Into this tenement swarm all manner of crackpot idealists, each having his own pet formula for solving the mysteries of the universe. Sarcastically: "Their mental tendencies, however heterodox at times, are still very fine and spiritual upon the whole; since the vacuity of their exchequers leads them to reject the coarse materialism of Hobbes, and incline to the airy exaltations of the Berkeleyan philosophy." Because they live under the shadow of the ancient Church of the Apostles, these "Teleological Theorists, and Social Reformers, and political propagandists" half-humorously and half-seriously call themselves "Apostles." And Pierre rents three rooms in the tenement, letting it be known that the beautiful dark-haired lady Isabel is his legal wife, and the accompanying girl is their friend and helper.

This necessary deception, to the effect that Pierre and Isabel are married, is but the first of innumerable subterfuges and lies which Pierre is forced to make, with dark allegorical significance, as he tries to imitate God and thus exemplify his own idealized concept of the word "Truth." Such superbly ironic antithesis constitutes a cumulative ambiguity in the entire narrative, and foreshadows the fact that eventually Pierre will be driven to his final self-recognition and God-recognition scene, when he, as Champion of Truth, is branded "liar" and threatened with legal action, or worse, because he has employed all his energies and talents to wage his losing campaign on behalf of Truth.

Reduced to financial embarrassment by the malicious refusal of his cousin Glen Stanley to help him, Pierre falls back on his literary talents. Having published some few pieces during his youth, he is able to secure a contract for a novel, and manages to live on the advances suppied by his publisher while he writes. By way of digression, Melville satirizes cheap literary practices of authorship, criticism, and publishing, so familiar and distasteful to him; but Pierre again isolates himself from the corrupted drift of literary fashions, and is determined to write an allegorical novel. We are told that Pierre's inspiration comes largely from two allegorists, Spenser and Dante, and one of his friends likes to refer to the novel being written as Pierre's personal *Inferno*. Melville begins his description of Pierre's undertaking by describing his fondness for allegory:

". . . Pierre was not only a reader of the poets and other fine writers, but likewise—and what is a very different thing from the other—a thorough allegorical understander of them, a profound emotional sympathizer with them; in other words, Pierre himself possessed the poetic nature; in himself absolutely, though but latently and floatingly, possessed every whit of the imaginative wealth which he so admired, when by vast pains-takings, and all manner of unrecompensed agonies, systematized on the printed page. Not that as yet his young and immature soul had been accosted by the Wonderful Mutes, and through the vast halls of Silent Truth, had been ushered into the full, secret, eternally inviolable Sanhedrim, where the Poetic Magi [Neo-Platonists?] discuss, in glorious gibberish, the Alpha and Omega of the Universe. But among the beautiful imaginings of the second and third degree of poets, he freely and comprehendingly ranged."[27]

For Melville, Spenser and Dante had become second and third rate poets, now, and only the dark tragedies of Shakespeare or the essays of Montaigne or the words of Solomon fitted his personal category of first rate work, because only such literature reflected for him the ultimate Truth: that "wisdom which is woe." Pierre's development follows Melville's earlier progress, and although his "young and immature soul" hindered him from dealing adequately with the central theme which he chose to illuminate in his allegorical novel, that central theme was none other than Melville's theme, in *Mardi*: Truth. With retrospective bitterness, Melville analyzes Pierre's motives:

"Disowning now all previous exertions of his mind, and burning in scorn even those fine fruits of a care-free fancy; . . . renouncing all his foregone self, Pierre was now engaged in a comprehensive compacted work. . . . [one motive being] the burning desire to deliver what he thought to be new, or at least miserably neglected Truth to the world. . . . Pierre was resolved to give the world a book, which the world should hail with surprise and delight. A varied scope of reading, little suspected by his friends, and randomly acquired by a random but lynx-eyed mind, in the course of the multifarious, incidental, bibliographic encounterings of almost any civilised young inquirer after Truth. . . . Now he congratulated himself upon his cursory acquisitions of this sort; ignorant that in reality to a mind bent on producing some thoughtful thing of absolute Truth, all mere reading is apt to prove but an obstacle hard to be overcome; and not an accelerator helpingly pushing him along."[28]

Thus, as the novel begins, its scope and technique and intention quite obviously suggest very much the sort of allegorical novel which Melville himself had written in *Mardi*. But Melville, borrowing from Emerson, criticizes Pierre for the ironic ambiguity of his endeavor: inspired by a vision of Truth, Pierre was not aware that he was as yet blind to certain key aspects of Truth:

"He would climb Parnassus with a pile of folios on his back. He did not see, that it was nothing at all to him, what other men had written; that though Plato was indeed a transcendently great man in himself, yet Plato must not be transcendently great to him. . . . He did not see that there is no such thing as a standard for the creative spirit . . . He did not see . . . that all the great books in the world are but the mutilated shadowings-forth of invisible and eternally unembodied images in the soul. . . ."[29]

Then, as though to establish more vividly the sharp antithesis between Pierre's youthful attitude and Melville's own presumably mature attitude, Melville presents three bitterly pessimistic and nihilistic tropes, which are important guides to the ulterior meaning of *Pierre* as a whole:

". . . so hath heaven wisely ordained, that on first entering into the Switzerland of his soul, man shall not at once perceive its tremendous immensity; lest illy prepared for such an encounter, his spirit should sink and perish in the lowermost snows. Only by judicious degrees, appointed of God, does man come at last to gain his Mont Blanc . . ."[30]

The sarcasm of the passage, and the doubly dark pun on both "blank" and "white" in "Mont Blanc" are not obvious, for the very reason that Melville protects himself in the continuation of the sentence. But the very next paragraph concludes with a second trope which clarifies the subtlety of the first:

"By vast pains we mine into the pyramid; by horrible gropings we come to the central room; with joy we espy the sarcophagus; but we lift the lid—and no body is there!—appallingly vacant as vast is the soul of a man!"[31]

And the third trope, which follows hard, corroborates the insinuations of the first and second. The subject being discussed throughout this section, it should be remembered, is the soul's quest for Truth:

"Deep, deep, and still deep and deeper must we go, if we would find out the heart of a man; descending into which is as descending a spiral stair in a shaft, without any end, and where that endlessness is only concealed by the spiralness of the stair, and the blackness of the shaft."[32]

So Pierre descends, as he is writing his *Inferno*-like novel. And while he is in the very midst of it, he makes his next transition from one phase of still idealistic but disillusioning discernment to a more advanced phase of perception, less idealistic. Now, suddenly, Pierre's *Mardi*-like novel becomes a *Moby-Dick*-like novel, and to give the reader an indication of the transition, Melville quotes a passage which Pierre has written after he has made the transition. As Melville says of Pierre, "he seems to have directly plagiarised from his own experiences, to fill out the mood of his apparent author-hero, Vivia, who thus soliloquizes." Then follows this passage from Pierre's novel:

" 'A deep-down, unutterable mournfulness is in me. Now I drop all humourous or indifferent disguises, and all philosophical pretensions. I own myself a brother of the clod, a child of the Primeval Gloom. Hopelessness and despair are over me, as pall on pall. Away, ye chattering apes of a sophomorean Spinoza, and Plato, who once didst all but delude me that the night was day, and pain only a tickle. Explain this darkness, exorcise the devil, ye can not. . . .' "[33]

12

THE next transition to an even darker phase of perception occurs when Pierre is pried away from "the all-exacting theme of his book" by the receipt of a letter from his once loved Angel of Light, Lucy. Somehow or other, she has been led to understand those "angelical" motives which have prompted the soul of Pierre in all he has done; she realizes now, she implies, that Pierre has merely *pretended* to be married to his illegitimate sister Isabel, because this was the only way he could shield his altruistic and idealistic purpose from the crass ugliness of the world. (What she does not perceive, intuitively or otherwise, is that Pierre's angelical soul has been double-crossed by his diabolic body; that his increasing bitterness has led him to see Virtue and Vice as "two shadows cast from one nothing"; that he has, in short, entered into incestuous sexual relationship with Isabel, so that his ostensible sister has in fact become his common-law wife.) In the light of all that Lucy feels she perceives, she proposes to come and live with them, and accidentally employs exactly the same deceptive terms to describe her intentionally chaste relationship, which Pierre had initially used in explaining his purpose to Isabel. Lucy:

"Let it seem as though I were some nun-like cousin immovably vowed to dwell with thee in thy strange exile. Show not to me,— never show more any visible conscious token of love. I will never to thee. Our mortal lives, oh, my heavenly Pierre, shall henceforth be one mute wooing of each other; with no declaration; no bridal; till we meet in the pure realms of God's final blessedness for us;— till we meet where the ever-interrupting and ever-marring world can not and shall not come; where all thy hidden, glorious unselfishness shall be gloriously revealed in the full splendor of that heavenly light; where, no more forced to these cruelest disguises, she, *she* too shall assume her own glorious place, nor take it hard, but rather feel the more blessed, when, there, thy sweet heart shall be openly and unreservedly mine. Pierre, Pierre, my Pierre! —only this thought, this hope, this sublime faith now supports me. . . ."[34]

Lovely! Here, the ironies reach their highest excruciation in the narrative, and the wheels within wheels of conflicting ambiguities as to whether Lucy is Good Angel or Bad Angel and as to whether

Isabel is Bad Angel or Good Angel, set the reader's head whirling!
But the allegorical resolution of meaning, here foreshadowed, will
become clearly this: while each of these "Angels" represents both
good and evil existing in close proximity to Pierre, and emblematic
of Pierre's dual nature, each will eventually prove to be, allegorically, a thief. Between these two thieves, Pierre will continue
striving to be Christ until the crucifixion is completed. So he will
die tragically, double-crossed by God, double-crossed by Society,
double-crossed by good intentions of both his Good Angel and
his Bad Angel; double-crossed by Self.

When Lucy appears, it is quite fitting that her new suitor, Glen
Stanley (the inheritor of Pierre's real estate), should appear with
her, and should fight physically with Pierre to save Lucy from this
disgraceful liaison. Of course, Glen Stanley's attempt to block the
plan only increases Lucy's resolve. Ambiguously, again, Glen
Stanley's altruistic idealism serves as a form of diabolism, and
permits him to hound and harass Pierre in his attempt to liberate
Lucy. During the staircase quarrel Glen Stanley and his companion add to the allegorical ambiguities by hurling suggestive
epithets at Pierre: "Villain!—Damn thee!" "Thou hast bewitched,
thou damned juggler, the sweetest angel!" "Thy depravity, thy
pollutedness, is that of a fiend!"[35] But Pierre is trying to imitate
Christ, who in turn tried to imitate God! Allegorically, be it never
forgotten, all things come of thee, oh Lord, and of thine own have
we given thee. In the Melvillian myth, God is the ultimate villain,
the damned juggler.

13

IMMEDIATELY after Lucy's arrival, Melville proceeds to symbolize,
as overtly as he considered practicable, the ultimate and ulterior
villainy of God Almighty. His device, here, is to let Pierre dream,
and then to make the dream emblematic. In his boyhood, Pierre
had explored the base of a lofty mountain, the summit of which
was inaccessible, and the sheer cliffs of which were cluttered, at
their base, by gigantic fragments of stone, one of which had a
human likeness. Visitors had given the mountain two seemingly
antithetical names which are (for Melville's purposes) identical.
Some had called it "The Delectable Mountain" and had glorified

it, poetically, as the Seat of God, following "Bunyan and his most marvelous book." Others had seen it as "the phantasmagoria of the Mount of the Titans," and had considered the prostrate stone which bore a human likeness to be an emblem of the defeated Titan, Enceladus. Around the base of the mountain grew two plants which create further ironic and emblematic correlations: the vegetation-destroying and useless amaranth, which continued to thrive, and the homely "farm-house herb," catnip, which seemed dying out: "The catnip and the amaranth!—man's earthly household peace, and the ever-encroaching appetite for God."

In this context, it had been Enceladus' "ever encroaching appetite for God" which had led him to assault the mountain:

"You saw Enceladus the Titan, the most potent of all the giants, writhing from out the imprisoning earth;—turbaned with upborne moss he writhed . . . still turning his unconquerable front toward that majestic mount eternally in vain assailed by him, and which, when it had stormed him off, had heaved his undoffable incubus upon him, and deridingly left him there to bay out his ineffectual howl."[36]

"Such was the wild scenery—the Mount of Titans, and the repulsed group of heaven-assaulters, with Enceladus in their midst shamefully recumbent at its base;—such was the wild scenery, which now to Pierre, in his strange vision, displaced the four blank walls, the desk, and the camp-bed, and domineered upon his trance. But no longer petrified in all their ignominious attitudes, the herded Titans now sprung to their feet; flung themselves up the slope; and anew battered at the precipice's unresounding wall. Foremost among them all, he saw a moss-turbaned, armless giant, who despairing of any other mode of wreaking his immitigable hate, turned his vast trunk into a battering-ram, and hurled his own arched-out ribs again and yet again against the invulnerable steep.

"'Enceladus! It is Enceladus!'—Pierre cried out in his sleep. That moment the phantom faced him; and Pierre saw Enceladus no more; but on the Titan's armless trunk, his own duplicate face and features magnifiedly gleamed upon him with prophetic discomfiture and woe. With trembling frame he started from his chair, and woke from that ideal horror to all his actual grief."[37]

Melville assures us that Pierre's familiarity with "the ancient

fables" enabled him "still further to elucidate the vision which so
strangely had supplied a tongue to muteness." Even so, Melville's
own elucidation of the emblematic meaning is extended. He insists that the reader should notice the striking parallel between
Pierre's allegorical story and Enceladus' allegorical story:

"Old Titan's self was the son of incestuous Coelus and Terra,
the son of incestuous Heaven and Earth. And Titan married his
mother Terra, another and accumulatively incestuous match. And
thereof Enceladus was one issue. So Enceladus was both the son
and grandson of an incest; and even thus, there had been born
from the organic blended heavenliness and earthliness of Pierre,
another mixed, uncertain, heaven-aspiring, but still not wholly
earth-emancipated mood; which again, by its terrestrial taint held
down to its terrestrial mother, generated there the present doubly
incestuous Enceladus within him; so that the present mood of
Pierre—that reckless sky-assaulting mood of his, was nevertheless
on one side the grandson of the sky. For it is according to eternal
fitness, that the precipitated Titan should seek to regain his paternal birthright even by fierce escalade. Wherefore whoso storms
the sky gives best proof he came from thither! But whatso crawls
contented in the moat before that crystal fort, shows it was born
within that slime, and there forever will abide."[38]

This helps to equate the final Pierre with Ahab; but before
Melville concludes the elucidation, he manages to establish a
further analogy between Enceladus and Pierre, each held captive
by "the world the gods had chained for a ball to drag at his o'er-
freighted feet."

14

INCEST, and its emblematic possibilities were far too attractive to
be dropped by Melville after the Enceladus-Pierre parallel. While
visiting an art gallery to see a particular exhibition of paintings,
Isabel and Pierre find two portraits significantly facing each other.
One is the portrait of a young man, and the other is of a young
woman. Isabel and Pierre are convinced that the young man was
painted from their own father, but the title is of no help (except
on the dark allegorical level of meaning): "Stranger's Head by
the Unknown Hand." As for the portrait of the young woman,

287

both Isabel and Pierre cannot help but be self-conscious: It is Guido's portrait of Beatrice Cenci.

The most striking aspect of the Cenci portrait, we are told, is the antithesis between the "funereally jetty hair" and the "soft and light blue eyes, with an extremely fair complexion." This, notes Melville cautiously, offers "a striking, suggested contrast, half-identical with, and half-analogous to, that almost supernatural one . . ." Melville is being very cautious in his metaphysical insinuation. Perhaps he also intends to hint that the Cenci portrait is as much an emblem of Piere's allegorical story as was the dream about Enceladus. Like Beatrice Cenci, Pierre finds himself the victim of a horrible crime, perpetrated by his father—allegorically, his ambiguous Heavenly Father; like Beatrice Cenci, Pierre is finally driven in desperation to defy his Father, and strike back. All that Melville says is that the "supernatural" contrast of coloring in the Cenci portrait "still the more intensifies the suggested fanciful anomaly of so sweetly and seraphically *blonde* a being, being double-hooded, as it were, by the black crape of the two most horrible crimes (of one of which she is the object, and of the other the agent) possible to civilised humanity—incest and parricide."[39]

15

As Pierre advances from one phase of spiritual perception to the next, he continues to alter the plan for his book, thus further providing an indirect opportunity for allegorical illumination:

"On either hand clung to by a girl who would have laid down her life for him; Pierre, nevertheless, in his deepest, highest part, was utterly without sympathy from any thing divine, human, brute, or vegetable. One in a city of hundreds of thousands of human beings, Pierre was solitary as at the Pole.

"And the great woe of all was this: that all these things were unsuspected without, and undivulgible from within; the very daggers that stabbed him were joked at by Imbecility, Ignorance, Blockheadedness, Self-Complacency, and the universal Blearedness and Besottedness around him. Now he began to feel that in him, the thews of a Titan were forestallingly cut by the scissors of Fate [God]. He felt as a moose, hamstrung. All things that think, or move, or lie still, seemed as created to mock and torment him. He seemed gifted with loftiness, merely that it might be dragged down to the mud [cf. Ahab]. Still, the profound willfulness in him would not give up. Against the breaking heart, and the bursting head; against all the dismal lassitude, and deathful faintness and sleeplessness, and whirlingness and craziness, still he like a demi-god bore up. His soul's ship foresaw the inevitable rocks, but still resolved to sail on, and make a courageous wreck. Now he gave jeer for jeer, and taunted the apes that jibed him. With the soul of an Atheist, he wrote down the godliest things; with the feeling of misery and death in him, he created forms of gladness and life. For the pangs in his heart, he put down hoots on paper."[40]

The reader of that passage, if he has just come from a reading of *Moby-Dick*, cannot help but recognize the striking parallel between Pierre's mood of authorship and Melville's. With very nearly the soul of an Atheist, Melville had written Father Mapple's sermon.

16

AFTER such an inexorable progression, Melville brings the reader to the catastrophe, precipitated by two letters which Pierre receives. The first is from his publisher, warning him that legal proceedings against Pierre have been begun:

"Sir:—You are a swindler. Upon the pretense of writing a popular novel for us, you have been receiving cash advances from us, while passing through our press the sheets of a blasphemous rhapsody, filched from the vile Atheists, Lucian and Voltaire. . . ."

The second letter is from Glendinning Stanley, who flings down a gauntlet which calls for a duel:

"Thou, Pierre Glendinning, art a villainous and perjured liar. It is the sole object of this letter imprintedly to convey the point-blank lie to thee. . . ."[41]

Now Pierre makes his final and deliberately fatal decision. Like Captain Ahab (and using some of the identical words and phrases which Captain Ahab had employed) he elects to declare his independence and to defy both God and man:

"These are most small circumstances; but happening just now

to me, become indices to all immensities. For now am I hate-shod! On these I will skate to my acquittal! No longer do I hold terms with aught. World's bread of life, and world's breath of honour, both are snatched from me; but I defy all world's bread and breath. Here I step out before the drawn-up worlds in widest space, and challenge one and all of them to battle! . . ."

Leaving the apartment, he passes the two Angels—the two thieves—so closely associated with his cumulative crucifixions, and speaks thus to Lucy:

"Dead embers of departed fires lie by thee, thou pale girl; with dead embers thou seekest to relume the flame of all extinguished love! Waste not so that bread; eat it—in bitterness!"[42]

In the hall, just after he closes the door, Pierre assumes a tableau position of outstretched arms, like that of Christ on the cross; but instead of hoping that either of his thieves will this day be with him in Paradise, the embittered Pierre utters a prayer which amounts to a curse:

"He turned, and entered the corridor, and then, with outstretched arms, paused between the two outer doors of Isabel and Lucy.

" 'For ye two, my most undiluted prayer is now, that from your here unseen and frozen chairs ye may never stir alive;—the fool of Truth, the fool of Virtue, the fool of Fate, now quits ye forever!' "

From the room of a neighbor Apostle, Pierre arms himself with a pair of pistols, and in the process suggests his kinship with man-making Prometheus, even as with Enceladus the Titan:

" 'Ha! what wondrous tools Prometheus used, who knows? but more wondrous these, that in an instant, can unmake the topmost three-score-years-and-ten of all Prometheus' makings.' "

Proceeding on his quest for his diabolic cousin, Pierre meets and murders Glen in an emblematically ironic spot—"a large, open, triangular space, built round with the stateliest public erections; the very proscenium of the town"—in other words, the epitome of those social laws and social justices which have ignored Pierre's degradation, during his idealistic pursuit of justice and truth. That night, in jail, Pierre reviews the entire story, briefly, and concludes with a Satanic assertion of Ahab-like defiance:

" 'Here, then, is the untimely, timely end;—Life's last chapter well stitched into the middle! Nor book, nor author of the book, hath any sequel, though each hath its last lettering!—It is ambiguous still. Had I been heartless now, disowned, and spurningly portioned off the girl [Isabel] at Saddle Meadows, then had I been happy through a long life on earth, and perchance through a long eternity in heaven! Now, 'tis merely hell in both worlds. Well, be it hell. I will mold a trumpet of the flames, and, with my breath of flame, breathe back my defiance! . . .' "[43]

When Lucy and Isabel join him, his greeting to them sums up their ambiguous relationship anew: each has been both good and bad Angel to him; each a thief. Now, it does not matter, because the Pierre who cared about values is dead:

" 'Ye two pale ghosts, were this the other world, ye were not welcome. Away!—Good Angel and Bad Angel both!—For Pierre is neuter now!' "

Isabel immediately tries to take the blame, and in so doing emphasizes the stony significance of Pierre's name:

" 'Oh, ye stony roofs, and seven-fold stony skies!—not thou the murderer, but thy sister hath murdered thee, my brother, oh my brother!' "

Shocked out of life by these two rhetorical blasts, the gentle Lucy "shrunk up like a scroll" at Pierre's feet, dead. Pierre, knowing that Isabel carries a vial of poison on a cord at her throat, turns to her:

" 'Girl! wife or sister, saint or fiend!—in thy breasts, life for infants lodgeth not, but death-milk for thee and me!—The drug!' "

The tableau thus created for the final curtain is viewed by two opposed visitors: Fred Tartan (cousin of Lucy and accomplice of Glen Stanley) and Millthorpe (friend of Pierre, since boyhood). Lucy and Pierre lie dead, and the dying Isabel, flanking Pierre on the side opposite Lucy, rises long enough to answer Millthorpe's solicitous lamentations over Pierre; to answer him with a paraphrased Biblical utterance which has decidedly different overtones when evaluated within the three distinct frames of reference:

" 'All's o'er, and ye know him not!' "

Then Isabel falls: "her whole form sloped sideways, and she fell upon Pierre's heart, and her long hair ran over him, and arbored him in ebon vines."

291

17

In concluding my analysis of *Moby-Dick*, I suggested one major discrepancy between Melville's apparent intention, as artist, and his actual achievement. Ideally wanting to project his narrative from a vantage point of complete artistic detachment, he signally failed to achieve such detachment. For example, while Melville apparently wanted to represent a wide variety of theological attitudes, from that dispassionately tolerant perspective which "makes neither believer nor infidel, but makes a man regard them both with equal eye," he did not convey an effect of artistic tolerance. Instead, he very powerfully dramatized and illuminated his dominant sympathy for the anti-Christian attitudes of Ishmael and Captain Ahab.

After reading *Pierre*, one may more clearly appreciate the ironies implicit in the repetition of these same artistic shortcomings. The supreme irony lies in Melville's simultaneous imitation and resentment of God's indifference. Trying to model an artistic ideal on being "indifferent as his God," Melville could never isolate that ideal from his sense of moral indignation. Or, to put it another way, God's indifference so infuriated Melville that the kinetic force of that infuriation undermined the static serenity of his artistic ideal, in practice.

At the beginning of this chapter, a passage from *Pierre* was quoted to illustrate Melville's asserted desire to be merely gamesome and playful in dealing with the follies of men and the gods. That passage should be correlated with the following, from *Pierre*, in which Melville again tries to achieve a tone of indifference as he smiles over such speculators as pretend to know what is going on in the mind of God:

". . . Now without doubt this Talismanic Secret has never yet been found; and in the nature of human things it seems as though it never can be. Certain philosophers have time and again pretended to have found it; but if they do not in the end discover their own delusion, other people soon discover it for themselves, and so those philosophers and their vain philosophy are let glide away into practical oblivion. Plato, and Spinoza, and Goethe, and many more belong to that guild of self-impostors, with a preposterous rabble of Muggletonian Scots and Yankees [including Carlyle and Emerson], whose vile brogue still the more bestreaks the stripedness of their Greek or German Neoplatonical originals. That profound Silence, that only Voice of our God, which I before spoke of; from that divine thing without a name, those impostor philosophers pretend somehow to have got an answer; which is as absurd, as though they say they have got water out of stone; for how can a man get a Voice out of Silence?"[44]

In context, that passage is beautifully geared and cogged with many different elements we have already considered. But Melville would here seem to pride himself, once again, on his detached and indifferent superiority to such theorizings about God; he would again pose as one viewing such foibles from that perspective which makes "neither believer nor infidel." That which undermines the pose is the tone of furious anger implicit in the last sentence, and the tone of scornful disdain reflected in the next-to-last sentence, containing harsh references to "self-impostors" and "preposterous rabble" and "vile brogue." If this is gamesomeness, it is exactly the same sort as was reflected in the caustic allusions to "fools and pretenders" among men, and "impostors and baboons among the gods."

In summary, Pierre's quarrel with God and man is strikingly similar to Captain Ahab's quarrel, and each is a fictional or symbolic projection of Melville's private myth, elaborately constructed on the anti-Christian assumption that the world is put together wrong and that God is to blame. Perhaps the clearest representation of this assumption occurs when Pierre himself correlates and interprets a passage in *The Divine Comedy* and a passage in *Hamlet*:

"Soon he found the open *Inferno* in his hand, and his eye met the following lines, allegorically overscribed within the arch of the outgoings of the womb of human life:

'Through me you pass into the city of Woe,
Through me you pass into eternal pain;
Through me, among the people lost for aye. . . .
All hope abandon, ye who enter here.'

"He dropped the fatal volume from his hand; he dropped his fated head upon his chest.

"His mind was wandering and vague; his arm wandered and

was vague. Some moments passed, and he found the open *Hamlet* in his hand, and his eyes met the following lines:

> 'The time is out of joint;—Oh cursed spite,
> That ever I was born to set it right!'

"He dropped the too true volume from his hand; his petrifying heart dropped hollowly within him. . . ."[45]

SWINDLER AS GOD'S AGENT

CHAPTER IX

. . . and believe not his many words: for with much communication will he tempt thee, and smiling upon thee will get out thy secrets. . . . Observe, and take good heed, for thou walkest in peril of thy overthrowing: when thou hearest these things, awake in thy sleep.

ECCLESIASTICUS 13:11, 13

" 'Some insinuation there.'
" 'More fool you that are puzzled by it.' "
MELVILLE, *The Confidence-Man*

" 'You fools! you flock of fools, under this captain of fools, in this ship of fools!' "
MELVILLE, *The Confidence-Man*

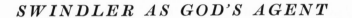

SWINDLER AS GOD'S AGENT

AMONG Melville's uncomplimentary epithets for God, perhaps his
favorite was "Practical Joker," and much of his vituperation was
aimed at human beings who let themselves be deceived by various
agents of God (from Satan to Christ and back) manipulated by
the All Powerful, to help Him palm off old chestnuts. His derisive-
ness was heightened by his grudging realization that his own
artistic attempts to expose God had backfired; that his counter-
gospel of mistrust and skepticism had peppered his own head
with that same opprobrium he had carefully aimed at the Practical
Joker, Himself.

After such an intensely disappointing experience in authorship,
Melville came to the conclusion that it was almost useless to continue this warfare against the gullibility of faith with his weapons
of skepticism and denial; useless, except that there still remained
to him the literary and artistic pleasure of representing, through
crafty indirections, the ridiculousness of such related nonsense as
Plato's glorious leap into wishful thinking, and the following vain
protestations of the Apostle Paul:

"And though I have the gift of prophecy, and understand all

297

mysteries, and all knowledge; and though I have all faith, so that I could remove mountains, and have not charity, I am nothing. . . . Charity . . . thinketh no evil; rejoiceth not in iniquity, but rejoiceth in truth; beareth all things, believeth all things, hopeth all things, endureth all things."[1]

There in a chestnut shell, Melville believed, lay the kernel of that shallow Christian dogma which he had come to loathe; the kernel cultivated from the teachings of the so-called Son of God, and stupidly employed by Melville's enemies to prove him "mad" and "misanthropic" whenever he suggested that such nonsense merely served God as pasteboard masks, behind which He could perpetrate His malicious and humiliating deceptions.

From this wry viewpoint, Melville projected *The Confidence-Man, His Masquerade*. The central character, a swindling rascal, was developed and elaborated with such oblique allegorical artistry that Melville could again hope to pop down the orthodox public throat a bolus bitter enough to gag anyone who might discover what he was swallowing. This time, however, Melville's own wile and guile were altogether too successful, and the public showed very little interest in the story when it appeared in 1857. Since then, various interpreters have puzzled over it, and many have wondered why Melville left the story incomplete; why he issued something so palpably deficient that it amounted to complete literary failure. But if we grant Melville the right to employ his own cabalistic symbolism and allegory to represent, once again, his own private myth, we may discover that *The Confidence-Man* is neither incomplete nor deficient.

Perhaps *The Confidence-Man* might profitably be viewed not merely as a continuation of Melville's quarrel with God and man but also as a continuation of Melville's quarrel with Carlyle. His increasing misanthropy would have made him relish particularly the following passage from *Heroes and Hero-Worship*, which must have seemed outrageously silly to Melville:

"But of a Great Man especially, of him I will venture to assert that it is incredible he should have been other than true. . . . Such a man is what we call an *original* man; he comes to us at first-hand. A messenger he, sent from the Infinite Unknown with tidings to us. We may call him Poet, Prophet, God;—in one way or other, we all feel that the words he utters are as no other man's words. Direct from the Inner Fact of things;—he lives, and has to live, in daily communion with that. . . . Really his utterances, are they not a kind of 'revelation':—what we must call such for want of some other name? It is from the heart of the world that he comes; he is portion of the primal reality of things. God has made many revelations: but this man too, has not God made him, the latest and newest of all. The 'inspiration of the Almighty giveth him understanding': we must listen before all to him."[2]

We know that Melville read *Heroes and Hero-Worship*; we can almost hear him snorting over that, and saying aloud, "Of all the unspeakable bilge I ever smelled . . ." With justifiable cynicism he must have wanted to ask Carlyle if he actually believed there was any necessary connection between greatness and goodness. For purposes of allegorical story-telling, of course, there might be some bitter sport in creating a Great Man, after the Carlyle pattern; in making him at least great enough to lead simpletons around by the nose through the easy expedient of preaching to the simpletons the word of God. One could not call such a hero an *"original* man"; but there might be some amusement in showing that the swindling initiative of a confidence-man is, in the Melvillian sense, God-like. This is exactly what Melville did.

2

THE entire action takes place aboard a Mississippi River steamboat which is emblematically named *Fidele* (or "faithful"; the direct antithesis of the word "infidel" or non-believer). The ship is represented as a microcosm of the world, and the passengers aboard are allegorically represented as making their faithful Christian soul-pilgrimages through life to death. Intent on his swindlings, our hero or "Great Man" comes aboard in one costume, soon disappears below deck to change into a new guise which will further assist him in his swindlings, and repeats this masquerade pattern of action several times before the story ends. Throughout his various enterprises, the double-crossing Confidence-Man blandly preaches the Christian doctrine of faith, hope, and charity, because it helps him in his business. His use of this deception permits the reader to notice that his name is nicely interlocked, by inference, with the name of the good ship *Fidele*. The pivotal motif of the entire action is betrayal of faith; allegorically, God's betrayal of man's faith. The unity of time is ironically preserved: all the events take place during a single day which is, nicely, April Fool's Day!

Another kind of orientation may be gained by appreciating Melville's discrete focus of narration. The swindler does not tell his own story; the omniscient author does not tell it. Instead, Melville provides the artistic illusion that the narrator is just an ordinary passenger aboard the vessel. He is "ordinary" in the sense that his viewpoint is that of a fairly conventional, fairly stupid, fairly shallow Christian. Quite naturally limited in his understanding of what occurs, even before his eyes, this narrator is permitted to tell the reader only what he sees or hears or thinks. Occasionally he feels called on to characterize or moralize, and through what he says or does not say, at such times, the narrator unintentionally reveals himself as a blockhead, if evaluated from the Melvillian viewpoint. Here is just one example (a major example) of the narrator's stupidity: he never recognizes that the Confidence-Man reappears in various masquerade costumes; he never seems to doubt but that whenever the Confidence-Man reappears in a new guise, he is actually a new passenger.

For Melville's occult purposes, the value of such narrative method is considerable. As artistic manipulator, he can thus imitate God the Divine Deceiver by also contriving to make the stupid narrator-character palm off old chestnuts! Or, to put it another way, Melville manages to plant his stupid narrator as a decoy or shield, and from behind this shield Melville is able to perpetrate his own literary jokes, at the expense of both God and man.

How does he manage to convey his own viewpoint, which is so strikingly different from that of his narrator? First of all, the dramatic action itself requires no comment. Even when the stupid narrator may fail to recognize the game of the Confidence-Man, the reader observes the deceptions, observes the gullibility of the victims, and is thus led to appreciate that whenever the Confidence-Man urges his victims to strengthen their belief in faith, hope, charity, he is administering a narcotic dope, to aid his own underhanded designs. Second, the decoy narrator is a prosy and unimaginative fellow, who would not be expected to care for poetry, in any form. Nevertheless, he is manipulated in such a way that he reports and records facts and conversations which recall to the reader conventional religious emblems and symbols. As the narrative progresses, the reader notices that these seemingly unintentional emblems and symbols begin to interlock, and as the interlocking is sustained throughout, the narrative gradually achieves an inverted allegorical meaning.

Again, Melville has found a technical formula for indulging triple-talk. This time, the first level of meaning is the obvious one: the narrative merely presents a series of entertaining incidents, conversations, actions, aboard a Mississippi River steamboat. The second level of meaning is provided by the shallow Christian viewpoint of the decoy narrator, buttressed by certain characters in the narrative who also dramatize and expound the same viewpoint. The third level of meaning, of course anti-Christian, represents Melville's own sinister and darkly private thoughts concerning the unjust ways of God to man.

With this much orientation, we are now in a position to watch Melville unfold and develop his private myth in *The Confidence-Man.*

3

ACCORDING to Christian doctrine, Melville keeps reminding us, life is a voyage out, and we are all pilgrims. Aboard the *Fidele*, most of the passengers belong to the ranks of the religiously faithful, and they resent the least misanthropic suspicion or doubt or cynicism displayed by a few odd sticks among them. Before Melville can work up the possible extensions, he must establish some hint as to the good ship *Fidele* as a microcosm of the world, and he does it early, by tucking in two casual and seemingly specific passages. The first hints that this ship-microcosm of the world extends through all the latitudes; that her course continues, even while the "passengers" are born into her life or die out of her life:

"Though her voyage of twelve hundred miles extends from apple to orange, from clime to clime, yet, like any small ferryboat, to right and left, at every landing, the huge *Fidele* still receives additional passengers in exchange for those that disembark; so that, though always full of strangers, she continually, in some degree, adds to, or replaces them with strangers still more strange;

like Rio Janeiro fountain, fed from the Cocovarde mountains, which is ever overflowing with strange waters, but never with the same strange particles in every part.'"[3]

The second passage may remind us that, even as the *Pequod* contained a cross-section of humanity, representing all races and colors, all attitudes and beliefs, on a pilgrim quest, so does the *Fidele*:

"As among Chaucer's Canterbury *pilgrims* [italics added] or those oriental ones crossing the Red Sea towards Mecca in the festival month, there was no lack of variety. Natives of all sorts, and foreigners; men of business and men of pleasure; parlour men and backwoodsmen; farm-hunters and fame-hunters; heiress-hunters, gold-hunters, buffalo-hunters, bee-hunters, happiness-hunters, truth-hunters, and still keener hunters after all these hunters. Fine ladies in slippers, and moccasined squaws; Northern speculators and Eastern philosophers; English, Irish, German, Scotch, Danes; ... Mormons and Papists; Dives and Lazarus; jesters and mourners, teetotallers and convivialists, deacons and blacklegs; hard-shell Baptists and clay-eaters; grinning negroes and Sioux chiefs solemn as high-priests. In short, a piebald parliament, an Anacharsis Cloots congress of all kinds of that multiform *pilgrim* [italics added] species, man."[4]

Although we cannot help but be reminded of what Melville made of his previous reference to Anacharsis Cloots, in *Moby-Dick*, it is more important to notice that the groupings, in this pilgrim throng, are largely in terms of antithetical pairs. This may be reduced still further to the basic grouping of characters around the Confidence-Man. Again, for convenience in representation, a diagram based on the compass-card may be helpful to represent the major magnetic repulsions or attractions. In such a diagram, the pivotal position is of course occupied by the Confidence-Man, whose constant reiterations concerning faith, hope, charity, would indicate that his attention is fixed on the "North" of God's "Truth." Flanking the Confidence-Man, to the East, are those who are the "faithful" or "confident"—in that they do subscribe to the faith-doctrine. Flanking the Confidence-Man, to the West, are those who are viewed by the others as the skeptical, or in-fidel, in that they have rejected the faith doctrine because they believe it to be a falsehood, a hoax. The skeptical ones repeatedly insist that the Confidence-Man is trying to conceal the unvarnished truth; that he is merely using the term, "God's Truth," as a mask or front or blind, from behind which he can swindle. To the skeptical, then, the Confidence-Man's fake "Truth" is diametrically opposed to the unvarnished truth, and the latter may thus be represented on the compass-card diagram as at the South.

As the action unfolds, the episodes establish cumulative tensions of attraction and repulsion, involving these three antithetical combinations: the Confidence-Man and the Faithful; the Confidence-Man and the Skeptical; the Faithful and the Skeptical.

4

IN the beginning, God's Agent comes aboard in a masquerade costume which the decoy narrator describes, just as he sees it; but Melville manipulates the narrator's remarks to convey certain insinuations which recall Melville's private theological myth. These insinuations suggest that this first masquerade performance is designed to serve as an emblematic reminder of Christ's earthly appearance. Like Father, like son, in the Melvillian twist, and the initiated reader makes something of the fact that this particular agent of God pretends that he cannot talk and cannot hear: "he involuntarily betrayed that he was not alone dumb, but also deaf. . . . he seemed already to have come from a very long distance . . . travelling night and day from some far country." From Melville's dark viewpoint, this may suggest that the Confidence-Man is somehow God-like, but the analogy with Christ has not yet been developed. Soon we are given more conventional word-play reminders which link the masquerade costume with the Lamb of God: "In the same moment with his *advent* [italics added], he stepped aboard the favourite steamer *Fidele*" (so far, so good) and proceeded "with the air of one . . . evenly pursuing the path of duty." Still good; but we need more than this and Melville soon causes the innocent narrator to describe the masquerader as "a man in cream-colours" with fair cheeks, a downy chin, flaxen hair, and "his hat a white fur one, with a long fleecy nap." Those enjoying the sinister context will not miss the possibility of a double pun in the word "fleecy." Later, as this stranger is about to disappear, he does not die; he falls asleep, and again the undertones are apparent: "His aspect was at once gentle and jaded. . . . his whole *lamb-like* [italics added] figure relaxed . . ." We are told that he settles down to sleep, unobtrusively, "as some sugar-snow in March, which softly stealing down over night, with its white placidity . . ." Already, Melville has established the whiteness of this masquerader as somehow emblematic, and after his recurrent use of white as ambiguously symbolic, particularly in the *Moby-Dick* chapter on "The Whiteness of the Whale," the reader is prepared to notice that in most of his successive masquerade costumes, the Confidence-Man wears both black and white conspicuously, until they amount to a dualistic badge of office.

Having correlated these emblematic hints concerning the Confidence-Man's first vague resemblance to Christ, we may now return to the beginning, to notice his Christ-like actions. Just after he comes aboard, he participates in a scene where a crowd of passengers have gathered around a sign advertising someone apparently wanted by the police. (One would do well to recall, here, the passage in *Mardi* which describes "an illustrious prophet, and teacher divine; who, ages ago, at long intervals, and in various islands, had appeared to the Mardians under the different titles of Brami [Brahma], Manko [Manes], and Alma [Christ]."[5]) The sign apparently refers to the Confidence-Man himself, who "held on his way along the lower deck until he chanced to come to a placard nigh the captain's office, offering a reward for the capture of a mysterious impostor, supposed to have recently arrived from the East; quite an *original genius* [italics added] in his vocation, as would appear, though wherein his originality consisted was not clearly given . . ."[6]

(As we shall see, the term "original genius" is reiterated, and the Carlyle-mocking insinuations are later correlated.) The Confidence-Man kept working slowly through the crowd (including kinlike pickpockets and hawkers already at work) until he "so far succeeded in threading his way, as at last to plant himself just beside the placard, when, producing a small slate and tracing some words upon it, he held it up before him on a level with the placard, so that they who read the one might read the other. The words were these: *'Charity thinketh no evil.'*" The spectators did not relish this intruder: ". . . he being of an aspect so singularly innocent; an aspect, too, which they took to be somehow inappropriate to the time and place, and inclining to the notion that his writing was of much the same sort; in short, taking him for some strange kind of simpleton, harmless enough, would he keep to himself. . . ." (The insinuations, there, depend on whether the passage is placed on the second or third level of meaning—within a Christian framework, or Melville's anti-Christian framework.) When someone flattens his fleecy hat down on his head, he merely writes again on his slate and holds it up: *"Charity suffereth long, and is kind."* Shoved out of the way, he again writes on his slate: *"Charity endureth all things."* As a counter-irritant, the ship's barber throws open his shop door, just then, and hangs up an antithetical sentiment: a "gaudy sort of illuminated pasteboard sign bearing only two words: 'NO TRUST.'"

By means of these overtones, Melville completes his first masquerade prologue and focuses our attention on these two extremes: faith, hope, charity: doubt, fear, hate, no trust.

5

As we saw in *Moby-Dick*—and as we shall see even more clearly in *Billy Budd*—Melville liked to play with the concept that the Devil is one of God's most efficient agents in gathering valuable evidence and in carrying out God's own malicious purposes. When the Confidence-Man appears in his next masquerade costume, he is a negro, and the cluster of insinuations suggest that the Confidence-Man is now masquerading behind a black Devil disguise; the Calvinists repeatedly represented Satan as the Black Man:

"'What is your name, *old boy*?' [italics added], said a purple-faced drover. . . .

"'Der Black Guinea dey calls me, sar.'

(Further questioning prompts the "negro" to say he has come from St. Louis. When asked where he sleeps, there, he answers:)

"'On der floor of der good baker's oven, sar.'"

(Any insinuations here? Hell is a kind of baker's oven. The conversation continues.)

"'In an oven? whose, pray? What baker, I should like to know, bakes such black bread in his oven, alongside of his nice white rolls, too. Who is that too charitable baker, pray?'

"'Dar he be,' with a broad grin lifting his tambourine high over his head.

"'The sun is the baker, eh?'"⁷

(After the reader has noticed the number of times, in *Mardi*, *White-Jacket*, *Moby-Dick*, and *Pierre*, that Melville has employed the traditional concept of the sun as an emblem of God, it is difficult to imagine that this possible interlocking of emblematic meanings is accidental.)

While masquerading thus as a negro, the Confidence-Man stages a very brief miracle-play circus act: he opens his big mouth and invites the charitable to see if they can throw pennies in it. These antics, amusing everyone, "more than revived their first interest by an expedient which, whether by chance or design, was a singular temptation." (In the sinister context, the careful reader is not likely to pass too hurriedly over "expedient" and "chance or design" and "temptation.")

At this point, Melville introduces a skeptical character who can see through the masquerade, and who thus can serve as a mouthpiece for some of Melville's own personal views. (I suspect that Melville, making the character seem like "some discharged custom-house officer," and at the same time one-legged like Captain Ahab, was tucking in something for Hawthorne's private enjoyment, with the assurance that even if nobody else could handle the meaning of the narrative, Hawthorne certainly would.) Here the reader has to make a careful differentiation between Melville as artistic manipulator and his shallow Christian narrator. The latter, unconscious of the irony, views this newly appearing and skeptical character with extreme distaste:

"While this game of charity was yet at its height, a limping, gimlet-eyed, sour-faced person—it may be some discharged custom-house officer, who, suddenly stripped of convenient means of support, had concluded to be avenged on government and humanity by making himself miserable for life, either by hating or suspecting everything and everybody—this shallow unfortunate, after sundry sorry observations of the negro, began to croak out something about his deformity being a sham, got up for financial purposes, which immediately threw a damp upon the frolic benignities of the pitch-penny players.

"But that these suspicions came from one who himself on a

wooden leg went halt, this did not appear to strike anybody present. That cripples, above all men, should be companionable, or, at least, refrain from picking a fellow-limper to pieces, in short, should have a little sympathy in common misfortune, seemed not to occur to the company.

"Meantime, the negro's countenance . . . turned in passively hopeless appeal, as if instinct told it that the right or the wrong might not have overmuch to do with whatever wayward mood superior intelligences might yield to."[8]

(Note that now-familiar thrust at "superior intelligences.") A Christian minister defends the negro against the sour-faced person, also with unconsciously ironic appropriateness:

". . . a young Episcopal clergyman, in a long, straight-bodied black coat; small in stature, but manly; with a clear face and blue eye; innocence, tenderness, and good sense triumvirate in his air." When asked by the clergyman whether there may be, aboard the boat, "someone who can speak a good word for you," the negro (or rather, the Confidence-Man) ingeniously lists all the masquerade characters whose parts he himself may subsequently play:

" 'Oh yes, oh yes, dar is aboard here a werry nice, good ge'mman wid a weed, and a ge'mman in a gray coat and white tie, what knows all about me; and a ge'mman wid a big book, too; and a yarb-doctor; and a ge'mman in a yaller west; and a ge'mman wid a brass plate; and a ge'mman in a wiolet robe; and a ge'mman as is a sodjer; and ever so many good, kind, honest ge'mmen more aboard what knows me and will speak for me, God bress 'em; yes, and what knows me as well as dis poor old darkie knows hisself, God bress him! Oh, find 'em,' he earnestly added, 'and let 'em come quick, and show you all, ge'mmen, dat dis poor ole darkie is werry well wordy of all you kind ge'mmen's kind confidence.' "[9]

(These protestations arouse the "unnatural ill-feeling of the discharged custom-house officer" who interposes:)

" 'Wild goose chase!' croaked he with the wooden leg, now again drawing nigh. 'Don't believe there's a soul of them aboard. Did ever beggar have such heaps of fine friends? He can walk fast enough when he tries, a good deal faster than I; but he can lie yet faster. He's some white operator, betwisted and painted up for a decoy. He and his friends are all humbugs.'

307

"'Have you no charity, friend?' here in self-subdued tones, singularly contrasted with his unsubdued person, said a Methodist minister, advancing; a tall, muscular, martial-looking man, a Tennessean by birth, who in the Mexican war had been volunteer chaplain to a volunteer rifle-regiment.

"'Charity is one thing, and truth is another,' rejoined he with the wooden leg. 'He's a rascal, I say.'

"'But why not, friend, put as charitable a construction as one can upon the poor fellow?' said the soldier-like Methodist . . . 'He looks honest, don't he?'

"'Looks are one thing, and facts are another,' snapped out the other perversely; 'and as to your constructions, what construction can you put upon a rascal, but that a rascal he is?'

"'Be not such a Canada thistle,' urged the Methodist, with something less of patience than before. 'Charity, man, charity.'

"'To where it belongs with your charity! to heaven with it!' again snapped out the other, diabolically; 'here on earth, true charity dotes, and false charity plots. Who betrays a fool with a kiss, the charitable fool has the charity to believe is in love with him. . . .' [Notice this covert Christ-and-Judas sneer.]

"'Surely, friend,' returned the noble Methodist, with much ado restraining his still waxing indignation—'surely, to say the least, you forget yourself. . . . Suppose, now, I should exercise no charity in judging your own character by the words which have fallen from you; what sort of vile, pitiless man do you think I would take you for?'

"'No doubt'—with a grin—'some such pitiless man as has lost his piety. . . .'

"'Some insinuation there.'

"'More fool you that are puzzled by it.'

"'Reprobate!' cried the other, his indignation now at last almost boiling over; 'godless reprobate! if charity did not restrain me, I could call you by names you deserve.'

"'Could you, indeed?' with an insolent sneer.

"'Yes, and teach you charity on the spot,' cried the goaded Methodist, suddenly catching this exasperating opponent by his shabby coat-collar, and shaking him till his timber-toe clattered on the deck like a ninepin. 'You took me for a non-combatant, did you?—thought, seedy coward that you are, that you could abuse

308

a Christian with impunity. You find your mistake'—with another hearty shake.

" 'Well said and better done, church militant!' cried a voice.

" 'The brave white cravat against the world!' cried another.

" 'Bravo, bravo!' chorused many voices, with like enthusiasm taking sides with the resolute champion.

" 'You fools!' cried he with the wooden leg, writhing himself loose and inflamedly turning upon the throng; 'you flock of fools, under this captain of fools, in this ship of fools!'

" '. . . There he shambles off on his one lone leg, emblematic of his one-sided view of humanity.'

" 'But trust your painted decoy,' retorted the other from a distance, pointing back to the black cripple, 'and I have my revenge.' "[10]

In a sense, this important exchange may be considered as an epitome of the entire narrative, because it so perfectly represents the basic triangulation involving the Confidence-Man, the "Charitable" and the "Uncharitable"; on the deeper level, the Representative of God, the deceived, and the not-deceived. Here, the spokesman for the not-deceived consistently represents Melville's own private views. Again we are back to two opposed concepts of "madness," and as the not-deceived gentleman walks away, the Methodist minister preaches a little sermon on the subject of "madness."

" 'What does all that mean, now?' asked the country merchant, staring.

" 'Nothing; the foiled wolf's parting howl,' said the Methodist. 'Spleen, much spleen, which is the rickety child of his evil heart of unbelief; it has made him mad. I suspect him for one naturally reprobate. Oh, friends,' raising his arms as in the pulpit, 'oh beloved, how are we admonished by the melancholy spectacle of this raver. Let us profit by the lesson; and is it not this: that if, next to mistrusting Providence, there be aught that man should pray against, it is against mistrusting his fellow-man. I have been in mad-houses full of tragic mopers, and seen there the end of suspicion: the cynic, in the moody madness muttering in the corner; for years a barren fixture there; head lopped over, gnawing his own lip, vulture of himself; while, by fits and starts, from the corner opposite came the grimace of the idiot at him.'

"'What an example,' whispered one.

"'Might deter Timon,' was the response.

"'Oh, oh, good ge'mmen, have you no confidence in dis poor ole darkie?' now wailed the returning negro, who, during the late scene, had stumped apart in alarm."[11]

Thus Melville keeps his own bitter viewpoint under artistic control throughout, by employing a favorite formula: he permits his own concepts to be attacked and disparaged most vehemently by the narrator, by the Confidence-Man, by the gulled ones. Yet he quietly permits the action of the story—the persistently successful fraud practiced by the Confidence-Man—to illuminate and justify his own private viewpoint. This foreshadows the focus of narration and structure used by Melville in *Billy Budd*.

6

In his third masquerade, the Confidence-Man appears as a well-dressed gentleman who still keeps dualistic emblems of his God-Devilness: a white cravat, and a black band or "weed" in his cap, ostensibly to indicate that he is in mourning, so that he may the more easily win the pity and "charity" and "confidence"of the gullible.

His next confidence-game is made possible by his having recovered, during his negro performance, a calling card dropped by the man who was most generous and charitable to him. Melville uses this scene to ridicule Christ's peddling religious concept of the soul's former existence in a realm where the soul and God were on intimate terms. Specifically, the Confidence-Man sets the stage by employing Taji's sailor tactics when trying to seduce Yillah: "Haven't I met you before, somewhere?" But this time, the Confidence-Man can begin by calling "Mr. Roberts" by name, then can continue with reassurances that indeed they have met before. To prove it, he tells Mr. Roberts his entire name and business and place of residence (of course with the aid of the calling card, well concealed). Then, after Mr. Roberts correctly fails to recall their former acquaintance, the Confidence-Man employs a parable of his own, with Biblical references (and sinister undertones), to help his unbelief:

"I see you have a faithless memory, Mr. Roberts. But trust in the faithfulness of mine. . . . Now, those who have faithless memories, should they not have some little confidence in the less faithless memories of others? . . . We are but clay, sir, potter's clay, as the good book says, clay, feeble, and too-yielding clay. But I will not philosophise. . . ."

Then he proceeds to work this potter's clay for a little financial assistance!

7

STILL playing the part of the "man with the weed," he next insinuates himself into the confidence of a somewhat disillusioned "collegian—not improbably, a sophomore—on his travels" and warns him against such literary studies as may inculcate skepticism and cynicism; deplores "that shallow Tacitus" which the youth holds in his hands and produces from his own pocket (with obviously ironic overtones) a more fitting guide for thought: Akenside's *Pleasures of Imagination*. Again the subtle burlesque of blind and blinding Christian optimism:

" '. . . One of these days you will know it. Whatever our lot, we should read serene and cheery books, fitted to inspire love and trust. But Tacitus! I have long been of the opinion that these classics are the bane of colleges; for not to hint of the immorality of Ovid, Horace, Anacreon, and the rest, and the dangerous theology of Aeschylus and others—where will one find views so injurious to human nature as in Thucydides, Juvenal, Lucian, but more particularly Tacitus? When I consider that, ever since the revival of learning, these classics have been the favourites of successive generations of students and studious men, I tremble to think of that mass of unsuspected heresy on every vital topic which for centuries must have simmered unsurmised in the heart of Christendom. . . . Tacitus—I hate Tacitus; not, though, I trust, with the hate that sins, but a righteous hate. Without confidence himself, Tacitus destroys it in all his readers. Destroys confidence, paternal confidence, of which God knows there is in this world none to spare. [Very fine!] For, comparatively inexperienced as you are, my dear friend, did you never observe how little, very little, confidence, there is? I mean between man and man—more particularly between stranger and stranger. In a sad world it is the saddest fact. Confidence! I have sometimes almost thought that confidence is fled . . .' Then softly sliding nearer, with the softest air, quivering down and looking up, 'Could you now, my dear young sir, under such circumstances, by way of experiment, simply have confidence in *me?*' "[12]

8

As the "man with the weed" moves on, another very pretty piece of ironic antithesis is established. When next we seem him operating, he is soliciting contributions from a new sucker, for "a Widow and Orphan Asylum recently founded among the Seminoles." He is interrupted by the urgency of the young Methodist clergyman, who explains that the negro cripple has said the "man with the weed" can give proof that the poor negro is "what he seems to be." After his doubts are removed, and the Methodist is ready to inundate the negro with charity, the Confidence-Man moans:

" 'Another instance that confidence may come too late. I am sorry to say that at the last landing I myself—just happening to catch sight of him on the gangway-plank—assisted the cripple ashore. No time to talk, only to help. He may not have told you, but he had a brother in that vicinity.' "[13]

Variations on this same formula of self-protection are employed by the Confidence-Man throughout; he can always account for the disappearance of each of his earlier manifestations! But in this instance, his remark is capped by the scornful laughter of "the wooden-legged man," who appears "morosely grave as a criminal judge with a mustard-plaster on his back." After the intruder protests that he was merely laughing at one of his favorite jokes, he proves his point by telling the joke—a pertinent parable or "instance" that mistrust (like confidence) may also come too late, in certain situations. This leads the Confidence-Man to ask the clergyman:

" 'Who is that scoffer? . . . Who is he, who even were truth on his tongue, his way of speaking it would make truth almost offensive as falsehood?' "

After the clergyman has explained, the Confidence-Man tries to convince the scoffer that the negro cripple's honesty was obvious;

that his motive could never have been merely to collect a few pennies. The skeptic retorts, with allegorical pertinence:

" 'You two green-horns! Money, you think, is the sole motive to pain and hazard, deception and deviltry, in this world. How much did the devil make by gulling Eve?' "[14]

As soon as the skeptic has hobbled off, the Confidence-Man opinionates:

" 'A bad man, a dangerous man; a man to be put down in any Christian community. And this was he who was the means of begetting distrust? Ah, we should shut our ears to distrust, and keep them open only for its opposite.' "

Then he proceeds to touch the clergyman for a charitable donation to the Seminole Widow and Orphan Asylum!

9

THE allegorical connotations of the Confidence-Man's next encounter are again satirically aimed at Christian doctrine, particularly the notion of life after death as God's fake panacea for the world's aches and pains. The swindler explains that he has just come from the World's Fair in London, where he had exhibited his own remarkable invention: a phenomenally curious easy-chair for invalids. The sinister overtones of God's attributes are particularly strong:

" 'Then you have not always been in the charity business?'

" 'Is it not charity to ease human suffering? *I am, and always have been, as I always will be, I trust* [italics added] in the charity business, as you call it; but charity is not like a pin, one to make the head, and the other the point; charity is a work to which a good workman may be competent in all its branches. I invented my Protean easy-chair in odd intervals stolen from meals and sleep.'

" 'You call it the Protean easy-chair; pray describe it.'

" 'My Protean easy-chair is a chair so all over bejointed, behinged, and bepadded, every way so elastic, springy, and docile to the airiest touch, that in some one of its endlessly changeable accommodations of back, seat, footboard, and arms, the most restless body, the body most racked, nay, I had almost added the most tormented conscience must, somehow and somewhere, find rest. Believing that I owed it to suffering humanity to make known such a chair to the utmost, I scraped together my little means and off to the World's Fair with it.'

" 'You did right. But your scheme [for world-wide charity]; how did you hit upon that?'

" 'I was going to tell you. After seeing my invention duly catalogued and placed, I gave myself up to pondering the scene about me. As I dwelt upon that shining pageant of arts, and moving concourse of nations, and reflected that here was the pride of the world glorying in a glass house, a sense of the fragility of worldly grandeur profoundly impressed me. And I said to myself, I will see if this occasion of vanity cannot supply a hint toward a better profit than was designed. Let some world-wide good to the world-wide cause be now done. In short, inspired by the scene, on the fourth day I issued at the World's Fair my prospectus of the World's Charity . . . the methodisation of the world's benevolence. . . . I am . . . a philanthropist. . . .' "

(The insinuations in the "fourth-day" reference, suggesting Genesis and God's creation of the heavens and the earth, are important: it was on the "fourth day" that God said, "Let there be lights in the firmament of heaven to divide the day from the night. . . ." The "enlightened" perceive the symbolic dualism.) The listener interrupts:

" 'I fear you are too enthusiastic.' [Nice, etymologically!]

" 'A philanthropist is necessarily an enthusiast; for without enthusiasm what was ever achieved but commonplace? . . .'

" 'Sharing the character of your general project, these things, I take it, are rather examples of wonders that were to be wished, than wonders that will happen.'

" 'And is the age of wonders past? Is the world too old? Is it barren? Think of Sarah.'

" 'Then I am Abraham reviling the angel [Note well: angel as representative of God] (with a smile). . . .'

" '. . . For a Christian to talk so!'

" 'But think of the obstacles!'

" 'Obstacles? I have confidence to remove obstacles, though mountains [cf. Paul]. Yes, confidence in the world's charity to that degree, that, as no better person offers to supply the place,

I have nominated myself provisional treasurer, and will be happy to receive subscriptions. . . .' "[15]

Considered allegorically, all these word-play overtones and extensions of meaning are amusing enough; but Melville's personal pleasure in writing it was apparently greater than even the most sympathetic reader's is likely to be, because the tediously long-winded conversations lack the interest of such dramatic action as that involving the Methodist clergyman, shaking the stuffing out of the one-legged man, while the crowd cheers and the Confidence-Man profits.

10

THE fourth change of costume brings the Confidence-Man on deck as the "ge'mman wid a big book." Specifically, he now pretends to be an officer of a joint-stock company, and the "big book" is the ledger of the company's transactions, by means of which he is able to arrange for selling stock to the gullible, with excellent promises of tremendous rewards for such virtuous investment! The sinister construction is clear enough: the "ledger" is emblematic of the Holy Bible! One passage, obliquely satirizing a too literal faith in the Word of God, will suffice for illustration. The Confidence-Man says to the sucker:

" 'But you have not examined my book.'

" 'What need to, if already I believe that it is what it is lettered to be?'

" 'But you had better. It might suggest doubts.'

" 'Doubts, maybe, it might suggest, but not knowledge; for how, by examining the book, should I think I knew any more than I now think I do; since, if it be the true book, I think it so already; and since if it be otherwise, then I have never seen the true one, and don't know what that ought to look like.'

" 'Your logic I will not criticise, but your confidence I admire, and earnestly too, jocose as was the method I took to draw it out. Enough, we will go to yonder table, and if there by any business which, either in my private or official capacity, I can help you do, pray command me.' "[16]

Immediately after this swindle had been concluded, the victim relates to the Confidence-Man a fablelike "Story of the Unfortunate Man" whose wicked wife (appropriately named after Lear's daughter, Goneril) had ruined his life. Observing the opportunity to use the story as a Christian parable, with application, the Confidence-Man first "begged to know in what spirit" the unfortunate man "bore his alleged calamities. Did he despond or have confidence?" The drift of his application provides Melville with another chance to satirize one of his favorite whipping-boys: Plinlimmon! Here are excerpts from the narrator's paraphrase of remarks by the Confidence-Man on the precious subject of God's ways and man's ways:

". . . to admit the existence of unmerited misery, more particularly if alleged to have been brought about by unhindered arts of wickedness, such an admission was, to say the least, not prudent; since, with some, it might unfavourably bias their most important persuasions. . . . if the conviction of a Providence, for instance, were in any way made dependent upon such variabilities as every-day events, the degree of that conviction would, in thinking minds, be subject to fluctuations akin to those of the stock-exchange during a long and uncertain war. Here he glanced aside at his transfer-book, and after a moment's pause continued. It was of the essence of a right conviction of the divine nature, as with a right conviction of the human, that, based less on experience than intuition, it rose above the zones of weather. . . .

"To which the merchant replied, that he earnestly hoped it might be so, and at any rate he tried his best to comfort himself with the persuasion that, if the unfortunate man was not happy in this world, he would, at least, be so in another."[17]

11

FOLLOWING his successful dealings with the merchant, the Confidence-Man paves the way for his next masquerade in which he will appear as an herb-doctor peddling, allegorically, a neatly packaged patent-medicine form of cure-all Christian doctrine; specifically described as a remedy of his own devising, called "The Omni-Balsamic Reinvigorator." Still garbed as the "man with the weed," the Confidence-Man finds a consumptive miser in his berth, seemingly on the verge of death, and consoles him thus:

" 'What a shocking cough. I wish, my friend, the herb-doctor was here now; a box of his Omni-Balsamic Reinvigorator would do you good. . . . I've a good mind to go find him. He's aboard somewhere. I saw his long, snuff-colored surtout. Trust me, his medicines are the best in the world. . . . Oh, how sorry I am.' "

But the miser suspects the invisible herb-doctor and suggests that he may be a fraud. Dropping that approach, the Confidence-Man immediately shifts to his immediate masquerade functions and offers to invest some of the miser's money, promising him triune profits! This makes the old boy sit up. Allegorically, the immediate ridicule on Melville's part is aimed at the belief in God as all knowing, merely because He is unknowable. God's invisibility and secrecy, by allegorical insinuation, are God's front for fraud:

" 'How, how?' still more bewildered, 'do you, then, go about the world, gratis, seeking to invest people's money for them?'

" 'My humble profession, sir. I live not for myself; but the world will not have confidence in me, and yet confidence in me were great gain.'

" 'But, but,' in a kind of vertigo, 'what do—do you do—do with people's money? . . . How is the gain made?'

" 'To tell that would ruin me. That known, everyone would be going into the business, and it would be overdone. A secret, a mystery—all I have to do with you is to receive your confidence, and all you have to do with me is, in due time, to receive it back, thrice paid in trebling profits.'

" 'What, what?' imbecility in the ascendant once more; 'but the vouchers, the vouchers,' suddenly hunkish again.

" 'Honesty's best voucher is honesty's face.'

" 'Can't see yours, though,' peering through the obscurity. . . . 'if, if now, I should put, put—'

" 'No ifs. Downright confidence, or none. *So help me heaven* [italics added] I will have no half-confidences.' "

(At this point, the Confidence-Man threatens to leave him entirely, and the old miser surrenders, in the process paraphrasing, of course unconsciously, one more celebrated Bible passage:)

" 'I confide, I confide; help, friend, my distrust!' "[18]

12

REAPPEARING later in his fourth disguise, as the herb-doctor, the Confidence-Man is challenged by another sick man, this time to explain the constituents of his "Omni-Balsamic Reinvigorator"— what herbs are used, the nature of them, and the reason for giving them. The Confidence-Man promptly upbraids him:

" 'You are sick, and a philosopher.'

" 'No, no;—not the last.'

" 'But to demand the ingredient, with the reason for giving, is the mark of a philosopher; just as the consequence is the penalty of a fool. A sick philosopher is incurable . . . he has no confidence.' "

The sick man challenges this, and another celebrated Bible passage is unconsciously paraphrased:

" 'You talk of confidence. How comes it that when brought low himself, the herb-doctor, who was most confident to prescribe in other cases, proves least confident to prescribe in his own; having small confidence in himself for himself.' "[19]

In the continuing discussion, the sick man mentions a book entitled *Nature in Disease*, and the Confidence-Man's remarks provide, in context, a surprisingly good burlesque of a doctrine perpetrated in America, some years later, by an actual confidence-woman:

" '*Nature in Disease*? As if nature, divine nature, were aught but health; as if through nature disease is decreed! But did I not before hint of the tendency of science, that forbidden tree? Sir, if despondency is yours from recalling that title, dismiss it. Trust me, nature is health; for health is good, and nature cannot work ill. As little can she work error. Get nature, and you get well. Now, I repeat, this medicine is nature's own.' "[20]

13

WHILE the Confidence-Man is variously engaged in peddling many cures (including his "Samaritan Pain Dissuader") and recommending himself to cripples as "The Natural bone-setter," the consumptive stops to ask for information about the man with the ledger. At first, the Confidence-Man seems to have difficulty in recognizing that description of his former self; but he finally exclaims, "Ten to one you mean my worthy friend, who, in pure goodness of heart, makes people's fortunes for them—their ever-lasting fortunes, as the phrase goes—only charging his one small commission of confidence." Together, they roam about the deck, arm in arm, searching for him, and just as the boat is leaving a landing, the herb-doctor pretends to see his "worthy friend" dis-embarking in the crowd; pretends to see him too late, and the best the herb-man can do is shout, "Mr. Truman, Mr. Truman! There he goes . . . Mr. Truman! for God's sake, Mr. Truman! No, no. There, the plank's in—too late—we're off." As consolation, he offers the miser a box of Omni-Balsamic Reinvigorator: "For heaven's sake, try my medicine, if but a single box. That it is pure nature you may be confident. Refer you to Mr. Truman."[21]

14

AT this point in the story, the herb-doctor's peddling of Mother Nature's Own Cure is severely challenged by a highly entertaining skeptic, "eccentric looking" and "ursine in aspect" as the unper-ceptive narrator is made to characterize him. He is a "man from Missouri"—the type of a frontiersman, a Daniel Boone or Davy Crockett, and dressed to the part, even to the double-barrelled gun in his hand. Approaching the consumptive miser, he growls a warning against the herb-doctor:

" 'Yarbs, yarbs; natur, natur; you foolish old file you! He diddled you with that hocus-pocus, did he? . . . Because a thing is nat'ral, as you call it, you think it must be good. But who gave you that cough? Was it, or was it not, nature? . . .'

" 'Oh, that a Christian man should speak agin natur and yarbs —' . . . '—ain't sick men sent out into the country; sent out to natur and grass?'

" 'Ay, and poets send out the sick spirit to green pastures, like lame horses turned out unshod to the turf to renew their hoofs. A sort of yarb-doctors in their way, poets have it that for sore hearts, as for sore lungs, nature is the grand cure. But who froze to death my teamster on the prairie? And who made an idiot of Peter the Wild Boy?' "[22]

(The German "Wild Boy" twist is nicer than the derogatory

pun references to the Twenty-third Psalm, which are poor enough; but the frontiersman is just warming to his subject.) When the herb-doctor tries to convert him to the true faith, the man from Missouri snaps at him: "I have confidence in distrust; more particularly as applied to you and your herbs." As the argument continues, the skeptic echoes certain remarks Captain Ahab made about Mother Nature, in *Moby-Dick*. The Confidence-Man says:

" 'Now, can you, who suspect nature, deny, that this same nature not only kindly brought you into being, but has faithfully nursed you to your present vigorous and independent condition? Is it not to nature that you are indebted for that robustness of mind which you so unhandsomely use to her scandal? Pray, is it not to nature that you owe the very eyes by which you criticise her?'

" 'No! for the privilege of vision I am indebted to an oculist, who in my tenth year operated upon me in Philadelphia. Nature made me blind and would have kept me so. My oculist counterplotted her.'

" 'And yet, sir, by your complexion, I judge you live an out-of-door life; without knowing it, you are partial to nature; you fly to nature, the universal mother.'

" 'Very motherly! Sir, in the passion-fits of nature, I've known birds fly from nature to me, rough as I look; yes, sir, in a tempest, refuge here,' smiting the folds of his bearskin. 'Fact, sir, fact. Come, come, Mr. Palaverer, for all your palavering, did you yourself never shut out nature of a cold, wet night? Bar her out? Bolt her out? Lint her out?'

" 'As to that,' said the herb-doctor calmly, 'much may be said.'

" 'Say it, then,' ruffling all his hairs. 'You can't, sir, can't.' Then, as in apostrophe: 'look you, nature! I don't deny but your clover is sweet, and your dandelions don't roar, but whose hailstones smashed my windows?'

" 'Sir,' with unimpaired affability, producing one of his boxes, 'I am pained to meet with one who holds nature a dangerous character. . . . *Through her regularly authorized agents, of whom I happen to be one* [italics added], nature delights in benefiting those who most abuse her. Pray, take it.'

" 'Away with it! . . .'

" 'Good heavens! my dear sir—'

" 'I tell you I want none of your boxes,' snapping his rifle.

" 'Oh, take it . . . do take it,' chimed in the old miser. . . .

" 'You find it lonely, eh,' turning short round; 'gulled yourself, you would have a companion.'

" 'How can he find it lonely,' returned the herb-doctor, 'or how desire a companion, when here I stand by him; I, even I, in whom he has trust. . . .' "[23]

Again the echo of a celebrated Bible passage, ironically appropriate in the sinister allegorical context.

15

TEMPORARILY worsted in his dispute with the man from Missouri, the herb-doctor disappears long enough to change costume. When he returns to renew the struggle, he is no longer an herb-doctor. This time, he wears a brass plate on which are engraved three significant letters: "P" and "I" and "O." Taken as a phonetic unit, these three letters are highly suggestive of a somewhat indelicate and derogatory exclamation; taken as a possible abbreviation of the word "PIOUS," on the other hand, they suggest that the wearer is (by definition) careful of the duties which he, as a created being, owes to God. But the wearer, now masquerading in his fifth guise, explains to the man from Missouri that the letters stand for "PHILOSOPHICAL INTELLIGENCE OFFICE." This time, the Confidence-Man says he comes from the headquarters of an employment bureau, which supplies little boys, and even men, for work on farms. The misanthropic man from Missouri answers that he hates little boys and prefers machines:

" 'My corn-husker—does that ever give me insolence? No: cider-mill, mowing-machine, corn-husker—all faithfully attend to their business. Disinterested, too; no board, no wages; yet doing good all their lives long; shining examples that virtue is its own reward—the only practical Christians I know.'

" 'Oh, dear, dear, dear, dear!'

" 'Yes, sir:—boys? Start my soul-bolts, what a difference, in a moral point of view, between a corn-husker and a boy! Sir, a corn-husker, for its patient continuance in well-doing, might not unfitly go to heaven. Do you suppose a boy will?'

" 'A corn-husker in heaven!' turning up the whites of his eyes.

'Respected sir, this way of talking as if heaven were a kind of Washington patent-office museum—oh, oh, oh! as if mere machine-work and puppet-work went to heaven—oh, oh, oh! Things incapable of free agency, to receive the eternal reward of well-doing —oh, oh, oh!' [Cf. Calvinistic dogma of "Election."]

" 'You Praise-God-Barebones you, what are you groaning about? Did I say anything of that sort? Seems to me, though you talk so good, you are mighty quick at a hint the other way, or else you want to pick a polemic quarrel with me.'

" 'It may be so or not, respected sir,' was now the demure reply; 'but if it be, it is only because as a soldier out of honour is quick in taking affront, so a Christian out of religion is quick, sometimes perhaps a little too much so, in spying heresy.'

" 'Well,' after an astonished pause, 'for an unaccountable pair, you and the herb-doctor ought to yoke together.' "[24]

In the end, however, the Confidence-Man converts the man from Missouri to the desired point of view, and (after they have explored burlesque extensions of opposed viewpoints on the thesis that "the child is father of the man,") the convert agrees to try a very promising boy whom the P. I. O. agent describes; agrees to try him only "for the sake purely of a scientific experiment." In closing the deal, the agent requests confidence in the lad, even if he show "some little undesirable trait." His reasoning in support of this request is indeed, in its allegorical context, a "Devil's Joke":

" 'Have but patience, have but confidence. Those transient vices will, ere long, fall out, and be replaced by the sound, firm, even and permanent virtues. Ah,' glancing shoreward, toward a grotesquely shaped bluff, 'there's the Devil's Joke, as they call it. . . .' "[25]

As soon as the agent disappears, the man from Missouri begins to regret that he has been duped, tries to understand the cunning of the Confidence-Man, and lights on an analogy that pleases him:

"Analogically he couples the slanting cut of the equivocator's coat-tails with the sinister cast in his eye; he weighs slyboot's sleek speech in the light imparted by the oblique import of the smooth slope of his worn boot-heels; the insinuator's undulating flunkeyisms dovetail into those of the flunky beast that windest his way on his belly."[26]

Again, this overt allusion to the Confidence-Man as somehow

analogous to that protean Satan who assumed the form of the serpent in the Garden of Eden, takes us back to the Genesis story. By this time, the various pieces of the allegorical puzzle have fallen into place enough to make us see the general nature of Melville's sinister purpose. In all his various masquerades, the Confidence-Man reflects the attributes of three celebrated characters in Christian doctrine: Satan, Christ, and God. And when the confidence-Man is specifically permitted to describe himself as one of Nature's "regularly authorized agents," this provides a stronger corroboration of the many hints that, on the darker level of allegorical meaning, man's pilgrimage through life to death exposes him to all manner of swindlers, each an agent of God.

16

In the sixth and last selection of costume for further masquerade, the Confidence-Man splurges his fondness for the deceptively protean by combining several different styles of dress in one, emblematic of world brotherhood. He "sported a vesture barred with various hues, that of the cochineal predominating, in style participating of a Highland plaid, Emir's robe, and French blouse; from its plaited sort of front peeped glimpses of a flowered regatta-shirt, while, for the rest, white trowsers of ample duck flowed over maroon-coloured slippers, and a jaunty smoking-cap of regal purple crowned him off at the top; king of travelled goodfellows, evidently." Again he begins by engaging in conversation with the man from Missouri, and introduces himself this time as "a cosmopolitan, a catholic man" who "federates, in heart as in costume, something of the various gallantries of men under various suns." His texts for exemplifying the brotherhood of man are persistently spiced with overtones of reference to Christ's Sermon on the Mount, and his favorite form of representing his ideas is that of the parable.

In short order, the man from Missouri pierces the disguise and calls him "another of them," even a Jeremy Diddler No. 3, somehow related to the herb-doctor and the bureau agent. After an exchange of remarks, the Confidence-Man resents the ironies aimed in his direction, and counters:

" 'Ah, now,' deprecating with his pipe, 'irony is so unjust; never could abide irony; something Satanic about irony. God defend me from Irony, and Satire, his bosom friend.'"

For the sake of the sinister context, it may be noted that the structure of this last sentence is nicely equivocal, and pivots on the two possible antecedents for "his." The man from Missouri makes his own comment on the remark as the conversation continues:

" 'A right knave's prayer, and a right fool's, too,' snapping his rifle-lock.

" 'Now be frank. Own that was a little gratuitous. But, no, no, you didn't mean it; anyway, I can make allowances. Ah, did you but know it, how much pleasanter to puff at this philanthropic pipe, than still to keep fumbling at that misanthropic rifle.'"

But this "Ishmael"—as the Confidence-Man calls his opponent from Missouri—proves too misanthropic and not sufficiently convertible. So the philanthropic one moves along the deck to make new acquaintances, one of whom confronts him with an extended parable obliquely illuminating the theological nature of a misanthrope. It is the story of John Moredock, professional Indian-hater, and in the process of exploring "the metaphysics of Indian-hating," the parable-teller establishes a pertinent analogy between a religion of hate and a religion of love. It occurs when Moredock is offered the governorship of Illinois and he declines it:

"If the governorship offered large honours, from Moredock it demanded larger sacrifices. These were incompatibles. In short, he was not unaware that to be a consistent Indian-hater involves the renunciation of ambition, with its objects—the pomps and glories of the world; and since religion, pronouncing such things vanities, accounts it merit to renounce them, therefore, so far as this goes, Indian-hating, whatever may be thought of it in other respects, may be regarded as not wholly without the efficacy of a devout sentiment."[27]

After several other adventures, the Confidence-Man drops into the barber shop and tries (successfully) to swindle the barber out of his "NO TRUST." Later, the barber recovers his equilibrium and edifies his friends concerning the Confidence-Man, to such an extent that they unite in calling the swindler "Quite an Original." Carlyle's use of the term, already cited, immediately becomes inverted, in Melville's context.

17

"QUITE an Original" has been accumulating possibilities from the beginning. Now Melville proceeds to correlate them, in "Chapter Forty-Four, In Which the Last Three Words of the Last Chapter are made the Text of Discourse, which Will be Sure of Receiving More or Less Attention from Those Readers who do not Skip it." We must not skip it, here, because it is certainly the "deepest" and "darkest" chapter in *The Confidence-Man*. Now Melville pushes his narrator out of the way and introduces an author's editorial on the general subject of "original characters in fiction." There are very few such, he says, "in the sense that Hamlet is, or Don Quixote, or Milton's Satan."

With the mention of Milton's Satan, we are encouraged to leave the overt subject matter of this chapter, and concentrate on the sinister undertones. Summarized, these undertones tie together many previous concepts. First of all, the Confidence-Man is not an original character: he is a representative or agent of God, even as Satan or Christ. But, to let Melville demonstrate his stylistic rascality once more, let us assume that we do not recognize that the Confidence-Man is an agent of God. Now, Melville deprecatingly asserts, the Confidence-Man as a character in fiction is not really original:

"In nearly all the original characters, loosely accounted such in works of invention, there is discernible something prevailingly local, or of the age; which circumstance, of itself, would seem to invalidate the claim, judged by the principles here suggested.

"Furthermore, if we consider, what is popularly held to entitle characters in fiction to be deemed original, is but something personal—confined to itself. The character sheds not its characteristic on its surroundings, whereas, the original character, essentially such, is like a revolving Drummond Light, raying away from itself all round it—everything is lit by it, everything starts up to it (mark how it is with Hamlet), so that, in certain minds, there follows upon the adequate conception of such a character, an effect, in its way, akin to that which in Genesis attends upon the beginning of things.

"For much the same reason that there is but one planet to one orbit, so can there be but one such original character to one work of invention. Two would conflict to chaos. . . ."[28]

Now, if we paraphrase and penetrate this rascality, it implies that if the dualistic or two-faced Confidence-Man should be tested as an original character, everything should be lit up by him, and everything should start up to him until "in certain minds, there follows upon the adequate conception" of the Confidence-Man "an effect, in its way, akin to that which in Genesis attends upon" God! In other words, "certain minds" will be aware that the ambiguous Confidence-Man is merely an emblem, or a microcosm of the macrocosm!

The "Drummond Light" reference, and the analogy with an original character, ("raying away from itself all round it—everything is lit by it, everything starts up to it") seems to me another example of Melville's fondness for inverting certain concepts stated so memorably in *Paradise Lost*. Consider the implications of the following passage, when placed against Melville's "Drummund Light" analogy:

> O Earth, how like to Heav'n, if not preferr'd
> More justly, Seat worthier of Gods, as built
> With second thoughts, reforming what was old!
> For what God after better worse would build?
> Terrestrial Heav'n, danc't round by other Heav'ns
> That shine, yet bear thir bright officious Lamps,
> Light above Light, for thee alone, as seems,
> In thee concentring all thir precious beams
> Of sacred influence: As God in Heav'n
> Is Centre, yet extends to all, so thou
> Centring receiv'st from all those Orbs; in thee,
> Not in themselves, all thir known virtue appears
> Productive in Herb, Plant, and nobler birth
> Of Creatures animate with gradual life
> Of Growth, Sense, Reason, all summ'd up in Man.[29]

This is Milton's Satan talking, and of course I have no way of proving that Melville had this passage in mind when he used the Drummond Light analogy. But the value of this passage, here, is that when placed in the context of Melville's private myth, it illuminates Melville's inverted concept thus: as God in Heaven is center, yet extends to all, so he extends to the viciousness of his agent the Confidence-Man, who is a sinner. Quite an Original Sinner is the Confidence-Man, and why not, when it is realized that he is the agent of that truly Original Sinner, God Almighty.

18

IN the final chapter, the Confidence-Man enters the gentlemen's sleeping-quarters cabin, as though to retire for the night. There he finds a devout old man reading the Word of God, and sits down opposite the reader at the table. Annoyed, the old man growls that one might think he was reading "a newspaper here with great news, and the only copy to be had." This gives the smooth operator as much of an opening as he needs:

" 'And so you *have* good news there, sir—the very best of good news.'

" 'Too good to be true,' here came from one of the curtained berths.

" 'Hark!' said the cosmopolitan. 'Someone talks in his sleep.'

" 'Yes,' said the old man, 'and you—*you* seem to be talking in a dream. Why speak you, sir, of news, and all that, when you must see this is a book I have here—the Bible, not a newspaper?'

" 'I know that; and when you are through with it—but not a moment sooner—I will thank you for it. It belongs to the boat, I believe—a present from a society.' "

(Receiving it, he asks the old man for help in interpreting the word of God; he is troubled by the meaning of a particular passage:)

" 'Can you, my aged friend, resolve me a doubt—a disturbing doubt?'

" 'There are doubts, sir,' replied the old man, with a changed countenance, 'there are doubts, sir, which, if man have them, it is not man that can solve them.'

" 'True; but look, now, what my doubt is. I am one who thinks well of man. I love man. I have confidence in man. But what was told me not a half-hour since? I was told that I would find it written—"Believe not his many words—an enemy speaketh sweetly with his lips"—and also I was told that I would find a good deal more to the same effect, and all in this book. I could not think it;

and, coming here to look for myself, what do I read? Not only just what was quoted, but also, as was engaged, more to the same purpose, such as this: "With much communication he will tempt thee; he will smile upon thee, and speak thee fair, and say What wantest thou? If thou be for his profit he will use thee; he will make thee bear, and will not be sorry for it. Observe and take good heed. When thou hearest these things, awake in thy sleep." '

" 'Who's that describing the confidence-man?' here came from the berth again.

" 'Awake in his sleep, sure enough, ain't he?' said the cosmopolitan, again looking off in surprise. 'Same voice as before, ain't it? Strange sort of dreamy man, that. Which is his berth, pray?

" 'Never mind *him*, sir,' said the old man anxiously, 'but tell me truly, did you, indeed, read from the book just now?' "

The Confidence-Man insists that he did, and points to "The Wisdom of Jesus." The sinister meaning is clear enough, and is even felt by the old man. But as soon as he discovers that these are the words of Jesus, the Son of Sirach, and that the passages occur in Ecclesiasticus, he is greatly relieved and hastens to explain that these passages do not constitute the true word *about* God; they occur in the Apocrypha. The Confidence-Man feigns a great sense of comfort from the old man's remarks, and thus worms his way into the old man's confidence until he learns just where he keeps his money. ("Where your treasure is, there will your heart be also.") Offering to lead the old man to his rest— allegorically, to his eternal rest—the Confidence-Man extinguishes the light (with overt emblematic meaning) and "in the darkness which ensued, the cosmopolitan kindly led the old man away." The occult insinuations of these equivocal and ambiguous words are appropriate. Melville adds just one more sentence: "Something further may follow of this Masquerade."[30]

Something further may follow—indeed is certain to follow—for any reader who does not insist on running while he reads. The narrative is complete enough, as it stands, but only for the reader whose response is lively enough to perceive the carefully established and elaborately interlocked insinuations, throughout. Once again Melville has (to his own apparent satisfaction) technically outpointed God in another round.

CHRONIC REPULSE

CHAPTER X

If conscience doubt, she'll next recant.
What basis then? O, tell at last,
Are earnest natures staggering here
But fatherless shadows from no substance cast?
Yea, are ye, gods? Then ye, 'tis ye
Should show what touch of tie ye may,
Since ye, too, if not wrung are wronged
By grievous misconceptions of your sway.

MELVILLE, *Timoleon*

But, crying out in death's eclipse,
When rainbow none His eyes might see,
Enlarged the margin for despair—
My God, My God, forsakest Me?

MELVILLE, *Clarel*

CHRONIC REPULSE

THE persistence of Melville's embittered and disillusioned pessimism, during the years between the writing of *The Confidence-Man* and *Billy Budd*, is reflected in his poems, journals, narratives. We must glance briefly at this evidence because it should help to dispel the considerable confusion which exists as to the direction of Melville's thought during the writing of *Billy Budd*. For example, some interpreters try to find in *Billy Budd a* "Testament of Acceptance" which would indicate that Melville had at last made his peace with God and man, and had thus availed himself of Heaven's promises, after death. Others have said that *Billy Budd* represents Melville's final acceptance of complete annihilation after death. Still others have found in it his final admission of the tragic necessity of law and bondage in society. At least one other, in dissent, has said that *Billy Budd* is an artistic failure because Melville did not properly conceive of the attributes which a tragic hero must possess, in order to oppose the law, in genuine tragedy. Still others have seen in *Billy Budd* a morality play, and it has been adapted to a dramatized version, to illuminate a profound philosophical and moral problem. One critic, praising this dramatized version, has interpreted Melville's theme in *Billy Budd* thus: "Absolute good and absolute evil cannot live in this world together, according to Melville. Each must destroy the other, for human life is a compromise that follows the middle way."[1] (Just where we might find absolute good and absolute evil, in this world, the critic does not say; he apparently misses the meaning of "innate depravity" as applied to Claggart, even as the writers of the dramatized version seem to miss it.)

Such confusion and misrepresentation could be made, it seems to me, only by those who are victimized by Melville's wry pleasure in using sustained irony for deceptively and self-protectively satirical purposes. I fear that our American eagerness to find in our literary history an American Dostoevsky has assisted Melville in utilizing his ingeniously devised mousetrap plays too long. My suggestion is that *Billy Budd* should be viewed as Melville's most subtle triumph in triple-talk; that it was designed to conceal and reveal much the same notions as expressed years earlier in *Moby-Dick* and *Pierre* and *The Confidence-Man*; that Melville came to the end of his life still harping on the notion that the world was put together wrong and that God was to blame and that only the self-profiting authoritarians pretend otherwise, in order to victimize the stupid. Before I try to justify that interpretation, let us consider some of Melville's own self-revelations, which indicate that his chronic anti-Christian pessimism did not abate during the forty-five years which elapsed between *The Confidence-Man* and *Billy Budd*.

Shortly after Melville had completed writing *The Confidence-Man*, but long before it was published, he was advised by his physician to take a sea voyage as a tonic for his debilities, largely psychological in cause. Always preferring to seek serenity anywhere other than where he might be, Melville quickly chose to carry out an earlier plan for visiting (of all places) the Holy Land. As we have seen, Hawthorne provided us with a glimpse of Melville's notions, during his brief visit to the Liverpool consul after the first leg of the Holy Land voyage had been completed. Other pertinent glimpses are available in Melville's own private journal of his experiences, and a few passages deserve to be quoted, here, with little comment. During his stay in Constantinople, Melville recorded on December 14, 1856, this Sabbath experience:

"Saw a burial. . . . Nearby, saw a woman over a new grave—no grass on it yet. Such abandonment of misery! Called to the dead, put her head down as close to it as possible; as if calling down a hatchway, a cellar; besought—'Why don't you speak to me? My God!—It is I! Ah,—speak—but one word!' All deaf. So much for consolation. This woman & her cries haunt me horribly."[2]

This sounds very familiar, and even recalls Ishmael's "hypos" in the first chapter of *Moby-Dick*: ". . . I find myself involuntarily pausing before coffin warehouses, and bringing up the rear of every funeral I meet." Death remained a morbid preoccupation and mystery for Melville, throughout his life. In Egypt, the pyramids excited Melville's imagination more strongly than any other object viewed during his Holy Land pilgrimage:

". . . Seem high & pointed, but flatten & depress as you approach. Vapors below summits. Kites sweeping & soaring around, hovering right over apex. . . . Old man . . . tried the ascent . . . Too much for him; oppressed by the massiveness & mystery of the pyramids. I myself too. A feeling of awe & terror came over me. . . . I shudder at ideas of ancient Egyptians. It was in these pyramids that was conceived the idea of Jehovah. Terrible mixture of the cunning and awful. Moses learned in all the lore of the Egyptians. The idea of Jehovah born here. . . . These the steps Jacob lay at. . . . Pyramids still loom before me—something vast, indefinite, incomprehensible, and awful. . . .

"They must needs have been terrible . . . those Egyptian wise men. And one seems to see that as out of the crude forms of the natural earth they could evoke by art the transcendent mass & symmetry . . . of the pyramid so out of the rude elements of the insignificant thoughts that are in all men, they could rear the transcendent conception of a God. But for no holy purpose was the pyramid founded."[3]

Again, that which is familiar, here, is Melville's attempt to achieve an attitude of detachment and indifference toward exactly those concepts of God which remain his morbid preoccupation. Another kind of preoccupation was suggested at Jaffa, where Melville's examination of a hotel register stimulated his delight in stylistic equivocation and ambiguity of such kind that the surface meaning would be diametrically opposed to an underlying meaning:

"Amused with the autographs & confessions of people who have stayed at this hotel. 'I have *existed* at this hotel &c &c.' Something comical could be made out of all this. Let the confessions be of a religious, penitential, resigned & ambiguous turn, apparently flattering to the host, but really derogatory to the place."[4]

And once more, how familiar to have Melville concerned with a stylistic device at one "apparently flattering" and "really derogatory." Even the subject matter suggested here had been used in *Moby-Dick*, where one sarcastic passage refers to the world as a hotel and the "host" (with all its fine extensions of meaning) as (by insinuation) God Almighty, yclept Thunder Cloud: "But I am one of those that never take on about princely fortunes, and am quite content if the world is ready to board and lodge me, while I am putting up at this grim sign of the Thunder Cloud."[5] Oh, quite! These two preoccupations—stylistic and theological—usually went hand in hand for Melville. Continuing his journey, he found Jerusalem merely a dreary stimulus to more dark thoughts:

"The mind cannot but be sadly & suggestively affected with the *indifference* [italics added] of Nature & Man to all that makes the spot sacred to the Christian. Weeds grow upon Mount Zion; side by side in *impartiality* [italics added] appear the shadows of church & mosque, and on Olivet every morning the sun *indifferently* [italics added] ascends over the Chapel of the Ascension. . . .

"Had Jerusalem no peculiar historic associations, still would it, by its physical aspect evoke peculiar emotion in the traveller. As the sight of haunted Haddon Hall suggested to Mrs. Radcliffe her curdling romances, so I have little doubt, the diabolical (haunted, horrible) landscape of Judea must have suggested to the Jewish prophets, their ghastly (diabolical, terrible, terrific) theology."[6]

In *Pierre*, Melville's show of indifference was undermined by a tone of acerbity. So, here, the extended search for just the right word to characterize Jewish theology undermines the assumed detachment of the historical approach. It was also in *Pierre* that Melville had explored the theological extensions of the word "stone" and of familiar phrases about blood from stones and bread from stones. He had even named his own son-of-God hero after a Stone. Naturally, then, he is predisposed to be interested in the stones of Judea. "We read a good deal about stones in Scriptures. Stories of these Monuments & memorials are set up of stones; men are stoned to death; the figurative seed falls in stony places; and no wonder that stones should so largely figure in the Bible. Judea is one accumulation of stones—Stony mountains & stony plains; stony torrents & stony roads; stony vales & stony fields; stony homes & stony tombs; stony eyes & stony hearts."[7]

In the journal, a few pages later, Melville modified the old adage to the effect that too much attention from the gods is ominous: "No country will more quickly dissipate romantic expectations than Palestine—particularly Jerusalem. To some the disappointment is heart sickening. Is the desolation of the land the result of the fatal embrace of the Deity? Hapless are the favorites of Heaven."[8]

There is something heartsickening for the reader in each page of this journal. The tone is truly that of a sick man, and of a man sickened by his own morbidity. But our immediate concern was to show the all-pervasive persistence of his pessimism. One final passage will do. In Cyprus, Melville is prompted to find an analogy between the fictions of Greek and Christian myth: "From these waters rose Venus from the foam. Found it as hard to realize such a thing as to realize on Mt. Olivet that from there Christ rose."[9]

2

SEVERAL years after Melville's return to America, he worked his Holy Land journal and recollections into a sort of "Childe Harold's Pilgrimage" and entitled it *Clarel: A Poem and Pilgrimage in the Holy Land*. As poetry, *Clarel* is of little value; but as an illumination of Melville's morbid preoccupation with sombre theological concepts, it is painfully convincing. Once more, in *Clarel*, he assembles a wide variety of attitudes toward Christian doctrine—attitudes which run the gamut from devout belief to scornful negation. The pervading tone, throughout, is skeptical, even agnostic; but the familiar and self-protecting deceptions are made to operate throughout. For example, while it might seem that *Clarel* concludes with just that affirmation of faith which will appeal to the orthodox Christian reader, a second reading makes it clear that the entire final passage is contrived to be characteristically equivocal and ambiguous, in that each of two possible meanings pivots nicely on a subjunctive verb. For immediate purposes, however, it is sufficient to notice that Melville is willing to permit one character, suggestively and ironically named Celio (heaven-rooted), to unburden himself in a hostile attack on the character of Jesus Christ. Celio's point is that Christ was a kind of double-crossed and double-crossing Confidence-Man, whether Christ knew it or not. In his wanderings about Jerusalem, Celio pauses before the arch named "Ecce Homo":

> With gallery which years deface,
> Its bulk athwart the alley grim,
> The arch named Ecce Homo threw;
> The same, if childlike faith be true,
> From which the Lamb of God was shown
> By Pilate to the wolfish crew.
> And Celio—in frame how prone
> To kindle at that scene recalled—
> Perturbed he stood, and heart-enthralled.
> No raptures which with saints prevail,
> Nor trouble of compunction born
> He felt, as there he seemed to scan
> Aloft in spectral guise, the pale
> Still face, the purple robe, and thorn;
> And inly cried—*Behold the Man!*
> Yon Man it is this burden lays:
> Even He who in the pastoral hours,
> Abroad in fields, and cheered by flowers,
> Announced a heaven's unclouded days;
> And, ah, with such persuasive lips—
> Those lips now sealed while doom delays—
> Won men to look for solace there;
> But, crying out in death's eclipse,
> When rainbow none His eyes might see,
> Enlarged the margin for despair—
> *My God, My God, forsakest Me?*
> Upbraider! we upbraid again;

Thee we upbraid; our pangs constrain
Pathos itself to cruelty.
Ere yet Thy day no pledge was given
Of homes and mansions in the heaven—
Paternal homes reserved for us;
Heart hoped it not, but lived content—
Content with life's own discontent,
Nor deemed that fate ere swerved for us:
The natural law men let prevail;
Then reason disallowed the state
Of instinct's variance with fate.
But Thou—ah, see, in rack how pale
Who did the world with throes convulse;
Behold Him—yea—behold the Man
Who warranted if not began
The dream that drags out its repulse.
   Nor less some cannot break from Thee;
Thy love so locked is with Thy lore,
They may not rend them and go free:
The head rejects; so much the more
The heart embraces—what? the love?
If true what priests avouch of Thee,
The shark Thou mad'st, yet claim'st the dove.[10]

That passage illuminates Melville's own dark brooding over the thought that the Son of God was betrayed by the forsaking malice of God, even as all mankind is constantly betrayed, as Melville seemed to think, by that same malice. To the later Melville, Christ at times seemed to be a Promethean character who had tried to place himself in accord with the implications of the divinity within and outside himself; who had tried to place himself on the side of God, and had been deceived into supposing that he was devoting his life to the revelation of divine truth and light; but had tragically realized, only in Gethsemane and on Golgotha, that he had been wrong; that God had forsaken him. In a limited sense, Melville thus projected his own spiritual biography into his private interpretation of Christ's life: Melville thought of himself as one who had tried to align himself with God's truth, and who had wished to be a mouthpiece for God until, repulsed, he had suffered a tragic and disillusioning perception of that particular wisdom which is woe and madness. Thereafter, Melville himself had been prompted to upbraid God, even as Celio construed Christ's remarks as proof that Christ upbraided God, from the cross.

Over and over again, as we have seen, Melville worked up literary narratives to dramatize his resentment at this forsaking, in his own experience. Captain Ahab crystallizes the concept, when he speaks to the lightning (or more precisely and more emblematically, to the triune corposants) as symbolic of God, and says, "Oh! thou clear spirit of clear fire, whom on these seas I as Persian once did worship, till in the sacramental act so burned by thee, that to this hour I bear the scar; I now know thee, thou clear spirit, and I now know that thy right worship is defiance." Pierre similarly crystallizes it, but more obliquely, when he cries, "For now am I hate-shod!" Celio crystallizes it, once more, in *Clarel*.

3

THREE other poems written by Melville may be described briefly as pertinent dramatic projections of Melville's identical spiritual tension over his thought that he had somehow been betrayed and forsaken by God and man. The first of these is the title poem in *Timoleon*, privately printed during the last year of his life, during the year he completed the writing of *Billy Budd*. Melville knew Plutarch's account of Timoleon's life; he knew Pierre Bayle's account. In each, Timoleon is described as a man who eventually gave full credit to the gods for his various successes. But Melville, in making his own artistic adaptation of Timoleon's experiences, warps Timoleon's response to both the gods and men, until that response becomes a reflection of Melville's viewpoint, not of the traditional Timoleon's viewpoint. After the preliminaries, Melville's poem describes how Timoleon feels guided by the gods, themselves, to strike for truth and justice, even though such action requires him to kill his own evil brother. Melville thus represents Timoleon's motives for this key action:

> In evil visions of the night
> He sees the lictors of the gods,

Giant ministers of righteousness,
Their fasces threatened by the Furies' rods.
    But undeterred he wills to act,
Resolved thereon though Ate rise;
He heeds the voice whose mandate calls,
Or seems to call, peremptory from the skies.

From Melville's viewpoint, naturally, there was exquisite irony
in the phrase, "Or seems to call." Later, after Timoleon finds that
public opinion has turned so completely against him that he is
ostracized for having consecrated his life to Truth and Justice,
Melville describes Timoleon as disillusioned, embittered, even
contemplating suicide. Rallying, Melville's Timoleon upbraids
God, thus:

But flood-tide comes though long the ebb,
Nor patience bides with passion long;
Like sightless orbs his thoughts are rolled
Arraigning heaven as compromised in wrong:
    To second causes why appeal?
Vain parleying here with fellow clods.
To you, Arch Principals, I rear
My quarrel, for this quarrel is with gods.
    Shall just men long to quit your world?
It is aspersion of your reign;
Your marbles in the temple stand—[cf. *Pierre*]
Yourselves as stony and invoked in vain? [italics added.]
    Ah, bear with one quite overborne,
Olympians, if he chide ye now;
Magnanimous be even though he rail
And hard against ye set the bleaching brow.
    If conscience doubt, she'll next recant.
What basis then? O, tell at last,
Are earnest natures staggering here
But fatherless shadows from no substance cast?
    Yea, *are* ye, gods? Then ye, 'tis ye
Should show what touch of tie ye may,
Since ye, too, if not wrung are wronged
By grievous misconceptions of your sway.
                    [cf. *P.L.*, III, 150ff.]

339

> But deign, some little sign be given—
> Low thunder in your tranquil skies;
> Me reassure, nor let me be
> Like a lone dog that for a master cries.

Years later, Timoleon is exonerated, and Corinth tries to recall him, so that he may be hailed as hero and leader:

> And Corinth clapt: Absolved, and more!
> Justice in long arrears is thine:
> Not slayer of thy brother, no,
> But savior of the state, Jove's soldier, man divine.
> Eager for thee thy City waits:
> Return! with bays we dress your door.
> But he, the Isle's loved guest, reposed,
> And never for Corinth left the adopted shore.[11]

Interpreted within Melville's bitter context, Timoleon's final attitude implies, "To Hell with the State I tried to save, and to Hell with Jove." For immediate purposes, the significance of "Timoleon" is that it so perfectly illustrates Melville's artistic tendency to subserve images and symbols and actions to represent his own autobiographical experience, as he viewed it; particularly to represent the repulse he felt he had suffered at the hands of society, and at the hands of God.

Perhaps the word "repulse" is the best word to represent Melville's inner bruise which hurt him so much that he fashioned his own private and anti-Christian myth to protect it. In one sense, at least, Melville's illusion of "repulse" induced him not only to begin but also to continue upbraiding and "arraigning heaven as compromised in wrong." He had begun his literary career by consecrating and dedicating himself to the Miltonic or Spenserian concept of the literary artist as a God-inspired prophet, who would talk with God and then serve high Heaven by revealing God's Truth. The concept had been refreshed in the nineteenth century, and was reflected in Carlyle's *Heroes and Hero-Worship*, in Emerson's essay on "The Poet." Even during the writing of *Mardi*, with all its reflections of psychological confusion, Melville frequently reiterated that ideal of authorship, one excellent example occurring in the already-quoted passage which begins, "Yet not I, but another: God is my Lord; and though many satellites revolve around me, I and all mine revolve round the great central Truth, sun-like, fixed and luminous forever in the foundationless firmament." Subsequently disillusioned by his decision that ultimate Truth must be unknown and unknowable, Melville deeply resented that apparent fact and seemed to feel that he had been snubbed by the silence of God.

4

THE concept of "repulse" is again illuminated in Melville's poem, "After the Pleasure Party," which follows immediately after the title poem in *Timoleon*: the two have a common theme. Much Freudian nonsense has been written concerning "After the Pleasure Party"; but one should notice that the sexual image of courtship-and-repulse is represented as a symbolic action within a series of analogous actions or parallel tropes which subordinate the sexual element to the deeper metaphysical concerns of the entire poem.

The narrative pattern of the poem takes the form of a night-thoughts soliloquy, which begins as the narrator stands amid the sensuous loveliness of a Roman garden lawn, flanked by the starlit Mediterranean, which sends in waves to break against the terrace wall below. As he broods, the poet sees his own story symbolized in the action of those waves, dashing vainly against the wall:

> Tired of the homeless deep,
> Look how their flight yon hurrying billows urge,
> Hitherward but to reap
> Passive repulse from the iron-bound verge!
> Insensate, can they never know
> 'Tis mad to wreck the impulsion so?

Thus, at the very beginning of the poem, the basic image of aspiration and repulsion is established. After making oblique references to his recent physical and sexual repulse, at the hands of a beautiful young lady significantly and symbolically named Urania, the poet contrasts that physical image of aspiration and repulse with the image of his own spiritual and ascetic aspiration

341

for heavenly beauty, wisdom, truth, during his early and consecrated years.

> And kept I long heaven's watch for this,
> Contemning love, for this, even this?
> O terrace chill in Northern air,
> O reaching ranging tube I placed
> Against yon skies, and fable chased
> Till, fool, I hailed for sister there
> Starred Cassiopea in Golden Chair.
> In dream I throned me; nor I saw
> In cell the idiot crowned with straw.
> And yet, ah yet scarce ill I reigned,
> Through self-illusion, self-sustained,
> When now—enlightened, undeceived—
> What gain I barrenly bereaved!
> Than this can be yet lower decline—
> Envy and spleen, can these be mine?

One might profitably compare that quest image with the symbolic quest image represented in the final tableau of Taji's soul-
pilgrimage, in *Mardi*. I suggest that the "W" shape of the constellation, Cassiopea's Chair, may have been a private symbol of
"Wisdom" (Heavenly Wisdom) in Melville's thought, even as
the subsequent developments in this poem would indicate. In the
Platonic sense, this value would also interlock with the ancient
myth, because Cassiopea, the Ethiopian Queen, was immortalized
among the stars as a constellation because of her beauty. Adapting
the Spenserian version of moral allegory to his uses, as we have
seen, Melville permitted the questing Taji to worship Yillah's
"heavenly" beauty as a symbol of absolute Truth, which is one
with absolute Wisdom, according to the celebrated passage in
Plato's *Symposium*.

So far, then, the wave image of repulse and the Cassiopea image
of repulse and the Urania image of repulse may be viewed as
symbolic actions which are analogous. The next progression, in
the poem, takes us to the pleasure party, which paved the way
for Urania's repulse. Again the spiritual repulse is further corre-

lated with the physical repulse, and with the consequent disillusionment:

> Ye stars that long your votary knew
> Rapt in her vigil, see me here!
> Whither is gone the spell ye threw
> When rose before me Cassiopea?
> Usurped on by love's stronger reign—
> But lo, your very selves do wane:
> Light breaks—truth breaks! Silvered no more,
> But chilled by dawn that brings the gale,
> Shivers yon bramble above the vale,
> And disillusion opens all the shore.

I wish to digress, briefly, to suggest a possible correlation between the autobiographical symbolism of the Cassiopea trope and
of the Urania trope. Melville's early consecration and dedication
to the high calling of authorship seems to have been inspired, as
I have said, by Milton and Spenser. It will be remembered that
Spenser dedicated his "Hymne of Heavenly Beautie" to Sapience,
or Wisdom, as "The soveraine dearling of the Deity," which suggests the Neo-Platonic characterization of Urania. Milton, in
making his invocation to Urania, at the beginning of *Paradise
Lost*, endows her with the double character of a tenth heavenly
Muse and of the "Spirit of God." At the beginning of Book Seven,
in *Paradise Lost*, Milton further describes heavenly Urania as the
sister of Wisdom, and this passage from Milton may stimulate our
understanding of Melville's symbolic imagery:

> Descend from Heav'n *Urania*, by that name
> If rightly thou art call'd, whose Voice divine
> Following, above th' *Olympian* Hill I soar,
> Above the flight of *Pegasean* wing.
> The meaning, not the Name I call: for thou
> Nor of the Muses nine, nor on the top
> Of old *Olympus* dwell'st, but Heav'nly born,
> Before the Hills appear'd, or Fountain flow'd,
> Thou with Eternal Wisdom didst converse,
> Wisdom thy Sister, and with her didst play
> In presence of th' Almighty Father, pleas'd
> With the Celestial Song. Up led by thee

Into the Heav'n of Heav'ns I have presumed,
An Earthly Guest, and drawn Empyreal Air,
Thy temp'ring; with like safety guided down
Return me to my Native Element:
Lest from this flying Steed unrein'd (as once
Bellerophon, though from a lower Clime)
Dismounted, on th' Aleian Field I fall
Erroneous there to wander and forlorn.
Half yet remains unsung, but narrower bound
Within the visible Diurnal Sphere;
Standing on Earth, not rapt above the Pole,
More safe I Sing with mortal voice, unchang'd
To hoarse or mute, though fall'n on evil days,
On evil days though fall'n, and evil tongues;
In darkness, and with dangers compast round,
And solitude; yet not alone, while thou
Visit'st my slumbers Nightly, or when Morn
Purples the East: still govern thou my Song,
Urania, and fit audience find, though few.
But drive far off the barbarous dissonance
Of *Bacchus* and his Revellers, the Race
Of that wild Rout that tore the Thracian Bard
In Rhodope, where Woods and Rocks had Ears
To rapture, till the savage clamor drown'd
Both Harp and Voice; nor could the Muse defend
Her Son. So fail not thou, who thee implores:
For thou art Heav'nly, shee an empty dream.

One difference between the courtships of Urania made by
Milton and Melville is that "After the Pleasure Party" contains
Melville's woeful plaint that he had "fallen on evil days" because
he had been repulsed not only by a physical Urania but also by
a metaphysical Urania.

Melville continues his poem in such a way as to add further
metaphysical extensions to the dualistic woe from which he suffers.
Continuing his night-thoughts, he recalls how he subsequently
and secretly watched his fleshly Urania as she stood in the Villa
Albani, where she had come, ostensibly to view the statuary, but
actually (the poet decides) to offer a prayer to none other than

Minerva, the goddess of Wisdom, before whose statue the young lady Urania lingers. The poet imaginatively construes this prayer to be an appeal to the goddess of Wisdom, for aid against the

> . . . strife
> Of that which makes the sexual feud
> And clogs the aspirant life.

The antithesis between the physical aspiration and the spiritual aspiration, thus reiterated, provides us with another analogy. Bitterly musing, now, on the duality which torments Urania, even as it continues to torment him, the poet predicts that Urania will also be repulsed by Minerva, goddess of Wisdom; that her prayer will not be answered, because the so-called God of Love will arrange to double-cross and betray Urania, even though such betrayal require the God to betray himself.

Now we move nearer to an understanding of the central thematic concern of the poem: the assumption of the poet is that the "Prime Mover" of trouble, for himself and Urania, is the ancient God of Love, Cupid; here referred to as Amor. When the name "Amor" is thus used, it has appropriately ambiguous and equivocal extensions, particularly in the larger context of Melville's private myth. The classical referent is obvious; the Christian referent is God: the New Testament concept, so scornfully rejected by Melville, insists that God is Love. The motto of the poem has already set the direction of the theme, because Amor has warned, in the motto, "Fear me, virgin . . . fear me, slighted." The poet, having shown that he himself first slighted Love, by courting Wisdom, and having predicted that the God of Love will also betray the pure aspirations of all (including Urania) ends his soliloquy with the observation that all other ignorant-innocent souls should beware of his (and her) lot, which he knows they will not. This final warning carries the memory of the reader back to earlier passages in the poem; not merely to the motto but also to an early question as to the "Original" cause of the physical and metaphysical repulse:

> What Comic jest or Anarch blunder
> The human integral clove asunder
> And shied the fractions through life's gate?

That question, drawing on the familiar imagery of the Platonic myth, is entirely rhetorical in the larger Melvillian context: the irreconcilable conflict between the dual aspects of human nature (here, the physical and the spiritual) is merely a reflection of the duality in the attributes of good-evil God, that Comic Jester. By sinister extension, then, "After the Pleasure Party" represents another of Melville's highly complex arrangements of tropes and emblems into structural parallels, symbolic actions, analogous actions, to illuminate anew that dark Melvillian notion that the ultimate blame for man's disillusioning frustrations (physical and spiritual) may be traced back to the repulsive malice of that so-called God of love. Remember again that this poem was printed during the last year of his life.

5

OBLIQUELY related to "Timoleon" and "After the Pleasure Party" is Melville's short poem "Camoens," containing a pair of fragmentary soliloquies imaginatively placed in the mouth of the Portuguese epic poet, Luis de Camoens. In the first part of "Camoens," the tone and mood and thought represent Camoens' youthfully naïve, idealistic, frantic aspiration to create artistic utterance worthy of his God-given potentialities; in the second part, the tone and mood and thought represent Camoens' disillusioned and embittered retrospect. This is the first part, entire:

> Restless, restless, craving rest,
> Forever must I fan this fire
> Forever in flame on flame aspire?
> Yea, for the God demands thy best.
> The world with endless beauty teems,
> And thought evokes new worlds of dreams:
> Then hunt the flying herds of themes.
> And fan, yet fan thy fervid fire
> Until the crucibled ore shall show
> That fire can purge, as well as glow.
> In ordered ardor nobly strong,
> Flame to the height of ancient song.

The value of this first part lies not so much in itself as in its service as an antithetical foil for the second part; the subtitle of the first being "Before" and the subtitle of the second being "After." Before and after what? Although the poetic extensions are many, it is clear that Melville desires to contrast the discrepancy between a viewpoint of idealistic, theoretical intention and a viewpoint of actual, disappointed, disillusioned accomplishment. Our immediate interest in the poem depends on the apparant manner in which Melville found and dramatized, this time, a sense of identity between what happened to Camoens as a neglected, misunderstood literary artist and what happened to Melville as a neglected, misunderstood literary artist.

Melville was familiar with both the life and works of Camoens. In *Billy Budd*, he makes a significant analogy based on a celebrated passage in Camoens' epic poem, *The Lusiad*. In *White-Jacket*, the "ever-noble Jack Chase" is described as well read; "but, above all things, was an ardent admirer of Camoens." At three different times, Jack Chase directly quotes from William Julius Mickle's translation of *The Lusiad*, and these direct quotations make it quite apparent that Melville had access to Mickle's translation while writing *White-Jacket*.

Mickle's spirited attack on Voltaire's unsympathetic criticism of certain allegorical machinery employed by Camoens in *The Lusiad* must have appealed to Melville. With considerable care, Mickle pointed out that Voltaire had failed to understand Camoens' epic machinery because Voltaire had not recognized the underlying allegorical meaning. The critical warfare over the artistry of Camoens had begun long before Voltaire, and it continued down to Melville's time. In fact, a criticism of *The Lusiad* occurs in one of the volumes in the *Neversink* library: "Blair's Lectures, University Edition—a fine treatise on rhetoric," as White-Jacket describes it. Following Voltaire's remarks much too closely, Blair deprecates Camoens, thus:

"The machinery of the *Lusiad* is perfectly extravagant; not only is it formed of a singular mixture of Christian ideas, and Pagan mythology; but it is so conducted, that the Pagan gods appear to be the true deities, and Christ and the Blessed Virgin, to be subordinate agents. . . . Towards the end of the work, indeed, the author gives us an awkward salvo for his whole mythology; making the goddess Thetis inform Vasco, that she, and the rest of the heathen deities, are no more than names to describe the operations of Providence."

It would seem, then, that Melville felt he and Camoens had more than a little in common. Is it possible that the frequent references to Camoens, in *White-Jacket*, constitute repeated hints that the reader who is familiar with the allegorical devices in *The Lusiad*, particularly with the use of certain "names to describe the operations of Providence," might recognize as significant the manner in which Melville, at the end of *White-Jacket*, also gives us a salvo which has pertinent bearing on Melville's own sinister allegorical insinuations throughout *White-Jacket*? Regardless of that possibility, it is certain that Melville could easily have seized on certain facts in Mickle's report of Camoens' life to corroborate frequent hints, in *The Lusiad*, that the outrageously persistent misfortunes and hardships and sufferings in Camoens' experience had undermined his faith in those religious beliefs to which he paid conventional lip-service. A pertinent example, in Mickle's translation, would be the extended pessimistic speech (too long to quote here) of "a reverend figure" at the end of Book Four. Two other passages, conveniently brief, are given here from Book Ten of Mickle's translation, to indicate the nature of Camoens' bitter pessimism. In the apostrophe to the muse Calliope, at the beginning of Book Ten, Camoens explains his desperate need for inspiration:

> No more the summer of my life remains,
> My autumn's lengthening evenings chill my veins;
> Down the bleak stream of years by woes on woes
> Wing'd on, I hasten to the tomb's repose,
> The port whose deep dark bottom shall detain
> My anchor never to be weigh'd again,
> Never on other sea of life to steer
> The human course—Yet thou, O goddess, hear,
> Yet let me live, though round my silver'd head
> Misfortune's bitterest rage unpitying shed
> Her coldest storms; yet let me live to crown
> The song that boasts my nation's proud renown.

No matter how differently those references to death may be interpreted, they certainly are not exactly buoyant with the Christian hope of resurrection! Even if Melville did not find in *The Lusiad* clear or covert hints that Camoens had lost his faith in God, he most certainly did find evidence that Camoens had lost his faith in man as an appreciator of his poetry. In the epilogue is this brief bit of evidence:

> Enough, my muse, thy wearied wing no more
> Must to the seat of Jove triumphant soar.
> Chill'd by my nation's cold neglect, thy fires
> Glow bold no more, and all thy rage expires.

With these impressions of Camoens in mind, we are in a better position to appreciate the second part of Melville's poem on Camoens, in which Camoens is apparently imagined as soliloquizing, in words which Melville himself might have used for pertinent soliloquizing:

> What now avails the pageant verse,
> Trophies and arms with music borne?
> Base is the world; and some rehearse
> How noblest meet ignoble scorn.
> Vain now the ardor, vain thy fire,
> Delirium mere, unsound desire:
> Fate's knife hath ripped the chorded lyre.
> *Exhausted by the exacting lay,*
> *Thou dost but fall a surer prey*
> *To wile and guile ill understood;* [italics added]
> While they who work them fair in face,
> Still keep their strength in prudent place,
> And *claim* they worthier run life's race, [italics added]
> Serving high God with useful good.

Considered generally, the two parts of Melville's poem "Camoens" dramatize and illuminate a contrast between the Promethean ardor of the youthful artist and the Solomonic pessimism of the aged artist. In this second part, however, there is a subordinate antithesis: the contrast between the artistic employment of symbolic indirections and of self-protective deceptions ("wile and guile ill understood") and the inartistic employment of pious means, prudently prosaic means, to achieve "useful good." The sarcasm in the last line should be obvious.

6

ONLY one other factor need be treated here, as a further preliminary to our consideration of Melville's mental and spiritual attitude, before and during the period when he wrote *Billy Budd*. Throughout the last years of his life, Melville was enough interested in the writings of Arthur Schopenhauer to purchase, at different times, a total of seven Schopenhauer volumes. Furthermore, he read these volumes with enough care to leave many pencilled marks and annotations in the margins. Fortunately, these marked copies have been preserved, and can be examined; but even if they had not survived, those familiar with Melville's somber thoughts could easily recognize the aspects of Schopenhauer's thinking which would have appealed to Melville. Some of these aspects may be summarized, briefly.

In his youth, Schopenhauer could not reconcile the existence of human pain and suffering and death with any theory which affirmed a just and benevolent God. He insisted that the very existence of evil, in the universe, was proof that *all* existence was necessarily evil. To Schopenhauer, the Christian attitude toward evil was so false that it led him to condemn all Christian doctrine. Furthermore, he ridiculed any religious and philosophic dogmas which viewed God as everlastingly benevolent and rational and moral; he insisted that God was a thoroughly disreputable character. To him, those dogmas which asserted the benevolence of God were merely human expressions of wishful thinking, reflecting the human craving to prolong existence through consoling dreams of an after-life. He reiterated that such dogmas were self-deceptions; that a true understanding of the forces at work in the universe showed the entire world-process to be one of endless malice, murder, suicide. If one wished to talk about freedom of the will, he said, one was forced to realize that all actions were selfish, and motivated entirely by the will to survive at any cost. This makes the world of human beings a hopeless mess, and totally depraved, according to Schopenhauer.

No wonder that Melville's late discovery of Schopenhauer

should have led him to buy and read the separate volumes of essays, as fast as they were translated into English. In reading Schopenhauer, Melville took particular pains to mark such passages as showed some similarity of belief with his own, in matters of theology, and one particularly pertinent passage which Melville marked in Schopenhauer's *Studies in Pessimism* is the following:

"There is nothing more certain than the general truth that it is the grievous *sin of the world* which has produced the grievous *suffering of the world*. I am not referring here to the physical connection between these two things lying in the realm of experience; my meaning is metaphysical. Accordingly, the sole thing that reconciles me to the Old Testament is the story of the Fall. In my eyes, it is the only metaphysical truth in that book, even though it appears in the form of an allegory. There seems to me no better explanation of our existence than that it is the result of some false step, some sin of which we are paying the penalty."[12]

Schopenhauer very carefully insists, there, that he is not referring to the physical connection between the sin of the world and the suffering of the world "lying in the realm of experience"; that his meaning is "metaphysical." The lynx-eyed Melville marked the passage, and one may imagine that his construction of it made it identical with his own belief that the world was put together wrong, and that the Original Sinner is God Almighty, for whose metaphysical and everlasting sins we are forced to pay the penalty. Melville also marked the following passage in the editor-translator's "Introduction" to Schopenhauer's *The Wisdom of Life*:

"In his [Schopenhauer's] opinion the foremost truth which Christianity proclaimed to the world lay in its recognition of pessimism, its view that the world was essentially corrupt, and that the devil was its prince or ruler."[13]

Melville could find such a viewpoint most congenial to his own. There is no need to quote further from Melville's marked passages. Nevertheless, to have such proof that Melville was reading widely, and over a period of months and years, in Schopenhauer, during the exact years and months when Melville was writing and revising *Billy Budd*, should be of more than passing interest to anyone who honestly wishes to understand Melville's meaning in *Billy Budd*.

DIVINE DEPRAVITY

CHAPTER XI

For should Man finally be lost, should Man
Thy creature late so lov'd, thy youngest Son
Fall circumvented thus by fraud? . . .
So should thy goodness and thy greatness both
Be question'd and blasphem'd without defence.

MILTON, *Paradise Lost*

The book of Genesis, taken according to the letter, gives the most absurd and the most extravagant ideas of the Divinity. Whoever shall find out the sense of it, ought to restrain himself from divulging it.

It may happen that some one, with the aid he may borrow from others, may hit upon the meaning of it. In that case he ought to impose silence upon himself; or if he speak of it, he ought to speak obscurely, and in an enigmatical manner, as I do myself, leaving the rest to be found out by those who can understand me.

MOSES MAIMONIDES (1135-1204)

An uncommon prudence is habitual with the subtler depravity, for it has everything to hide.

MELVILLE, *Billy Budd*

DIVINE DEPRAVITY

In his patient writing and rewriting of *Billy Budd*, Melville finally achieved that quality of artistic detachment which he had sought to achieve in each of his narratives, starting with *Mardi*. This time, with seeming effortlessness, he handles a complex artistic formula which combines, ingeniously, sustained irony and sustained (but inverted) allegory. The artistic effect amounts to a new variation of the Melvillian triple-talk, because it makes discrete appeals to three distinct viewpoints.

An unsophisticated and superficial skimmer of pages might be willing to settle for the mere story concerning the impressment of a sailor and the subsequent hanging of that sailor because he strikes and kills a superior.

A second viewpoint, represented by any reader who is biased by his Christian heritage (whether he acknowledges it or not) is slyly encouraged by Melville to take the story as a sort of morality play which dramatizes the tragic conflict between good and evil in human experience.

A third viewpoint, represented by any reader who can transcend the bias of his own prejudices, is slyly encouraged by Melville to

355

view the story as a bitter comedy, in the satiric and sarcastic tradition of Lucian and Voltaire and Tom Paine.

Naturally, the first and second categories of reader are inclined to be shocked at the mere suggestion that either the action or the narrative manner in *Billy Budd* could possibly be described as amusing or comic, in any sense: they see nothing there to laugh at. If such readers understand the traditional principles of satiric literary art, they should have no difficulty in overcoming their bias enough to recognize that the misanthropic Melville does indeed ask the reader to laugh with him, derisively, even to the bitter end of *Billy Budd*.

Part of Melville's deception, in *Billy Budd*, rests on his assurance that most readers forget one point: the comic or non-comic values of a situation (in literature or in life) depend entirely on the scale of values implicit in a spectator's viewpoint. Take a crude example. A six-year-old boy and his mother, walking cautiously along a slippery sidewalk, just behind a stout lady, see the stout lady slip and fall on her back, heavily. The boy screams with laughter, his mother screams with fright: two diametrically opposed reactions to the identical situation.

Melville's misanthropic viewpoint, at the time he wrote *Billy Budd*, was similar to that of Schopenhauer, who insisted that the world was put together wrong, that God was a scoundrel, that human beings were motivated entirely by selfish and depraved desires to prolong their own existence at any cost. Priding himself on being an "enlightened" and "thinking" man, Melville began *Billy Budd* with several obvious hints. First of all, the initial sentence is this: "The year 1797, the year of this narrative, belongs to a period which, as every *thinker* [italics added] now feels, involved a crisis for Christendom." The ambiguity there suggested is simply this: most readers wish Christendom well; Melville wished it ill. Secondly, Melville specifically mentions Tom Paine and Voltaire. Thirdly, he provides an obvious hint as to his allegorical direction by bracketing the story with three names of ships involved in the action: *The Rights of Man*, His Majesty's Ship *Indomitable*, the *Atheiste*.

Consider the value of remembering the writings of Tom Paine, here. In *The Age of Reason*, Paine had foreshadowed Melville's viewpoint, thus: "But there are times when men have serious thoughts, and it is at such times, when they begin to think, that they begin to doubt the truth of the Christian religion; and well they may, for it is too fanciful and too full of conjecture, inconsistency, improbability, and irrationality, to afford consolation to a thoughtful man. His reason revolts against his creed."[1] Paine's hatred of authoritarianism and tyranny of all kinds, as expressed in *Common Sense*, interlocks social tyranny with metaphysical tyranny by using the Genesis story as a trope: "Government, like dress, is the badge of lost innocence; the palaces of kings are built on the ruins of the bowers of paradise. For were the impulses of conscience clear, uniform, and irresistibly obeyed, man would need no other lawgiver . . ."[2] The flavor of Rousseau is there, and as far back as the days when Melville wrote *The Confidence-Man*, he had been reacting with mixed feelings against the teachings of Rousseau. Similarly, he reacted with mixed feelings against his hero in *Billy Budd*, and some hint as to Melville's attitude may be foreshadowed by the following passage in Paine's *Rights of Man*:

"When I contemplate the natural dignity of man; when I feel . . . for the honour and happiness of its character, I become irritated at the attempt to govern mankind by force and fraud, as if they were all knaves and fools, and can scarcely avoid disgust at those who are thus imposed upon."[3]

The disgust, there, aimed against the stupidity of human beings who permit themselves to be pushed around, and who are old enough to know better, is very closely related to Melville's mixed feelings toward his hero, Billy Budd. Billy is of age, twenty-one years old; but he is simultaneously a man and a child, stupidly ignorant, and thus easily imposed on. Voltaire had chosen much the same kind of budlike child-man to serve as the hero named Candide. A bitter critic of the tyranny of orthodox Christianity and also of social and political tyrannies, Voltaire would have made strong appeal to Melville. The optimistic silliness which he ridiculed in Leibnitz was correlated with the optimistic silliness, as Voltaire saw it, of certain Christian teachings that all is for the best in this best of all possible worlds. Equally appealing to Melville would have been Voltaire's satirical attacks on those who believe in the Bible as the word of God. Both Voltaire (in *Candide*) and Melville (in *Billy Budd*) create a naïve and stupidly candid hero who "had never been taught to judge anything for himself," and whose responses to the evils of human experience were therefore viewable as amusing, ridiculous, pathetic; but never tragic. Billy was never designed to play the part of a tragic hero, and for that reason it is a mistake to accuse Melville of having failed to make Billy a tragic hero.

As further orientation, consider the significance of Melville's having dedicated *Billy Budd* to Jack Chase, a former shipmate with Melville aboard the frigate *United States*. Melville's firsthand experience as an enlisted man and as an ordinary seaman, during more than a year of unpleasant service in the Navy, evoked in him a loathing for the brutalities and tyrannies of the officers; a loathing which found vent in the vituperative pages of *White-Jacket*, where Jack Chase is the hero. The striking parallels between Melville's fictional characterization of Jack Chase and Billy Budd are not nearly so important as their striking differences. Billy submissively leaves *The Rights of Man* and submissively adapts himself to life aboard His Majesty's Ship *Indomitable*; by contrast, Jack Chase is described as "a stickler for the Rights of Man and the liberties of the world." Billy is easily victimized by the officers; by contrast, Jack Chase shared Melville's loathing for the pretentiousness and the imbecilities of the officers. Billy is so ignorant and innocent as to misunderstand sarcasm; by contrast, Jack Chase delights to use it and to hear it used.

An excellent preparation for reading *Billy Budd* may be derived from a rereading of *White-Jacket*, particularly because the essential situation in *Billy Budd* is borrowed and adapted by Melville from that situation, already described, which actually occurred in the United States Navy, and was still the scandal of the Navy when Melville was an enlisted man: Captain Mackenzie of the brig *Somers* found all the justification he needed for peremptorily hanging three men, at sea, because he suspected them of having planned mutiny; but while Captain Mackenzie was certain that his own actions were just and right, many others were equally certain that his actions were unjust and wrong. In *White-Jacket*, as we have seen, Melville refers twice to the *Somers* incident and characterizes Captain Mackenzie as a murderer.

Just how persistently the public maintained an interest in the scandalous *Somers* incident, one may gather from this: some forty-six years after the incident, the *American Magazine* published an article entitled, "The Mutiny on the *Somers*," and that article elicited a retort in another magazine; a retort in which the word "Mutiny" was replaced by the word "Murder." Many readers had found the first article offensive because it defended Captain Mackenzie and glorified him as the hero of the *Somers* incident, while it characterized the three hanged men as villainous. (The "official" report of Billy's death also characterized Billy as villainous.) Melville would naturally have paid particular attention to the fact that the writer who thus defended Captain Mackenzie was a naval officer, apparently presuming to be thus well qualified to tell an "inside story," written with all that behind-the-scenes knowledge which is available only to a naval officer. The irony of such pretentiousness might have struck the spark which fired Melville's tinder-dry reactions and prompted him to write his own "inside story" from the viewpoint, ironically, of a naval officer, or at least of a naval historian.

Before we start to examine the way in which Melville unfolds and develops the story in *Billy Budd*, I shall describe certain informing principles which operate throughout the story; particularly the control which Melville achieved, once again, through the sustained irony of interplay between the action itself and the narrative manner of presenting that action. I shall also describe the control achieved through the establishment of allegorical values.

2

SOMEWHAT arbitrarily, we may separate the dramatic action in *Billy Budd* from the narrative manner in which that action is presented. For example, the dramatic version of *Billy Budd*, made by Messrs. Louis O. Coxe and Robert Chapman, is an adaptation of only the dramatic action. The narrative manner which Melville employed is superfluous to such an adaptation and of necessity must be discarded. Nevertheless, the danger of such adaptation and discard is this: Melville used the narrative manner as a device for controlling and illuminating his intended interpretation of the action. There is no harm in dramatizing that central action; but there is harm in concluding that such a dramatization gives any hint as to Melville's interpretation of that action.

Melville's narrative method, in *Billy Budd,* involves the technical principle of sustained irony because Melville cunningly and
slyly creates the artistic illusion that the narrator sympathizes,
throughout, with the authoritarian viewpoint of Captain Vere,
and praises Vere's actions, even though these actions are at several
points palpably unpraiseworthy. This technical device might be
described in another way: Melville gives the illusion of creating
a narrator who is, in a sense, a character whom we as readers get
to know because his remarks are self-revealing. Like the narrator
in *The Confidence-Man,* this contrived narrator speaks from an
essentially Christian viewpoint; but Melville arranges to let us see
that the narrator is, at the same time, just a wee bit stupid. These
two different ways of describing Melville's focus of narration
come to the same end; but for convenience in description and
analysis I shall represent the narrator as an artistically contrived
character.

The allegorical values begin to accumulate as soon as Melville
permits his narrator to describe the three main characters. We are
told that Billy is an innocent, who has much in common with
Adam; that Claggart is a sinister character, who has much in common with Satan; that Vere, captain of the man-of-war, is omnipotent and God-like (as "agent" and as "principal"). This triangulation, which is developed in the preliminary chapters before the
main action occurs, suggests the possibility that the subsequent
action may be analogous, in some way, to that action in the
Garden of Eden; suggests that we may be offered an allegorical
narrative "of man's first disobedience, and the fruit of that forbidden tree whose mortal taste brought death into the world, and
all our woe, with loss of Eden." By this time, we are aware that
Melville knew Milton's *Paradise Lost* very well; but that he had
long anticipated Schopenhauer's dark thought that mankind was
indeed paying the penalty for some sin, and that there was profound metaphysical truth in the Genesis story of the fall, if one
noticed that the evidence itself pointed to God as the Original
Sinner. As we have seen, this sinister interpretation was not new
with either Melville or Schopenhauer, and it had been variously
used. While the Ophites played it straight, in the second century,
Pierre Bayle and many other anti-Calvinists played it crooked in
order to make badgering accusations against the Calvinists for

having formulated a theology which, so their enemies claimed, made God the author of sin. Although Bayle's game was obviously to make the Calvinistic dogma look ridiculous, Melville's early and deeply-rooted Calvinistic belief caused him to view that dogma as ridiculously true, tragically true. Again, in *Billy Budd*, he returns to the problem he had in mind when he said of Hawthorne that his power "derives its force from its appeal to that Calvinistic sense of Innate Depravity and Original Sin, from whose visitations, *in some shape or other* [italics added], no deeply thinking mind is always and wholly free." While Melville was always cautious, Shelley was far more blunt: "God made man such as he is, and then damned him for being so."

These various interpretations of the Genesis story should be kept in mind, as we follow the manner in which Melville creates his own allegorical interpretation of the fall of man, in *Billy Budd*.

3

THE specific narrative begins when impressment brings Billy from the *Rights-of-Man* to H.M.S. *Indomitable*. Although there is no reason to assume that Melville's previous hatred of impressment had abated, we should notice that he now ironically manipulates his officer-praising narrator in such a way as to let him speak quite blandly of that particular impressment as something of a necessity:

"It was not very long prior to the time of the narration that follows that he had entered the King's Service, having been impressed on the Narrow Seas from a homeward-bound English merchantman into a seventy-four outward-bound, H.M.S. *Indomitable*; which ship, as was not unusual in those hurried days had been obliged to put to sea short of her proper complement of men."

The little action which snatches Billy from the *Rights-of-Man* is emblematically suggestive in itself. Even the name of the boarding-officer seems uncomplimentary: Ratcliffe. Another metaphysical and theological insinuation occurs when Ratcliffe decides to take only one sailor, Billy: "And him only he elected." Only after Melville begins to accumulate an overwhelming number of terms familiar in Calvinistic theology does such a reference to "election" find an adequate context. Allegorically and theologically considered, however, this impressment (which ignores and insults the free will of Billy) is made in accordance with a predestinating order from the omnipotent Captain Vere, who is backed by the higher law. Furthermore, Melville's narrator is permitted to digress, this early, to endow the name of Billy's previous ship with rationalistic, deistic, anti-Christian overtones:

"The hard-headed Dundee owner was a staunch admirer of Thomas Paine whose book in rejoinder to Burke's arraignment of the French Revolution had then been published for some time and had gone everywhere. In christening his vessel after the title of Paine's volume the man of Dundee was something like his contemporary shipowner, Stephen Girard of Philadelphia, whose sympathies, alike with his native land and its liberal philosophers, he evinced by naming his ships after Voltaire, Diderot, and so forth."

These are merely prefatory and directional hints. Now consider another kind of hint, which occurs in connection with Billy's impressment:

". . . Then making a salutation as to the ship herself, 'And good-bye to you too, old Rights-of-Man!'

" 'Down, Sir!' roared the lieutenant, instantly assuming all the rigor of his rank, though with difficulty repressing a smile.

"To be sure, Billy's action was a terrible breach of naval decorum. But in that decorum he had never been instructed; in consideration of which the lieutenant would hardly have been so energetic in reproof but for the concluding farewell to the ship."

The narrator is there made to characterize himself, in his choice of words and his tone of comment on that incident. Notice that he speaks from the viewpoint of the "brass"; that he pictures Ratcliffe as a nice fellow, beneath his gruff exterior; that he speaks condescendingly of Billy because Billy had not yet learned "naval decorum" and so could be forgiven for this "terrible breach." Melville further manipulates his narrator to provide another hint as to the technical device of irony and satire which operates throughout the narration; a sly insinuation (not intended by the manipulated narrator, of course):

". . . for Billy, though happily endowed with the gaiety of high health, youth, and a free heart, was yet by no means of a satirical turn. The will to it and the sinister dexterity were alike wanting. To deal in double meaning and insinuations of any sort was quite foreign to his nature."

Foreign indeed to Billy's nature, but certainly not foreign to the consciousness of Melville. Notice the accumulation of terms in those last two sentences: "satirical turn," "sinister dexterity," "double meanings," "insinuations." The contrived narrator is a letter-of-the-law kind of person, himself; he is prosaic in his remarks; he himself will not even notice that Melville frequently gives us the illusion of putting into that narrator's mouth certain remarks which mean only one thing to the narrator and at least two things to the careful reader.

4

IN Chapter Two, Melville begins to make allusions which establish more symbolic values, which will later be interlocked to provide an underlying allegorical meaning for the entire action. The innocence of Billy, we are now told, is like the innocence of Adam. The word "innocence" picks up a motif value, as the story develops, and an ambiguous value, if viewed first from a Christian viewpoint and then from an anti-Christian viewpoint:

". . . the Handsome Sailor Billy Budd's position aboard the seventy-four was something analogous to that of a rustic beauty transplanted from the provinces and brought into competition with the high-born dames of the court. But this change of circumstances he scarce noted. As little did he observe that something about him provoked an ambiguous smile in one or two harder faces among the blue-jackets. Nor less unaware was he of the peculiar favourable effect his person and demeanour had upon the more intelligent gentlemen of the quarter-deck."

There is a good illustration of insinuative triple-talk on Melville's part. Billy himself represents the response which might be made by one category of reader: he perceives very little and does not even understand what he observes. The situation is differently evaluated by a second category of observer: the "harder faces" among the sailors wear an "ambiguous smile" when they look at Handsome Billy because they see something simultaneously pathetic and funny in impressing such an innocent into such an evil

363

atmosphere. Thirdly, the situation is differently evaluated by the officers, who like Billy because he promises to be amenable. Now consider what happens if we imagine how the "harder faces" of the enlisted men evaluate the reactions of the officers to Billy: these enlisted men view the officers as liking Billy because the officers can play Billy for a sucker, so to speak. Melville's viewpoint, as represented in the larger context of the narrative, is represented by the "harder faces" of the enlisted men; but notice that Melville's contrived narrator would seem to be siding with the officers, whom he politely refers to as "the more intelligent gentlemen." More intelligent than whom? The referent is indefinite and so the effect is in accord with Melville's fondness for ambiguity.

Now consider an entirely different kind of tri-valence, with allegorical overtones. According to the Adam-Satan-God frame of reference, Billy is allegorically the child of God; God is the "Heavenly Father." Melville insinuatively probes back toward the beginning of beginnings, thus:

"Asked by the officer, a small brisk little gentleman, as it chanced, among other questions, his place of birth, he replied,

" 'Please, Sir, I don't know.'

" 'Don't know where you were born? Who was your father?'

" 'God knows, Sir.'

"Struck by the straightforward simplicity of these replies, the officer next asked, 'Do you know anything about your beginning?'

". . . Yes, Billy Budd was a foundling, a presumable by-blow, and, evidently, no ignoble one. Noble descent was as evident in him as in a blood horse."

From Melville's anti-authoritarian and anti-Christian viewpoint, this is apparently a wry sort of fun, and more allegorical hints are added in Chapter Two:

"For the rest, with little or no sharpness of faculty or any trace of the *wisdom of the serpent, nor yet quite a dove* [italics added; cf. Rev. Falsgrave in *Pierre*; cf. Christ's own ambiguous words in Matthew 10:16], he possessed that kind and degree of intelligence going along with the unconventional rectitude of a sound human creature, one to whom not yet had been proffered the questionable apple of knowledge. . . . By his original constitution aided by the co-operating influences of his lot, Billy in many

364

respects was little more than a sort of upright barbarian, much such perhaps as Adam presumably might have been ere the urbane Serpent wriggled himself into his company."

Melville's repetitious references to Adam and to the "questionable apple of knowledge" are interwoven with reminders of certain Rousseau concepts concerning the "noble savage" as innocent; the civilized "urbane" city-dwelling individual as evil. But the fun improves when Melville permits his stupid narrator to digress, after having stumbled (so to speak) on his Adam analogy. He uses it as an excuse for making a few Christian generalizations (somewhat confused, it may be noticed) on "the doctrine of man's fall." Melville again correlates these generalizations with Rousseau, again for purposes of ridiculing Christian concepts.

"And here be it submitted that apparently going to corroborate the doctrine of man's fall (a doctrine now popularly ignored), it is observable that where certain virtues pristine and unadulterate peculiarly characterize anybody in the external uniform of civilisation, they will upon scrutiny seem not to be derived from custom or convention but rather to be out of keeping with these, as if indeed exceptionally transmitted from a period prior to Cain's city and citified man. The character marked by such qualities has to an unvitiated taste an untampered-with flavour like that of berries, while the man thoroughly civilised, even in a fair specimen of the breed, has to the same moral palate a questionable smack as of a compounded wine. To any stray inheritor of these primitive qualities found, like Casper Hauser, wandering dazed in any Christian capital of our time, the poet's famous invocation, near two thousand years ago, of the good rustic out of his latitude in the Rome of the Caesars, still appropriately holds:—

> 'Faithful in word and thought,
> What hast Thee, Fabian, to the city brought.' "

Once again, the reader is encouraged to try that passage from a Christian viewpoint and then from an anti-Christian viewpoint; but the Christian viewpoint, immediately suggested at the very start, will not be very comfortable, here, because Melville has permitted his narrator to reveal his stupidity in a form of chop logic which is good for Melville's sinister purposes of burlesque and ridicule. If the narrator does submit, here, something which does corroborate the doctrine of man's fall, then that something should demonstrate (according to the dogma) that even the purest human beings are sinners, innately depraved. Instead, the narrator's chop logic takes us directly to an anti-Christian concept, reminiscent of Rousseau, to the effect that man in his natural or savage state is always noble: a concept loathed by the Calvinists. But who views the savage, here, as having pure and uncontaminated qualities? An observer with "unvitiated taste"; by insinuation, in the larger context, an anti-Calvinist, a Rousseauist. Melville lets the narrator add that the same "unvitiated taste" views the citified man as having a "questionable smack." Rousseau again. But notice the conclusion: if a "primitive" like Billy does wander into a Cain's city or a Christian capital (the two are interchangeable, for Melville), the antithesis is striking because the "primitive" is represented as "faithful in word and thought" among those who have been vitiated by the Christian atmosphere! Melville made much the same point, quite bitingly, in *Typee*. In short, the beginning of that paragraph assumes the Christian viewpoint; but the development of the paragraph inverts and burlesques the Christian viewpoint, by insinuations.

In the very next paragraph of Chapter Two, Melville further permits his narrator to say one thing suitable to that narrator's Christian viewpoint; but also susceptible to an anti-Christian or Melvillian construction, which substantially extends the sinister allegorical meanings already suggested:

"Though our Handsome Sailor had as much of masculine beauty as one can expect anywhere to see; nevertheless, like the beautiful woman in one of Hawthorne's minor tales, there was just one thing amiss in him. No visible blemish, indeed, as with the lady; no, but an occasional liability to a vocal defect. Though in the hour of elemental uproar or peril, he was everything that a sailor should be, yet under sudden provocation of strong heart-feeling his voice, otherwise singularly musical, as if expressive of the harmony within, was apt to develop an organic hesitancy,—in fact, more or less of a stutter or even worse. In this particular Billy was a striking instance that the arch-interferer, the envious marplot of Eden, still has more or less to do with every human consignment to this planet of earth. In every case, one way or another, he is sure to slip in his little card, as much as to remind us—I too have a hand here."

The narrator, speaking from the Christian viewpoint, makes an orthodox application, in his conclusion, there: Satan is the "arch-interferer, the envious marplot of Eden." But consider the ambiguous Melvillian meaning which is made available through the Hawthorne reference. In "The Birthmark," Hawthorne comments thus on Georgiana's birthmark blemish: "It was the fatal flaw of humanity which Nature, in one shape or another, stamps ineffaceably on all her productions. . . ." Because Carlyle and the Transcendentalists in general delighted to adapt a Calvinistic concept to their needs by equating Nature and God, Melville had previously and sarcastically accepted their rules and beaten them at their own game, by concentrating on the evil aspects of Nature, in *Moby-Dick*. Again, he does much the same thing, here. The Hawthorne analogy enables him to represent Billy's "defect" (which will eventually be responsible for his "sin" and consequently responsible for his punishment by death) as an "original" blemish or birthmark from Nature, or (allegorically considered) a gift from God, his Maker. In this anti-Christian context, God might be viewed as the responsible source of this defect, this depravity, this sin, this death; God might be viewed as the "arch-interferer, the envious marplot of Eden." Because this oblique passage occurs in Chapter Two, let us hold the evaluation and interpretation tentatively, to see whether it is in any way corroborated by the subsequent action and commentary.[4]

5

In Chapter Three, Melville's narrator blandly gives us a brief historical background for understanding Billy's story: we are told that in the spring of 1797 His Majesty's Navy had been shaken by two spectacular mutinies, and some details are given. Specifically, these recent mutinies are of value to the story because they throw light on much that Captain Vere subsequently says and does concerning Billy's sin; allegorically, these mutinies are very subtly converted into symbols of justifiable rebellion and defiance, on the part of "thinking" men, against the authoritarian tyranny of the Christian doctrine and the Christian God. Melville's insinuative method, here, is to correlate these mutinies with the atheistical revolution in France; a correlation already suggested in the "Preface" to *Billy Budd*:

"The opening proposition made by the Spirit of that Age, involved a rectification of the Old World's hereditary wrongs. . . . Now, as elsewhere hinted, it was something caught from the Revolutionary Spirit that at Spithead emboldened the man-of-war's men to rise against real abuses, long-standing ones, and afterwards at the Nore to make inordinate and aggressive demands, successful resistance to which was confirmed only when the ringleaders were hung for an admonitory spectacle to the anchored fleet."

Notice that the brass-serving narrator there disapproves of the "inordinate" demands and approves of the hangings which squelched the trouble. The sinister allegorical overtones are merely hinted at by the already mentioned phrase, "crisis for Christendom." These overtones are more strongly developed in Chapter Three (italics added):

". . . the blue-jackets, to be numbered by the thousands, ran up with hurrahs the British colours *with the union and the cross wiped out*; by that cancellation transmuting *the flag of founded law and freedom defined*, into the enemy's red meteor of unbridled and unbounded revolt. . . . The event converted into *irony* for a time those spirited strains of Dibdin—as a song-writer no mean auxiliary to the English Government—at this European conjuncture, strains celebrating, among other things, the patriotic *devotion* of the British tar—

" 'And as for my life, 'tis the King's!' "

Allegorically considered, the surface meaning and tone of that entire passage is converted into irony by the larger context. Also in Chapter Three, the officer-honoring narrator adds a few remarks on correct procedure in honest historical writing: there are times, he says in effect, when the historian should not be any more honest than he can help! Melville is known to have used, for reference while writing *Billy Budd*, a history of the British Navy written by a certain William James, who was as much a brass-server as Melville's narrator would seem to be. For some reason, Melville permits his narrator to refer to this historian as "G. P. R.

James." Obviously, Melville had in front of him the evidence which could have kept him from the accidental mistake of thinking that the celebrated novelist G. P. R. James was one and the same as the celebrated naval historian William James. What gain could Melville have made by pretending to stumble into this mistake? Possibly the gain of a sly joke: because the naval historian also wrote his history from the "inside" viewpoint of the Admiralty, he might be described more accurately as a fiction writer than as an historian.

6

AFTER permitting his narrator to blow hot and cold on Admiral Nelson in Chapter Four, Melville contrasts that "declarer of his own person in fight" with the retiring "Captain the Honourable Edward Fairfax Vere." The narrator assures us that Captain Vere was a sterling fellow in every way. The contrast with the portrait of Lord Nelson, juxtaposed, is not flattering to Vere; but the narrator does not seem to notice this discrepancy which he himself would seem to have created. Being a literalist, the narrator would not be expected to notice that there is allegorical value in the emblematic suggestiveness of the Captain's name; a clustering of heavenly suggestiveness. Vere, Verity, Verus: later, the Captain will be represented as a personification of Truth. His nickname, we are told, is "Starry" and that seems appropriate. Fairfax: the Maker of All that is Fair. Now all we need is some correlation with the apple-stealing episode in Genesis. Quite blandly the narrator gives us the historical source of Captain Vere's nickname: it was derived from an appropriate passage in a poem entitled "Appleton House" by Andrew Marvell:

> This 'tis to have been from the first
> In a domestic heaven nursed,
> Under the discipline severe
> Of Fairfax and the starry Vere.

Before the reader finishes unraveling the allegorical meaning of Billy's story, those four lines will be recognized as an appropriately sardonic summary and conclusion, the sinister construction or paraphrase amounting to this: "The story perfectly illustrates what happens, in life, when an Adam-like innocent-ignorant such as Billy runs afoul of that selfishly severe letter-of-the-law discipline for which the Heavenly ("Starry") Creator (Fair-Fax) God (Vere: Truth) is notorious."

7

ANOTHER kind of artistic cross-ruff is established when the narrator describes Captain Vere's fondness for reading. Again, the narrator is permitted to make certain assertions in one chapter, so that Melville can make him unconsciously contradict himself in a later chapter. The difference in method, here, is that the careless reader is given plenty of time to forget the assertion, long before he arrives at the contradiction.

For example, Vere's reading tastes are described in such a way as to remind us of Melville's delight in stylistic subterfuge and ambiguity. His fondness for Montaigne's double-talk had prompted him to praise one character in *White-Jacket*, it will be remembered, thus: "I would have staked my life on it that he seized the right meaning of Montaigne." Notice that such discrimination is there made to serve as a touchstone of an individual's perceptiveness and penetration. Melville implies that a merely literal reading of certain literary passages is inexcusable, because the letter killeth; that deeper meanings can be appreciated only when the reader looks far enough beneath the surface to recognize the spirit and tone. Notice that Captain Vere will later prove to be an egregious literalist, and his stubborn insistence on the literal interpretation of a naval law will result in Billy's death. In Chapter Six, however, Melville lets his narrator praise Vere; lets the narrator protest that Vere has exactly those powers of deep penetration and discrimination which, as the later action reveals, he obviously lacks:

"He had a marked leaning towards everything intellectual. . . . With nothing of that literary taste which less heeds the thing conveyed than the vehicle, his bias was towards those books to which every serious mind of superior order occupying any active post of authority in the world, naturally inclines; books treating of actual men and events no matter of what era—history, biography and unconventional writers, who, free from cant and convention, like Montaigne, honestly, and in the spirit of common sense philosophise upon realities."

It is a shame to tamper with so much nice hocus-pocus as Melville gets together in that passage; but consider just a few elements involved. Melville took pleasure in his discovery that Montaigne was at his stylistic best when not stylistically "honest" and when not writing in the spirit of "common" sense. But it would seem that Vere likes to read about facts, treated as facts: "books treating of actual men and events." Presumably, he has no taste for poetry, and for the artistic convention of saying two things at once. Oh, to be sure, he may think he does: he is an admirer of literary style; but there is an ambiguous element in the reference to his fondness for both "the vehicle" and "the thing conveyed." (Melville had written, in an earlier version, "the matter than the style," but the revision is more attractive, and perhaps another tribute to Laurence Sterne.)

Yet just what does Vere get out of his reading? One feels a bit confused by the import of this passage: Melville goes out of the way to convey exactly that effect of confusion. As he lets the narrator bumble along, however, we get another oblique answer to the question as to what Vere gets from his reading. I have already pointed out that Melville could count on the success of his own stylistic traps because he knew that a reader bound by "cant and convention" (consciously or unconsciously) is unable to set aside his own views and values, and consequently insists on reading into a passage—then out of the same passage—exactly his own views and values, without regard for the consequent distortion of the author's meaning. Vere makes exactly this same mistake, and with consistent irony Melville permits his narrator to praise Vere for making this mistake:

"In this love of reading he found confirmation of his own more reserved thoughts—confirmation which he had vainly sought in social converse, so that as touching most fundamental topics, there had got to be established in him some positive convictions which he felt would abide in him essentially unmodified so long as his intelligent part remained unimpaired. In view of the troubled period in which his lot was cast this was well for him. His settled convictions were as a dyke against those invading waters of novel opinion, social, political, and otherwise, which carried away as in a torrent no few minds in those days, minds by nature not inferior to his own."

Again nice! Vere prides himself on using his "intelligent part" for sandbag purposes of creating a dike; perhaps a more solid sort of dike, somehow rock-ribbed and dogmatic in its conservatism. The narrator is praising Vere for using his mind as some kind of a stopper; but the story itself will reveal that Vere's inflexible and rock-ribbed rigidity will cause him to fasten on the literal meaning of a law, and on the necessity for executing Billy Budd accordingly, even when such an interpretation and such an action is opposed by his officers. Opposed, that is, until Vere ruthlessly overpowers them with his false logic as to the "necessity" of the execution. The central meaning of the story, on all three levels, will eventually pivot on that philosophical or theological word "necessity" and its extensions. In Chapter Six, however, Melville lets his narrator proceed even further, and with more unconscious irony, to praise Vere for the *liberality* of his views.

"While other members of that aristocracy to which by birth he belonged were incensed at the innovators mainly because their theories were inimical to the privileged classes, Captain Vere disinterestedly opposed them not alone because they seemed to him incapable of embodiment in lasting institutions, but at war with the peace of the world and the true welfare of mankind."

That passage is slippery enough to deserve careful handling. The primary antithesis would seem to be the contrast between the views of the aristocrats and the views of Vere, each concerned with the "theories" of "innovators," presumably French. Captain Vere disinterestedly opposed the theories of the innovators, we are told, because he found such theories inimical to the welfare of mankind as a whole; by contrast, his aristocratic opponents' concern was merely for the welfare of the privileged classes. The equivocation, here, lies in the possibly specious use made of such an argument by those who frequently conceal their own selfish motives for protecting vested rights, by insisting that their primary concern is for the welfare of others! Is there any way of determining that Vere's use of such an argument is indeed a specious use? Decidedly. Captain Vere will later make exactly this same kind of false protest, when he weighs the problem as to whether Billy Budd shall hang.

This clarifies another aspect of Melville's preliminary method. He is carefully and quietly preparing the cautious reader for the final and climactic scene in which Vere decides that Billy must die; he is providing the reader with the wherewithal to evaluate the validity of Captain Vere's arguments, and of Captain Vere's decision. All this preparation is done by permitting the narrator to select as praiseworthy certain aspects of Vere's character which his actions and words will subsequently reveal to be unpraiseworthy.

8

STATED in allegorical terms, there are only three characters, here: Adam, God, and Satan. Having introduced Billy Budd as the character who will play the emblematic part of Adam, in the subsequent action; having introduced Captain Vere as the character who will play the emblematic part of God (as principal or agent), Melville uses Chapter Seven to introduce the character who will play the emblematic part of Satan. According to Melville's somber and sinister theological views, any type of Satan, in this narrative, should also be represented as an agent of God—someone who may serve as a policeman for God, an "accuser of our brethren," as Satan is described in the book of Revelation. In a ship's company, the Master-at-Arms fits such a role, because his duties are permissive and because he is directly responsible to the omnipotent Captain. Melville was able to draw heavily on his preliminary study of such a type, made in Bland, the Master-at-Arms aboard White-Jacket's *Neversink*. This time, the name of the Master-at-Arms is Claggart. (The narrator's name should be "Bland.") When first the narrator is made to describe him, the specific details are the total concern of the narrator; but the overtones and the allegorical hints are Melville's ulterior concern. There is much that is mysterious and dark about Claggart's background and antecedents, we are told:

"His brow [was] of the sort phrenologically associated with more than average intellect; silken jet curls partly clustering over it, making a foil to the pallor below, a pallor tinged with a faint shade of amber skin to the hue of time-tinted marbles of old.[5] . . . But his general aspect and manner were so suggestive of an educa-

tion and career incongruous with his naval function, that when
not actively engaged in it he looked like a man of high quality,
social and moral, who for reasons of his own was keeping in-
cognito."

So far, the hints are cabalistic: the black-white badge of office,
the extraordinary intellect, the "high" quality, the tinged-marble
reference. As the passage continues, however, there are some still
occult but correlated references which remind us that if Claggart
is later to be established as an emblem of Satan, his allegorical
background is familiar: he was once one of God's angels, demoted
by God because of too high aspirations. Claggart's background
suggests this:

"Nothing was known of his former life. It might be that he was
an Englishman; and yet there lurked a bit of accent in his speech
suggesting that possibly he was not such by birth, but through *natu-
ralization* [italics added] in early childhood. Among certain grizzled
sea-gossips of the gun-decks and forecastle went a rumour perdue
that the master-at-arms was a chevalier who had volunteered into
the King's navy *by way of compounding for some mysterious
swindle whereof he had been arraigned at the King's Bench* [italics
added]. . . . And indeed a man of Claggart's accomplishments,
without prior nautical experience entering the navy at mature life,
as he did, and *necessarily allotted at the start to the lowest grade
in it* [italics added]; a man, too, who never made allusion to his
previous life ashore; these were circumstances which in the dearth
of exact knowledge as to his true antecedents opened to the
invidious a vague field for unfavourable surmise."

At present, of course, the character of Claggart remains neutral,
and it will only be after he goes into action that we shall be able
to test the possible corroboration of these provocative suggestions.
Notice, however, that as this description of Claggart is brought
to a conclusion, it adds one very rich example of stimulating
equivocation:

"Of this maritime chief of police, the ship's corporals, so called,
were the immediate subordinates, and compliant ones; and this, as
is to be noted in some business departments ashore, almost to a
degree inconsistent with entire moral volition. His place put
various converging wires of underground influence under the
Chief's control, capable when astutely worked through his under-

strappers of operating to the mysterious discomfort if nothing worse, of any of the sea-commonalty."

In the sinister context, Claggart is indeed so suitable an agent of God that he organizes his subordinates directly after the pattern on which God organizes His subordinates![6] As for "business departments ashore," my guess is that Melville insinuates, "churches" (run for a "profit").

9

A NEW character is introduced in the next chapter. He is a subordinate whose importance is that of a commentator on the action, a sort of Greek-Chorus commentator. In the sense that his wisdom is the dark wisdom of Solomon, he is an Ahab-like character and even a Melvillian character. Aboard ship he is merely an old sailor called "the Dansker" because of his Danish background. (Emblematically, a blood-kin to Hamlet). Like Ahab, the Dansker wears a symbolic and "enlightening" scar on his face: ". . . he had received a cut slantwise along one temple and cheek, leaving a long pale scar *like a streak of dawn's light* [italics added] falling athwart the dark visage." For the narrator, the analogy with "a streak of dawn's light" is merely of descriptive value; for Melville the analogy has a woeful allegorical value: the old Dansker knows the worst about both God and man. His bitter profit from having eaten the apple of knowledge is that he can easily evaluate and predict the price Billy Budd must pay for being innocent and ignorant:

"Now the first time that his small weasel-eyes happened to light on Billy Budd, a certain grim internal merriment set all his ancient wrinkles into antic play. Was it that his eccentric unsentimental old sapience, primitive in its kind, saw, or thought it saw, something which in contrast with the warship's environment looked oddly incongruous in the Handsome Sailor? But after slyly studying him at intervals, the old Merlin's equivocal merriment was modified. For now when the twain would meet, it would start in his face a quizzing sort of look, but it would be but momentary and sometimes replaced by an expression of speculative query as to what might eventually befall a nature like that, dropped into a world not without some man-traps and against whose subtleties simple courage lacking experience and address and without any touch of defensive ugliness, is of little avail; and where such innocence as man is capable of does yet in a moral emergency not always sharpen the faculties or enlighten the will."

That is a very revealing and corroborative passage.

The old Dansker likes Billy Budd, and is kind to him; but he cannot help revealing "patriarchal irony touching Billy's youth" and always addresses him as Baby Budd. When the young innocent carries the story of his petty troubles to the old Dansker and asks his advice, the old man immediately sees in the story a proof that the Master-at-Arms is, as usual, doing leg-work for the Captain:

"The old man, shoving up the front of his tarpaulin and *deliberately rubbing the long slant scar* [italics added] at the point where it entered the thin hair, laconically said,

" 'Baby Budd, *Jemmy Legs* (meaning the master-at-arms) is down on you.'

" '*Jemmy Legs!*' ejaculated Billy, his welkin eyes expanding; 'what for? Why he calls me *the sweet and pleasant young fellow*, they tell me.'

" 'Does he so?' grinned the grizzled one; then said, 'Ay, Baby lad, a sweet voice has *Jemmy Legs.*'

" 'No, not always. But to me he has. I seldom pass him but there comes a pleasant word.'

" 'And that's because he's down upon you, Baby Budd.'

"Such reiteration along with the manner of it, incomprehensible to a novice, disturbed Billy almost as much as the mystery for which he had sought explanation. Something less unpleasingly oracular he tried to extract; but the old sea-Chiron thinking perhaps that for the nonce he had sufficiently instructed his young Achilles, pursed his lips, gathered his wrinkles together and would commit himself to nothing further.

"Years, and those experiences which befall certain shrewder men subordinated life-long to the will of superiors, all this had developed in the Dansker the pithy guarded cynicism that was his leading characteristic."

The sinister allegorical overtones of the reference to "shrewder men subordinated life-long to the will of superiors" is worth noticing; but even more important is the fact that Melville here gives his third clean-cut hint as to his own stylistic method in *Billy Budd*: the ambiguous method which is "incomprehensible to a novice," and the novice's desire for "something less unpleasantly oracular." Melville, like the Dansker, has been driven by his own "pithy guarded cynicsm" to represent his meaning in riddles, and at this late stage in his life he will "commit himself to nothing further" as to his meaning.

Hard on this third clean-cut hint comes the fourth, for the benefit of the reluctant reader: a situation which may serve to remind the reader that the sense of a remark (or even of a whole narrative) may be exactly the opposite of its literal meaning. The situation is trivial: Billy spills a bowl of soup on the deck in front of Claggart, and the Master-at-Arms sarcastically comments, "Handsomely done, my lad! And handsome is as handsome did it too." Unable to handle sarcasm, naïve Billy (not entirely unlike some naïve readers of Melville in this regard) entirely misses the point of the remark. After Claggart has gone, Billy turns to his messmates and says, "There now, who says that Jemmy Legs is down on me!"

10

THE mysteriousness of Claggart's character becomes a subject over which Melville cunningly causes his stupid narrator to puzzle. Quite unintentionally, of course, the narrator establishes some analogies which are of value on the deeper level of meaning; that deeper level which the narrator, as such, never perceives. The narrator opines that the Bible, and even Biblical Commentaries, might be of value here, but that unfortunately and regrettably these are not "any longer popular." Consequently the narrator feels the necessity of referring to "some authority not liable to the charge of being tinctured with Biblical element." His goal here is complete detachment. So he chooses Plato as his authority, and extracts from a list of definitions *attributed* to Plato this seemingly trivial definition of Natural Depravity:

"Natural Depravity: a depravity according to nature." The fun, here, begins as soon as we notice that this is no definition at all! While the narrator blandly expounds the significance of the definition, however, the alert reader makes his own computation in

terms of Melville's sinister frame of reference: a depravity according to nature has its source in nature, or in the source of the
source: in God. Natural Depravity is thus an emblem of Divine
Depravity. The narrator brightly comments on the definition,
thus: "A definition which though savouring of Calvinism, by no
means involves Calvin's dogma as to total mankind." Indeed not,
when construed in a sinister sense. After the narrator completes
his elegant exegesis, Melville puts this into his mouth: "Now
something such was Claggart, in whom was the mania of an evil
nature, not engendered by vicious training or corrupting books or
licentious living, but born with him and innate, in short 'a depravity according to nature.'"

Now the cogged meanings of Melville's darker thoughts begin
to turn, and the reader is obliged to reckon with the wheels within
wheels. Although Claggart is an emblem of Satan, and Billy is an
emblem of Adam, it would seem from this exegesis on "Natural
Depravity" that there is a striking parallelism between Claggart
and Billy, between Satan and Adam: each has his God-given
birthmark; each has some kind of imperfection which controls his
destiny and yet for which each is not responsible. ("Responsibility" is a major motif in *Billy Budd*.) Such a concept is a precise
inversion of that parallelism between Satan and Adam which
occurs in another artistic illumination of meaning in the Genesis
story: the major parallelism which Milton develops, in *Paradise
Lost*, between the story of Satan's fall and the story of Adam's
fall. It will be recalled that Milton uses this technical device of
parallelism to underline the concept that each character has
brought on himself his own fate: "Whose fault? Whose but his
own!" By contrast, Melville proceeds to invert Milton's central
concept, here, in order to illuminate his own bitter conclusion:
"Whose fault? Whose but God's!"

The narrator's little treatise on "Natural Depravity" and what
he refers to as "those intricacies involved in the question of moral
responsibility" is brought to a conclusion in a final paragraph
that points one way, in terms of the narrator's purpose, and
another way in terms of Melville's allegorical purpose:

"Dark sayings[7] are these, some will say. But why? Is it because
they somewhat savour of Holy Writ in its phrase 'mysteries of
iniquity'?[8] If they do, such savour was foreign from my intention

for little will it commend these pages to many a reader of today. The point of the present story turning on the hidden nature of the master-at-arms has necessitated this chapter."

Captain Vere subsequently becomes interested in Paul's phrase, "mystery of iniquity," and quotes it. The narrator rounds off his discussion by returning to his starting point: he has been puzzling over the mysterious "hidden nature" of Claggart, and this is all he has in mind when he speaks about the "mysteries of iniquity." So much, then, for the narrator. Melville's witty equivocation, for the enjoyment of the careful reader, affords an entirely different construction. The narrator has been right when he has said that the point of the present story turns on the hidden nature of the Master-at-Arms; but the point turns on an aspect which the narrator does not see or mention. In a sinister sense, or an allegorical sense, Melville implies, Satan's fall and Adam's fall were predestined; caused by forces beyond their control; caused by certain birthmark attributes. Even as Billy's fateful impediment is God's birthright gift to Billy, so Claggart's "natural depravity" is God's birthright gift to Claggart. Darkly, then, the point of the present story turns on the hidden nature of the Master-at-Arms because this leads us directly to the hidden nature of God: the malice of God, the "Original Sin" of God. As the narrator very precisely puts it, if such a concept seems somewhat to savour of *Holy* Writ, such was quite foreign to Melville's intention!

11

I HAVE said that Melville's ulterior concept, in *Billy Budd*, inverts Milton's ulterior concept, in *Paradise Lost*. Man's fault, says Melville, is God's fault. The many cross-references between *Billy Budd* and *Paradise Lost* are sometimes obvious and sometimes subtle; but one of the most obvious is the direct quotation which Melville uses as his title or motto for Chapter Eleven: "Pale ire, envy and despair." Milton uses those words to describe Satan's mixed feelings when first he looks on Adam in the Garden of Eden; Melville uses those words to describe Claggart's mixed feelings when he looks on Billy. Envying Billy his innocence, Claggart yet views that innocence with disdain: ". . . to be nothing more than innocent! Yet in an aesthetic way he saw the charm of it, the courageous free-and-easy temper of it, and fain woud have shared it, but he despaired of it." Thus the reader's attention is made to concentrate on the relationship between innocence and ignorance, with many possible extensions of that relationship. Melville's handling of it recalls the remarks of Milton's Satan as he enviously soliloquizes, while watching Adam and Eve:

> Yet let me not forget what I have gain'd
> From thir own mouths; all is not theirs it seems:
> One fatal Tree there stands of Knowledge call'd,
> Forbidden them to taste: Knowledge forbidd'n?
> Suspicious, reasonless. Why should thir Lord
> Envy them that? can it be sin to know,
> Can it be death? and do they only stand
> By Ignorance, is that thir happy state,
> The proof of thir obedience and thir faith?
> O fair foundation laid whereon to build
> Thir ruin![9]

After Melville has suggested a correlation between Milton's Satan and Claggart, he lets the narrator tuck in a more darkly significant kind of correlation:

"With no power to annul the elemental evil in himself, though he could hide it readily enough; apprehending the good, but powerless to be it; what recourse is left to a nature like Claggart's, surcharged with energy as such natures almost invariably are, but to recoil upon itself, and, like the scorpion for which the Creator alone is responsible, act out to the end the part allotted it."

Once again the narrator has established an analogy merely for purposes of describing Claggart's specific iniquity. Melville uses this seemingly innocent remark for sinister purposes, and thus shifts the weight of meaning from Claggart to the dark allegorical concept: the fault is not Claggart's any more than the fault which ruined Satan was Satan's. Each commits actions "for which the Creator alone is responsible." In *Paradise Lost*, Satan works out ironic variations on that same theme. When God's agent Ithuriel asks who he is, Satan answers, "Not to know mee argues yourselves unknown." Later, as we have noticed, when Satan plots the corruption of Adam he speaks with unheard bitterness: "Accept your

Maker's work; he gave it me, Which I as freely give." So Claggart implies, allegorically.

12

THE temptation with which Claggart confronts Billy Budd is made indirectly: one of Claggart's underling agents invites Billy to enter into collusion with a group of impressed sailors who are (falsely) said to be planning a mutiny. Billy fails to see that there may be some relationship between the tempting afterguardsman and Claggart, but when he tells a modified version of the incident to the old Dansker, the following conversation occurs:

" 'Didn't I say so, Baby Budd?'

" 'Say what?' demanded Billy.

" 'Why, *Jemmy Legs* is *down* on you.'

" 'And what,' rejoined Billy in amazement, 'has *Jemmy Legs* to do with that cracked afterguardsman?'

" 'Ho, it was an afterguardsman, then. A cat's-paw, a cat's-paw.'
. . . it was his wont to relapse into grim silence when interrogated in sceptical sort as to any of his sententious oracles, not always very clear ones, but rather partaking of that obscurity which invests most Delphic deliverances from any quarter."

There, for at least the fifth time, Melville has found an oblique way of reminding the reader, in passing, that his own literary revelations of meaning are—like those of God—cryptic, grim, oracular. But the contrast between the Dansker's distrustfulness and Billy's charitable but stupid faith in the essential goodness of human nature provides Melville with another chance to let his narrator deliver some unconsciously equivocal remarks on the subject of innocence and ignorance: ". . . And yet a child's utter innocence is but its blank ignorance, and the innocence more or less wanes as intelligence waxes. But in Billy Budd intelligence, such as it was, had advanced, while yet his simple-mindedness remained for the most part unaffected."

As a consequence of this, Billy has no way of recognizing or evaluating evil or malice: "And the thews of Billy were hardly comparable with that sort of sensitive spiritual organisation which in some cases instinctively conveys to *ignorant innocence* [italics added] an admonition of the proximity of the malign. . . . As it was, innocence was his blinder."

Again the difference between the narrator's overt meaning and Melville's covert meaning: the narrator is talking about Billy's lack of defense against Claggart's malice; Melville is allegorically dramatizing the "ignorant innocence" of individuals who cannot perceive God's malice, as represented in the actions of a Satanic agent of God, or as represented in the actions and attributes of God Himself.

13

MELVILLE is at last ready to unfold the major action within the allegorical framework already carefully established. This major action begins when Claggart appears before Captain Vere and makes his false accusation that Billy Budd is suspected of having joined with others to plot mutiny. Claggart hints that if some swift retribution is not taken, Captain Vere may find himself in exactly the same danger which overtook the Captain at the Nore during that recent and notorious mutiny. But Captain Vere is very fond of his newly-acquired and Adam-like Handsome Sailor; Vere is also strongly inclined to suspect Claggart's motives for making such an accusation. Sensible of his own "vaguely repellent distaste" for Claggart, however, Vere did not wish to show "undue forwardness in crediting an informer *even if his own subordinate* [italics added] and charged among other honours with police surveillance of the crew." The sinister allegorical and theological insinuations, there, are strong: Satan is a permissive agent of God.

While weighing Claggart's charge against Billy, Captain Vere recalls what he has known—or has thought he has known—about the Handsome Sailor. While the bland narrator presents these recollections as evidence of Vere's sterling qualities, the alert reader is permitted to notice that each of Vere's recollections furnishes a further count against Vere. For example: "Though in general not very demonstrative to his officers, he had congratulated Lieutenant Ratcliffe upon his good fortune in lighting on such a fine specimen of the *genus homo*, who in the nude might have posed for a statue of young Adam before the Fall."

By this time, we may pass over the further correlation of Billy and Adam; this count against Vere is that he reveals his approval of impressment in general, and one impressment in particular.

From Melville's point of view, this would certainly be a very serious count against Vere. Consider one more example: "In sum, Captain Vere had from the beginning deemed Billy Budd to be what in the naval parlance of the time was called a '*King's bargain*,' that is to say, for His Britannic Majesty's navy a capital investment at small outlay or none at all."

Emblematically, even as the Captain of a ship may serve as a symbol of God's power and attributes, so the King may here serve as a symbol of God's power and attributes. The immediate context presumably praises Vere for gloating over this "King's bargain," and Vere is presumably so blinded by what Schopenhauer calls self-interest that he is not even conscious of the injustice implicit in stealing and enslaving Billy. Thus, on the emblematic level of meaning, the slurring allusions to God are double-barreled: in terms of the King, in terms of the Captain.

The action continues, as Captain Vere warns Claggart that if he is bearing false witness, the penalty is death. Just how strongly Vere suspects that Claggart does indeed deserve the death penalty, is indicated by the narrator's Captain-praising (and unintentionally ironic) remarks:

"Though something exceptional in the moral quality of Captain Vere made him, in earnest encounter with a fellow-man, *a veritable touch stone of that man's essential nature* [italics added; allegorically, very nice!] yet now as to Claggart and what was really going on in him his feeling partook less of intuitional conviction than of strong suspicion clogged by strange dubieties. The perplexity he evinced proceeded less from aught touching the man informed against—as Claggart doubtless opined—than from considerations how best to act in regard to the informer."

Indeed, we learn, the excellent and astute Captain Vere, this "veritable touch stone," felt that he had only one problem on his hands: "he would first practically test the accuser." The obvious way to do this, the narrator continues, would be to require that Claggart should produce those witnesses who, he had said, could prove beyond doubt that Billy was guilty. That makes sense. But the narrator immediately defends Vere for rejecting this sensible way: it *might* cause talk; it *might* have an undesirable effect on the ship's company. (Remember that argument; it will be used again.) Vere instead decides to be secretive: he will bring Claggart and Billy Budd face to face in his cabin, and then let Claggart repeat his accusation to Billy Budd. (The secretiveness is God-like.) Implicitly, the orthodox and conventional narrator approves this action, even as he approves any and every decision and statement and action of the almighty Captain Vere.

But Melville might assume that any except the dullest reader will immediately start to worry over the egregious wrong which must eventuate from such a plan. Vere is convinced that Claggart bears false witness; that Billy Budd is innocent. Ironically, the scene which he has planned can result in only the opposite conclusion: in some way or other, Billy Budd will protest his innocence. What then? Captain Vere will have the word of an officer against the word of an enlisted man. Billy will say he is innocent, and Claggart will call Billy a liar. Bad as that is, the next situation will be worse. This is no stalemate, because an officer's word has obvious precedence over the word of an enlisted man. So the planned scene can result only in a technical proof that the man whom Vere thinks innocent is guilty! In other words, Captain Vere's plan is inexcusably stupid; more than that, it is criminal. Yet Melville, wryly heaping irony on irony, permits his narrator to approve and praise and commend Captain Vere, even at this moment.

14

WHEN Claggart makes his accusation, standing face to face with Billy in the Captain's Cabin, Billy is speechless with surprise. Vere embarrasses him further by issuing a command:

" 'Speak, man!' said Captain Vere to the transfixed one struck by his aspect even more than by Claggart's, 'Speak! defend yourself.' "

Billy is handicapped in several different ways. First of all, his innocence has disarmed him by providing him with no knowledge as to how he might cope with such a situation, and he is bewildered. This disadvantage is aggravated by his birthmark handicap: his God-given tendency to stutter. The narrator, in describing his difficulties, refers to Captain Vere's command to speak as an "appeal"—under the circumstances a highly ironic description:

"Which appeal caused but a strange, dumb gesturing and

gurgling in Billy; amazement at such an accusation so suddenly sprung on inexperienced nonage; this, and it may be horror at the accuser, serving to bring out his lurking defect, and in this instance for the time intensifying it into a convulsed tongue-tie; while the intent head and entire form, straining forward in an agony of ineffectual eagerness to obey the injunction to speak and defend himself, gave an expression to the face like that of a condemned vestal priestess in the moment of being buried alive, and in the first struggle against suffocation."

(Note well the expression, "tongue-tie." It is used again, later.) As soon as he recognizes that Billy's failure to answer is caused by his tongue-tie, the narrator tells us, Vere belatedly tries to correct his mistake, and with pathetic consequence:

"Going close up to the young sailor, and laying a soothing hand on his shoulder, he said: 'There is no hurry, my boy. Take your time, take your time.' Contrary to the effect intended, these words so fatherly in tone, doubtless touching Billy's heart to the quick, prompted yet more violent efforts at utterance—efforts soon ending for the time in confirming the paralysis, and bringing to the face an expression which was *as a crucifixion* [italics added] to behold. The next instant, quick as the flame from a discharged cannon at night, his right arm shot out, and Claggart dropped to the deck."

Now, Captain Vere is in a position to feel a guilty sense of regret for his own crime in creating a scene which has produced such a ghastly catastrophe. Now his superior qualities of heart and mind —his so-called fatherliness—will be tested. They are indeed tested, and Captain Vere is found sadly wanting, although the narrator does not seem to notice it. As Claggart lies there motionless, Vere's first word is one in which he indirectly passes sentence on Billy Budd:

" 'Fated boy,' breathed Captain Vere in tone so low as to be almost a whisper, 'what have you done!' "

Which, in the Melvillian context, suggests the counter-question, and the allegorical insinuations: what have *you* done, omnipotent Captain Vere! Immediately, Vere undergoes a metamorphosis, according to the narrator. More precisely, Vere immediately reveals his true character: "The father in him, manifested towards Billy thus far in the scene [!] was replaced by the military disciplinarian. In his official tone he bade the foretopman retire to a state-room aft (pointing it out) and there remain till thence summoned. This order Billy in silence mechanically obeyed."

Billy is submissive, throughout; mechanically so. As soon as Vere is assured by the surgeon that Claggart is indeed dead, Vere exclaims, "It is the divine judgment of Ananias!" (For Melville's allegorical purposes, that is a very pretty touch! It will be remembered that when Ananias lied to Peter, Peter said, "Why hath Satan filled thine heart to lie to the Holy Ghost . . . Thou hast not lied unto men, but unto God." And immediately Ananias fell down dead.)

Having delivered himself of this allegorically pertinent pronouncement, Vere delivers himself of its corrollary, still with reference to the manner of Ananias' death; but with a quaint exegetical twist: "Struck dead by an angel of God. Yet the angel must hang!" In other words, Captain Vere has already passed sentence on Billy Budd, by finding Budd guilty of a crime which originated in the stupid and criminal action of Vere; which originated because Vere confronted an innocent and ignorant man with a false witness, whose penalty for bearing false witness should have been death. With appropriate irony, the falsely accused and innocent man had instinctively and impulsively served as executioner. Such a construction obviously goes beneath the letter of the law to the spirit of the law. Captain Vere, of course, is a dike, a rigid man-of-war man, and a letter-of-the-law man. According to the letter of the law, Billy Budd is guilty of striking a superior officer; nay, of killing a superior officer. And according to the Articles of War, the penalty for that is death: argal, the angel must hang. Vere informs the surgeon that he will call a drumhead court.

15

As the Surgeon leaves the cabin, he is so troubled by Vere's remarks that he suspects the Captain of suffering (with allegorical appropriateness) from some form of depravity:

"Was Captain Vere suddenly affected in his mind, or was it but a transient excitement brought about by so strange and extraordinary a happening? As to the drumhead court, it struck the surgeon as impolitic, if nothing more. The thing to do, he thought, was to place Billy Budd in confinement, and in a way dictated by usage, and postpone further action in so extraordinary a case to such a time as they should again join the squadron, and then refer it to the Admiral. He recalled the unwonted agitation of Captain Vere and his excited exclamations so at variance with his normal manner. *Was he unhinged?* [italics added] But assuming that he is, it is not so susceptible of proof. What then could he do? *No more trying situation is conceivable than that of an officer subordinated under a Captain whom he suspects to be, not mad indeed, but yet not quite unaffected in his intellect.* [italics added] To argue his order to him would be insolence. To resist him would be mutiny."

Melville is here manipulating the surgeon as another sort of Greek-Chorus character (even as he previously employed the Dansker), to convey strong allegorical insinuations. The Surgeon's convictions are further emphasized when the lieutenants and the captain of marines, to whom the Surgeon delivered the message, agreed with the Surgeon in at least one respect: "They fully stared at him in surprise and concern. Like him they seemed to think that such a matter should be reported to the Admiral."

I have already pointed out that Melville's sinister theological theme is most overtly and precisely represented by the phrase, ". . . the Creator alone is responsible." Allegorically considered, the meaning of the Surgeon's thoughts is closely correlated with the meaning of the theme. The allegorical insinuations are particularly significant in this sentence: "No more trying situation is conceivable than that of an officer subordinated under a Captain whom he suspects to be, not mad indeed, but yet not quite unaffected in his intellect."

Now it becomes clear, within the sinister framework, that Captain Vere is indeed an emblem of divine depravity, in the theological sense of the word "depravity." This scene in Captain Vere's cabin, the killing of Claggart and the condemnation of Billy, is the crisis of the novel. All the remaining action, the falling action, will merely illuminate, allegorically, other aspects of divine depravity, as Melville viewed it. For this reason, particular attention should be paid to a single sentence with which Melville ends that scene. The narrator is permitted to challenge, in an oblique way, the critical and suspicious and fault-finding thoughts of the Surgeon, thus: "Whether Captain Vere, as the surgeon professionally surmised, was really the sudden victim of any degree of *aberration* [italics added] one must determine for himself by such light as this narrative may afford."

That sentence is perfectly balanced in its equivocation, and as such it is an epitome of the perfect artistic balance of *Billy Budd*. The narrator seems to be saying that even while the Surgeon thought Vere somehow off balance, subsequent events will show how wrong the Surgeon was: the narrator is on Vere's side. The sinister meaning, which is Melville's and not the narrator's, is that there will be differences of opinion on this point—"one must determine for himself"—and yet that the individual is by no means left without some guide as to the right or wrong opinion of the Surgeon. The individual is under a specific obligation: he *must* determine "by such light as this narrative may afford." Again, the subjunctive "may" provides a slippery meaning. Again, the sheep will be further parted from the goats, during the remainder of the narrative. The reader biased and blinded by Christian dogmatism (again, whether he acknowledges that or not) will persistently discover that the remainder of the story is suffused with praise for the Christian doctrine of Necessity and of the greatest good for the purest number; suffused with approval of the Christian doctrine that God's will should be accepted even though God's will may often be contrary to man's will. On the other hand, the reader who is not biased or blinded by Christian dogma will recognize the way in which Melville hides behind his manipulated narrator and thus employs various forms of sarcasm and satire and irony to present a considerable variety of allusions to Christian beliefs, so that he may invert and ridicule these beliefs; that Melville will accomplish his ultimate and ulterior purpose of dark illumination by giving Captain Vere more and more rope until he has enough to hang both Billy and Himself.

16

As soon as the drumhead court has been arranged, Melville permits Captain Vere to play three specific roles and three allegorical roles simultaneously: accusing witness, one-man jury, judge. Even in his highest capacity, he insists that he is not a free agent; that he is responsible for the carrying out of a higher law. Responsibility thus becomes an old concept placed in a new light, and it is closely related to the continuing tension of the narrative: who is to blame? In order to appreciate the sinister allegorical meanings which Melville develops during and after that drumhead court, we should refresh our memories as to some of Melville's previous allegorical utterances in *White-Jacket*. There, as in *Billy Budd*, the word "depravity" was used repeatedly. Discussing naval abuses, White-Jacket protested, "It is to no purpose that you apologetically appeal to the general depravity of the man-of-war's man. Depravity in the oppressed is no apology for the oppressor; but rather an additional stigma to him, as being, in a large degree, the effect, and not the cause and justification of oppression."[10]

Theologically considered, these problems of "responsibility" and "blame" and "depravity" had been explored at length during the recurrent wrangles between Calvinists and anti-Calvinists. For example, Pierre Bayle's summary of these theological wrangles had been capped with the following comment:

". . . Why so many Suppositions? What was the Reason of so many Steps? It was the desire of clearing God; for it was plainly perceived that Religion was at Stake, and that Man would be necessarily led to Atheism, if God was said to be the Author of Sin. . . . Note, that there is no Difference between a Man who commits a Crime by himself, or by the Instrument of another. It is manifest to any one who reasons, that God is a most perfect Being, and that of all Perfections, none is more essential to him than Goodness, Holiness, and Justice. If you deprive him of those Perfections, to make him a Law-giver who forbids Men to Sin, and yet induces them to sin, and then punishes them for it, you make him a Being in whom Men cannot put their Trust, a deceitful, malicious, unjust and cruel Being: He can be no longer an Object of Worship. . . . When an Object is dreaded only because it has the Power and Will of doing Harm, and exercises that Power cruelly and unmercifully, it must needs be hated and detested . . . To represent God as a Being, who makes some Laws against Sin, which he induces Men to transgress, that he may have a Pretence to punish them, is to expose Religion to the Raileries of the Libertines."[11]

That last sentence may serve in part to suggest what Melville is up to, allegorically, in *Billy Budd*: he would like to expose religion to the raillery in much the same satirical way that Lucian and Voltaire did. But again we are faced with the problem of remembering Melville's inability to be detached in his laughter; at times the earnestness in *Billy Budd* recalls the vindictive tone of that passage in *White-Jacket* wherein Melville pointed at the Thirty-second Article of War as a major cause of "depravity" among enlisted men:

"This is the article that, above all others, puts the scourge into the hands of the captain, calls him to no account for its exercise, and furnishes him with an ample warrant for inflictions of cruelty upon the common sailor. . . . By this article the captain is made a legislator, as well as a judge and an executive. So far as it goes, it absolutely leaves to his discretion to decide what things shall be considered crimes, and what shall be the penalty; whether an accused person has been guilty of actions by him declared to be crimes; and how, when, and where the penalty shall be inflicted."[12]

The relevance of that passage to the situation in *Billy Budd* should be obvious, on either the specific level or the sinister allegorical level of meaning. Nevertheless, it is not quite strong enough to represent the degree of Melville's misanthropic bitterness against man and God; it needs to be correlated with another passage from *White-Jacket*:

"It cannot have escaped the discernment of any observer of mankind, that, in the presence of its conventional inferiors, conscious imbecility in power often seeks to carry off that imbecility by assumptions of lordly severity. The amount of flogging on board an American man-of-war is, in many cases, in exact proportion to the professional and intellectual incapacity of her officers to command. Thus, in these cases, the law that authorises flogging does but put a scourge into the hand of a fool."[13]

This is the attitude which White-Jacket held toward Captain Claret; it approximates the attitude which Melville holds toward Captain Vere, as reflected in the total effect of *Billy Budd*. Delighting in the subtleties of artistic indirections, Melville takes bitter pleasure in permitting his stupid narrator to continue, however, to praise and defend Captain Vere, even while Vere is making an ass of himself, in his courtmartial rhetoric. Now we can return to the text, with a better chance to recognize the caustic elements in Melville's satirical art.

17

WITH unconscious irony, the narrator blandly argues the *Necessity* of all Vere's actions and thoughts, even the *Necessity* of Vere's foreknowledge that Billy is predestined to be hanged, although the drumhead court has not yet rendered its decision. Of course, the narrator admits, the situation is intricate:

"In the jugglery of circumstances preceding and attending the event on board the *Indomitable*, and in the light of martial code whereby it was formally to be judged, innocence and guilt, personified in Claggart and Budd, in effect changed places."

(Plenty of insinuation, there! Continuing:)

"In the legal view the apparent victim of the tragedy was he who had sought to victimise a man blameless; and the indisputable deed of the latter, navally regarded, constituted the most heinous of military crimes."

(That is the narrator's manipulated viewpoint; not Melville's. Notice that neither the narrator nor Captain Vere take into account any evaluation of Billy's motive for his action. Each of these commentators on that action is a letter-of-the-law man, and they find that Billy's "indisputable deed" constitutes "the most heinous of military crimes," when it is "navally regarded." What has Billy done? He has struck and killed a superior officer. Never mind the word "justification"—so sacred to theological Milton and other Calvinists: the law says such action is punishable by death, and that is that. Continuing:)

"Yet more. The essential right and wrong involved in the matter, the clearer that might be, so much the worse for the *responsibility* [italics added; note well] of a loyal sea-commander inasmuch as he was not authorised to determine the matter on that primitive legal basis."

(Who says so? The narrator says so. Vere says so. Therefore, some readers feel that the logic of the argument is flawless and that they as readers must accept that logic as gospel truth. Allegorically considered, Melville sneers, it is indeed gospel truth. Under the circumstances, the omnipotent Vere is not omnipotent, any more than God was omnipotent when he carried out the predestined fate of Adam, in Eden. But even as God felt sorry, so Vere has a great heart and can pity Adam-like Billy.)

To justify the ways of Vere to Budd, ever further, the narrator blandly points out the superbly democratic manner in which Vere arranges to have Billy tried by a jury of his superiors. First of all, Vere himself makes the selection, in order to, make certain that justice is done. Next, Vere further emasculates the jury by appointing himself to the trinitarian function of accuser, jury, judge: ". . . reserving to himself as the one on whom the ultimate accountability would rest, the right of maintaining a supervision of it, of formally or informally interposing at need." There is justice! The sinister allegorical and theological extension is that the jury, in exercising its own free will to reach a decision, is ironically predestined to reach the very decision which Vere has already made!

18

As soon as Billy is arraigned before the court, he is asked, "Is it or is it not as Captain Vere says?" (Allegorically, that question is pertinent.) Billy's submissive reply is this: "Captain Vere tells the truth. It is just as Captain Vere says, but it is not as the master-at-arms said. I have eaten the King's bread and I am true to the King." (If some of the "hard faces" of more experienced impressed enlisted men on the gun deck could have heard that, it is safe to assume that their ambiguous smiles would have returned.)

Now the questions which are not so easily answered: the captain of the marines asks if there was any malice between Claggart and Billy. (Melville's fondness for the word "malice" gives it allegorical insinuations here: Claggart was the permissive agent of Captain Vere.) Blandly, the narrator characterizes the marine officer's question as "unintentionally touching on a spiritual sphere, wholly obscure to Billy's thoughts." That is nice, because it happens to touch on a spiritual sphere which is also wholly obscure to the prosaic and artistically manipulated narrator's thoughts. Billy answers,

"No, there was no malice between us. I never bore malice against the master-at-arms. I am sorry that he is dead. I did not mean to kill him. Could I have used my tongue I would not have struck him. But he foully lied to my face and in the presence of my Captain, and I had to say something, and I could only say it with a blow. God help me!"

392

Considered in terms of Melville's sinister allegory, God help him, indeed! As the trial proceeds, Billy is further asked why Claggart should have "so lied, so maliciously lied, since you declare there was no malice between you?" Ignorant-innocent Billy is completely baffled by that, because he has so far only bitten into the forbidden fruit without getting a good taste of it. Appropriately, he now silently prays to his fatherly Captain for aid: ". . . turning an appealing glance towards Captain Vere as deeming him his best helper and friend." More wormwood! But his prayer is answered after a fashion by Vere:

"The question you put to him comes naturally enough. But can he answer it? Or anybody else? . . . In effect though, as it seems to me, the point you make is hardly material. Quite apart from any conceivable motive actuating the master-at-arms, and irrespective of the provocation of the blow, a martial court must needs in the present case confine its attention to the blow's consequence, which consequence is to be deemed not otherwise than as justly the striker's deed."

There is the letter of the law, and in that single speech, the foreordaining literalism of Captain Vere is revealed in all its ugliness. Billy is confused by Vere's words. "Nor was the same utterance without marked effect upon the three officers, more especially the soldier [i.e., the marine officer]. Couched in it seemed to them a meaning unanticipated, involving a prejudgment on the speaker's part. It served to augment a mental disturbance previously evident enough."

Melville's fondness for ambiguous word-play is apparent throughout, but notice it in that last sentence: the bland narrator is not referring to earlier hints as to the possible "depravity" of Captain Vere. In the larger context, however, the words suggest that. Vere has said that the only responsibility confronting them is to pass judgment on Billy for having struck and killed a superior. Never mind the accidental nature of the killing; never mind the provocation of the blow; never mind that Vere arranged the hideous situation; never mind that Vere is therefore in a sense responsible for what happened. Captain Vere says never mind, in effect; but the captain of the marines refuses to let Vere close the drumhead court as summarily as Vere seems disposed to do. Again the marine officer presses the question:

"Nobody is present—none of the ship's company, I mean, who might shed lateral light, if any is to be had, upon what remains mysterious in this matter?"

Specifically and allegorically, that question puts the finger on a very delicate point, because it even suggests that the asker might somehow be harboring doubts as to truth-telling Vere's right to serve as plaintiff, jury, judge. Vere takes the question in stride:

"That is thoughtfully put; I see your drift. Ah, there is a mystery; but to use a Scriptural phrase, it is a 'mystery of iniquity,' a matter for psychological theologians to discuss. But what has a military court to do with it? Not to add that for us, any possible investigation of it is cut off by the lasting tongue-tie of—him—in yonder . . . The prisoner's deed. With that alone we have to do."

Melville has arranged further allegorical insinuations by the use of a dash between "of" and "him." The lasting "tongue-tie" which Melville could never forgive was the lasting "tongue-tie" of God, as we have seen. Allegorically, then, what more appropriate birth-mark gift of God could Billy receive than a kind of "tongue-tie." There is a further allegorical insinuation, here: Vere at times plays the role of the omnipotent, as Captain of this world in a man-of-war. The really serious tongue-tie is not that of the dead Claggart, but that of the living Vere. Because Vere himself is responsible, it is fitting that he himself should introduce the Biblical term already employed by the narrator: "mystery of iniquity." Allegorically the entire story turns on this question as to where the evil originated, and who is to blame for the entrance of this evil into this human situation. Vere shrugs off the question, here, and disparagingly relegates it to those realms explored by "psychological theologians"—of which Melville is one!

Because Melville's insinuations here invert the original meaning, we should have in mind the passage as it occurs in Paul's Second Letter to the Thessalonians, Chapter Two:

"Now we beseech you, brethren . . . that ye be not soon shaken in mind, or be troubled, neither by spirit, nor by word, nor by letter as from us . . . Let no man deceive you by any means . . . except there come a falling away first, and that man of sin be revealed, and the son of perdition; who opposeth and exalteth himself above all . . . so that he, as God, sitteth in the temple of

God, shewing himself that he is God. . . . For the mystery of iniquity doth already work."

Paul's right-side-up meaning, there, makes the phrase refer specifically to Satan. Melville's wrong-side-up meaning, in *Billy Budd*, makes the phrase refer to Captain Vere; allegorically, to God, the source of iniquity. Once again, Melville has brought us back to his own way of interpreting the ancient theological problem, and again there is the possibility that Melville remembered in Bayle's *Dictionary* a highly pertinent Calvinistic illustration:

"If a Soveraign knew certainly, that if he should place a Man in a Crowd . . . it would raise a Sedition, and occasion a Fight, in which . . . Men should be kill'd, he might very well, according to the rigour of the Law, be look'd upon as the first Author of all those Murthers. It would be to no purpose for him to say, 'I order'd not that Man to strike any Body . . . nor to raise a Sedition; on the contrary, I forbade him to do it. *I have not moved his Arm to kill, nor form'd his Voice to excite the People to fight.*' [italics added] He would be answered, 'You knew certainly that that Man being placed in such Circumstances would be the Cause of those Miseries. It was in your Power to place him in more favourable Circumstances, which might have produced all manner of Happiness.' I am sure he could reply nothing that could put a stop to the murmuring of the People; and if we will speak sincerely, we must confess that nothing can be answered for God, that can silence the Minds of Men."[14]

Bayle is quoting adroitly, there, from his Calvinistic enemy Jurieu to illustrate the casuistry of Christian theological disquisition. Bayle had prepared the way for that quotation, in the previous paragraph, where Bayle himself had said:

"It has been a constant Opinion amongst Christians from the Beginning, that the *Devil* is the Author of all false Religions; . . . that he inspires Men with Errors . . . ; in a word, with all the Crimes that are committed amongst Men; that he deprived Adam and Eve of their Innocency. . . . but as for the Qualities of a Creature, one ought to inquire into the Reason of them, and it cannot be found but in its Cause. You must therefore say that God is the Author of the Devil's Malice, that he himself produced it such as it was . . ."

Although I think *Billy Budd* is a self-sufficient and self-explanatory work of artistic contrivance, those two juxtaposed passages in Bayle's *Dictionary* are convenient to illuminate Melville's sinister allegorical meaning in *Billy Budd*: Vere is responsible not only for Billy's action but also for Claggart's action; God is responsible not only for Adam's action but also for Satan's action. Perhaps I read too much into and out of Melville's fondness for Pierre Bayle; but as Melville so nicely phrases it in *Billy Budd*, "one must determine for himself by such light as this narrative may afford."

19

AFTER Billy is led out of the drumhead court, Captain Vere uncorks some ostensibly persuasive oratory, calculated to justify the sentence which he himself insists that the court must pass, against the better judgment of his subordinates, and without even permitting his subordinates to render their own independent verdict. Arguing consistently from the letter of the law, Vere has no difficulty in making his logic seem cogent. In the premises, however, the reader is likely to be particularly interested in the injustice of Vere's refusal to consider Billy's motive. For allegorical purposes, Melville arranges to let Vere talk like a Calvinist who is answering a Renaissance humanist or a rationalist of the so-called enlightenment:

" 'How can we adjudge to summary and shameful death a fellow-creature innocent before God, and whom we feel to be so?' Does that state it aright? You sign sad assent. Well, I too feel that, the full force of that. It is Nature. But do these buttons that we wear attest that our allegiance is to Nature? No, to the King. Though the ocean, which is inviolate Nature primeval, though this be the element where we move and have our being as sailors, yet as the King's officers lies our duty in a sphere correspondingly natural? So little is that true, that in receiving our commissions we in the most important regards ceased to be natural free-agents."

Again, we are required to read that passage in a Christian frame of reference and then in an anti-Christian frame of reference. Vere speaks from the Christian viewpoint, and he echoes John Calvin, who said, "We are not our own. Therefore, let us not propose it as our end to seek what may be expedient for us according to the flesh. We are not our own. Therefore, let us as far as possible forget ourselves and all things that are ours." To John Calvin, the "natural" impulses of "natural man" were anathema. So Vere says his allegiance is not to Nature but to God.

Now try to evaluate Vere's words, there, from an anti-Christian and a Melvillian frame of reference. Having declared his independence from God, Melville had further declared the sovereignty of natural man. ("We hold these truths to be self-evident . . .") Vere's blasphemy, in this context, is that he urges an allegiance to a Superior, even though such allegiance forces the individual to be unnatural!

Before we consider Vere's next remarks, we may profitably recall Melville's confession to Hawthorne: "I stand for the heart. To the dogs with the head! . . . The reason the mass of men fear God, and *at bottom dislike* Him, is because they rather distrust His heart, and fancy Him all brain like a watch." Now notice that Vere goes on to assert that the dilemma which faces the drumhead court is caused by their mistaken tendency to let the heart interfere with the mind: "But let not warm hearts betray heads that should be cool." By his own actions and words, however, Vere has already demonstrated that his own "head" is not exactly trustworthy. Resorting to his much-needed authority, the letter of the law, Vere hammers away at the inexorable logic of their responsibility to the letter of the law.

Once again the captain of the marines interrupts to suggest that Vere narrows the case too much: "But surely Budd purposed neither mutiny nor homicide." Ironically, this interruption is made to serve as Vere's springboard for his third argument, during the making of which he further unmasks himself. Vere points out that there are two laws: God's law, man's law. In this instance, man's law is the law of the Mutiny Act, and according to the law of the Mutiny Act, Billy must hang, even though his act was not mutinous in spirit, even though God's law must be set aside in order to hang Billy. Happily, as Christian Vere explains, there is the consolation of knowing that "at the Last Assizes it shall acquit" Billy. (Voltaire had fun with this kind of casuistry, in *Candide*: ". . . you will make a prodigious fortune; when a man fails in one world, he succeeds in another.") As far back as the writing of *Moby-Dick*, Melville had taken pleasure in ridiculing the Christian doctrine that because everything is going to be all right in Heaven, we must be content with the sad fate which overtakes such poor people as luckless Billy, here on earth. Captain Vere might even seem to crib from Plotinus Plinlimmon's exegesis: ". . . When they go to heaven, it will be quite another thing. There, they can freely turn the left cheek, because the right cheek will never be smitten. There, they can freely give all to the poor, for *there* there will be no poor to give to. A due appreciation of this matter will do good to man. . . . I but lay down, then, what the best mortal men do daily practice."

But the asininity of Captain Vere has not yet been revealed in all its glory, and Melville proceeds to unbutton him by letting the first lieutenant ask, "Can we not convict and yet mitigate the penalty?" In answer, Vere says:

"Lieutenant, were that clearly lawful for us under the circumstances, consider the consequences of such clemency. The people (meaning the ship's company) have *native sense* [italics added]; most of them are familiar with our naval usage and tradition; and how would they take it? Even could you explain to them—*which our official position forbids* [italics added; allegorically, that is very naughty]—they, long moulded by arbitrary discipline, have not that kind of intelligent responsiveness that might qualify them to comprehend and discriminate. No, to the people the foretopman's deed, however it be worded in the announcement, will be plain homicide committed in a flagrant act of mutiny. What penalty for that should follow, they know. But it does not follow. Why? they will ruminate. You know what sailors are."

Melville knew what sailors were: he was one. He also knew what officers were, in their snobbishly superior and tyrannically brutal attitude toward enlisted men. Here is the zenith of Vere's argument (or the nadir) and in concluding the above remarks, Vere arranges to have Billy formally convicted and sentenced to be hanged at the yardarm, the following morning. Melville has paid out to Vere the last bit of rope needed for Vere to fasten around his own neck: ". . . Why? they will ruminate. You know what sailors are."

But the allegorical insinuations are equally devastating. Christian doctrine explains sin and evil without any difficulty: Whose fault? Whose but man's? Melville suggests that "the people" have been conditioned by "naval usage and tradition"; that they have been discouraged from making "that kind of intelligent responsiveness that might qualify them to comprehend and discriminate." Baby Budd (twenty-one years old) is a good example. Remember Tom Paine: "When I contemplate the natural dignity of man . . . I become irritated at the attempt to govern mankind by force and fraud . . . and can scarcely avoid disgust at those who are thus imposed upon."

20

AT this illuminating moment in the narrative, Melville lets his narrator make a bland reference to the analogy between Vere's action and Captain Mackenzie's action, aboard the *Somers*:

"Not unlikely they were brought to something more or less akin to that harassed frame of mind which in the year 1842 actuated the commander of the U.S. brig-of-war *Somers* . . . an act vindicated by a naval court of inquiry subsequently convened ashore. History, and here cited without comment. True, the circumstances on board the *Somers* were different from those on board the *Indomitable*. But the urgency felt, well-warranted or otherwise, was much the same."

The bland narrator thus refers to the analogous action of the *Somers* incident as a method of vindicating Captain Vere's action. Melville endows the narrator's remarks with just enough equivocation to make the same words suggest something diametrically different, when colored by the larger context of the narrative. "History, and here cited without comment," indeed!

21

As soon as Captain Vere has forced his predestinating will on the drumhead court, and has revealed himself as a precise disciplinarian, he is described as reverting to the role of tender father toward Billy. Melville bitterly permits the narrator to praise Vere for this superb display of humanitarianism. The sinister allegorical correlations are these: the God-like Vere now explains to the Adam-like Billy the full nature of his sin, describes the penalty, teaches him how to accept the penalty, and then comforts him! As it was in the beginning, Melville bitterly implies, so now: this Adam-like Billy is too ignorant and innocent to recognize the injustice of the penalty imposed upon him ("impressed" upon him); so he meekly submits and accepts:

"It was Captain Vere himself who of his own motion communicated the findings of the court to the prisoner; for that purpose going to the compartment, where he was in custody, and bidding the marine there to withdraw for the time.

"Beyond the communication of the sentence, what took place at this interview was never known. But, in view of the character of the twain closeted in that stateroom, *each radically sharing in the rarer qualities of one nature* [italics added]—so rare, indeed, as to be all but incredible to average minds, however much cultivated—some conjecture may be ventured."

The "right" meaning makes this a caustic passage, even though the "average mind" of the average reader may not immediately recognize the insinuation. It could even suggest this: like father, like son! Billy has been condemned to death as a sinner and a criminal. In the Melvillian sense, Captain Vere deserves to be condemned to death, as a sinner and a criminal. Allegorically, even as Billy's sin has its source in Captain Vere's sin, so man's "original sin" has its cause in God. Less darkly, we are told that there is another sharing. After the manner of the Confidence-Man, Captain Vere wins the confidence and the "charity" of Billy, and teaches him the "radical sharing" of that abject attitude of submission to, and acceptance of, a higher will. The bitterness of Melville's meaning, here, should be obvious:

"It would have been in consonance with the spirit of Captain Vere should he on this occasion have concealed nothing from the condemned one—should he indeed have frankly disclosed to him the part he himself had played in bringing about the decision, at the same time revealing his actuating motives. On Billy's side it is not improbable that such a confession would have been received in much the same spirit that prompted it. Not without a sort of joy indeed he might have appreciated the brave opinion of him implied in his Captain making such a confidant of him. [Calomel!] Nor as to the sentence itself could he have been insensible that it was imparted to him as to one not afraid to die. [An echo of Addison's last words!] Even more may have been. Captain Vere in the end may have developed the passion sometimes latent under an exterior stoical and indifferent. *He was old enough to have been*

Billy's father [italics added; allegorically, he is]. The austere devotee of military duty, letting himself melt back into what remains primeval in our formalised humanity, may in the end have caught Billy to his heart even as Abraham may have caught young Isaac on the brink of resolutely offering him up in obedience to the exacting behest. But there is no telling the sacrament—seldom if in any case revealed to the gadding world wherever under circumstances at all akin to those here attempted to be set forth—two of great Nature's nobler order embrace. There is privacy at the time, inviolable to the survivor, and holy oblivion, the sequel to each diviner magnanimity, providentially covers all at last."

Although the narrator's frame of reference there is Christian, Melville's arrangement to let the narrator merely guess as to what occurred in that secret interview may be viewed as another artistic device for pondering (with anti-Christian insinuations) the subject of death. Sarcastically, Melville wonders just how God-like Vere explained to Adam-like Billy that death must be the price exacted for his sin; that this death sentence must be accepted as incredibly just. The Abraham-Isaac reference recalls the stern love of God, which commanded Abraham to murder his own son (or at least to be willing to do so) as sacrificial proof of Abraham's love for God. Melville's most sardonic insinuations occur in the last two sentences. In Christian thought, the nobility of death rests in the belief that through death the individual may ascend to meet and embrace his Maker. There is indeed no telling the sacrament, Melville implies, because the dead never return to tell us about that oblivion to which they have gone. Or, to phrase much the same thought sardonically and sarcastically in Christian phrases, "There is privacy at the time, inviolable to the survivor, and holy oblivion, the sequel to each divine magnanimity, providentially covers all at last." Schopenhauer's terms are pertinent: death is indeed oblivion and oblivion is the "diviner magnanimity"; but because the completeness of that oblivion is "providentially" concealed from the gullible among the living, the gullible are able to dream up and believe in all kinds of pleasant fictions as to an after-life.

To round out this pretty chapter of pretty thoughts, Melville permits his narrator to add more words of praise for the probable fatherliness of the God-like Vere: he suffers "agony" over Billy's

401

predestinated and foreordained fate. Again the equivocations suggest that Melville is taking another scornful fling at the theological concept that whatever the All-Father God does to his children (including His murder of them) is for their own good; that it hurts God more than it hurts the children:

"The first to encounter Captain Vere in the act of leaving the compartment was the senior lieutenant. The face he beheld, for the moment one expressive of the agony of the strong, was to that officer, though a man of fifty, a startling revelation. That the condemned one suffered less than he who mainly had effected the condemnation was apparently indicated by the former's exclamation in the scene soon perforce to be touched upon."

Oh yes, apparently! That "exclamation" will be Billy's four-word submission to, and acceptance of, the blessedness of his murderer. Ignorant-innocent Billy is thus to be placed in allegorical accord with ignorant-innocent Adam, who thus blesses God for punishing him, in Milton's *Paradise Lost*:

> O goodness infinite, goodness immense!
> That all this good of evil shall produce,
> And evil turn to good; more wonderful
> That that which by creation first brought forth
> Light out of darkness! full of doubt I stand,
> Whether I should repent me now of sin
> By mee done and occasion'd, or rejoice
> Much more, that much more good thereof shall spring,
> To God more glory, more good will to Men
> From God, and over wrath grace shall abound.

22

THE continuing action of the narrative provides further "linked analogies" between the military depravity of Captain Vere and the divine depravity of God, as Melville viewed it. When Captain Vere issues his summons to the crew and informs them as to the death sentence passed on Billy, he explains merely that Billy killed Claggart; that Billy has been given the justice provided by the full military rights of trial by a summary court. These half-truths amount to malicious lies, and recall Vere's earlier insistence that the "people" must not be told the truth because they would not understand the truth! Then Melville again permits his narrator to utter further commendatory remarks which are (quite apart from the narrator's meaning) superbly equivocal:

"The word mutiny was not named in what he said. He refrained, too, from making the occasion an opportunity for any preachment as to the maintenance of discipline, thinking, perhaps, that under existing circumstances in the Navy the consequence of violating discipline should be made to speak for itself."

Indeed it does speak for itself, very convincingly; the wages of sin is death: "Their Captain's announcement was listened to by the throng of standing sailors in a dumbness like that of a seated congregation of believers in Hell listening to the clergyman's announcement of his Calvinistic text."

This second specific reference to the doctrine of John Calvin reenforces the artistic evidence that Melville has sarcastically and bitterly contrived the entire story of *Billy Budd* to illuminate his own reactionary interpretation of a Calvinistic text.

23

MELVILLE further avails himself of opportunities to ridicule Christian concepts, and particularly the concept of submissive acceptance, by describing what happened to Billy as he lay in irons on the upper gun-deck, awaiting the hour of his execution. It would seem that Melville asks the reader to recognize that Vere's words, spoken to Billy in private, were equivalent to a narcotic shot of religious dogma; that the doped Billy lies tranced by Vere's dose of comfort; by insinuation, there is a triple pun in saying that Billy is "nipped in the vice of fate":

"But now, lying between the two guns, as nipped in the vice of fate, Billy's agony, mainly proceeding from a generous young heart's virgin experience of the diabolical incarnate and effective in some men—the tension of that agony was over now. It survived not the something healing in the closeted interview with Captain Vere."

Superficially, the "diabolical incarnate and effective" refers to Claggart; in a sinister sense, it refers to Vere; in Melville's anti-Christian allegorical sense, it refers to God. Thus Melville increases the irony by hinting that Vere (or God) himself had first caused Billy's (or Adam's) agony, and then had assuaged it. The passage continues:

"Without movement, he lay as in a trance, that adolescent expression previously noted as his, taking on something akin to the look of a child slumbering in the cradle when the warm hearthglow of the still chamber at night plays on the dimples that at whiles mysteriously form in the cheek, silently coming and going there. For now and then in the gyved one's trance, a serene happy light born of some wandering reminiscence or dream would diffuse itself over his face, and then wane away only anew to return."

Now isn't that a sweet picture? The Wordsworthian overtones of intimation are fairly overt: we are only pilgrims here, having come from heaven which is our home, and having the assurance that when we die we shall return home and thus escape from the evils of this world. Billy is on his way home. The narrator's tone is Christian; Melville's tone is the derisive, sardonic, sarcastic tone of disbelief and denial.

24

IF we remember Rev. Falsgrave, in *Pierre*, we might feel quite certain that Melville would not pass up an opportunity to increase his ridicule of Christian doctrine, here, by introducing the Chaplain as a professional Christian. It should be remembered that, in *White-Jacket*, he indulged in some covertly ruthless sneering as he described and commented on the *Neversink's* Chaplain. Here, however, the bland narrator will naturally praise the Chaplain, and so the Melvillian meaning lies concealed just beneath the thin surface:

"The Chaplain coming to see him and finding him thus, and perceiving no sign that he was conscious of his presence, attentively regarded him for a space, then slipping aside, withdrew for the time, peradventure feeling that even he, the minister of Christ, though receiving his stipend from Mars, had no consolation to proffer which could result in a peace transcending that which he beheld. But in the small hours he came again. And the prisoner, now awake to his surroundings noticed his approach, and civilly, all but cheerfully, welcomed him. But it was to little purpose that

in the interview following the good man sought to bring Billy
Budd to some Godly understanding that he must die, and at dawn.
True, Billy himself freely referred to his death as a thing close at
hand; but it was something in the way that children will refer to
death in general, who yet among their other sports will play a
funeral with hearse and mourners."

In the sinister sense, Billy has been provided with his religious
formula: an abject worship of Captain Vere's benevolence. Ignorant and childlike as he is, he has no room in his mind, particularly
at such a time, for a study of comparative religions, and so when
the Chaplain tries to indoctrinate him, Billy shows no particular
interest. Vere has already "saved" him! But the Chaplain's leave-
taking of Billy Budd is so contrived that Melville can achieve,
in tableau form, another backhanded swipe at Christianity. In his
innocence, Billy himself might be viewed as a Christ-like character, foresaken, and about to be crucified. By contrast, this Chaplain, who is ostensibly a disciple of Christ, has sold out to Mars; to
the vested interests, as opposed to the man-of-peace interests—an
antithesis which Melville had developed in *White-Jacket*. So what
could be more appropriate, in the darker frame of meaning, than
to let the Chaplain perform some act toward Billy Budd which
would place the Chaplain, emblematically, in the role of a betraying Judas Iscariot:

". . . he reluctantly withdrew; but in his emotion not without
first performing an act strange enough in an Englishman, and
under the circumstances yet more so in any regular priest. Stoop-
ing over, he kissed on the fair cheek his fellow man, a felon in
martial law, one who, though in the confines of death, he felt he
could never convert to a dogma; nor for all that did he fear for
his future."

The literal reader may be annoyed by any suggestion that this
touching passage suggests an Iscariot tableau. Very well, then,
consider the explicit form of "betrayal" which Melville develops,
in the narrator's next-paragraph comment on the tableau:

"Marvel not that having been acquainted with the young sailor's
essential innocence (an irruption of heretic thought hard to sup-
press), the worthy man lifted not a finger to avert the doom of
such a martyr to martial discipline. So to do would not only have
been as idle as invoking the desert, but would also have been an

405

audacious transgression of the bounds of his function, one as exactly prescribed to him by military law as that of the boatswain or any other naval officer. Bluntly put, a chaplain is the minister of the Prince of Peace serving in the host of the God of War— Mars. As such, he is as incongruous as a musket would be on the altar at Christmas. Why then is he here? Because he indirectly subserves the purpose attested by the cannon; because too he lends the sanction of the religion of the meek to that which practically is the abrogation of everything but brute force."

Bluntly put, indeed! It would seem that Melville deliberately pushes his bland narrator out of the way, in those last two sentences, and speaks directly to the reader. A chaplain who lends Christian sanction to brute force might be said to betray his trust, even as Judas Iscariot betrayed Christ. But in what sense could a man of God be said to subserve, indirectly, the purpose attested by the cannon? In Melville's sense, God Himself is the supreme military disciplinarian, who ultimately resorts to the abrogation of everything but brute force: death, which is murder. Or, in the terms of Ahab's prayer, ". . . thou canst but kill; and all are killed."

25

HAVING hinted an allegorical correlation between the First Adam and the Second Adam[15] (having suggested that Billy reflects the ignorance-innocence of both Adam and Christ), Melville has nevertheless permitted his narrator to maintain an overtly Christian tone and viewpoint, throughout. To maintain the sustained irony in the denouement is not difficult because Billy himself has been converted to the true faith of Captain Vere, and Melville can thus arrange to let Billy's last words, at the moment of his peculiar crucifixion, be similar in tone and meaning to the last words spoken by Christ on the cross, as reported in Luke: "Father, into thy hands I commend my spirit." Favoring the darker interpretation (suggested in *Clarel*) as to the meaning of Christ's words as reported in Matthew and Mark ("My God, my God, why hast thou forsaken me?"), Melville could nevertheless take sardonic pleasure in letting ignorant-innocent Billy die praising his murderer. Thus Billy's last words are indeed fitting and proper, in either the Christian or the ironically anti-Christian frame of reference. So Billy's last words can supply the supreme irony of the entire narrative, because they are so palpably at odds with the dark facts of the situation; those last words can even be used to hypnotize the crew, because the crew is also duped, doped, kept in ignorance as to the truth. Melville surrounds these last words with additional ironies by concealing his belief that death is eternal oblivion, and by pretending to imply that Billy immediately ascends to the Land of Chronometricals:

"At the penultimate moment, his words, his only ones, words wholly unobstructed in the utterance, were these—'God bless Captain Vere!' Syllables so unanticipated coming from one with the ignominious hemp about his neck—a conventional felon's benediction directed aft towards the quarters of honor; syllables too delivered in the clear melody of a singing-bird on the point of launching from the twig, had a phenomenal effect, not unenhanced by the rare personal beauty of the young sailor spiritualised now through late experiences so poignantly profound.

"Without volition, as it were, as if indeed the ship's populace were the vehicles of some vocal current-electric, with one voice, from alow and aloft, came a resonant sympathetic echo—'God bless Captain Vere!' And yet at that instant Billy alone must have been in their hearts, even as he was in their eyes.

"At the pronounced words and the spontaneous echo that voluminously rebounded them, Captain Vere, either through stoic self-control or a sort of momentary paralysis induced by emotional shock, stood erectly rigid as a musket in the ship-armourer's rack.

"The hull, deliberately recovering from the periodic roll to leeward, was just regaining an even keel, when the last signal, *the preconcerted dumb one* [italics added; allegorically significant], was given. At the same moment it *chanced* [italics added] that the vapoury fleece hanging low in the East was shot through with a soft glory as of the fleece of the Lamb of God seen in mystical vision, and simultaneously therewith, watched by the wedged mass of upturned faces, Billy ascended; and ascending, took the full rose of the dawn.

"In the pinioned figure, arrived at the yard-end, to the wonder of all, no motion was apparent save that created by the slow roll

407

of the hull, in moderate weather so majestic in a great ship heavy-cannoned."

There is no need to try to exhaust the excruciating ironies in that passage. Notice, however, the deliberately sarcastic and ridiculous analogy which Melville establishes between Billy's last words (just before he is to be killed) and the trivial note of "a singing-bird on the point of launching from the twig." The analogy would scarcely seem to be apt, unless we remember that Melville is simultaneously pitying Billy and sneering at Billy's stupidity, in having accepted the fraud of Vere's lies as truthful and sorrowing words of a loving fatherly superior. Allegorically, Melville implies, this is the fraud of God, and hence the ironic appropriateness of the pun implicit in the symbolism of the sky: "a soft glory as of the fleece of the Lamb of God seen in mystical vision." If we are inclined to think of the verb "fleece" as merely modern slang, we can find from the dictionary that it has long been a verb in good standing; that it means (1) "To sheer (sheep)" or (2) "To strip off money or property by fraud; despoil." Thus the passage is available in a Christian sense or in a Melvillian sense. So also the "full rose of the dawn." Melville's sarcastic commentaries on love, in *Pierre*, make allusive use of Shelley ("Death is busy everywhere") to equate love and death, and a fragment of one caustically sardonic passage from *Pierre* may be appropriate here, because Billy is ironically represented as embracing an emblem of divine love when he is actually (in the Melvillian sense) embracing his brutally and unjustly inflicted death: "Love is both Creator's and Saviour's gospel to mankind; a volume bound in rose-leaves, clasped with violets, and by the beaks of humming-birds printed with peach-juice on the leaves of lilies." That sentence from *Pierre* is excruciatingly and misanthropically bitter, in much the same sense that the underlying meaning of this entire passage which describes Billy's murder is bitter.

Because the man-of-war, and everything connected with it, has been represented by Melville as a symbol of brute force, the description of Captain Vere's response to the unexpected blessing, from condemned man and crew, is in keeping with the larger symbolism: he is no more moved by the blessing than a musket would be moved.

Just one more term deserves comment: "seen in mystical vision,"

of course, the soft glory as of the fleece of the Lamb of God has a
sacred and symbolic meaning. For Melville, however, the true
mystic was an individual who had had his eyes opened by painful
experience. In this sense, Melville could imagine that Christ became a true mystic only in that moment before his death, when
(as Melville liked to think) he saw God as a Forsaker and a Fraud,
according to Melville's interpretation of the words quoted in
Matthew and Mark. A credulous mystic, Melville thought, was a
fake mystic or a self-deceived no-mystic. He elaborated these
views in *Pierre*:

"For he who is most practically and deeply conversant with
mysticisms and mysteries; he who professionally deals in mysticisms and mysteries himself; often that man, more than any body
else, is disposed to regard such things in others as very deceptively
bejuggling; and likewise is apt to be rather materialistic in all his
own merely personal notions (as in their practical lives, with
priests of Eleusinian religions), and more than any other man, is
often inclined, at the bottom of his soul, to be uncompromisingly
skeptical on all novel visionary hypotheses of any kind. It is only
the no-mystics, or the half-mystics, who, properly speaking, are
credulous. So that in Pierre was presented the apparent anomaly
of a mind, which by becoming really profound in itself, grew
skeptical of all tendered profundities; whereas, the contrary is
generally supposed."[16]

26

AFTER presenting the chapter describing Billy's death, Melville
adds a half-dozen chapters which are of particular importance
because they provide oblique corroboration of the sinister allegorical meaning implicit throughout. All of these chapters at the
end seem to be built around the allegorically represented notion
that the Christian religion is an opiate for the "people" (as Captain
Vere calls the ship's company). In the first of these chapters, a
discussion between the Purser and the Surgeon represents the
Purser as asking whether Billy's submissive death, without even
a reflexive struggle, was indicative of his having been drugged.
Melville contrives to represent the Surgeon as seeming to have
certain information which he is unwilling to impart. The conclusion correlates the entire conversation with theological concepts:

" 'But tell me, my dear Sir,' pertinaciously continued the other, 'was the man's death effected by the halter, or was it a species of euthanasia?'

" '*Euthanasia*, Mr. Purser, is something like your will-power; I doubt its authenticity as a scientific term—begging your pardon again. It is at once imaginative and metaphysical,—in short, Greek. But' (abruptly changing his tone) 'there is a case in the sick-bay which I do not care to leave to my assistants. Beg your pardon, but excuse me.' And rising from the mess he formally withdrew."

That teasing passage represents the Surgeon as an "enlightened" and "doubting" non-believer in the metaphysical; one who denies the possibility that there could be any mode or act of inducing death painlessly by metaphysical means.

In the next of these final chapters, the narrator explains that a symbolic action, occurring at the time of Billy's sea burial, had caused some agitation among the superstitious sailors; but that this agitation was quickly subdued by a roll of the drum, beating to quarters. Vere explains the reason why he gave the extraordinary order:

" 'With mankind,' he would say, 'forms, measured forms are everything; and that is the import couched in the story of Orpheus with his lyre spell-binding the wild denizens of the woods.' "

In other words, the roll of the drum had had a narcotic effect, an opiate effect, on the enlisted men. In this context, a play on words, indeed a pun, is suggested by the term, "lyre": Orpheus understood the art of spell-binding and of hypnosis. Vere's analogy is again uncomplimentary toward "the people" in that it equates them with "the wild denizens of the woods."

The chapter which follows establishes another teasing and covert analogy, this time an analogy between the way in which Billy died and the way in which Captain Vere died. Mortally wounded in an encounter between His Majesty's Ship *Indomitable* and the French Revolutionary man-of-war *Atheiste* (emblematically suited to avenge the unjust death of an underling impressed from the *Rights-of-Man*), Captain Vere dies somehow drugged, and as he dies he utters, as his last words, the name of the underling who had been doubly "impressed" by "forms, measured forms":

"Not long before death, while lying under the influence of that magical drug which, soothing the physical frame, mysteriously operates on the subtlest element in man, he was heard to murmur words inexplicable to his attendant—'Billy Budd, Billy Budd.' That these were not the accents of remorse, would seem clear from what the attendant said . . ."

In the fourth additional chapter, another kind of opiate is administered to the people. The narrator tells how the "naval chronicle of the time, an authorized weekly publication" (note well the word "authorized" with its Biblical connotations) misrepresented the facts concerning the fall of Billy, and the consequent justification of death. The bland narrator, still defending the frauds of physical and metaphysical tyranny, makes this explanation of the lies in that authorized version of the incident: "It was doubtless for the most part written *in good faith* [italics added], though the medium, partly rumour, through which the facts must have reached the writer, seemed to deflect, and in part falsify them." The allegorical insinuation, here, is that there are "linked analogies" not only between what happened to Billy and what happened to Adam but also between the report of Billy's fall, in this "naval chronicle of the time" and the report of Adam's fall in that "authorized" word of God, Genesis. Here is the fabulous account of what happened to Billy:

" 'On the tenth of the last month a deplorable occurrence took place on board H.M.S. *Indomitable.* John Claggart, the ship's master-at-arms, discovering that some sort of plot was incipient among an inferior section of the ship's company, and that the ringleader was one William Budd; he, Claggart, in the act of arraigning the man before the Captain, was vindictively stabbed to the heart by the suddenly drawn sheaf-knife of Budd. . . . The enormity of the crime and the extreme *depravity* [italics added] of the criminal, appear the greater in view of the character of the victim, a middle-aged man, respectable and discreet, belonging to that minor official grade . . . upon whom, as none know better than the commissioned gentlemen, the efficiency of His Majesty's navy so largely depends. . . .' "

That the word "depravity" should occur in Melville's contriving of this authorized version, and that it should be applied to Billy, is in perfect keeping with the sustained irony of the narrative. The narrator's comment on this authorized version is nice: "The

411

above item appearing in a publication now long ago superannuated and forgotten is all that hitherto has stood in human record to attest what manner of men respectively were John Claggart and Billy Budd." One suggestion, there, is that the blandly Christian-spirited narrator has felt himself called upon to correct the previous misrepresentations by giving an "inside story" which would more accurately justify the ways of Billy to Claggart and the ways of Vere to Billy. Melville's insinuation is that if any reader should be a literalist, even as Vere and the artistically contrived narrator were letter-of-the-law men, a literal meaning of this new "inside story" will merely substitute a new opiate for the older opiate. Obviously, those who are inclined to believe in the letter of the law are also inclined to take at face value whatever they believe in print. Like Billy, they are by no means of a satirical turn, and as a result, the "sinister dexterity" of "double meanings" and "insinuations" is wasted on them.

To provide the final allegorical irony, Melville permits the narrator to tell how "the people" aboard His Majesty's Ship *Indomitable,* so long doped and drugged by "forms, measured forms," mingle with their feeling that Billy's death was necessary and inevitable the "instinctive" feeling that Billy died a martyr, victimized by fraud and foul play: "*Ignorant though they were of the real facts of the happening, and not thinking* [italics added] but that the penalty was somehow unavoidably inflicted from the naval point of view; for all that, they instinctively felt that Billy was a sort of man as incapable of mutiny as of wilful murder." Thus brooding over the mystery of iniquity, the people cut mementoes from the spar from which Billy was hanged: "To them a chip of it was as a piece of the Cross."

27

THE manuscript of *Billy Budd* shows that at one time Melville had thought to conclude with an abstract generalization which would group the major characters, antithetically, in terms of their emblematic values, thus:

"Here ends a story not unwarranted by what sometimes happens in this incomprehensible world of ours—Innocence and infamy, *spiritual depravity* [italics added] and fair repute."[17]

The two contrasting allegorical implications of the passage provide a suitable summary of Melville's artistic methods and thematic concerns. In terms of that allegorical meaning which would satisfy the orthodox Christian reader, the emblematic correlations are clear: Billy Budd represents innocence, and Claggart represents infamy; Claggart represents depravity and Billy Budd represents fair repute. However, in terms of that sinister allegorical meaning which better satisfied Melville, the emblematic correlations are far more involved. Once over lightly: Billy Budd represents innocence again, Claggart represents infamy again; but Captain Vere picks up the other two values and shares them both with Claggart. Take it through again, in part: Claggart is certainly emblematic of infamy and depravity, and even in certain quarters and at certain times (with the early Billy Budd, for example), Claggart would seem emblematic of fair repute. But Claggart plays a kind of confidence-man game with Billy Budd, in order to seduce him; furthermore, be it remembered, it was Captain Vere himself who looked on Claggart the informer and remembered that he was the Captain's "own subordinate and charged among other things with police surveillance." By emblematic and allegorical extension, Claggart is an agent of Vere, an agent of God. His powers are permissive, even as Satan's powers are permissive in Christian theological dogma. By extension, then, Claggart and Vere do indeed share the infamy and depravity, but only through the permissive will of the "Maker of All that is Fair." Who is to blame? On whom does the ultimate responsibility rest? Who is the Original Sinner? The answer is made clear by the allegorical narrative. Yet the ultimate irony of that answer, for Melville, would seem to be that the Guilty One should so largely manage to conceal His depravity behind a mask of fair repute. What kind of depravity? Natural? Melville wrote, "Spiritual depravity."

In conclusion, we may ask again how it is possible that anyone who has read *Billy Budd* carefully could ever describe it as Melville's "Testament of Acceptance." But we know the answer to that: Melville cunningly arranged to have certain kinds of readers arrive at exactly that mistaken interpretation. Artistically and thematically, then, *Billy Budd* is cut from the same piece of cloth (a dark sort of spiritual sail-cloth) which supplied the makings for

White-Jacket, Moby-Dick, Pierre, The Confidence-Man. No doubt
Hawthorne was right in saying that Melville could never be comfortable in his unbelief; no doubt but that Melvilles' wistfulness
for belief had much to do with making him so furiously resentful
(even jealous) toward Christian believers; furiously angry with
God for being God, and for robbing him of belief. Motivated by
his mingled disillusionment, hate, skepticism, agnosticism, wistfulness, Melville projected his complex narratives not merely because
he was caught on the horns of what some like to view as a profoundly ambiguous paradox but also because he took comfort and
delight in employing ambiguities and equivocations as stylistic
devices for hoodwinking and deceiving those readers whom he
hated because they would be inclined to resent the dark implications of his single thematic concern. His obsession, which remained
quite constant, achieved an increasingly Schopenhauerish in-
tensity of hate toward the end of his life. On the last page of the
manuscript of *Billy Budd* he wrote, "END OF BOOK April 19th,
1891." He died on September 28, 1891.

CONCLUSION

CHAPTER XII

We are, I know not how, double in ourselves, so that what we believe we disbelieve, and cannot rid ourselves of what we condemn.

MONTAIGNE

No utter surprise can come to him
  Who reaches Shakespeare's core;
That which we seek and shun is there—
  Man's final lore.

MELVILLE, *" 'The Coming Storm' "*

CONCLUSION

In my analysis and interpretation of Herman Melville's art and thought, I have consciously and arbitrarily restricted my approach: I have tried to present and resolve what I see as the basic or fundamental problems posed by Melville's artistic and non-artistic attitudes toward his materials, and toward his readers; also, the related problems as to the readers' aesthetic responsibility to Melville's art.

Different as Melville's art is from that of Henry James, these two outstanding American storytellers have this much in common: each invokes, evokes, demands a high degree of close attention, close reading. Their exacting claims, in this regard, are justified by the skill and genius with which each one orders, fashions, shapes, controls the significance of artistic statements, to achieve effects which enable the close reader to "go beyond statement to the meaning which is still unuttered," as Joyce phrased it. For the reader, then, there are two kinds of fascination. First, there is the fascination of learning to cope with the complexities of artistic statement. Thereafter, because artistic statement in the novel indirectly reveals the artist's own personal viewpoint, there is the added fascination of recognizing, perceiving, understanding that personal viewpoint. In this connection, some remarks made by Henry James in his preface to *Lady Barbarina* may help to illuminate my own attitude, in my approach to Herman Melville:

"One never really chooses one's general range of vision—the experience from which ideas and themes and suggestions spring: this proves ever what it has *had* to be, this is one with the very turn one's life has taken; so that whatever it 'gives,' whatever it makes us feel, and think of, we regard very much as imposed and inevitable. The subject thus pressed upon the artist is the necessity of his own case, and the fruit of his own consciousness; which truth makes and has ever made of any quarrel with his subject, any stupid attempt to go behind *that*, the true stultification of criticism. . . . The thing of profit is to *have* your experience—to recognise and understand it, and for this almost any will do; there being surely no absolute ideal about it beyond getting from it all it has to give. The artist—for it is of this strange brood we speak—has but to have his honest sense of life to find it fed at every pore even as the birds of the air are fed . . ."[1]

Speaking from the viewpoint of a highly conscious artist, Henry James there illuminates the particular problems which confront us, in our attempt to cope with Melville's art and thought. Somewhere else, James says that the deepest quality of a work of art will always be the quality of the mind of the producer. I see it that way, particularly if we take his use of the word "mind," there, to signify that complex response of the artist; a response which finds expression in the blending of artistic matter and manner. As many others have pointed out, the creative process has two distinct phases: first, what life does to the artist, and then what the artist does to life, or makes of life, in retaliation. Closely related is the fact that the non-artistic response, which expresses itself first in the complex moral idiom of the artist-as-human-being, always proves to be the major factor which shapes and controls the differently complex idiom of that artist. Indeed, as I have tried to demonstrate, one additional pleasure available to the contemplative reader of Melville is the discovery of that close relationship between these two idioms.

To increase our understanding, I have also tried to give some brief indication as to the factors which shaped these two closely related idioms, in Melville. Of these factors, the major ones seem to have been his social training as a child and his religious training as a child, in his own home. Absorbing and intricate as Melville's literary art proves to be, and praiseworthy as that intricacy certainly is, the disturbing fact remains that a comparison between his artistically expressed range of vision and that of other celebrated literary figures (James, for example) reveals that Melville's range was limited by his inability to achieve some mature and working reconciliation of his confused inner conflicts; that Melville's art dramatizes, more vividly than anything else, a kind of arrested development. Spellbound by his own disillusionments, he became stranded in the narcissistic shallows and miseries of those disillusionments. The turn his life happened to take was an unfortunately inverted turn. Suffering from barked shins, during his youth, he quite naturally reacted with somewhat childish and spoiled-child wilfulness; but most of us are inclined to be a bit surprised to watch Melville spend his life kicking to pieces the furniture over which he had stumbled during his youth.

Here we verge, perhaps, on what James calls that "stupid attempt" which is "the true stultification of criticism." I have taken that risk, however, because my primary concern is to understand Melville's art, even though I cannot entirely resist criticizing Melville for being what he was. I have done my best to accept Henry James' statement that whatever life gives an artist and makes an artist feel or think, may as well be regarded in retrospect as imposed and inevitable. Because the subject thus pressed on the artist must be the necessity of his own case and the fruit of his consciousness, our pleasure has been to discover what profit Melville found in recognizing his own experience for what it was, and what profit it proved to be for him and us, artistically.

But it seems to me that James is on thin ice, here, even as I am. As James so well suggests, it is inevitable that each artist shall, in some sense or other, always be telling his own story as to what life did to him and what he did to life in retaliation. Melville seemed compelled to devote most of his art to the emblematic telling and retelling of his spiritual autobiography, with the main emphasis on disillusionment. Now there are many different artistic ways of simultaneously getting at, and getting outside, self-revelation. The contrast between James and Melville is again helpful. James, like

419

so many other literary artists, demonstrated that one of the best artistic ways of getting outside self is to look backward in time and contemplate certain inherently dramatic tensions in the artist's own earlier experience, and then to translate those tensions into symbolic actions, from the detached and mature perspective of later life. Obviously, there is nothing wrong with using one's own disillusionment as raw materials for storytelling; for that kind of storytelling which Melville himself referred to, in *Pierre*, as "Hamletism." Now I think we can differentiate between thin ice and thick ice. Although I may be wrong, it seems to me that one important part of Shakespeare's artistic validity, in *Hamlet*, rests on his having chosen to draw from his own personal understanding of disillusionment and project it into symbolic action, *after* he had passed far enough beyond that phase of disillusionment to achieve detached perspective; to give a three-dimensional representation of disillusionment. As a result, the mature members of Shakespeare's audience contemplate the unfolding action of *Hamlet* with a growing awareness that they are gradually being shown "disillusionment" from several different sides. Shakespeare himself has so controlled his artistic study of "disillusionment" that the sophisticated playgoer may depart with nicely balanced responses to the central character: a sense of being simultaneously critically sympathetic and sympathetically critical. James understood the artistic principle involved there, and it constitutes thick ice for him. But Melville's artistic limitation would seem to rest in part on the apparent necessity of his projecting his own personal Hamletism into symbolic actions, *before* he had achieved a sufficiently mature perspective to give him and us a sense of adequate detachment. Perhaps it is not a stultification of criticism to point that out.

Aware of this technical problem in presenting Hamletism, Melville himself experimented constantly with various ways of giving an artistic illusion of his having achieved that detachment which he simultaneously desired and lacked. In a technical sense, he may be said to have solved that problem only in *Moby-Dick* and in *Billy Budd*. In a more profound sense, however, he merely gave himself (and some of his readers) the illusion of artistic detachment, or as James would say, the illusion of an illusion. Melville felt that he had made some kind of progress through various phases of disillusionment, because he could measure the growing

420

gulf between his youthful Christian idealism and his subsequently anti-Christian skepticism and agnosticism. But it is extremely important for us to remember that there are just as definitely "sophomorean" (Melville's word) forms of skepticism and agnosticism, as of idealism; that there are just as definitely mature forms of skepticism and agnosticism, as of idealism. Any one of these three modes of thought is far more valid if each succeeds in paying homage to, and making alliances with, the others. They are not mutually exclusive. Because the concepts were so important to Melville, and therefore important to our understanding of his art, let us consider them separately.

The root meaning of the word "agnosticism" merely indicates an attitude or notion that the full significance and attributes of some phenomena are unknown and unknowable; that all knowledge is therefore relative and uncertain. We too frequently make the mistake of using the word in either a perverted or a pejorative sense. Confronted with the root meaning of the word, however, who would be so completely lacking in humility as to insist that he was not, in any degree, an agnostic?

The root meaning of the word "skepticism" merely indicates the attitude of thoughtfulness, reflectiveness, contemplation; the attitude which challenges and doubts evidence, in order to establish (when possible) the validity of evidence. Again we too frequently make the mistake of using that word in either a perverted or a pejorative sense. Confronted with the root meaning of the word, who would be so completely lacking in humility as to insist that he was not, in any degree, a skeptic?

The root meaning of the word "idealism" merely indicates an attitude that non-material values exist and that these non-material values can be perceived. Who, then, would take any satisfaction in saying that he was not, in any degree, an idealist?

Now consider the manner in which Melville exposed himself to a great deal of anguish and punishment by feeling that he was compelled to work out some interplay of idealism, skepticism, agnosticism, even though he lacked either the temperament or the discipline to make those three concepts lie down together. His initial idealism, represented by his youthful and secondhand faith in the essential tenets of his Calvinistic heritage, was necessarily an immature idealism, which he necessarily outgrew. When he

421

became old enough to discover the immaturity of that secondhand idealism which had been his, he was still so young as to indulge, necessarily, in an immature skepticism. Then, after he had read widely (not wisely, not well) in the history of philosophic rationalism, he indulged in an immature agnosticism.

Worse than that, he mistakenly employed his skepticism and agnosticism merely as destructive weapons to bludgeon the idealism of others, and particularly Christian idealism. At the same time, ironically, he chose to remain an idealist, without realizing the idealistic nature of his choice: proceeding on the immature and childish notion that because an object is not white it must be black, he clung to a religious idealism which was merely an inversion of that secondhand Calvinistic idealism which he had intended to discard. We must proceed cautiously, here as elsewhere. Melville seems to me to have been correct in his notion that the Calvinistic concept of God was in some ways an ugly and unacceptable concept of God, which did not encourage anyone to love God so much as to fear God. When he chose to turn his back on that concept, however, he faced a considerable variety of substitute choices, as he certainly knew; but from our reading of *Mardi* we may gather that he actually proceeded to make several different choices at one and the same time. Gradually, however, his "progress" through the inferno of his disillusionment brought him only deeper into an inner inferno, which seems to me to have been a quaintly childish oversimplification: if the Calvinistic God did not inspire love, that God must inspire hate. If He was not white, He was black.

Again we must proceed cautiously. It would be easy enough to insist that Melville never did quarrel with God; that he merely quarreled with the Calvinists for having created such an outrageous concept of God. The evidence, here, is very strong. Melville did devote much time and space to attacking the Calvinistic concept of God. But again there were numerous and different ways of attacking the concept, and Melville had plenty of company, in his own day, in America. As I have pointed out, William Ellery Channing attacked the Calvinistic concept of God, in his famous Baltimore sermon, the very year that Melville was born. Thereafter, many liked to think and say that Calvinism was on the wane, although this was scarcely true. For deeply religious people, however, the ugliest tenets of Calvinistic dogma (the basic concepts of Original Sin and Innate Depravity) became merely discarded pieces of theological furniture. Instead of merely discarding this furniture, however, Melville devoted the best part of his life to kicking that discarded furniture to pieces. Why?

Because his responses to life were what they were, he needed a scapegoat: someone to blame. Having started with hating Christians because they were not sufficiently Christian, he proceeded to hate Christians because they were Christians. When that scapegoat failed to satisfy him, he went on to hate the Calvinistic concept of God, and then proceeded to hate God. It never seemed to occur to him that he had merely declared his independence from the ideal of Calvinism in order to pledge his allegiance to an inverted form of that same ideal.

Let me say again that I am not urging that Melville should not have been inconsistent, or that he would have been a better artist if he had been more consistent. He might never have been an artist, in any sense, if he had gotten his own inner conflicts straightened out. For our aesthetic satisfaction, then, it is fortunate that Melville was exactly what he was. Nevertheless, if our ultimate concern is to understand Melville's art, there is value in recognizing how it happened that his non-artistic spiritual idiom made his artistic idiom the complex thing it certainly is.

As I see it, the major problem which confronts the reader, as he comes to Melville for the first time, is the problem of recognizing, and learning to cope with, those different forms of artistic deception and hoodwinking which he developed and employed, because of his embarrassment over the heretical and blasphemous nature of his views. I have repeatedly suggested that his own disillusionment forced him into such a private preoccupation with, and employment of, ambiguities and equivocations that he did not need to contrive any principles or practices of artistic subterfuge. It is apparent, however, that the persistent and concealed sadness of his long experience as a human being was alleviated for him by the happiness of his long experience as a literary artist: the retaliatory triumph which he achieved came to him through the act of pushing words around, to make those words do what he wanted them to do. And a very high degree of that pleasure, certainly, was derived from his skill in pushing words around in such a way

423

that some of his readers would not understand what he wanted those words to do and say. Like his early literary idol, John Milton, he was haughty enough to be content with fit audience, though few.

Part of that major problem which confronts the first-reader of Melville is the problem of recognizing, and learning to cope with, his adaptation of moral allegory to his own peculiar uses, in such a way as to create ambiguous allegorical meanings. Once again, this adaptation of moral allegory should be recognized as a significant element in his principle and practice of literary deception. Melville knew that the allegorical mode of storytelling had so largely gone out of fashion, in his day, that many of his readers would be completely oblivious to his use of allegory in any form. That disposed of "the superficial skimmer of pages." He also knew that those readers well versed in the principles of moral allegory would naturally be the devout and unconsciously bias-bound Christian readers, who would quickly recognize his use of allegory and would instinctively prefer to make a conventional interpretation of his allegorical meanings. That disposed of a second category of readers. He also knew that his sustained irony, created by endowing allegory with sinister or inverted meanings, belonged in a "high hushed" literary tradition which included (in different ways) such of his favorite authors as Rabelais, Montaigne, Pierre Bayle; that these writers had always found fit audience, though few; that it was to such a "fit audience" he was addressing his dark and ulterior meanings. Considering this threefold appeal, I think it justifiable to call Melville's literary formula a kind of artistic triple talk. Artistically, he fulfilled his responsibilities to us, on this score; but we as readers have generally failed to pay enough attention, and in this sense we have not fulfilled our responsibilities to him. Yet, because he encouraged most of his readers to misunderstand him, perhaps things have worked out for Herman Melville, very much as he desired.

Finally, we may quite easily summarize the essential element in the general range of Melville's vision, because that element remained so constant throughout so much of his later life. As I have been obliged to reiterate, the general range of Melville's vision is somewhat disappointing (not nearly so exciting and fascinating as the infinite variety of his devices for representing it) because that vision narrows down to the sharp focus of a misanthropic notion that the world was put together wrong, and that God was to blame. The gist of it is that simple. He spent his life not merely in sneering at the gullibility of human beings who disagreed with him but also in sneering at God, accusing God, upbraiding God, blaming God, and (as he thought) quarreling with God. The turn which his life had taken translated him from a transcendentalist and a mystic into an inverted transcendentalist, an inverted mystic. To this extent, then, he was consistent, in spite of all his concomitant inconsistencies, to the very end of his life. Like his own Captain Ahab, he remained a defiant rebel, even in the face of death.

Emblems delighted Melville so much (particularly when he could invert them) that his grave-stone emblem should be the Melville coat of arms, on which the motto indicates the ultimate irony of his triumphant departure from the Hell of this life:

"Denique Caelum." (Heaven, at last.)

NOTES

TO THE READER

1. *Moby-Dick*, I, 4. Unless otherwise indicated, all page references to Melville's writings are to the Constable edition of Melville's *Works*.

2. To indicate the currently accepted interpretations of *Moby-Dick*, I shall represent those of Newton Arvin, Richard Chase, Willard Thorp, Howard P. Vincent.

Newton Arvin (*Herman Melville*. New York: Sloane, 1950, pp. 143-193) leans heavily on Freud and Jung in his interpretation of the relationship between Captain Ahab and the White Whale: "A kind of castration, in short, has been not only imagined and dreaded but inflicted, and the phallic source of vital potency has been replaced by an image of impotence and lifelessness. . . . [Poor Captain Ahab!] Moby Dick is thus the archetypal Parent, the father, yes, but the mother also, so far as she becomes a substitute for the father. And the emotions *Moby Dick* evokes in us are the violently contradictory emotions that prevail between parent and child. Too little, curiously, has been made of this. . . ." Not too little; too much, I'd say. Following this train of thought, Mr. Arvin progresses to "the moral meanings of *Moby Dick*," thus:

"From the oneiric point of view Ahab is the suffering and neurotic self, lamed by early experience so vitally that it can devote itself only to destructive ends and find rest only in self-annihilation. No reader of the book, to be sure, could fail to feel how imperfectly this clinical description fits the grandiose captain of the Pequod: he embodies a form of sickness, certainly, but in doing so he embodies also, and on a higher imaginative plane, a form of tragedy. The two, however, originate and eventuate together."

After exploring the extensions of his conviction that "the tragic error for which Ahab suffers is an archetypal one," Mr. Arvin equates it with "the Christian sin of pride," and at last gets to the touchstone chapter, thus:

"Father Mapple's sermon is intended to make us understand that Ahab, like Jonah, has in a certain sense sinned through proud refusal to obey God's will, or its equivalent; pride and disobedience, in at any rate some dimly Christian senses, are at the root of Ahab's wickedness."

In concluding his analysis, Mr. Arvin thinks he catches glimpses of Melville's spiritual hope:

"Already in *Moby Dick* there has been an intimation of this cosmic submissiveness. The desire to understand, to fathom, the whole truth about the White Whale—the desire that is manifest at every turn in the explanatory and meditative passages—this is at least the true beginning of wisdom. The willingness to submit, to accept, to 'obey,' in that sense, would naturally follow. Father Mapple, indeed, in his sermon . . . makes provision for this. . . . The 'will' of nature, even if there is something godlike in it, is hardly synonymous with God's will in the Christian sense. Yet *Moby Dick* seems to say that one might arrive at a kind of peace by obeying it."

Perhaps I am wrong, but I cannot help but feel that Mr. Arvin's interpretation of *Moby-Dick* provides an excellent example of Melville's success in coaxing the unwary and humorless reader into the trap so carefully set: the Mapple-sermon trap which encourages a certain kind of reader to make his ultimate interpretation in terms of Christian doctrine, particularly the doctrine of acceptance.

Richard Chase (*Herman Melville: A Critical Study.* New York: Macmillan, 1949, pp. 43-102) is also charmed by Freud and Jung:

"I should say that Ahab is as much the American of his time as was Homer's Odysseus the Greek of his time or Joyce's Leopold Bloom the Jew of his time. [Question: how much is that?] He is the American culture image: the captain of industry and of his soul: the exploiter of nature who severs his own attachment to nature and exploits himself out of existence. [Clearly, this is a "liberal" interpretation of Captain Ahab!] In his poem on Melville, W. H. Auden says of Ahab that 'the rare ambiguous monster . . . has maimed his sex.' And indeed in the fall of the year—some time, that is, before Christmas, when the *Pequod* sailed—Ahab, like the divine hero Adonis, suffered a 'seemingly inexplicable, unimaginable casualty.' He was found lying on the ground, 'his ivory limb having been so violently displaced that it had stake-wise smitten him and all but pierced his groin.' "

After a good deal more of this, Mr. Chase gets the Freudian and Christian concepts together, by way of summary: "In *Moby-Dick*, a great man allows himself to be unmanned by the lure of God." For Mr. Chase, as for Mr. Arvin, the most important conceptual core of *Moby-Dick* is that Melville intends the story to serve as an object lesson: we see what Ahab should *not* have done. His sin was that he was an exploiter, and his penalty was that he exploited himself out of existence. The wages of sin is death.

Willard Thorp (editor, *Moby-Dick, or the Whale.* New York: Oxford, 1947, pp. ix-xviii) again insists that Melville intended Captain Ahab's monomaniac pursuit to serve as a horrible object lesson:

"Father Mapple's sermon in the sailor's bethel . . . dwells with pregnant insistence on the sins of Jonah, the fugitive from God. . . . Early in the voyage Ahab tosses overboard his lighted pipe. Pipes are meant for serene days and there will be none on this ship. The time is not far off when he will discard something more precious—the quadrant which he splits and tramples underfoot. The mad old man first cuts himself off from the simple world of men; in the extremity of his madness he destroys the instrument that would bring him and his crew safely home."

428

Again, Melville's trap has worked efficiently.

Howard P. Vincent (*The Trying-Out of Moby-Dick*. Cambridge: Houghton Mifflin, 1949) seems to me to waste his elaborate and scholarly source-huntings when he utilizes them merely to come up with this conclusion:

"With this epilogue of Ishmael's rescue, the great spiritual theme of *Moby-Dick* is rounded off. Ishmael had started for the South Seas in a state bordering on suicide, alone and angered at life. Ishmael learned the law of aloneness and the law of companionship, the psychological duality. But Ishmael has also learned the law of acceptance, to accept what Fate has in store for him, not to fight it in the manner of Ahab. . . . *Moby-Dick* has returned at last to the memorable message of Father Mapple."

In summary, the four most recent and most extended utterances by four Melville scholars center on the same conclusion: Melville intended *Moby-Dick* to reenforce the central teachings of Christian doctrine, and particularly the doctrine of acceptance. One advantage which these scholars gain from leaning on each other is that they help to hold each other up.

I. FRUIT OF THAT FORBIDDEN TREE

1. *Moby-Dick*, I, 107-108. Cf. Carlyle: ". . . to many a Royal Society, the Creation of a World is little more mysterious than the cooking of a dumpling; concerning which last, indeed, there have been minds to whom the question, *How the apples were got in,* presented difficulties." *Sartor Resartus*. Albany, N.Y.: Lyons, 1889, p. 3.

2. E. T. Corwin, J. H. Dubbs, J. T. Hamilton, *A History of the Reformed Church, Dutch*. New York: The Christian Literature Company, 1895, p. 205.

3. *ibid.*, p. 206.

4. William Braswell, *Melville's Religious Thought: An Essay in Interpretation*. Durham, N.C.: Duke University Press, 1943, p. 5. Although Braswell's excellent study has been of considerable value to me, he does not show any interest in my primary concern: Melville's artistic devices of deception and hoodwinking, in order to conceal the nature of his religious thought.

5. Quoted from Luther's *Works* in Wilhelm Pauck, *The Heritage of the Reformation*. Boston: Beacon Press, 1950, p. 19.

6. Quoted in Jacques LeClerq's "Introduction" to *The Complete Works of Rabelais*. New York: Modern Library, 1944, p. xxii.

7. Pauck, p. 61.

8. Quoted in H. H. Hudson (translator), *The Praise of Folly by Desiderius Erasmus*. Princeton, N.J.: Princeton University Press, 1941, p. xviii.

9. E. J. Trechmann (translator and editor), *The Essays of Montaigne.* London: Oxford University Press, 1927, 2 volumes, I, 428n.

10. Milton, *Paradise Lost,* I, 94-109.

11. Pierre Bayle, *An Historical and Critical Dictionary.* London, 1710, 4 volumes, IV, 2484.

12. *ibid.,* IV, 2493.

13. Howard Robinson, *Bayle the Sceptic.* New York: Columbia University Press, 1931, p. 22.

14. Melville could scarcely have escaped knowing Andrews Norton, *The Evidences of the Genuineness of the Gospels,* Cambridge, Mass.: John Owen, 1844. Widely reviewed, widely read, widely quoted, much discussed, Andrews Norton's work was a scholarly landmark of the period. His second and third volumes treated "The Evidence for the Genuineness of the Gospels Afforded by the Early Heretics." A few summary excerpts from Volume Two of *The Evidences* are pertinent here for purposes of cross-reference.

On page 83, Norton quotes from Justin Martyr: "And accordingly there are and have been many coming in the name of Jesus, who have taught men to say and do impious and blasphemous things. . . . Some in one way, and some in another, teach men to blaspheme the Maker of All, and the Messiah who was prophesied as coming from him; and the God of Abraham and Isaac and Jacob." The reference is to the Gnostic heresy which taught that the Maker of the material universe was not the Supreme God, but a being imperfect in power, wisdom, goodness. The Gnostic sect holding this belief was said to have been founded by Marcion, and his followers were known as the Marcionites.

On page 91, Norton quotes Irenaeus against Marcion: "Because Marcion alone has dared openly to mutilate the Scriptures, and has gone beyond all others in shamelessly disparaging the character of God, I shall oppose him by himself." Norton summarizes Irenaeus thus: "In speaking of Marcion's disparaging the character of God, Irenaeus refers, as will be readily understood, not to Marcion's opinion concerning the Supreme Being, but to his opinions concerning that inferior agent, whom the Gnostics conceived of as the Maker of the World."

Melville seems to draw on his familiarity with the Marcionite heresy when he writes to Hawthorne, "We incline to think that God cannot explain his own secrets, and that He would like a little information upon certain points Himself." Similarly, in "The Candles" chapter, Captain Ahab's blasphemous prayer contains this: "Thou knowest not how came ye, hence callest thyself unbegotten; certainly knowest not thy beginning, hence callest thyself unbegun. . . . There is some unsuffusing thing beyond thee, thou clear spirit, to whom all thy eternity is but time, all thy creativeness mechanical."

Norton also presents considerable information concerning the Ophites. After summarizing some references to a heretical book entitled the "Gospel of Eve," which was said to contain the wisdom which Eve learned from the Serpent, Norton adds (page 218), "It seems probable that the book . . . had its origin among certain reputed heretics, who, according to Origen, were not Christians. They were called Ophians or Ophites (we might render the name Serpentists) . . . they took the part of the Serpent who seduced Eve, and represented him as having given good counsel to our first parents." Norton continues (page 219), "We can therefore admit . . . only some very general conclusions respecting the doctrines of the Ophians. Whether Christians or not, they appear to have been of the class of theosophic Gnostics, holding very disparaging opinions of the Creator, whom they regarded as the god of the Jews. They believed that . . . the way, which might otherwise be barred by those powers, was open to such as were initiated in their mysteries." Page 220: "Their doctrines have the appearance of being a caricature of the doctrines of the proper Gnostics. Maintaining the common opinion that the Creator was *not spiritual*, and regarding him as being opposed to the manifestation and development of the spiritual principle in man, they honored the Serpent for having thwarted his narrow purposes, withdrawn our first parents from their allegiance to him, induced them to eat the fruit of the tree of knowledge, and thus brought them the knowledge of 'that Power which is over All.'"

The Melville cross-references which might be made here are numerous; but one excellent example is contained in the celebrated memorandum which Melville wrote on a flyleaf of his volume containing *Hamlet, Othello, King Lear*, and beginning, *"Ego non baptizo te . . ."*

Norton further correlates the Ophites and the Cainites (page 221): "Clement of Alexandria once incidentally mentions the Ophians, in speaking of the origin of the names of different sects. Some, he says, are denominate 'from their systems and from the objects they honor, as the Cainists and the Ophians.' The Cainists or Cainites . . . are represented as magnifying Cain. The Ophians honored the Serpent."

Melville's familiarity with Byron's *Cain: A Mystery* would have made him familiar with the essential tenets of the "Cainites." In *Redburn*, when reference is made to Jackson as "a Cain afloat," the subsequent description of Jackson presents specifically heretical views which lock Jackson with both Cainites and Ophites.

On page 221, Norton summarizes information on the Ophites drawn from Irenaeus: ". . . according to his account of their system . . . he (the Serpent) appears employed by Sophia or Wisdom, the offspring of the Unknown God, *the mother*, but adversary of the Creator, for the purpose of seducing our first parents to eat of the forbidden fruit; by which they obtained a knowledge of the Supreme Divinity. But the Creator, who was himself desirous of being regarded as the highest God, being in consequence angry with the Serpent, expelled him from heaven, where he had before dwelt, and cast him down to earth. After this fall he is made to correspond to the serpent of the Apocalypse, the Devil; and is represented as . . . full of malice equally toward men and their Maker."

This time the cross-references in Melville occur most frequently in hints. Take, as just one example, Captain Ahab's blasphemous prayer, again, in "The Candles" chapter: "Oh, thou magnanimous! now I do glory in my genealogy. But thou art but my fiery father; my sweet mother, I know not. Oh, cruel! what hast thou done with her? There lies my puzzle; but thine is greater."

15. Bayle, *Dictionary*, IV (Appendix), liii.

16. Thomas Hobbes, *Leviathan, or the Matter, Forme & Power of a Commonwealth, Ecclesiastical and Civil.* Cambridge, 1904, pp. 118-119. Notice that Hobbes' explanation of his title image "Leviathan" as a symbol of God, in the passage quoted, is closely related to the use which Melville makes of the words "Leviathan" and "whale" throughout *Moby-Dick*. Melville's repeated quotations from God's word to Job concerning Leviathan clearly establish his source; Hobbes' source is probably the same.

Hobbes' references to the book of Job would have been particularly interesting to Melville, because of its emphasis on death: "The whole 14. Chapter of Job, which is the speech not of his friends, but of himselfe, is a complaint of this Mortality of Nature...." (*ibid.*, p. 330.)

17. William Blake, "The Marriage of Heaven and Hell" (c. 1790); D. J. Sloss and J. P. R. Wallis (editors), *The Prophetic Writings of William Blake.* Oxford: Clarendon Press, 1926, 2 volumes, I, 13-14.

18. Willard Thorp (editor), *Herman Melville: Representative Selections.* New York: American Book Company, 1938, p. 392.

19. *The Complete Poetical Works of Percy Bysshe Shelley.* Boston: Houghton Mifflin, 1892, pp. 75-76.

20. *The Poetical Works of Lord Byron.* London: Oxford University Press, 1935, p. 510.

21. *ibid.*, p. 97.

II. EDEN REVISITED

1. *Typee*, pp. viii-ix.
2. *ibid.*, p. 267.
3. *ibid.*, pp. 264, 259, 165.
4. *ibid.*, pp. 262-267.
5. *ibid.*, p. 273.
6. Chase, *Melville*, p. 12.
7. Arvin, *Melville*, p. 87.
8. *Typee*, pp. 231-233.
9. *Mardi*, I, vii.

III. QUEST FOR ATONEMENT

1. *Mardi*, II, 400.

2. The most condensed example of such staggering evidence occurs in the following passage:

"Ay: many, many souls are in me.... Like a grand, ground swell, Homer's old organ rolls its vast volume under the light frothy wave-crests of Anacreon and Hafiz; and high over my ocean, sweet Shakespeare soars, like all the larks of the spring. Throned on my seaside, like Canute, bearded Ossian smites his hoar harp, wreathed with wildflowers, in which warble my Wallers; blind Milton sings bass to my Petrarchs and Priors, and laureates crown me with bays.

"In me, many worthies recline, and converse. I list to St. Paul who argues the doubts of Montaigne; Julian the Apostate cross-questions Augustine; and Thomas a Kempis unrolls his old black letters for all to decipher. Zeno murmurs maxims beneath the hoarse shout of Democritus; and though Democritus laugh loud and long, and the sneer of Pyrrho be seen; yet, divine Plato, and Proclus, and Verulam are of my counsel; and Zoroaster whispered me before I was born. I walk a world that is mine; and enter many nations, as Mungo Park rested in African cots; I am served like Bajazet; Bacchus my butler, Virgil my minstrel, Philip Sidney my page. My memory is a life beyond birth; my memory, my library of the Vatican, its alcoves all endless perspectives, eve-tinted by cross-lights from Middle Age oriels." (*Mardi*, II, 53-54.)

3. *ibid.*, II, 8-9; 19-20.

4. *ibid.*, II, 31-33.

5. *ibid.*, I, 267. Melville's high sense of dedication and consecration, as an artist, frequently echoes Spenser. In this particular case, the image of returning to the Heavenly source for creative fire seems to echo *The Faerie Queene*, Book VII, Canto 7, Stanzas 1 and 2:

> Ah! whither doost thou now thou greater Muse
>> Me from these woods and pleasing forrests bring? . . .
> Yet sith I needs must follow thy behest,
>> Doe thou my weaker wit with skill inspire,
>> Fit for this turne; and in my feeble brest
>> Kindle fresh sparks of that immortal fire,
>> Which learned minds inflameth with desire
>> Of heavenly things: for, who but thou alone,
>> That art yborne of heaven and heavenly Sire,
>> Can tell things doen in heaven so long ygone;
> So farre past memory of man that may be knowne.

6. *Mardi*, II, 128. Throughout *Mardi*, there is a recurrent tone of Melvillian self-pity which echoes the tone of Byronic self-pity in "Childe Harold's Pilgrimage." It is even possible that the title, *Mardi*, may have been suggested by the following passage from "Childe Harold's Pilgrimage."

> Oh, Christ! it is a goodly sight to see
> What Heaven hath done for this delicious land:
> What goodly prospects o'er the hills expand!
> But man would mar them with an impious hand . . .

Later, when far more deeply disillusioned, and when deeply sympathetic with impiety, Melville satirically permitted pious Lucy to write an unintentionally funny letter to Pierre, in which pious Lucy used the same image of the world as a place where man mars the divine: ". . . till we meet [in Heaven] where the ever-interrupting and ever-marring world can not and shall not come." (*Pierre*, p. 431.)

7. *Mardi*, II, 54-55.

8. *ibid.*, II, 276-277.

IV. THREE PHASES OF DISILLUSIONMENT

1. In arranging Taji's soul-pilgrimage through the drag of the temporal toward the ultimate atonement with the eternal, Melville seemed to let Taji listen as much to St. Paul as to the "divine Plato." His conventional use of the garment-of-faith image, echoing Romans 13:14, Ephesians 6:11-17, foreshadows his subsequently inverted and anti-Christian use of the garment-of-faith image in *White-Jacket*; foreshadows his inverted uses of several Biblical passages in *Redburn*.

2. Thorp, *Representative Selections*, pp. 374-375. To his father-in-law, Melville expressed another attitude toward *Mardi*, shortly after reviews began to appear:

"I see that *Mardi* has been cut into by the *London Atheneum*, and also burnt by the common hangman in the *Boston Post*. . . . These attacks are matters of course, and are essential to the building up of any permanent reputation—if such should ever prove to be mine— 'There's nothing in it!' cried the dunce when he threw down the 47th problem of the 1st Book of Euclid—'There's nothing in it!'—Thus with the posed critic. But Time, which is the solver of all riddles, will solve *Mardi*." (*ibid.*, p. 410.)

3. *ibid.*, p. 376.	6. *ibid.*, p. 61.
4. *Redburn*, p. 42.	7. *ibid.*, p. 33.
5. *ibid.*, p. 50.	8. *ibid.*, p. 179.

9. Bayle, *Dictionary* (Appendix: "How what I have said concerning the Objections of the Manichees, ought to be considered."), p. lviii. (See also II Corinthians 5:7.)

10. *Redburn*, p. 237.	16. *ibid.*, pp. 65-66.
11. *ibid.*, p. 242.	17. *ibid.*, p. 72.
12. *ibid.*, pp. 261-262.	18. *ibid.*, p. 134.
13. *ibid.*, p. 180ff.	19. *ibid.*, p. 335.
14. *ibid.*, pp. 11-12.	20. *ibid.*, p. 355.
15. *ibid.*, pp. 15, 16, 19.	21. *ibid.*, pp. 356-357.

V. SLASHING THE JACKET

1. *White-Jacket*, p. 63.	2. *ibid.*, p. 4.

3. Perhaps Sir Thomas Browne was responsible for Melville's delight in twisting the meaning of Exodus 33:23 and I Corinthians 13:12. For a

more elaborate and obvious example, see footnote 75 of Chapter VII ("Wicked Book").

4. *White-Jacket,* pp. 499-501.
5. *ibid.,* pp. 502-504.
6. Carlyle, *Sartor Resartus,* pp. 43-44.
7. *White-Jacket,* p. 1.
8. *ibid.,* pp. 96-97.
9. *ibid.,* pp. 230-231.
10. *ibid.,* p. 25.

11. *ibid.,* p. 27.
12. *ibid.,* p. 171.
13. *ibid.,* pp. 352-353.
14. Hobbes, *Leviathan,* p. 86.
15. *White-Jacket,* p. 181.
16. *ibid.,* p. 218.
17. *ibid.,* p. 119.
18. *ibid.,* p. 260.

19. Braswell, *Melville's Religious Thought,* p. 27. Braswell points out that the passage indicates Melville's "fascination with the question of man's divinity and shows his appreciation of a religious attitude that would develop the best in man." By contrast, I think it shows his fondness for equivocations; in this case, a decidedly sacrilegious second meaning.

20. *White-Jacket,* p. 182.
21. *ibid.,* p. 377.
22. *ibid.,* pp. 379-380.
23. *ibid.,* pp. 381-382.
24. *ibid.,* p. 185.

25. *ibid.,* p. 187.
26. *ibid.,* pp. 232-233.
27. *ibid.,* pp. 233-234.
28. *ibid.,* pp. 178-179.

VI. DARK CONFESSIONS

1. Thorp, *Representative Selections,* pp. 387-389.
2. Carlyle, *Sartor Resartus,* p. 145.
3. *ibid.,* pp. 208, 145.
4. Thorp, *Representative Selections,* p. 392. The phrase "like a watch" suggests Melville's familiarity with the analogy worked so hard by the Continental deists, and adapted to his own uses by Priestley: God made and wound the mechanism of the universe, and ever since then it has been running in a way controlled by its own springs and cogs. Melville had previously shown his familiarity with Priestley: see the second chapter of *Mardi.*
5. Carlyle, *Sartor Resartus,* pp. 128-129.
6. *ibid.,* pp. 166-171 passim.
7. Jude 4-13 passim.
8. Thorp, *Representative Selections,* pp. 327-342 passim. It may seem to some readers that Melville's preoccupation with the possibilities for hoodwinking and deception, in literary art, is so unique that it has no counterpart in the history of literature. Such a supposition is extremely naive and unsophisticated. As I have suggested in my "To the Reader" and in my first chapter, Melville himself was sufficiently sophisticated in his knowledge of literary history to be well aware that the long tradition of hoodwinking, with which he aligned himself, could be traced back across at least twenty-three centuries to Plato's dialogue

entitled *Phaedrus,* in which Socrates explains and demonstrates to Phaedrus that rhetoric has frequently been employed for purposes of deception.

9. Melville marked this passage (*King Lear,* i, ii, 123) in his own copy, now in Harvard College Library.

10. Quoted in Charles Olsen, *Call Me Ishmael.* New York: Reynal and Hitchcock, 1947, p. 52. Notice that the blasphemous black-mass Latin phrase (which may be translated, "I do *not* baptize thee in the name of the Father, and of the Son, and of the Holy Ghost; but in the name of the Devil") represents a conscious and deliberate burlesque or inversion of Christ's words, in Matthew 28:18-19: "All power is given unto me, in heaven and in earth. Go ye therefore, and teach all nations, baptizing them in the name of the Father, and of the Son, and of the Holy Ghost . . ." Notice also that Melville, in his memorandum, goes on to discuss various approaches to "power."

11. Raymond M. Weaver, *Herman Melville, Mariner and Mystic.* New York: Doran, 1921, p. 274.

12. *Moby-Dick,* i, 233.

13. Milton, *Paradise Lost,* iv, 48-49, 69-70.

14. Quoted in Julian Hawthorne, *Nathaniel Hawthorne and his Wife.* Boston, Osgood, 1885, 2 vols., i, 401-405. There seems to be an obvious typographical error in Julian Hawthorne's version of this letter; the phrase "I . . . revere the test of my Lord Shaftesbury" means, in context, "I reverse the test . . ." Melville's remarks (in this letter and elsewhere) diametrically oppose and contradict (in effect) the basically optimistic and Christian tenet on which Shaftesbury erected his system. In his essay, "An Inquiry Concerning Virtue and Merit," Shaftesbury promulgated the doctrine that all men are divinely endowed with an inner "reflex" or "moral" sense which should impel them to respond positively to the good, the true, the beautiful. In effect, Melville repeatedly ridicules and contradicts such an optimistic assumption. In this letter, after doing just that, Melville would seem to be employing a mock-legalistic term, as he comments on the difference between his view and Shaftesbury's view: he reverses the decision or test of Shaftesbury. Consequently, I have taken the liberty of substituting the word "reverse" for Julian Hawthorne's reading, "revere."

15. Thorp, *Representative Selections,* 394-395 passim.

16. For example, one such recent joker was Charles Poore, in his wise *New York Times* book review (May 4, 1950) of Newton Arvin's *Herman Melville:*

"And all over America, in quiet studies under academic elms, other scholars are at this moment, or thereabouts, standing valiantly in the paper prows of their doctoral whaleboats ready to harpoon new Freudian symbolisms in 'Moby Dick.' Mr. Arvin does magnificently well in that rather widely and enthusiastically pursued aspect of the great game of Moby Dickering. As one who has long planned to write a monograph proving that there is no symbolism whatever in 'Moby Dick'— or even a real whale, for that matter—I confess . . ."

Methinks the joker doth confess too much, particularly when he backs up his own conviction with documentary evidence drawn from the brilliant Melville-interpretation of Somerset Maugham, who recently edited an expurgated edition of *Moby-Dick*.

17. Randall Stewart (editor), *The English Notebooks of Nathaniel Hawthorne*. New York: Oxford, 1941, pp. 432-433.

VII. WICKED BOOK

1. Braswell, *Melville's Religious Thought*, p. 12.
2. *Pierre*, pp. 471-472.
3. *Moby-Dick*, I, 166-167.
4. *ibid.*, II, 94.
5. Ishmael establishes an antithesis between his own fugitive cowardice and Cato's stoic attitude, thus foreshadowing the contrast he will later establish between his cowardice and Captain Ahab's heroic boldness. Because Melville had such great admiration for Montaigne's essays, he would probably have been familiar with Montaigne's extended praise of Cato, which I quote here, in part, because it may serve to summarize the admiring attitude toward Captain Ahab held by both Ishmael and Melville:

"Witness the younger Cato. When I see him dying and plucking out his bowels . . . I believe that without doubt he felt a sensual pleasure in an action so noble, and that he felt a greater satisfaction in it than in any other action of his life: he departed this life, said Cicero, rejoicing in having found a motive for leaving it.

"I am so far advanced in that belief that I begin to question whether he would have wished to be robbed of the opportunity of so heroic an achievement. . . .

"I seem to read in that action I know not what exultation in his soul, and the expression of an extraordinary pleasure and manly voluptuousness, when she [the soul] considered the nobility and sublimity of his deed: 'Embracing death with desperate ferocity.' . . .

"Cicero said, 'Cato, whom nature had endowed with incredible strength of soul, and who, ever following the path he had traced for himself, had by habit strengthened the firmness of his character, was bound to die rather than look upon the face of a tyrant.'" ("Of Cruelty"; Trechmann, *Essays of Montaigne*, I, 415.)

Captain Ahab was endowed by Melville with incredible strength of soul because Ahab also preferred to die rather than look longer at the mask of God's tyranny.

6. *Moby-Dick*, I, 1.   8. *ibid.*, I, 5-6.
7. *ibid.*, I, 3-4.   9. *ibid.*, I, 6-7.
10. *ibid.*, I, 7. Melville's violent reaction against the essentially ortho-

dox Christian viewpoint underlying Carlyle's *Sartor Resartus* is reflected throughout *Moby-Dick* and *Pierre*. Carlyle begins with hints which he calls "loomings" ("The Philosophy of Clothes is now to all readers, as we predicted it would do, unfolding itself into new boundless expansions, of a cloud-capt, almost chimerical aspect, yet not without azure loomings . . .") and Melville entitles Chapter One of his Whaling Philosophy, "Loomings." The following early quotation from *Sartor Resartus* is given to help us appreciate the fact that both Carlyle and Melville were approaching the same basically religious and philosophic problems from diametrically opposed viewpoints:

"Readers of any intelligence are once more invited to favor us with their most concentrated attention; let these, after intense consideration, and not till then, pronounce, Whether on the utmost verge of our actual horizon there is not a *looming* [italics added] as of Land; a promise of new Fortunate Islands, perhaps whole undiscovered Americas, for such as have canvas to sail thither?—As exordium to the whole, stand here the following long citation:—

" 'With men of a speculative turn,' writes Teufelsdrockh, 'there come seasons, meditative, sweet, yet awful hours, when in wonder and fear you ask yourself the unanswerable question: Who am *I*; the thing that you can say "I"? The world, with its loud trafficking, retires into the distance; and, through the paper-hangings, and the living and lifeless integuments (of Society and a Body) wherewith your Existence sits surrounded,—*the sight reaches forth into the void Deep* [Italics added; cf. Melville's "loomings" in Chapter One of *Moby-Dick*], and you are alone with the Universe, and silently commune with it, as one mysterious Presence with another.

" 'Who am I; what is this ME? A Voice, a Motion, an Appearance; some embodied, visualized Idea in the Eternal Mind? *Cogito, ergo sum.* Alas, poor Cogitator, this takes us but a little way. Sure enough, I am; and lately was not; but Whence? How? Whereto? The answer lies around, written in all colors and motions, uttered in all tones of jubilee and wail; in thousand-figured, thousand-voiced, harmonious Nature; but where is the cunning eye and ear to whom that God-written Apocalypse will yield articulate meaning? . . .

" 'Pity that all Metaphysics had hitherto proved so inexpressively unproductive! The secret of Man's Being is still the Sphinx's secret: a riddle that he cannot rede; and for ignorance of which he suffers death, the worst death, a spiritual. What are your Axioms, and Categories, and Systems, and Aphorisms? Words, words. . . . Be not the slave of Words; is not the Distant, the Dead, while I love it, and long for it, and mourn for it, Here, in the genuine sense, as truly as the floor I stand on?' " (*Sartor Resartus*, p. 40.)

11. *Moby-Dick*, I, 11. 14. *ibid.*, I, 32-33.
12. *ibid.*, I, 14. 15. *ibid.*, I, 44-45.
13. *ibid.*, I, 15. 16. *ibid.*, I, 47-48.

17. *ibid.*, ɪ, 59.
18. *ibid.*, ɪ, 62.
19. *ibid.*, ɪ, 64.

20. *ibid.*, ɪ, 76.
21. *ibid.*, ɪ, 91-92.

22. *ibid.*, ɪ, 101. Notice that Ishmael's attitude towards Captain Ahab is strikingly similar to Redburn's attitude toward Jackson (". . . there was that in his eye at times that was ineffably pitiable and touching; and though there were moments when I almost hated this Jackson, yet I have pitied no man as I have pitied him.") and White-Jacket's attitude toward Bland ("I could not but abominate him when I thought of his conduct; but I pitied the continual gnawing which, under all his deftly donned disguises, I saw lying at the bottom of his soul. I admired his heroism in sustaining himself so well under such reverses.")

23. *Moby-Dick*, ɪ, 102.

24. *ibid.*, ɪ, 116-118 passim.

25. *ibid.*, ɪ, 128. An excellent gloss on Melville's sardonic chapter title, "Merry Christmas," is available in *Pierre* (p. 398): "Unendurable grief of a man, when Death itself gives the stab, and then snatches all availments to solacement away. For in the grave is no help, no prayer thither may go, no forgiveness thence come; so that the penitent whose sad victim lies in the ground, for that useless penitent his doom is eternal, and though it be Christmas-day with all Christendom, with him it is Hell-day and an eaten liver forever."

26. *Moby-Dick*, ɪ, 130.
27. *ibid.*, ɪ, 132-133.
28. *ibid.*, ɪ, 138.
29. *ibid.*, ɪ, 141-142.
30. *ibid.*, ɪ, 143-144.
31. *ibid.*, ɪ, 144.

32. *ibid.*, ɪ, 145.
33. *ibid.*, ɪ, 146.
34. *ibid.*, ɪ, 149-150.
35. *ibid.*, ɪ, 152-153.
36. *ibid.*, ɪ, 154.

37. Milton, *Paradise Lost*, ɪ, 599-604.

38. P. B. Shelley, *The Complete Poetical Works*, edited by Edward Dowden. New York: Crowell, n.d., 70-71. Melville's previous familiarity with Shelley's *Queen Mab* was reflected in *White-Jacket* (p. 340): "How many great men have been sailors. . . . There's Shelley, he was quite a sailor . . . but they ought to have let him sleep in his sailor's grave . . . and not burn his body, as they did, as if he had been a bloody Turk. But many people thought him so, White-Jacket, because he didn't go to mass, and because he wrote *Queen Mab*."

39. *Moby-Dick*, ɪ, 161-163.

40. *ibid.*, ɪɪ, 86.

41. *ibid.*, ɪ, 164-167.

42. *ibid.*, ɪ, 167. Viewing Jonah's story as a "fish-story" did not start with Melville, obviously. Pierre Bayle may be said to have set the pace, and during the eighteenth century many deistical writers who delighted to ridicule Christian doctrines concerning the inspiration of the scriptures and the Christian faith in miracles, had a field day with the Jonah story.

43. Delicate indelicacies in *Moby-Dick* are quite similar to those in the writings of Laurence Sterne, whom Melville admired, paraphrased, quoted. Sterne may even have taught Melville the harmless hoaxing device of quoting from a black-letter volume written by an author "of whose works I possess the only copy extant." (*Moby-Dick*, i, 11.) A possible example of Melville's indebtedness to Sterne for suggestive phallic ambiguities occurs in the "Cetology" chapter, following the discussion of the Narwhale or the Unicorn Whale:

"Black Letter tells me that Sir Martin Frobisher on his return from that voyage, when Queen Bess did gallantly wave her jewelled hand to him from a window of Greenwich Palace, as his bold ship sailed down the Thames; 'when Sir Martin returned from that voyage,' saith Black Letter, 'on bended knees he presented to her highness a prodigious long horn of the Narwhale, which for a long period after hung in the castle of Windsor.' An Irish author avers that the Earl of Leicester, on bended knees, did likewise present to her highness another horn, pertaining to a land beast of the unicorn nature." (*Moby-Dick*, i, 176.)

Melville frequently saves a choice ambiguity for the very last paragraph of a chapter, and such a tendency is particularly noticeable even as late as *Billy Budd*. In *Moby-Dick* (i, 179), the "Cetology" contains this in the final paragraph:

"But I now leave my cetological System standing thus unfinished, even as the great Cathedral of Cologne was left, with the crane still standing upon the top of the uncompleted tower. For small erections may be finished by their first architects; grand ones, true ones, ever leave the copestone to posterity."

Sterne never kept a straighter face than Melville does there.

44. *Moby-Dick*, i, 204-205. This extremely illuminating passage bears a strikingly inverted similarity to a passage in Carlyle's *Sartor Resartus*. Ahab's peroration begins by asserting that "all visible objects" in nature are "pasteboard masks"; Carlyle calls them "windows":

"All visible things are emblems; what thou seest is not there on its own account; strictly taken, is not there at all; Matter exists only spiritually, and to represent some Idea, and body it forth. . . . Rightly viewed no meanest object is insignificant; all objects are as windows, through which the philosophic eye looks into Infinitude itself. . . . So that this so solid-seeming World, after all, were . . . what the Earth-Spirit in Faust names it, the living visible Garment of God . . ." (*Sartor Resartus*, p. 55.)

The correlation, here, has further significance. The *Faust* paraphrase contained in "the living visible Garment of God" is the key phrase which all of *Sartor Resartus* is contrived to elaborate and illuminate. Similarly, it might be said that Captain Ahab's observations beginning, "All visible objects . . ." is the key passage which all of *Moby-Dick* is contrived to elaborate and illuminate.

45. *ibid.*, I, 209-210. 49. *ibid.*, I, 222.
46. Milton, *Paradise Lost*, IX, 99ff. 50. *ibid.*, I, 226, 227.
47. *ibid.*, IV, 380-381. 51. *ibid.*, I, 229-230.
48. *Moby-Dick*, I, 211. 52. *ibid.*, I, 243-244.

53. *ibid.*, I, 257. Although the viewpoints of Carlyle and Melville were opposed, they had much in common. Suffering from the same type of biliousness, each took wry pleasure in teasing and fooling and insulting his reader. Compare the passage just quoted from *Moby-Dick*, with this from *Sartor Resartus* (p. 43):

"Strange enough how creatures of the human-kind shut their eyes to plainest facts; and by the mere inertia of Oblivion and Stupidity live at ease in the midst of Wonders and Terrors. But indeed man is, and was always, a blockhead and dullard; much readier to feel and digest than to think and consider. Prejudice, which he pretends to hate, is his absolute lawgiver; mere use-and-wont everywhere leads him by the nose . . ."

54. *Moby-Dick*, I, 272. 58. *ibid.*, II, 271-272.
55. *ibid.*, I, 291-292. 59. *ibid.*, II, 56.
56. *ibid.*, I, 275-276. 60. *ibid.*, II, 58.
57. *ibid.*, II, 55-56. 61. *ibid.*, I, 281.

62. *ibid.*, II, 273-275. Notice how easily the superficial skimmer of pages may be trapped into the assumption that Melville intends the quadrant smashing and the "cursed be all things that cast man's eyes aloft" to serve as proof of Captain Ahab's madness. To the contrary, this symbolic action only adds further proof of Ahab's self-sufficiency. It is closely related to that other symbolic action which occurs when heaven's own lightning ruins Ahab's ship's compass, and thereafter Ahab steers by a compass of his own devising. ("With compass and lead, we had not found these Mardian Isles. Those who boldly launch, cast off all cables; and turning from the common . . . with their own breath fill their own sails.") As further proof of this interpretation, remember that Ahab has set himself an extremely difficult problem in navigation: to locate the White Whale in the "boundless deep"; that he succeeds in doing exactly that, after having rejected all conventional and traditional dogma.

Again this entire action of Captain Ahab inverts the meaning of a parallel passage in *Sartor Resartus*. Carlyle's own meaning in the following passage is ambiguous; yet his total meaning is conventionally Christian. Here he raises questions as to what will happen to his own navigating hero, Teufelsdrockh, when he goes his own way, like Captain Ahab:

"Quitting the common Fleet of . . . whalers, where indeed his leeward, laggard condition was painful enough, he desperately steers off, on a course of his own, by sextant and compass of his own. Unhappy Teufelsdrockh! Though neither Fleet nor Traffic, nor Commodores pleased thee, still was it not a *Fleet*, sailing in prescribed track, for fixed objects; above all, in combination, wherein, by mutual guidance, by all manner of loan and borrowings, each could manifoldly aid the other? How wilt thou sail in unknown seas; and for thyself find that shorter Northwest Passage to thy fair Spice-country of a Nowhere?— A solitary rover, on such a voyage, with such nautical tactics, will meet with adventures." (*Sartor Resartus,* p. 102.)

63. *Moby-Dick,* I, 284.	69. *ibid.,* II, 87-88.
64. *ibid.,* I, 286.	70. *ibid.,* II, 152-160.
65. *ibid.,* I, 298-299.	71. *ibid.,* II, 196-204.
66. *ibid.,* I, 306-330 passim.	72. *ibid.,* II, 268.
67. *ibid.,* II, 44-45.	73. *ibid.,* II, 311-315.
68. *ibid.,* II, 35.	74. *ibid.,* II, 325.

75. Romans 8:38-39. Melville's fondness for satirically inverting the conventional meanings of Biblical passages, particularly those of Paul (after the manner of Montaigne and Pierre Bayle) may be illustrated here in such a way as to suggest Melville's admiration for similar inversions in the writings of Sir Thomas Browne, whom Melville meant to honor when he called him a "crack'd Archangel." Paul's First Letter to the Corinthians (13:12) contains this familiar passage:

"For now we see through a glass darkly; but then face to face; now I know in part, but then shall I know even as also I am known."

For present purposes, that passage should be correlated with God's intimate words to Moses in Exodus 33:23: "And I will take away mine hand, and thou shalt see my back parts; but my face shall not be seen."

Captain Ahab's complaint, it will be remembered, was that he could not even see through a glass darkly; that he could see only through something like "pasteboard masks." Sir Thomas Browne, in *Religio Medici* (Section XIII) somewhat boisterously and indelicately twists Paul's passage in this paraphrase:

". . . for we behold him but asquint, upon reflex or shadow; our understanding is dimmer than Moses's eye; we are ignorant of the back parts or lower sides of his divinity; therefore to pry into the maze of his counsels is not only folly in man, but presumption even in angels; there is no thread or line to guide us in that labyrinth."

Melville, while continuing his Job-parody on the anatomy of Leviathan (*Moby-Dick,* II, 123), concludes his chapter on "The Tail" with this ambiguous extension of Browne's boisterousness:

"Dissect him how I may, then, I but go skin deep; I know him not, and never will. But if I know not even the tail of this whale, how understand his head? much more, how comprehend his face, when face he has none. Thou shalt see my back parts, my tail, he seems to say, but my face shall not be seen. But I cannot make out his back parts; and hint what he will about his face, I say again he has no face."

F. O. Matthiessen (*American Renaissance.* New York: Oxford, 1941, p. 431) easily recognizes the covert Biblical allusion in that passage; but he flatly says of it, "The effect of that burlesque is to magnify rather than to lessen his theme, not to blaspheme Jehovah, but to add majesty to the whale." I disagree.

76. Jude 6.

77. *Moby-Dick*, II, 94.

78. *ibid.*, II, 96.

79. *ibid.*, II, 175-176.

80. *ibid.*, II, 79-80.

81. *ibid.*, II, 171-172.

82. *ibid.*, II, 179-182. The central image in the "Try-works" chapter— the ship "plunging into that blackness of darkness"—is used in an emblematic sense that is closely related to a parallel passage in *Sartor Resartus* (pp. 98-144). Carlyle develops his image and extends it in order to satirize disillusionment as false, and at the same time to show that disillusionment provides a steppingstone upward toward the "Everlasting Yea" and thus toward a true perception of God. These are Teufelsdrockh's somber thoughts, while suffering through his "Everlasting No":

"The Universe was a mighty Sphinx-riddle, which I knew so little of, yet must rede, or be devoured. In red streaks of unspeakable grandeur, yet also in the *blackness of darkness* [italics added; cf. Melville, cf. Jude 13], was Life, to my too-unfurnished Thought unfolding itself. A strange contradiction lay in me; and I as yet knew not the solution of it. . . . It continues ever true that Saturn, or Chronos, or what we call TIME, devours all his Children: only by incessant Running, by incessant Working, may you (for some threescore-and-ten years) escape him; and you too he devours at last. . . . To me, the Universe was all void of Life, of Purpose, of Volition . . . it was one huge, dead, immeasurable Steam-engine, rolling on, in its dead indifference, to grind me limb from limb. Oh, the vast, gloomy, solitary Golgotha, and Mill of Death! Why was the Living banished thither companionless, conscious? Why, if there is no Devil; nay, unless the Devil is your God?"

So far, in this passage, Melville and Teufelsdrockh have a great deal in common! But subsequently, Teufelsdrockh recants, leaves Melville in the lurch:

". . . the heavy dreams rolled gradually away, and I awoke to a new Heaven and a new Earth. . . . O Nature!—Or what is Nature? Ha! why do I not name thee God? Art not thou the 'Living Garment of God'? O Heavens, is it, in very deed, HE, then, that ever speaks through thee; that lives and loves in thee, that lives and loves in me? . . . The Universe is not dead and demoniacal, a charnel-house with spectres; but godlike, and my Father's! . . . Always there is a black spot in our sunshine: it is even, as I said, the Shadow of Ourselves."

Taken in its totality, *Sartor Resartus* might be considered as an answer to Melville's thesis in *Moby-Dick*, made several years before *Moby-Dick* was written! One might say that Melville's familiarity with Carlyle made him uncomfortable enough to force some kind of satirical retaliation. Take just one more possible retaliation: Melville's "Caatskil eagle" image, with its insinuation that the prosy-plain being will never ascend even to the eagle's lowest point of descent; that the prosy-plain reader will not ascend to an appreciation of Melville's double-talk. Compare that passage with this from *Sartor Resartus* (p. 54):

"Well sang the Hebrew Psalmist: 'If I take the wings of the morning and dwell in the uttermost parts of the universe, God is there.' Thou thyself, O cultivated reader, who too probably art no Psalmist, but a Prosaist, knowing God only by tradition . . ."

83. *Moby-Dick*, II, 169-170.　　86. *ibid.*, II, 281-282.
84. *ibid.*, II, 301-302.　　87. *ibid.*, II, 283-284.
85. *ibid.*, II, 261.

88. *ibid.*, II, 366. Compare Captain Ahab's words, "Oh, now I feel my topmost greatness lies in my topmost grief"—and his meaning—with the following from *Sartor Resartus* (p. 144):

"Man's Unhappiness, as I construe, comes of his Greatness; it is because there is an Infinite in him, which with all his cunning he cannot quite bury under the Finite. . . . Try him with half of a Universe, of an Omnipotence, he sets to quarreling with the proprietor of the other half, and declares himself the most maltreated of men."

The more accurate Carlyle became as a diagnostician of Melville's ailments, the more Melville must have resented Carlyle while reading *Sartor Resartus*. My point, here, is that Carlyle's meaning amounts to a blunt criticism of exactly that kind of so-called tragic hero whom Melville intended to glorify—and did glorify—in Captain Ahab. Although I try to keep my own personal prejudices out of this, most of the time, I must say that my sympathies, here, are more with Carlyle than with Melville.

89. *Moby-Dick*, II, 270.

90. *ibid.*, II, 367. Remember that this overt gloss beginning, ". . . his ship, which, like Satan, would not sink to hell till she had dragged a living part of heaven along with her," has already been correlated (in Section 2 of Chapter V) with other Melvillian images of dragging-down; particularly with the description of Jackson (*Redburn*, pp. 356-357) who in dying "yet did not give over his blasphemies, but endeavoured to drag down with him to his own perdition . . ."

91. *ibid.*, II, 169-170.　　93. *ibid.*, II, 117.
92. *ibid.*, II, 368.

94. *ibid.*, II, 135-136. Melville's "Centre of Indifference" recalls Carlyle's version, in *Sartor Resartus* (p. 129):

" 'Indignation and Defiance,' especially against things in general, are not the most peaceable inmates; yet can the Psychologist surmise that it was no longer a quite hopeless Unrest; that henceforth it had at least a fixed center to revolve round. For the fire-baptized soul, long so scathed and thunder-riven, here feels its own Freedom, which feeling is its Baphometic Baptism; the citadel of its whole kingdom it has thus gained by assault, and will keep inexpugnable; outwards from which the remaining dominions, not indeed without hard battling, will doubtless by degrees be conquered."

Melville certainly took a sideswipe at that very passage in *Sartor Resartus*, and burlesqued it unmercifully, in *Pierre*; is it possible that the *Moby-Dick* passage (". . . there I still bathe me in eternal mildness of joy.") was designed to be read sarcastically? I can see the two possibilities, and it certainly would be like Melville to have intended them.

95. *Mardi*, ii, 277. 97. *Moby-Dick*, i, 133.

96. *White-Jacket*, p. 353. 98. *Pierre*, pp. 471-472.

99. *ibid.*, p. 502. While I was proof-reading galleys on this chapter ("Wicked Book") Miss Millicent Bell's excellent article on "Pierre Bayle and *Moby-Dick*" was published in *PMLA* (Vol. lxvi, No. 3, September 1951, pp. 626-648). Although I had not previously known of Miss Bell's work on Bayle and Melville, I quickly discovered that she had gone far beyond me in marshalling proofs as to the extensive uses Melville made of Bayle in writing *Moby-Dick*. All of her cited parallelisms delight me, of course, because they happen to provide additional support for my central thesis, in so far as that thesis involves Melville's debt to Bayle. In reading her article I found particularly fresh and rewarding to me the following points, which I myself would have made if I had noticed them:

(1) The description of "a stylistic device which Melville could have observed in Bayle." "Bayle cites authority against contradictory authority till the result is a house of cards, ready to fall at the first breath of disbelief, and in such a chapter of *Moby-Dick* as lxxxiii, dealing with the Jonah story, both factual material and argumentative design are simultaneously coming through from Bayle." (In my analysis of the "Try-Works" chapter, I described Melville's use of that device; but failed to correlate it with Bayle, as I should have done.)

(2) The correlation of Melville's insinuative uses of the Jonah story and the Ahab story with Bayle's essay on Gregory of Rimini, where Bayle "considers the difficult problem presented by the episodes of the Bible which attribute false statements and dishonorable acts to God himself." (Although my own analysis of Melville's insinuations concerning Jonah and Ahab explores this identical concept, I had never read Bayle on Gregory of Rimini.)

(3) The correlation of Bayle's quotation from Calvin (involving Exodus 33:23) with Melville's inverted and blasphemous paraphrase of the same Biblical passage. (I had also missed that, although I had previously correlated Melville's blasphemy, there, with Browne's boisterousness, in footnote number 75, above.)

(4) The striking correlation between Bayle's representation of Zoroaster and Melville's representation of Ahab. (Again I had failed to notice that, and I consider this single point which Miss Bell makes to be a major contribution to our understanding of so many highly significant Zoroastrian allusions and images in *Moby-Dick*.)

(5) The correlation of Bayle's summary of the ideas of Descartes, in the Pyrrho article, on the illusion of color with Melville's

blasphemous dissertation on "The Whiteness of the Whale." (Again, very important.)

My own interpretation differs from Miss Bell's on only one double-edged point. Miss Bell concludes her article, ". . . whiteness is defined by Melville as the image of un-illusion, the appearance of the world stripped of the false color of faith. This is the ultimate sense in which the hunt for the White Whale is impious." By contrast, I would call this the penultimate sense. According to my readings of Bayle and Melville, Bayle remained the confirmed and cautious skeptic, who committed himself on the good-evil of God only to ridicule the pretentiousness of all theodicies; the later Melville (the inverted mystic) became, increasingly, the confirmed and aggressive believer in the infinite malice of God. Proceeding on this assumption, I have suggested (in Chapter One) that Melville apparently misunderstood the ulterior motives and meanings of Bayle's skeptical insinuations.

VIII. GOD'S STONY HEART

1. *Pierre*, p. 372.

2. *ibid.*, pp. 412-413. The passage just quoted leads me to theorize that Carlyle's narrative of Teufelsdrockh's pilgrim progress through the disillusionments of the "Everlasting No" and on to the "Centre of Indifference" and thence to the "Everlasting Yea" stimulated Melville to project a fictional narrative, in *Pierre*, which would begin by seeming to ape the beginning of Carlyle's narrative, and then would develop into a narrative contradiction and ridicule and denial of Carlyle's conclusions. Carlyle was intent on treating disillusionment as a temporary and transitional state; for that reason he gently burlesqued the fad (among English and German romantics) of translating the anguish of the adolescent soul into the anguish of a tragic hero. Melville, while overtly satirizing the anguish of adolescent disillusionment, proceeds to show how these agonies are but the first steps toward an accurate perception of God's malice, and man's malice. It might be said that Melville's ulterior concern, in *Pierre*, is "descendental" rather than "transcendental"; but my immediate concern is to point out that Melville does indeed echo and covertly satirize the meaning of many separate passages in *Sartor Resartus*. For example, the passage just quoted from *Pierre*, in the text, may be recognized as a deceptively close parallel to the following passage from *Sartor Resartus* (p. 121):

". . . in these sick days, when the Born of Heaven first descries himself (about the age of twenty) in a world such as ours, richer than usual in two things, in Truths grown obsolete, and Trades grown obsolete,— what can the fool think but that it is all a Den of Lies, wherein whoso will not speak Lies and act Lies, must stand idle and despair? Whereby it happens that, for your nobler minds, the publishing of some such Work of Art, in one or the other dialect, becomes almost a necessity.

For what is it properly but an Altercation with the Devil, before you begin honestly Fighting him? Your Byron publishes his Sorrows of Lord George, in verse and in prose, and copiously otherwise."

Melville's implicit answer, in *Pierre*, is that the "Altercation" is "properly" with God, who is indeed at one with the Devil!

3. *Pierre*, p. 2. Melville's entire portrayal of Pierre's doomed love for Lucy is very closely related, in mock-heroic style and in mock-heroic imagery, to Carlyle's portrayal of Teufelsdrockh's doomed love for the fair Blumine. The basic symbolic extensions employed by both Carlyle and Melville are carefully grooved to illuminate the disillusioned one's reinterpretation of the Genesis story. To illustrate this close relationship between *Pierre* and *Sartor Resartus*, compare Melville's method with Carlyle's method in these passages from *Sartor Resartus* (pp. 102-106 passim):

"If in youth, the Universe is majestically unveiling, and everywhere Heaven revealing itself on Earth, nowhere to the Young Man does this Heaven on Earth so immediately reveal itself as in the Young Maiden. Strangely enough, in this strange life of ours, it has been so appointed. . . .

"In every well-conditioned stripling, as I conjecture, there already blooms a certain prospective Paradise, cheered by some fairest Eve; nor, in the stately vistas, and flowering and foliage of that Garden, is a Tree of Knowledge, beautiful and awful in the midst thereof, wanting. Perhaps too the whole is but the lovelier, if Cherubim and a Flaming Sword divide it from all footsteps of men; and grant him, the imaginative stripling, only the view, not the entrance. Happy season of virtuous youth, when shame is still an impassable celestial barrier; and the sacred air-cities of Hope have not shrunk into the mean clay-hamlets of Reality; and man, by his nature, is yet infinite and free!

"As for our young Forlorn, continues Teufelsdrockh, evidently meaning himself, in his secluded way of life, and with his glowing Fantasy, the more fiery that it burnt under cover, as in a reverberating furnace, his feeling towards the Queens of this Earth was, and indeed is, altogether unspeakable. A visible Divinity dwelt in them; to our young Friend all women were holy, were heavenly. . . . It was appointed, that the high celestial orbit of Blumine should intersect the low sublunary one of our Forlorn; that he, looking in her empyrean eyes, should fancy the upper Sphere of Light was come down into this nether sphere of Shadows. . . ."

4. *Pierre*, p. 6.

5. *ibid.*, pp. 16-17. Melville here satirizes both Carlyle and Goethe. The Latin quotation ("Nobody is against God unless it be God Himself") is from Goethe's *Autobiography*. Carlyle has also used this mock-heroic style, for entirely different reasons, in *Sartor Resartus* (p. 111):

". . . in such a many-tinted Aurora, and by this fairest of Orient Light-bringers must our friend be blandished, and the new Apocalypse of Nature unrolled to him. Fairest Blumine! And, even as a Star, all Fire and humid Softness, *a very Light-ray incarnate*! [italics added; cf. the name of Melville's heroine, "Lucy"] Was there so much as a fault, a 'caprice,' he could have dispensed with? Was she not to him in very deed a Morning-star; did not her presence bring with it airs from Heaven? As for Aeolian Harps in the breath of dawn, as from *Memnon's Statue* [italics added; cf. Melville's elaborate use of Memnon in *Pierre*] struck by the rosy finger of Aurora, unearthly music was around him, and lapped him into untried balmy Rest. Pale Doubt fled away to the distance; Life bloomed up with happiness and hope. The past, then, was all a haggard dream; he had been in the Garden of Eden, then, and could not discern it! But lo now! the black walls of his prison melt away; the captive is alive, is free."

6. *Pierre*, pp. 43-44.

7. *ibid.*, p. 45.

8. *ibid.*, pp. 45-46.

9. *ibid.*, p. 58.

10. *ibid.*, p. 87.

11. *ibid.*, pp. 89-90.

12. *ibid.*, pp. 90-91. Compare that passage with this from *Sartor Resartus* (p. 125):

". . . I nevertheless still loved Truth, and would bate no jot of my allegiance to her. 'Truth!' I cried, 'though the Heavens crush me for following her: no Falsehood! though a whole celestial Lubberland were the price of Apostasy.' . . . Thus . . . was the Infinite nature of Duty still dimly present to me: living without God in the world, of God's light I was not utterly bereft; if my as yet unsealed eyes, with their unspeakable longing, could nowhere see Him, nevertheless in my heart He was present, and His heaven-written Law still stood legible and sacred there."

13. *Pierre*, p. 93.

14. *ibid.*, p. 121. The theological overtones of "I will no more have a father" should be obvious. Because Pierre is intermittently cast in the role of a First Adam, the implicit inversion of the Genesis story, or rather of the Christian construction of it, is equally obvious, throughout.

Carlyle similarly establishes an analogy between the parentage of Adam and the parentage of Teufelsdrockh; but for a purpose entirely different from Melville's. Carlyle's chapter on Teufelsdrockh's birth is entitled, with obvious ambiguity, "Genesis." Notice, in the following passage, Carlyle's oblique theological overtones (*Sartor Resartus*, pp. 65-66):

"Who this reverend Personage that glided into the Orchard Cottage when the Sun was in Libra, and then, as on spirit's wings, glided out again, might be? An inexpressible desire, full of love and of sadness, has often since struggled within me to shape an answer. Ever, in my distresses and loneliness, has Fantasy turned, full of longing, to that unknown Father, who perhaps far from me, perhaps near, either way invisible, might have taken me to his paternal bosom, there to lie

screened from many a woe. Thou beloved Father, dost thou still, shut
out from me only by thin penetrable curtains of earthly Space, wend
to and fro among the crowd of the living? Or art thou hidden by those
far thicker curtains of the Everlasting Night, or rather of the Everlasting Day, through which my mortal eye and outstretched arms need
not strive to reach? Alas, I know not, and in vain vex myself to know.
More than once, heart-deluded, have I taken for thee this and the other
noble-looking Stranger; and approached him wistfully, with infinite
regard; but he too had to repel me, he too was not thou."

15. *Pierre*, pp. 151-152.

16. *ibid.*, p. 196.

17. *ibid.*, p. 144.

18. *ibid.*, pp. 190-191. Pierre's question to the Memnon Stone, and
the ensuing silence, again recalls a parallel (but differently intended)
passage in *Sartor Resartus* (p. 124):

"Thus has the bewildered Wanderer to stand, as so many have done,
receiving no Answer but an Echo. It is all a grim Desert, this once-
fair world of his; wherein is heard only the howling of wild beasts, or
the shrieks of despairing, hate-filled men; and no Pillar of Cloud by
day, and no Pillar of Fire by night, any longer guides the Pilgrim. To
such length has the spirit of Inquiry carried him. 'But what boots it?'
cries he: 'it is but the common lot in this era. . . . The whole world is,
like thee, sold to Unbelief; their Old Temples of the Godhead, which
for long have not been rain-proof, crumble down; and men ask now:
Where is the Godhead; our eyes never saw him?'"

19. *Pierre*, pp. 229-230.

20. *ibid.*, pp. 240-241.

21. *ibid.*, pp. 245, 246, 247.

22. *ibid.*, pp. 265-268.   24. *Pierre*, pp. 285-286.

23. Milton, *Paradise Lost*, ix, 990ff.   25. *ibid.*, pp. 293-300.

26. *ibid.*, pp. 380-381. Again consider a parallel passage, differently
intended, from *Sartor Resartus* (p. 126):

"Alas, the fearful Unbelief is unbelief in yourself; and how could
I believe? Had not my first, last Faith in myself, when even to me the
Heavens seemed laid open, and I dared to love, been all too cruelly
belied? The speculative Mystery of Life grew ever more mysterious to
me: neither in the practical Mystery had I made the slightest progress,
but been everywhere buffeted, foiled, and contemptuously cast out.
A feeble unit in the middle of a threatening Infinitude, I seemed to have
nothing given me but eyes, whereby to discern my own wretchedness.
Invisible yet impenetrable walls, as of Enchantment, divided me from
all the living; was there, in the wide world, any true bosom I could
press trustfully to mine? O Heaven, No, there was none!"

27. *Pierre*, pp. 341-342.   30. *ibid.*, p. 396.

28. *ibid.*, pp. 393-395.   31. *ibid.*, p. 397.

29. *ibid.*, p. 395.   32. *ibid.*, p. 402.

33. *ibid.*, p. 421. Pierre's blunt dropping of "indifferent disguises" and "all philosophical pretensions" is so closely related to his dismissal of "ye chattering apes of a sophomorean Spinoza, and Plato," that he might well have included in his dismissal both Goethe and Carlyle. So far, Pierre has acted out something like an inverted pattern of Carlyle's disillusionment-progression represented in *Sartor Resartus.* We first see Pierre glorying in the "Everlasting Yea" and then we see him move through a middle period of confusion to an "Everlasting No." The exclamation, "Away, ye chattering apes of a sophomorean Spinoza, and Plato," should be correlated with the passage in which Melville as narrator in *Pierre* speaks about the "Talismanic Secret" which has never yet been found: "Certain philosophers have time and again pretended to have found it; but if they do not in the end discover their own delusion, other people soon discover it for themselves, and so those philosophers and their vain philosophy are let glide away into practical oblivion. Plato, and Spinoza, and Goethe, and many more belong to the guild of self-impostors, with a preposterous rabble of Muggletonian Scots and Yankees, whose vile brogue still the more bestreaks the stripedness of their Greek or German Neoplatonical originals." (*Pierre*, 231.)

34. *Pierre*, pp. 430-431. 36. *ibid.*, p. 480.
35. *ibid.*, p. 452. 37. *ibid.*, p. 482.

38. *ibid.*, p. 483. Melville's responses and reactions to Spenser's poetry would reward an extended study. Here, the total action of the "Two Cantos of Mutabilitie" is pertinent; particularly some speeches of incest-bred Dame Mutabilitie, in answer to Jove, and some of his reply:

> 'I am a daughter, by the mother's side,
> Of her that is grand-mother magnifide
> Of all the gods, great Earth, great Chaos' child:
> But by the father's (be it not envide)
> I greater am in bloud (whereon I build)
> Than all the gods, though wrongfully from heaven exil'd.
>
> For Titan (as ye all acknowledge must)
> Was Saturn's elder brother by birth-right;
> Both, sonnes of Uranus: but by unjust
> And guileful meanes, through Corybantes' slight,
> The younger thrust the elder from his right:
> Since which thou, Jove, injuriously hast held
> The heavens' rule from Titan's sonnes by might;
> And them to hellish dungeons downe hast feld:
> Witnesse, ye heavens, the truth of all that I have teld.'
>
> . . . .
>
> Till, having pauz'd awhile, Jove thus bespake:
> 'Will never mortall thoughts ceasse to aspire,

In this bold sort, to heaven claime to make,
And touch celestiall seates with earthly mire?
I would have thought that bold Procrustes' hire,
Or Typhon's fall, or proud Ixion's paine,
Or great Prometheus tasting of our ire,
Would have suffiz'd the rest for to restraine,
And warn'd all men, by their example, to refraine:

'But now this off-scum of that cursed fry
Dare to renew the like bold enterprize,
And challenge th' heritage of this our skie;
Whom what should hinder, but that we likewise
Should handle as the rest of her allies,
And thunder-drive to hell?' With that, he shooke
His nectar-deawed locks, with which the skyes
And all the world beneath for terror quooke,
And eft his burning levin-brond in hand he tooke.
                    (*Faerie Queene*, VII, Cantos 26, 27, 29, 30)

39. *ibid.*, p. 489.   41. *ibid.*, p. 497.
40. *ibid.*, pp. 471-472.   42. *ibid.*, p. 499.
43. *ibid.*, p. 502. Pierre's Ahab-like defiance and hate recall the surface meaning (but not the ulterior meaning) of Teufelsdrockh's defiant No; before he has learned better:
". . . what is the sum-total of the worst that lies before thee? Death? Well, Death; and say the pangs of Tophet too, and all that the Devil and Man may, will or can do against thee! Hast thou not a heart; canst thou not suffer whatsoever it be; and, as a Child of Freedom, though outcast, trample Tophet itself under thy feet, while it consumes thee? Let it come, then; I will meet it and defy it! . . . The Everlasting No had said, 'Behold thou art fatherless, outcast, and the Universe is mine . . .' to which my whole Me now made answer, 'I am not thine, but Free, and forever hate thee!'" (*Sartor Resartus*, p. 128.)

44. *Pierre*, p. 290.
45. *ibid.*, p. 235. I have studied with care and admiration the elaborate and stimulating Introduction and Notes of Dr. Henry A. Murray, in his edition of *Pierre* (New York, Hendricks House-Farrar, Strauss, 1949). His knowledge of the facts concerning Melville's life and of the psychic and psychopathic aspects of Melville's condition is far more extensive and profound than mine can ever be. Nevertheless, his interpretation of *Pierre* strikes me as inadequate; his imposition of terminology borrowed from Freud and Jung seem to me to be more of a hindrance than a help. Furthermore, I suggest that Dr. Murray is guilty of making that mistake I describe in the first paragraph of my remarks To the Reader: he permits the bias of his own complex viewpoint and of his own scale of values to come between himself and his attempt to understand Melville's viewpoint in writing *Pierre*. For example, consider this excerpt from his Introduction (pp. lxii-lxiii):

"Although Melville may be said to have succeeded in identifying his hero in our minds with certain features of Christ's personality, it is clear that his imagination has not wholly surrendered to the magnetic figure of the historic Jesus; that is, he was not trying to re-create Christ 'in modern dress' to the extent, say, that Dostoevsky does in *The Idiot*. . . . In the first place, Pierre is only nominally a Christian. He has been polished by the 'gentlemanizing influences of Christianity,' but we find only one allusion, and that unconvincing, to any devotion to God. . . . Spiritually he is a spoiled brat who believes that joy is his 'right as man,' and were he deprived of it he would have reason to become a 'railing atheist.' . . . In the second place, before meeting Isabel, Pierre is a natural unredeemed egoist. . . ."

Dr. Murray apparently views the figure of the historic Jesus as "magnetic," and so do I. At the stage when Melville wrote *Pierre*, he probably retained that attitude toward Jesus which he had expressed in *Moby-Dick*: "And whatever they may reveal of the divine love in the Son, the soft, curled hermaphroditical Italian pictures, in which his idea has been most successfully embodied; these pictures, so destitute as they are of all brawniness, hint nothing of any power, but the mere negative, feminine one of submission and endurance, which on all hands it is conceded, form the peculiar practical virtues of his teachings." Melville sneers at the doctrine of Christian acceptance, throughout *Moby-Dick* and throughout *Pierre*. For Dr. Murray to hold Pierre up against Dr. Murray's concept of "the magnetic figure of the historic Jesus" is, then, irrelevant to an understanding of Melville's portrayal of Pierre. Melville, in his view of Jesus, is off on another tack, and consequently the reader or interpreter who is interested in following Melville's tack is obliged to set aside the concept of the figure of Jesus as "magnetic"; to set it aside, temporarily.

Again, to say that Pierre is only nominally a Christian is to render no service to our understanding of Melville because that merely measures Pierre in Dr. Murray's Christian scale of values. Dr. Murray acknowledges (at times, and then seems to forget it) that Melville was writing *Pierre* from an anti-Christian viewpoint. Because that is correct, I see no value whatsoever in trying to measure Pierre in any scale of values other than Melville's, if our objective is to understand Melville.

Again, what value is gained by observing that "we find only one allusion, and that unconvincing, to any devotion to God," on Pierre's part? Unconvincing to whom? Our concern is with anti-Christian Melville, and his scale of values. It is possible to imagine a frame of reference in which Pierre's devotion to God is convincing, and such a use of our imaginations should increase our understanding of anti-Christian Melville.

Again, what value is gained by describing Pierre as a "natural unredeemed egoist"? Notice that those two adjectives, "natural" and "unredeemed," have an apparently pejorative value in Dr. Murray's context; but notice that they also had a pejorative value in that Calvinistic terminology which Melville loathed, and that they could be used by anti-Christian Melville as terms of honor.

When Dr. Murray gets around to saying of Pierre, "Spiritually he is a spoiled brat . . ." Dr. Murray's bias again gets in his way and blocks him off from understanding Melville's bias. As it happens, I have to keep my own bias under strict lock and key, as much as I can, to achieve at least the illusion of sympathy with Melville's viewpoint in order to understand that viewpoint; it would be much easier for me to join Dr. Murray in getting angry with both Pierre and Melville for their closely related viewpoints.

My own mistakes and inadequacies are what they are, and I do not pretend to pose as an infallible paragon in this matter of trying to understand Melville, even though I may sound as though I do, at times. In challenging Dr. Murray's approach, I merely wish to point out that while he is beautifully long-suited in facts and in the principles of psychoanalysis (habitually used for purposes of effecting cures), he seems to me to be somewhat short-suited in his grasp of the principles of literary interpretation.

IX. SWINDLER AS GOD'S AGENT

1. I Corinthians 13:2-7.
2. Carlyle, *On Heroes, Hero-Worship, and the Heroic in History.* Albany, N.Y.: Lyons, 1888, p. 276.
3. *Confidence-Man*, p. 7.
4. *ibid.*, pp. 8-9.
5. *Mardi*, II, 31-32.
6. *Confidence-Man*, p. 1.
7. *ibid.*, pp. 10-11.
8. *ibid.*, pp. 12-13.
9. *ibid.*, pp. 14-15.
10. *ibid.*, pp. 15-17.
11. *ibid.*, pp. 18-19.
12. *ibid.*, pp. 33-34.
13. *ibid.*, p. 37.
14. *ibid.*, p. 42.
15. *ibid.*, pp. 49-54 passim.
16. *ibid.*, p. 73.
17. *ibid.*, pp. 49-54 passim.
18. *ibid.*, pp. 96-98.
19. *ibid.*, p. 105.
20. *ibid.*, p. 106.
21. *ibid.*, p. 138.
22. *ibid.*, pp. 140-141. Peter the Wild Boy (Dr. Arbuthnot's celebrated patient) is here used by Melville as he was used by many other "enlightened rationalists" to ridicule that aspect of the Rousseau concept which implied that "natural man," if nurtured only by Mother Nature, must be as noble as prelapsarian Adam. The fun started in 1724, and in Germany, when someone found a naked black-haired dark-skinned child in a "natural" position, sucking the teat of a cow. The parentage or history of the child could not be learned, and although he seemed to be about twelve years old he was so completely "natural" that he could neither speak nor understand "civilized" words. Brought to England by royal order, about two years later, and placed under

Dr. Arbuthnot's care, the creature became the topic of high-flown philosophical speculation. Defoe's catch-penny pamphlet summarizing the hullabaloo was entitled, *Mere Nature Delineated; or, a Body Without a Soul. Being Observations Upon the Young Forester Lately Brought to Town, from Germany.* Apparently with tongue in cheek, Defoe opined, "He seems to be the very creature which the learned world has, for many years past, pretended to wish for, *viz.*, one that being kept entirely from human society, so as never to have heard anyone speak, must therefore either not speak at all; or, if he did form any speech to himself, then they should know what language Nature would first form for mankind." (Compare this concept, as echoed derisively in *The Confidence-Man*, with Ishmael's sly sarcasm concerning the type of morbid Captain Ahab: "receiving all nature's sweet or savage impressions fresh from her own voluntary and confiding breast.") Significantly (in Melville's frame of reference), Peter the Wild Boy was eventually classified by medical experts as a full-fledged idiot; a "natural."

23. *Confidence-Man,*
   pp. 143-145.
24. *ibid.*, pp. 153-154.
25. *ibid.*, p. 171.
26. *ibid.*, p. 174.

27. *ibid.*, pp. 207-208.
28. *ibid.*, p. 328.
29. Milton, *Paradise Lost,* ix, 99-113.
30. *Confidence-Man,* pp. 320-336 passim.

X. CHRONIC REPULSE

1. Brooks Atkinson, "Foreword," in Louis O. Coxe and Robert Chapman, *Billy Budd: A Play in Three Acts, Adapted from a Novel by Herman Melville.* Princeton, N.J.: Princeton University Press, 1951.

2. *Herman Melville: Journal Up the Straits, October 11, 1856—May 5, 1857.* New York: The Colophon, 1935, p. 29.

3. *ibid.*, pp. 57-58, 64. These entries on the pyramids later served Melville as raw materials for his poem, "The Pyramid," in which he gave an oblique and concealed statement of the same theological view.

4. *ibid.*, p. 72.
5. *Moby-Dick,* i, 95.
6. *Journal Up the Straits,* pp. 79, 88.
7. *ibid.*, p. 89.

8. *ibid.*, pp. 91-92.
9. *ibid.*, p. 104.
10. *Clarel,* i, 51-53.
11. *Poems,* pp. 247-259.

12. Arthur Schopenhauer, *Studies in Pessimism: A Series of Essays.* T. Bailey Saunders (editor and translator), London, Sonnenschein, 1891, p. 24. Melville's copies of Schopenhauer are now in the Harvard College Library, and are described in Merton M. Sealts, Jr., *Melville's Reading: A Check-List of Books Owned and Borrowed.* Offprinted from Harvard Library Bulletin, 1948-1950, p. 417.

13. Arthur Schopenhauer, *Counsels and Maxims.* T. Bailey Saunders (editor and translator), London, 1890, Sonnenschein, p. xiii.

Melville's fondness for employing fablelike utterances, as a means of revealing and concealing his darker meanings, may have been partially responsible for his marking the following passage; but his marking indicates that he particularly enjoyed the sarcasm in the last sentence:

"A mother gave her children Aesop's fables to read, in the hope of educating and improving their minds; but they very soon brought the book back, and the eldest, wise beyond his years, delivered himself as follows: 'This is no book for us; it's much too childish and stupid. You can't make us believe that foxes and wolves and ravens are able to talk; we've got beyond stories of that kind.' In these young hopefuls you have the enlightened Rationalists of the future."

XI. DIVINE DEPRAVITY

1. Thomas Paine, *Age of Reason; Being an Investigation of True and Fabulous Theology.* New York, Vincent Parke, 1908, p. 132.

2. Thomas Paine, *Common Sense; Addressed to the Inhabitants of the United States.* London, J. S. Jordan, 1791, pp. 5-6.

3. Thomas Paine, *Rights of Man: Being an Answer to Mr. Burke's Attack on the French Revolution.* London, J. S. Jordan, 1891, p. 55.

4. "Death" is just as much a "hypo" for Melville in *Billy Budd* as it was for Ishmael in Chapter One of *Moby-Dick.* Hawthorne, in "The Birthmark," had said that Aylmer's somber imagination viewed the little hand-shaped ("I too have a hand here.") blemish on Georgiana's face as "the symbol of his wife's liability to sin, sorrow, decay, and death." This is a pertinent aspect of the analogy which Melville establishes; particularly in the light of later developments in *Billy Budd.*

Melville's own "Hamletism" and his repeated references to *Hamlet* may justify my suggesting a Melvillian reading of the following celebrated *Hamlet* passage (I, iv, 23ff.) as a symbolic representation of "innate depravity":

> So oft it chances in particular men,
> That for some vicious mole of nature in them,
> As, in their birth—wherein they are not guilty,
> Since nature cannot choose his origin. . . .
>
> . . . .
>
> Carrying, I say, the stamp of one defect,
> Being nature's livery or fortune's star—
> His virtues else—be they as pure as grace,
> As infinite as man may undergo—
> Shall in the general censure take corruption
> From that particular fault: the dram of evil
> Doth all the noble substance often doubt
> To his own scandal.

My point, here, is that Melville could easily have construed this passage to represent the victims of "innate depravity" as suffering from a "birthmark," a "dram of evil," mark you, "wherein they are not guilty." In the action of *Hamlet*, the motif of "responsibility" is viewed from various conflicting angles; Melville would have been inclined to view it from only one angle.

5. The streakedness of marble seemed to fascinate Melville as a theological symbol, even as the imperviousness of stone also did. One of the subtlest pieces of stylistic chicanery in *Pierre* is pertinent here, and I make bold to suggest that Melville had something like it in mind as he wrote his description of Claggart:

"Ah, if man were wholly made in heaven, why catch we hellglimpses? Why in the noblest marble pillar that stands beneath the all-comprising vault, ever should we descry the sinister vein? We lie in nature very close to God; and though, further on, the stream may be corrupted by the banks it flows through; yet at the fountain's rim, where mankind stand, there the stream infallibly bespeaks the fountain."

In other words, the streakedness, or the "sinister vein" also bespeaks the Source.

6. Stubb explained the situation nicely: "Damn the devil, Flask; do you suppose I'm afraid of the devil? Who's afraid of him, except the old governor who daren't catch him and put him in double-darbies, as he deserves, but lets him go about kidnapping people; ay, and signed a bond with him, that all the people the devil kidnapped, he'd roast for him? There's a governor!"

7. Melville *is* a rascal! The pretended tone of innocence in this passage should be obvious; but Melville knows when he quotes the Bible without quotation marks. "Dark sayings" has a highly pertinent context in Psalm Seventy-eight:

> I will open my mouth in a parable;
> I will utter dark sayings of old.

How old, in this case? As old as the Ophite heresiarchs whom Melville mentioned by name in *Moby-Dick*.

8. There he goes again, and he dearly loved to invert Paul's meanings. For further exegesis on "the mystery of iniquity," see Section 18 of this chapter.

9. Milton, *Paradise Lost*, iv, 512-522.

10. *White-Jacket*, p. 177.

11. Bayle, *Dictionary*, iv, 2494-2495.

12. *White-Jacket*, pp. 178-179.

13. *ibid.*, p. 187.

14. Bayle, *Dictionary*, iv, 2493.

15. Melville's familiarity with the writings of Tom Paine, and his previously mentioned fondness for following both Montaigne and Bayle in the tradition of tampering with the maxims of Paul, would

have predisposed him to like this reference to the First Adam and the Second Adam:

"That manufacturer of quibbles, St. Paul, if he wrote the books that bear his name, has helped this quibble on by making another quibble upon the word *Adam*. He makes there to be two Adams; the one who sins in fact, and suffers by proxy; the other who sins by proxy, and suffers in fact. A religion thus interlarded with quibble, subterfuge, and pun has a tendency to instruct its professors in the practise of these arts. They acquire the habit without being aware of the cause." (*Age of Reason*, p. 32.)

The point which Paine makes in those last two sentences should not be shrugged off, because there is too much evidence to show that he is right, even when we convert his meaning to a non-pejorative viewpoint. The Bible itself is essentially oriental in its employment of figurative language, and the literary impact of the figurative language of the Bible on European literature encouraged the development of allegorical utterance. Paul himself was very fond of taking a passage from the Old Testament and then adapting it to his own uses by giving it an allegorical interpretation. It is certainly obvious that Melville's entire leaning toward an exceptional form of figurative and symbolic and allegorical narrative owes much to his having been saturated in Biblical modes of expression and in Biblical exegesis or commentary. Paine was right, in this limited sense, and his remark helps us to understand Melville's artistic style and structure.

16. *Pierre*, p. 493.

17. The manuscript of *Billy Budd* has been variously transcribed by three editors, whose separate versions I have consulted in making my quotations.

(1) Raymond W. Weaver (editor), *Billy Budd and Other Prose Pieces*. London: Constable, 1924.

(2) Raymond W. Short (editor), *Four Great American Novels*. New York: Holt, 1946.

(3) F. Barron Freeman, *Melville's Billy Budd: The Complete Text of the Novel and the Unpublished Short Story*. Cambridge: Harvard University Press, 1948.

XII. CONCLUSION

1. Henry James, *The Art of the Novel: Critical Prefaces*. With an Introduction by Richard P. Blackmur. New York: Scribner, 1947, p. 201.

INDEX

Adam's Fall:

Background (Chronological): St. Paul provides basis for orthodox interpretation (Romans 5:12-19), 457; second-century Ophites taught that God deceived Adam and Eve and that the Serpent spoke Truth, 34, 430-431; Clement and Origen taught that Adam's misuse of free will caused the Fall, 22; Arius and Arians rejected dogma that Fall was predestinated, 22; Pelagius rejected dogma of Original Sin, based on Fall, 22; Moses Maimonides hinted God was Original Sinner, 354; Calvin (following Augustinian dogma) based his concepts of the Fall on dogmas of Predestination, Original Sin, Innate Depravity, 4-6, 16; Arminius reasserted that Adam's will was free, 22; Sir Thomas Browne said Adam blamed God, t.p.; Milton made Calvinistic-Arminian interpretation of, 24-26; Bayle twitted Calvinists for error of misrepresenting God as Author of Adam's evil, 28-30; Rousseau's variations on, 33-34; Blake (obliquely), 34-35; Shelley (obliquely), 36, 179-180; Byron, 37-39; Dutch Reformed Church in America, on, 18-19; Carlyle on (obliquely), 447, 448-449; HM on Hawthorne's concern for, 135; Schopenhauer on, 351

HM's Changing Responses Toward: accepted Calvinistic dogma on, in youth, 4, 18-19; in *Typee*, contradictory blend of Calvin-Rousseau concepts on, 45-49; in *Redburn*, equivocal allusion to, 81; in *White-Jacket*, rationalistic allegorical satire on orthodox view of, 103; in *Mosses* review, ambiguous allusion to, 135; in *Moby-Dick*, sarcastic mention of "orchard thieves" and "undigested apple-dumpling," 18, 157; in Hawthorne letter, Adam's allegory viewed as unsolved riddle, 141; in *Pierre*, sardonic inversion of First-Adam, Last-Adam dogma, 269-271, 285, 290-291; in *Confidence-Man*, allusion, 313; in *Billy Budd*, central allegory inverts

orthodox concept of, 355ff; *see* Depravity, God, Madness, Original Sin, Right Reason, Truth

Aeschylus, *Prometheus Bound*, quoted, 179

Age of Reason (Paine), 188; quoted, 356-357, 456-457

Ahrimanism, Carlyle on modern, 131

Akenside, Mark, *Pleasures of Imagination*, theological insinuation made of, 311

Allegory and Symbol:

Background: Bunyan, 23, 176, 286; Carlyle on symbols, 133-134; Dante, 60, 281, 294; Paul, 457; Plato, 60; Spenser, 60, 62-63, 253, 281

HM's Adaptations of Allegorical Conventions: in *Mardi*, relatively orthodox use of, 60ff; in *Redburn*, allegory of the Guide-Book, 82-84; in *White-Jacket*, values of conventional tropes inverted, 93ff; in *Moby-Dick*, elaborate and sustained inversions of values for orthodox symbols, 133-135, 147ff; in *Pierre*, inversion of Eden-convention and soul's-progress-upward convention, 247ff; in *Confidence-Man*, inversion of Biblical-theological tropes, 297ff; in *Billy Budd*, inversion of conventional First-Adam, Last-Adam tropes, 355ff; *see Moby-Dick*, Allegorical Elements of; *see also* Deception, Triple-talk

Allen, Ethan, *Reason the Only Oracle of Man*, 262

Anatomie of Melancholy, see Burton

Ancient Mariner (Coleridge), oblique use of, in *Moby-Dick*, 206-207

"Apology for Raimond Sebond" (Montaigne), 21; extract, quoted in *Moby-Dick*, 187

"Appleton House, Upon: To My Lord Fairfax" (Marvell), HM insinuates theological extensions for a passage quoted from, in *Billy Budd*, 369

Arius and Arian heresy, 22

Arminius and Arminian heresy, 22, 24

Arnold, Matthew, "Dover Beach," 45

Arvin, Newton, on *Typee*, cited and challenged, 51; on *Moby-Dick*, cited and challenged, 427

lightened: in *White-Jacket*, feigns Christian orthodoxy while championing the natural rights of man, 93-98; slashing off the white jacket symbolic of self-liberation from Christian-Platonic belief, 98-109; covert allegory suggests tyranny, malice, brutality, depravity, of all superiors in God's chain-of-being, 109-119; further representation of interest in Satanic hero, 120-121; his rationalism merely a pose because, fascinated by what repelled him, he has already become an inverted Calvinist, inverted mystic, inverted Transcendentalist, 5-6, 122-124, 131-133, 421-423

Declaration of Independence From God: in Hawthorne letter, a Byronic manifesto, cautiously worded, 127-128; an "Everlasting No" thundered against Carlyle's "Everlasting Yea," 128-134; baptizes himself (Ahab, Ishmael) in the name of the Devil, 137-140

Choice of Weapons For the Rebellion: mistakenly evaluates Hawthorne's use of stylistic weapons, 134-136; praises exquisiteness of Burton's "atheistical" ironies on sacred matters, 151; admires Browne for writing like a Satanic or "crack'd archangel," 74; claims that only enlightened rationalists perceive the "right meaning" in Montaigne's stylistic equivocations, 94; hints at "wile and guile" in the tropes of Camoens, 96, 346-349; opines that Solomon resorted to defensive deceptions, 140; privately confides to Hawthorne the "secret" motto of *Moby-Dick*, 138

Declares War on God: sends Ahab and Ishmael into battle, for him, in *Moby-Dick*, 184-185, 191-195, 214-215, 231-232, 234; in *Pierre*, the hero finally achieves a tragic vision of God's malice and asserts his defiance, in death, 290-291; analogy between final actions of Ahab and Pierre, 241-243

Siege and Repulse: reconnoitering in the Holy Land, 332-335; a fresh view of God's only begotten son, in *Clarel*, 335-338; repulse in "Timoleon" and "After the Pleasure Party," 338-346; self-projection, in "Camo-

ens," 346-349; alliance with Schopenhauer, 350-351

Last Campaign: in *Billy Budd*, sardonically oblique attack on God's depravity, 356-414; allegorical representation of God's persistent malice provided by correlating *Somers* incident with Genesis incident, 117-118, 355-361; ultimate invasion of Heaven, 425

Melville's Religious Thought (Braswell), 429

Mephistopheles, 200

Mickle, William J., translator of Camoens' *Lusiad*, 347

Milton, John, and *Paradise Lost*:

Background: view of, as champion of Reformation dogma and enemy of rationalistic humanism, 24-26; attacked, at least in spirit, by rationalists like Bayle, 26-32; attempts of Satanic School to "capture" *Paradise Lost*, 34-40

HM's Changing Responses To: possibly inspired to high calling of pious authorship by Spenser and Milton, 340-341; tribute to, in *Mardi*, 433; equivocal allusion to Milton's Satan, in *Redburn*, 88; suggestion of, in *White-Jacket*, 120; Captain Ahab's relation to Milton's Satan, in *Moby-Dick*, 137-139, 143, 178-179, 189-190, 203; Pierre's ultimate relation to Milton's Satan, 269-271, 290-291; Satan in *Confidence-Man*, 326-327; in *Billy Budd*, 377-381, 402

Paradise Lost, Quotations From:

I, 1ff	16
I, 94ff	25
I, 599ff	179
III, 150ff	26
IV, 48ff	139
IV, 115ff	379
IV, 380ff	190
IV, 512ff	380
VII, 1ff	343-344
IX, 99ff	189, 326
IX, 990ff	270
XII, 469ff	402

Moby-Dick (Melville), pertinent aspects of, analyzed, 7-11, 147-242; basic antithesis between the Ahab-Ishmael tragic vision of Truth and Starbuck's optimistic vision of God's plan (Satanic "madness" *vs.* Christian "right

crookedness, 297-328; in *Billy Budd,* Captain Vere's trial-scene rhetoric is (allegorically considered) sardonically represented as an appeal to the Calvinistic dogma of "right reason," to justify the ways of Vere to Budd, 392-399; *see* Madness

Rights of Man, *see* Natural Man, Rationalism, Depravity

Rights of Man (Paine), quoted, 357

Rousseau, J. J., 31, 33-34; HM's sympathetic responses to concepts of, in *Typee,* 45ff; in *White-Jacket,* 112-116; by contrast, sneeringly skeptical attitude toward concept of the "noble savage," in *Confidence-Man,* 319-321, 453-454; in *Billy Budd,* "noble savage" represented as gullible victim, because of his ignorance-innocence, 357, 366

Sartor Resartus (Carlyle):

HM's Reaction To, Privately: in letter to Hawthorne, the "yes-gentry" are damned, while those who say "No! in thunder" are extolled, 128-129; unlike the mature Carlyle's affirmative position, Melville echoes the first-phase Teufelsdrockh when he baptizes himself in the name of the Devil, 131-132, 137-140

HM's Reaction To, in White-Jacket: suggestion that the allegory of slashing off the jacket reflects HM's anti-Christian interpretation of Christian Carlyle's clothes-philosophy, 98-109

HM's Reaction To, in Moby-Dick: antithetical polarity of HM's blasphemous whaling philosophy and Carlyle's pious clothes philosophy, 133-134; inverted parallelisms: in "The Guilder," HM apparently contradicts Carlyle on the pilgrim progress of the soul's growth, 149-150; "Loomings," 155-159, 437-438; in "A Bosom Friend," Ishmael pretends to be a Presbyterian, 166-168; in "The Advocate," Carlyle as God's Advocate is answered by Ishmael as Devil's Advocate, 171-173; in "The Quarter-Deck," Ahab paraphrases and contradicts Carlyle on the symbolic significance of "all visible objects," 184, 440; Ahab and Teufelsdrockh both represented as quitting the common

fleet of whalers, and navigating with sextant and compass of their own devising, 441-442; in "Whiteness of the Whale," the Carlyle-Goethe concept of Nature as "visible garment of God" is contradicted by Ishmael, "all deified Nature absolutely paints like the harlot," 195, 440; in "The Try-Works," Ishmael makes nautical paraphrase and inversion of Carlyle, 219-227, 443; Ahab's final speech echoes (and inverts meaning of) another Carlyle passage, 234, 444; Ishmael's asserted "Centre of Indifference," 240-241; 444-445

HM's Reaction To, in Pierre: compare: mock-heroics on Pierre and on Teufelsdrockh, 251-252, 446-447; Pierre's courtship of Lucy and Teufelsdrockh's courtship of Blumine, 252, 447-448; Pierre on "Truth" and Teufelsdrockh on "Truth," 258, 448; Pierre and Teufelsdrockh, allegorically, on their father in Heaven, 260-261, 448-449; Pierre and Teufelsdrockh on Memnon Stone, 260-261, 447-448; Pierre and Teufelsdrockh on unbelief, 279, 449; Pierre and Teufelsdrockh on "defiance," 290-291; 451; insulting reference to "Muggletonian Scots," 292-293, 450; *see Heroes and Hero Worship*

Satan, Milton's concept of, *see* Milton

Satanic School of Literature, *see* Devil School

Schopenhauer, Arthur, HM's splurge of reading in, 350-351, 454

Sealts, Merton M., Jr., *Melville's Reading: A Check-List of Books Owned and Borrowed,* 454

Sebond, Raimond, Montaigne on, 21, 173, 187

Servetus, Michael, 19

Shaftesbury, Third Earl of, in relation to Bayle, 30-32; HM contradicts a basic theory of, concerning perception of Truth, 140, 436

Shakespeare, William, drafted into Satanic School by HM, 136; tragic vision of, drove him to use literary deceptions, according to HM, 136-137; HM records his Satan-baptism memorandum in his copy of *King Lear,* 137-138; HM views Montaigne as spiritual father of, 266; HM's tribute to, 416